Be Your Own Financial Adviser

About the author

Jonquil Lowe trained as an economist, worked for several years in the City as an investment analyst and is a former head of the Money Group at Consumers' Association. Jonquil now works as a freelance researcher and journalist. She writes extensively on all areas of personal finance and is the author of several other books, including *The Which? Guide to Giving and Inheriting, The Which? Guide to Planning Your Pension, Take Control of Your Pension* (an Action Pack), *The Which? Guide to Money in Retirement, The Which? Guide to Shares*, and, with Sara Williams, *The Lloyds-TSB Tax Guide*.

Be Your Own Financial Adviser

Jonquil Lowe

 CONSUMERS' ASSOCIATION

Which? Books are commissioned by
Consumers' Association and published by
Which? Ltd, 2 Marylebone Road, London NW1 4DF
Email address: books@which.net

Distributed by The Penguin Group:
Penguin Books Ltd, 80 Strand, London WC2R 0RL

First edition March 1996
Reprinted February 1997, September 1997
Second edition March 1998
Reprinted April 1998, May 1998, November 1999
Third edition July 2000
Fourth edition June 2002
This edition January 2004

British Library Cataloguing-in-Publication Data
A catalogue record for this book is available from the British Library

ISBN 0 85202 955 1

For a full list of Which? books, please write to Which? Books, Castlemead, Gascoyne Way,
Hertford X, SG14 1LH, or access our web site at www.which.net

Cover photograph by Jeff Smith/getty images
Editorial and production: Joanna Bregosz, Ian Robinson

Typeset by Saxon Graphics Ltd, Derby
Printed and bound in Great Britain by Creative Print and Design (Wales) Ebbw Vale

For information on the latest Budget see www.which.net (click on Bookshop and follow the
links).

Contents

Addresses, telephone numbers and, where applicable, Internet sites for those organisations marked with an asterisk (*) can be found in the address section starting on page 427.

Introduction

The most important event since the last edition of this guide has been the three-year fall in the stock market between December 1999 and January 2003. It has been a sharp reminder of the nature of risk and the need to be sceptical about deals that promise much. The stock-market slide has exposed the weaknesses of some financial products and the shortcomings of some financial advice. It has driven home forcibly the need to plan your finances and to ensure that you have not just a fair-weather plan but one that will withstand the storms as well. Ensuring you have a strong plan means anticipating what could happen and either taking steps to avoid unacceptable risks or having a contingency plan to cope with them.

This has been vividly demonstrated with millions of homeowners facing shortfalls on their endowment mortgages. With-profits policies that were supposed smoothly to grow and pay off the loan at the end of the mortgage term have failed to provide robust protection against a deep and prolonged fall in the markets. Of course, there never was a guarantee that these policies would grow by enough – but how many salespeople and advisers really brought that message home to their customers? How many took the time to ensure that borrowers were aware that they were taking a stock-market risk and understood what that risk might entail? Equally, how many customers who were warned preferred to turn a blind eye to the risks?

Income investors have been further casualties of the with-profits concept turned sour. Historically low interest rates prompted income seekers to cast around for extra returns that the secure bank or building society could no longer offer. As a result, sales of with-profits bonds boomed. Only belatedly did consumers realise that the cost of the higher income is often the loss of some savings.

Falling stock markets have also exposed behind-the-scenes changes to some split-capital investment trusts. One type of investment trust shares – 'zeros' – in particular had been marketed as a tax-efficient, low- to medium-risk way of planning ahead to meet expenses like school fees. That used to be a fairly reasonable description, but unknown to investors – and indeed most advisers – the managers of some of these trusts were upping the stakes by borrowing more money to invest and buying into the shares of other similarly structured trusts. If stock markets had continued rising, no-one would have been any the wiser, but the stock market slide plunged these trusts into debt, leaving them unable to pay out on the zeros as promised.

An understanding of risk lies at the heart of much financial planning. It breeds a healthy scepticism that makes you ask: how can this firm offer me such a high return – where is the catch? How is this firm able to maintain good returns when every other provider is cutting its rates? How genuine is this guarantee – in what circumstances would it fail? Why is this product so cheap – what is missing? In the financial world, there simply are no free lunches. If you want the prospect of a better return, you have to take on more risk. If you are uncomfortable with risk, you need to spread your money so that you manage the types and degrees of risk to which you are exposed.

A key aim of *Be Your Own Financial Adviser* is to give you a sound understanding of risk and the ability to apply that understanding to the financial decisions you will make throughout your life, whether you are borrowing to buy your home, insuring to protect your family, planning ahead for retirement, saving a small sum or making major investments. Understanding risk will help you to make better decisions and also to spot rogue or unsound deals.

Cracks in the pension system also appeared as stock-market returns vanished. If you have a 'money purchase' pension, you should have been aware that you were exposed to falling share prices. By contrast, if you belong to a 'final salary' scheme at work, you probably thought you had a pension promise regardless of the vagaries of stock markets. But someone always foots the bill for risk and many employers, faced with alarming and open-ended costs of providing pensions, decided to pull the plug. Schemes have been closed and in the worst cases wound up, leaving members with the prospect of much lower pensions than were originally promised. This highlights another important facet of financial planning. Your plan should be reviewed regularly and be flexible. A good adaptable plan will anticipate likely disasters. But it will also be flexible enough to help you cope with the unforeseen, such as rebuilding your pension plans.

Whether you want to be your own financial adviser or simply to engage more effectively with professional advisers, *Be Your Own Financial Adviser* aims to put you on the right road. It shows you how to assess and prioritise your financial goals and identify products to help you meet them, taking into account your personal circumstances and the degree of risk with which you are comfortable.

This edition has been updated to include the Budget 2003 measures and includes details of other proposed changes to the financial system, such as the regulation of mortgages, general insurance, the tax treatment of pensions and the introduction of new products including the child trust fund and stakeholder suite.

Chapter 1

Why be your own financial adviser?

A glance at your local telephone directory or a stroll down the high street will quickly tell you that there is no shortage of firms and individuals eager to help you organise your finances. So why choose to be your own financial adviser? Since you would not be reading this book if you had not already been tempted to handle your financial affairs yourself, one or more of the following reasons for choosing the d-i-y route has probably occurred to you. Some are good reasons, others less so.

Reason 1: I can't afford financial advice

In fact, with many financial products, you don't pay *extra*, because you are already paying for advice even if you haven't had any! Most advisers get paid only if they sell something. They receive commission from the company whose product you have bought or invested in. The commission is financed out of the charges you pay for the product. The advantage of this system is that the cost of advice is spread over the life of the product, making it easy to afford. The snag is, with many products, the charging structure is just the same even if you haven't had any advice. If you definitely don't want advice, it pays to shop around for products which do not have commission payments built in – see page 14.

Reason 2: I'm not wealthy enough to have an adviser

However large or small your savings are, you need to invest them wisely. Often, the smaller the amount you have, the more important it is to take the right financial decisions, since you can ill afford to make mistakes. Some financial advisers are willing to give time and attention to even the smallest of clients, but most are not because, if you have only small savings, the most suitable investments for you are likely to be schemes like building society accounts and National Savings & Investments. Advisers generally receive little or no commission if they recommend these types of investment. You are also unlikely to take up many of the health and other insurance products which are important sources of income for many advisers.

Some advisers charge you fees, rather than relying on commission income, and so do not suffer the above drawbacks, but the fees charged will often outweigh the benefits of the advice given to a client with only small means.

Reason 3: Financial advisers cannot be trusted

Pension transfers, endowment mortgages, top-up pensions, with-profits, split capital investment trusts – all are familiar from newspaper headlines and have fuelled the public's general mistrust of financial advisers in recent times. But it would be a mistake to tar all advisers with the same brush: there are many skilled, knowledgeable, conscientious and trustworthy advisers the length and breadth of the UK. The problem is that you have to spot and avoid their less honourable colleagues. Certainly, the more you find out about handling your finances, the less likely you are to fall prey to a fraudulent or incompetent adviser.

Reason 4: Advisers are just pushy salespeople

Outright fraud is thankfully rare but, sadly, there are other ways in which an adviser can let you down. The commission system described on page 11 is a less than ideal way of paying an adviser who is supposed to have your best interests at heart. It means there is a built-in incentive for advisers to recommend:

- products or courses of action which produce a commission rather than those which do not: for example, a personal pension rather than membership of an occupational pension scheme, or unnecessary switching from one company to another
- products which pay higher commission than others: for example, endowment mortgages rather than repayment mortgages, investment-type life insurance policies rather than unit trusts

- the product of a company paying higher commission than other companies
- that you invest more, or buy more insurance cover, than might really be ideal for you.

A good adviser will not be swayed by the lure of commission – not only would it be unethical, but it could be bad business if the adviser wants to build up a base of satisfied customers who will generate a steady stream of further business over the years. Unfortunately, not all advisers fit this mould.

You can avoid the possibility of advice biased due to commission by choosing an adviser who is instead paid by fees.

Reason 5: I don't know how to find an adviser

There are different sorts of adviser. Some act as agents of a company whose products they sell. Others act as your agent and can recommend products from the full range on the market – these are 'independent' advisers. Chapter 2 explains the different types of advice in more detail. In surveys, most people say they would prefer to have independent advice, but often they do not know how to find it. By default, many people turn to their trusted and familiar bank or building society for advice, but very few banks and building societies give independent advice and most offer only a narrow range of products. However, finding an independent adviser is not as difficult as you imagine. There are several directories that you can use to search for details of advisers in your area – see page 21.

Finding an adviser is one thing; finding a *good* adviser is quite another. *Which?* magazine keeps a check on the standard of advice being offered to consumers. Although the proportion of advisers giving poor advice has been falling in recent years, it is clear that choosing an adviser is still something of a lottery (see pages 15–16). *Which?* has generally found that independent advisers give good advice more often than other types of adviser.

Reason 6: The need for financial advice is overrated

There is no reason at all why you should not make an excellent job of handling your own financial affairs. But do not make the mistake of assuming that this is a trivial task. Superficially, your finances may seem simple, but you could be unaware of, or underestimate, the importance of certain aspects. If your circumstances genuinely are straightforward and your resources modest, it might not take long to sort out your finances – this time. But financial planning is not a one-off exercise: as your circumstances change, and as the economic and political climate alters, you will need to revise your affairs, which might become more, or less, complex. If you have substantial wealth or, for example, your family circumstances are complicated, understanding and organising your finances will already be a challenging task. Whatever your situation, proper financial planning requires adequate time, thought and care. If you are unable or disinclined to give the job the attention it demands, you should seriously consider consulting a professional financial adviser instead.

Reason 7: Handling my own finances will save me money

Whether you pay a fee or your adviser receives commission (see page 11), it's true that the cost of advice can run to hundreds of pounds. So can you save that money by doing the job yourself?

Obviously, if you choose not to go to a fee-charging adviser, you save the fee. The picture is more complicated when you look at commission-based advice.

The cost of paying the adviser commission is passed on to you, the customer, through the charges for the product you have bought. For example, the cost of commission might be taken as an upfront charge, leaving less of your money to be invested. Alternatively, the cost of commission might be taken gradually over the years through a variety of charges, but recouped through a single, large surrender penalty if you cash in or stop the product early.

With many products, these charges are exactly the same whether or not you use an adviser. So opting to buy without advice does not necessarily save you money. However, there are three ways to overcome this problem:

• Go to a 'direct company' – in other words, a provider that sells direct to the public (often by phone or via the Internet), by-passing advisers and other intermediaries. Often, the products from direct companies cost less, in part reflecting the fact that no commission is being paid.

Stake out

Stakeholder pensions are designed to be simple and good value, but many people still want advice before investing, for example, on how much to pay in and how to invest the resulting pension fund. Charges (and hence commissions to advisers) are capped at a low level – some firms say too low to make including advice economic. But many banks, building societies and life insurance companies, as well as independent financial advisers (IFAs) say they offer advice on stakeholder pensions without charging any extra.

In August 2001, Which? set out to test whether stakeholder pensions were being recommended and to test the advice being given. It sent four undercover researchers, wired for sound, to a total of 38 advisers: 12 from high street banks and building societies, 13 from life companies and 13 IFAs. Which? designed scenarios for the researchers where a stakeholder pension would be the most appropriate recommendation.

31 of the 38 advisers visited appropriately recommended a stakeholder pension. The low charges could have discouraged some advisers from recommending stakeholder pensions but Which? found little evidence of this.

It was not all good news though. The quality of advice was often poor. Which? found several advisers not doing the basics, like assessing attitude towards risk. Eight out of ten bank and building society advisers who recommended a stakeholder pension went for the default investment fund with little or no discussion about the investment options. Two bank advisers and two IFAs gave bad advice and at some of the life companies it was a struggle even getting to speak to an adviser.

While a stakeholder pension was the right product for the Which? researchers, in some cases the recommendation was reached more by luck than as a result of a thorough advice process. In general the bank and building society advisers tended to be worse than average.

Which? February 2002

(For information about stakeholder pensions, see Chapter 12.)

Mortgage lottery

Which? researchers posed as first-time buyers seeking mortgage advice. They hoped to start a family in the next few years, so would want to move again at that point to a larger home. They had a cautious attitude and didn't want to run any risk that they would be unable to repay the mortgage at the end of its term. If asked, they revealed that they expected to be able to pay off a lump sum within five years.

The researchers visited 40 branches of the top ten lenders as well as four estate agents and four independent financial advisers. The good news is that endowments have disappeared from the mortgage scene – none of the advisers suggested these, whereas two years previously half of the recommendations were for endowment mortgages.

Advisers can offer three different levels of service: information about a single product, information about several products, or advice and information on the most suitable mortgage for you. Nearly one-third of advisers failed to say what level of service they were offering.

Two-thirds of the advisers failed fully to establish the researchers' needs. Seven advisers pushed ISA mortgages which would not be appropriate given the researchers' attitude towards risk. Misleading advice was given about repayment mortgages, with 13 advisers badly underestimating the amount of the loan you would pay off in the early years and 14 wrongly claiming that repayment mortgages are inflexible. On the other hand, some advisers mentioned only repayment mortgages without having first made any check on the researchers' attitude towards risk – these advisers seemed too cautious to explore anything else.

Only one of the 48 advisers gave good all-round advice. *Which?* found that it's hit and miss when it comes to getting good mortgage advice. Much depends on the individual adviser you see rather than who they work for.

Which? May 2001

(For information about choosing mortgages, see Chapter 9.)

- Even where a company normally does sell through advisers, try approaching it direct and asking if it will refund to you some or all of the commission which would have gone to an adviser.
- Buying through a 'discount broker'. These are independent intermediaries that, as standard practice, rebate a large part of the commission you would normally pay (but don't usually offer advice). This results in lower product charges, ensuring that more of your money is invested. Examples of discount brokers are given in the Addresses section. 'Fund supermarkets' (see Chapter 17) – Internet sites where you can buy a range of different companies' unit trusts and similar investments – also rebate commission as standard. See Appendix III for a list of the main fund supermarkets.

Bear in mind that what you save by not using an adviser could be trivial compared with your losses if you choose the wrong product. If you have any doubts, it is usually better to pay up and take advice. But remember that, even if you use an adviser who gives you a full advice service, he or she might be prepared to cut the cost of the advice if you ask for a rebate (see page 33).

Reason 8: Handling my own finances would be fun

This is the best reason for being your own financial adviser. If you would not find it a satisfying and enjoyable experience, you would do better to concentrate your energies on finding a professional adviser whom you trust.

Chapter 2

What to expect from a professional adviser

Before deciding how far down the d-i-y financial planning road to go, you should have a clear understanding of the services that a professional can offer. You will then be in a position to assess which of those services you can provide for yourself. The factors you will need to look at include the following:

- Do you have the right temperament to undertake those activities for yourself? Financial planning could be stressful, for example, if you find figurework dull, are not reasonably decisive or find it hard to be objective about risks.
- Have you, or can you obtain, the skills needed to undertake those activities? This book will introduce you to basic financial planning. You can build on this to develop more sophisticated skills and understanding, if you decide to go further down the d-i-y road.
- Do you have access to the information you will need to make investment decisions? For example, having access to the Internet or living or working near a good reference library with a reasonable range of statistical and business sources could make all the difference. This book indicates what source materials are useful and where you can obtain them.
- Can you successfully complete your financial planning within an acceptable timescale? This does not simply mean having enough spare time *per se*. You should also consider whether d-i-y financial planning is an enjoyable way for you to spend your leisure hours, given that it may mean cutting back on other activities.

Where to go for professional advice and what the advisers offer depends largely on the type of financial products or services you are considering. Financial products are often complex, which opens the way for confusion, mis-selling and even fraud. To protect consumers, advisers must usually abide by rules that aim to ensure that advisers conduct their business in an honest and competent way, and that customers get the information they need and have access to redress if things go wrong. But the rules have grown up piecemeal, so different products are covered by different regulatory regimes and signing up to the rules is voluntary in some areas.

However, the regulation of advice is due to become much more coherent. By 2005, nearly all advisers will, by law, have to abide by regulations laid down by the Financial Services Authority (FSA). Although the detailed rules will still differ to some extent from one type of product to another, the broad framework will be the same. Advice about investments is already regulated by the FSA, though some of the rules are changing during 2004.

The sections below broadly describe the sort of advice you can expect from financial advisers both at the time of writing and once the new system starts. See Chapter 3 for guidance on the documents that advisers should give you during the advice and selling process.

Investment advice

How is investment advice regulated?

In general, any UK firm giving you investment advice must be regulated by the FSA or covered by broadly equivalent rules. To be 'authorised' to give advice, the firm will have to satisfy the FSA that it is fit for the job and will have to abide by the FSA's rules which, amongst other areas, deal with how the adviser conducts its business.

What are investments?

'Investments' for the purpose of the regulations include: pensions, investment-type life insurance (for example, endowment policies, with-profits bonds, single premium bonds and so on), unit trusts, open-ended investment companies (OEICs), investment trusts, shares, gilts, corporate bonds, traded options and so on.

Also included are some types of health insurance (such as income protection insurance and critical illness cover – see Chapters 6 and 7) where they have an investment element (not all policies do).

Simple savings products such as bank and building society accounts and National Savings & Investments products are not covered by the investment advice regulations. And, although the rules cover the investment part of a product, they do not extend to any non-investment part of the same product – for example, they do not cover a mortgage but do apply to an endowment policy or individual savings account linked to the mortgage.

There are special rules concerning 'packaged products' which are defined as investment-type life insurance, personal pensions, unit trusts, OEICs and investment trust savings schemes either held directly or through an individual savings account (ISA) or personal equity plan (PEP).

Who are the advisers?

Packaged products?

In the case of packaged products, you might go direct to the provider, to an independent financial adviser (IFA), or to an appointed representative who might be tied either to a provider or to an IFA.

A representative working for a provider is often called a 'tied agent' and can take many forms including, for example, banks and building societies that have agreed to sell a particular insurance company's products and estate agents arranging endowment mortgages. Appointed representatives are not directly authorised by the FSA but the authorised firm for which they work accepts responsibility for their actions and conduct.

At the time of writing, packaged product advisers are covered by a regime called 'polarisation' which means that they must either sell the products of a single provider (as would be the case if you went direct to the provider or its tied agent) or be totally independent and able to recommend any product on the market (which would apply if you went to an IFA or its representative).

Polarisation was introduced to protect consumers because previously some advisers had promoted themselves as able to give impartial, independent advice when in reality they pushed the products of just a small handful of companies to which they were tied. But, if you do not use an IFA, polarisation restricts your choice – for example, many people turn to their familiar bank for advice but are then limited to the products of the single company to which the bank is typically tied.

To widen consumer choice, polarisation is due to be scrapped during 2004. Once its abolition is complete, you will have a wider choice of investment advisers as follows:

- **advisers able to give advice about and sell the products of a single provider**. This will be the case if you go direct to the provider and that provider sells only its own products, or you go to a tied agent of such a provider. However, the provider can choose to let its employees and agents recommend 'out-of-range' products of other providers.
- **advisers able to give advice about and sell the products of several providers** (sometimes referred to as 'multi-tied' though this is not strictly an accurate description). Under the new rules, firms will be able to 'adopt' the products of other providers into their product range (retaining the other providers' brand names or co-branding them). If you go direct to such a firm or its tied agents, you will have a choice of products and providers from the range. The firm may have more than one range – for example, for different types of customer and the provider can also choose to let its employees and agents recommend 'out-of-range' products. The firm might itself be a provider and sell the adopted products alongside its own, or it might be a 'distributor firm' that does not have its own products at all. Rules allowing firms to adopt other providers' products already apply to stakeholder pensions and to any packaged product being sold by 'direct offer promotion', for example by mail order or over the Internet.
- **independent advisers able to advise on and sell any product on the market**. To use the name 'independent' these advisers must also give you the option of paying for the advice by fees (see page 23).

It is expected that, once the new rules come into effect, banks and building societies in particular will take the opportunity to widen the range of products and providers they offer. Although this means you will get a better choice, you will still not necessarily get the best deal on the market.

To have the widest choice, you should opt for independent advice. To find an independent adviser, contact IFA Promotion★, the Society of Financial Advisers (SOFA)★, the Institute of Financial Planning★, Matrix Data UK IFA Directory★, or the Money Management National Register of Independent Fee-Based Advisers★.

Other investments?

Non-packaged investments are mainly traded on various markets and you buy, sell and get advice by going to a specialist trader or broker, such as a stockbroker. A broker acts as your agent and should give you independent advice. IFAs can also advise on non-packaged investments.

To find a stockbroker, contact the Association of Private Client Investment Managers and Stockbrokers (APCIMS)★ or the London Stock Exchange★. If you have access to the Internet, several personal finance websites have search facilities to help you select an online stockbroker. Try, for example, Money Supermarket or FT Your Money (see Appendix III).

What an investment adviser must do

Investment advisers must have passed exams before they can advise you (or be supervised by a qualified person if they are still training). They must comply with a wide range of rules, including:

- **know the customer** The adviser must find out enough about your personal and financial circumstances to be able to give you sound advice. Usually this is done by taking you through a lengthy form called a 'fact find'. It will ask about your marital status, children, any other dependants, your income, how much you spend, what you can afford to save, your financial goals, your attitude towards risk, your existing insurances and investments, your pension arrangements, what financial benefits you can get through work, and so on. You aren't obliged to provide all this information, but if you don't the adviser's advice will be more limited. If the adviser fills in a fact find for you, you should check that it is correct before you sign it.
- **'suitable advice'** The adviser must only recommend courses of action and products that are suitable given your personal and financial circumstances. If your adviser is independent, this means selecting suitable products from the market as a whole. If the adviser is tied, it means recommending the most suitable products from the company's range. If the company does not offer anything suitable, the adviser must tell you so.

How investment advisers are paid

An adviser employed by a company may be paid by salary, often supplemented by commission or bonuses, or by commission alone. A tied agent or appointed representative of a particular company is paid by commission on each product sold.

Independent advisers may be paid by commission or a fee you pay direct to the adviser, or a combination of both. Some advisers offer you a choice. Once the polarisation rule is scrapped (see page 21), to use the description 'independent' an adviser will have to offer you the option to pay by fees. If the advice is fee-based, any commission received by the adviser is set off against the fee.

Appointed representatives (tied agents)

An appointed representative is tied to a particular firm (called the 'principal') and gives advice about and sells the products from that firm. These might be the products of a single provider, of several providers (for example, where the firm has adopted the products of other firms), or products drawn from the whole market where the representative is tied to a firm of independent advisers.

By 2005, the FSA will regulate most types of financial product. It has said that it proposes to allow appointed representatives to tie simultaneously to more than one firm, but only one firm at a time for each of these categories of product: investments (both packaged products and other investments); mortgages other than lifetime mortgages; lifetime mortgages (a type of equity release product). In each case, the principal is responsible for the actions of its appointed representatives.

The rules will be different for non-investment insurance products (meaning term insurance and general insurance, including health insurances other than long-term care insurance). A firm will be able – as now – to be an appointed representative for any number of firms at the same time, so it can have any number of principals. However, to ensure that you are properly protected, one of the firms it represents will be designated the 'lead principal' for the appointed representative. It is the lead principal who will handle any complaint you have against the representative. The lead principal is also responsible for ensuring there are arrangements between all the principals for agreeing liability when things go wrong. If the principals are unable to reach agreement, the Financial Ombudsman Service would step in.

At the outset, an investment adviser should provide you with a letter setting out his or her terms of business, including how he or she expects to be paid. If the adviser is to be paid by fee, before doing business get a clear idea of the amount you will be charged.

If you ask, an investment adviser must tell you how much commission he or she stands to make if you buy a recommended product. This information is also included in product details which the product provider must give you.

Life insurance advice

How is life insurance advice regulated?

Investment-type life insurance counts as an investment and therefore is regulated as described above. But term insurance – life insurance that just provides protection and has no investment element is treated differently. At the time of writing, term insurance advisers are unregulated. However, from 14 January 2005, they will be regulated by the FSA.

Who are the advisers?

You can get advice about term insurance from:

- **life insurance companies** Their advisers can tell you about the policies offered by that company.
- **tied agents** At the time of writing, these may be tied to one or more insurance companies and from 14 January 2005 the rules described in the box on page 23 will apply. Tied agents may be specialist insurance consultants but also include, for example, building societies selling term insurance in conjunction with mortgages.
- **independent intermediaries** These work as your agent and try to find you the best deal either from the whole market or a selection of companies. In practice, it would be unusual for an intermediary to look at the whole market. From 14 January 2005, to count as 'independent' recommendations must simply be based on a review of a sufficiently large number of contracts to amount to a 'fair analysis'.

Although term insurance is not an investment, IFAs and other investment advisers are usually happy to sort out your life insurance needs.

What term insurance advisers must do

There are no particular rules governing advice about term insurance, because it is considered to be a reasonably transparent and straight-forward product (see Chapter 5). However, as with many other types of life insurance, after taking out a policy, you do have the safeguard of a statutory 14-day cooling-off period during which you can change your mind and cancel the deal without any financial penalty.

When the FSA takes over regulating term insurance advisers in 2005, advisers will be required to give you suitable advice (but will not be required to seek out the *most* suitable contract). Advisers will not be required to have passed exams, but the firm they work for must ensure that they are competent and appropriately supervised. You will have a 30-day cooling-off period during which you can change your mind and cancel the contract.

How term insurance advisers are paid

Advisers employed by companies may be paid by salary, often supplemented by commission or bonuses, or by commission alone. Tied agents are paid by commission.

Intermediaries may be paid by commission, by a fee you pay direct to the adviser or a combination of both.

Even after the FSA starts to regulate these advisers, they will not be required automatically to tell you how much commission they receive. However, an intermediary acting as your agent (rather than acting for an insurance company) is required to disclose the amount of commission if you ask. There will be no restrictions on the use of the description 'independent' and no requirement for you to have the option to pay by fees.

Savings advice

How is savings advice regulated?

Savings products – mainly bank and building society accounts and National Savings & Investments products – are considered rela-tively straightforward. Therefore this type of advice is not regulated.

Who are the advisers?

You can get information about savings products from the banks and building societies which issue them, or from National Savings & Investments★ in the case of its products – see Chapter 15.

There are no independent advisers specialising in just savings accounts, but if you are in contact with an adviser anyway – for example an IFA who is looking at your whole financial position – he or she might also give you advice about the best home for your savings.

Only a few banks and building societies pay commission to advisers.

Mortgage advice

How is mortgage advice regulated?

At the time of writing, a voluntary code of practice – the Mortgage Code – covers mortgage advice. Most (but not all) lenders have agreed to abide by the code and those lenders have agreed to deal only with intermediaries that have also signed up to the code.

If you go to a lender or intermediary which does not subscribe to the code, then at the time of writing there are no rules concerning the mortgage advice given.

From 31 October 2004, the FSA is due to take over the regulation of mortgage advice.

Who are the advisers?

You can get advice about mortgages from:

* **lenders** These are often building societies and banks but also include specialist mortgage companies. Usually, these advisers base their advice just on their own products. The exception is where the lender is a 'mortgage packager' – a company which markets a brand of mortgages but does not actually provide the loans itself – where there may be a choice of loans from several lenders.

* **intermediaries** These range from estate agents and solicitors to IFAs and specialist mortgage brokers. At the time of writing, some intermediaries are tied to a single lender – for example, an estate agent might recommend the mortgages of a particular building society. Some intermediaries are 'multi-tied' and select mortgages from a panel of several lenders. Others are independent and will look at the whole market. When the FSA takes over regulating mortgage advice, the rules in the box on page 23 will apply to tied intermediaries. In addition, an intermediary

wishing to use the description 'independent' will have to base its advice on consideration of the whole mortgage market and give you the option of paying a fee for the advice.

Mortgage advisers might also offer advice about investments – for example, about an endowment policy or individual savings account (ISA) which you intend to use to pay off your mortgage. Any mortgage adviser giving investment advice must comply with the rules for investment advisers (see page 19). It is possible for an adviser simultaneously to give, say, independent advice about investments but be tied to just one or two lenders for mortgage advice. This will be still be possible even after the FSA takes over regulating mortgage advice, so it is important to check the status of the adviser for each type of financial product in which you are interested.

What a mortgage adviser must do

Provided your lender or intermediary is covered by the Mortgage Code, they should:

- **disclose the level of service they are giving** The code sets out three levels of service: advice and recommendation entails helping you to select a mortgage which suits your circumstances and aims; information on different types of mortgage entails telling you about the range of products the lender or intermediary offers so you can make an informed choice between them; and information about a single product is offered where the lender or intermediary has only one product or where you have already selected that particular mortgage. The lender or intermediary should at the outset tell you which levels of service they can offer and, before you take out a mortgage, they should confirm in writing the level of service they gave you.
- **assess your ability to repay the mortgage** Whatever level of service you are given, the lender should check that you are likely to be able to manage the mortgage payments. They should do this by taking into account your income and commitments, credit record and other information. In practice, these checks may overestimate your ability to manage the loan, so it's worth doing your own sums by realistically comparing your normal monthly spending with your income to see how much you could afford to earmark for mortgage payments. Be careful to leave

some allowance if your mortgage payments are the type which can increase (see Chapter 9).

Since 31 December 2002, the Mortgage Code requires advisers to have passed an exam before being able to give you advice. The FSA will extend this requirement to all mortgage advisers once it takes over regulating mortgage advice.

Under the FSA rules, advisers will be required to recommend to you the best product in their range. This will be based on a three-stage process:

- whether a mortgage is suitable for you at all – this will usually involve assessing whether you can afford a mortgage
- what type of mortgage would be suitable for you based on an assessment of your needs, circumstances, attitude towards risk and so on, and
- which specific mortgage and provider would best meet your needs and circumstances.

How mortgage advisers are paid

Advisers who are employed by a lender may be paid by salary, often supplemented by commission or bonuses, or by commission alone. Note that mortgage lenders often act as agents for insurance companies selling life insurance, house insurance or mortgage payment protection policies – this means that the lenders receive commission when they sell these products.

Advisers who act as agents for lenders are paid by commission. Advisers who are not tied to a particular lender may be paid by commission or by a fee you pay direct to the intermediary or a combination of both.

Under the Mortgage Code, intermediaries must tell you if they will receive commission for arranging your mortgage. Before you take out the mortgage, they must tell you the amount of commission if it is £250 or more. If it is less than £250, all they have to tell you is that they will receive a sum up to that amount.

If you do not follow a mortgage intermediary's recommendation within six months, under the Consumer Credit Act 1974, the maximum fee the intermediary can charge you is just £5. If you have already paid a larger fee, you can claim a refund.

When the FSA takes over from 31 October 2004, the amount of commission your adviser receives will be shown in the documents you are given (see Chapter 3) though the precise amount need not be disclosed if it does not exceed £250. At the same time, the Consumer Credit Act rule limiting the maximum fee to £5 where advice is not followed will be scrapped.

Equity release schemes

How is equity release advice regulated?

There are two broad types of equity release scheme (see Chapter 18 for details). With the first, now often called a 'lifetime mortgage', you take out a mortgage on your home and use the money raised as a lump sum, invest it to provide an income, or both. At the time of writing, the rules for investment advice (see page 19) apply to the investment part (if any) of the scheme and the mortgage advice rules (see above) apply to the mortgage part.

From 31 October 2004, the FSA is due to take over the regulation of lifetime mortgages and, because these are complex and some-times risky products, special rules will apply over and above those for standard mortgages. In addition, the FSA regime will integrate the investment and mortgage strands of the advice.

The second type of equity release is a 'home reversion scheme'. With this you sell part of your home and use the money raised as a lump sum, to provide income, or both. Again, any investment part of the scheme is subject to the rules for investment advice (see page 19). But there are no special rules applying to advice about the sale of your home or schemes that do not involve investments. There have been calls for home reversion schemes to be regulated by the FSA. This was not originally planned, but at the time of writing the government was reviewing whether they should be brought within the scope of the FSA's rules.

Some equity release providers belong to Safe Home Income Plans (SHIP)* – a voluntary trade body whose members observe a code of business conduct.

Who are the advisers?

For advice about a lifetime mortgage, you can go direct to the handful of insurance companies, banks and building societies which offer them. Similarly, for advice about home reversion schemes, you can go direct to the providers, which tend to be insurance companies or specialist firms. IFAs can advise on both types of scheme and recommend from the whole market the company that will best meet your needs.

What an equity release adviser must do

See page 19 for the rules applying to investment advice and page 26 for mortgage advice. SHIP members are required to explain their schemes fairly, simply and completely, including details of the limitations, costs, tax situation and so on.

When the FSA starts to regulate lifetime mortgages, advisers will be required to recommend to you the most suitable lifetime mortgage from their range. Although recommending particular home reversion schemes is not covered by the rules as proposed at the time of writing, advisers would still be required to consider their suitability in a general sense. The advice process would have three stages:

- whether equity release is suitable for you. This would involve considering, for example, whether you would lose state benefits, how your tax position would be affected and whether you could afford the monthly payments, if any, on the mortgage.
- what types of equity release could be suitable. The type of scheme would have to be selected to match your needs and circumstances and, for example, your wishes regarding inheritance.
- which particular lifetime mortgage(s) and provider(s) would best meet your needs and circumstances. At this stage, the adviser might recommend a home reversion scheme, but as the position stood at the time of writing no FSA rules would then apply.

How equity release advisers are paid

Advisers employed by an equity release provider might be paid by salary, commission and/or bonuses. Intermediaries are paid by commission and/or fees.

Under the FSA's rules, the amount of commission received would have to be disclosed in the scheme documents (see Chapter 3) though the precise amount would not need to be given if no more than £250. And advisers who want to call themselves 'independent' would have to give you the option of paying by fee.

General and health insurance advice

How is general and health insurance advice regulated?

At the time of writing, only voluntary regulation applies to general insurance (which includes, for example, car, home and travel insurance, mortgage payment protection insurance, private medical cover and so on). Advisers employed by insurance companies that belong to the Association of British Insurers (ABI)★ and intermediaries that choose to do so follow the ABI's code of practice and guidance notes. Intermediaries and insurers which belong to the General Insurance Standards Council (GISC)★ follow its code of practice for members. Membership of these bodies is not compulsory.

From 14 January 2005, nearly all general insurance advice will be regulated by the FSA. However, the FSA will not regulate travel agents selling travel insurance in conjunction with holidays or travel arrangements. At the time of writing a decision had yet to be taken on whether the FSA would regulate salespeople selling extended warranty insurance along with, for example, electrical goods.

Some types of health insurance (which includes products like income protection insurance and critical illness cover) have an investment element and so the investment advice rules apply (see page 19). Where there is no investment element, in most cases the rules described in this section apply.

The FSA intends to draw up a single set of rules (probably from 31 October 2004) for long-term care insurance. These would apply to policies both with and without an investment element. At the time of writing, the proposed rules had yet to be published.

Who are the advisers?

You can find out about general insurance from:

- **insurance companies** A company's own advisers can tell you about that company's policies.
- **tied agents** At the time of writing, these may be tied to one or more insurance companies, and from 14 January 2005 the rules described in the box on page 23 will apply. Tied agents may be specialist insurance consultants but also include, for example, building societies selling home insurance.
- **independent intermediaries** These work as your agent and try to find you the best deal either from the whole market or a

selection of companies. In practice, it would be unusual for an intermediary to look at the whole market and, from 15 January 2005, to count as 'independent' recommendations must simply be based on a review of a sufficiently large number of contracts to amount to a 'fair analysis'.

Independent financial advisers (IFAs), most often associated with investment advice (see page 20), often also offer advice about health insurance products.

What an insurance adviser must do

Both the ABI and GISC codes require advisers to:

- **ensure suitability** The adviser must make sure as far as possible that products and services match your needs. If practical, the adviser will identify your needs by asking you for relevant information.
- **explain the products and service** The adviser must explain all the main features, including any significant or unusual restrictions or exclusions, and the costs involved. If you don't have the product information at the time you buy (for example, you purchase over the phone), the information must be sent to you and you have 14 days from the time you receive the information during which you can change your mind and cancel the deal without penalty. Written quotations and sample policies should be given to you if you ask for them.
- **explain your duty to disclose material facts** This means your duty to provide the insurer with all relevant information that might influence the decision to cover you or the terms on which cover is offered. The adviser should also explain the consequences if you fail to disclose this information.

The rules once the FSA takes over will be similar. Advisers will be required to give you suitable advice (but will not be required to seek out the *most* suitable contract). Advisers will not be required to have passed exams, but the firm they work for must ensure that they are competent and appropriately supervised. You will still have a 14-day cooling-off period within which to cancel a deal. This will be extended to 30 days in the case of critical illness insurance and long-term care insurance.

How general insurance advisers are paid

Advisers employed by a company may receive salary, often supplemented by commission or bonuses, or commission alone. Tied agents are paid by commission.

Intermediaries representing you are usually paid by commission from the company whose product they have sold. Alternatively, you might pay a fee direct to the adviser.

Under the GISC code, if the adviser is acting for you (rather than as an agent for an insurer) and you ask, the adviser must tell you how much commission he or she will receive as a result of your purchase.

Even after FSA regulation starts, advisers will not be required automatically to tell you how much commission they receive. However, an intermediary acting as your agent (rather than acting for an insurance company) will be required to disclose the amount of commission if you ask. There will be no restrictions on the use of the description 'independent' and no requirement for you to have the option to pay by fees.

Commission rebates

Many advisers are willing to forgo part of their commission in order to attract your custom. The amount forgone – called the 'commission rebate' – is usually used to increase the amount invested in the product you are buying or enhance in some other way the benefits you'll get from the product. Occasionally, you receive a rebate as a cash lump sum. Some advisers (often called 'discount brokers') specialise in discount business and offer commission rebates as standard. With others, it's a matter for negotiation.

Do not be shy of asking about commission rebates. Nowadays most providers offer a 'commission menu' so that the adviser can choose either, say, a high commission or a lower one coupled with enhanced benefits for the client. There is often also a choice about the extent to which commission is paid 'upfront' (called 'initial commission') or spread over part or all of the lifetime of the policy (called 'renewal commission' or 'trail commission'). Moreover, the market for financial advice is very competitive, and you have a lot of consumer power – so use it. Just as haggling over the discount on a new car or the price of a jacket in your local market square is perfectly acceptable, so is negotiating a commission rebate. You should consider this course especially if you think that the commission the adviser stands to receive looks higher than the norm – though, in that case, you should be alert to the possibility that the advice might have been biased by the high commission and might not be the most suitable for you.

To negotiate a rebate, follow these steps:

- Ask what commission the adviser stands to get if you invest in or buy the recommended product.
- If you have seen the commission payable on similar products and know this commission looks high, or if you know the deal which a discount business could get for you, use this information as a basis for deciding on the rough amount of commission rebate you are seeking.
- Ask what rebate the adviser is willing to consider or what enhanced terms he or she can get for you.
- Be prepared to haggle.
- If you cannot get the commission rebate you think is reasonable, be prepared to take your custom elsewhere.

Could you be your own financial adviser?

Although different types of advice are covered by different rules and regulations, the process of giving advice is broadly the same whether you are buying investments, mortgages, savings or insurance. A financial adviser should:

- **get to know the customer** by finding out relevant information about their personal circumstances and financial arrangements
- **recommend a suitable course of action or product** given what is known about the customer.

As far as knowing the customer goes, an adviser is initially at a disadvantage to you. You know your circumstances intimately and you are in the best position to identify your financial aims. However, you could fail to recognise aims which you should be weaving into your financial structure, unless you take a dispassionate and systematic look at your finances. Chapter 4 will help you do this.

When it comes to giving suitable advice, be aware that there is seldom any one solution which is definitely the best. Usually, there is a range of options of broadly equal merit. Even so, recognising those options as the suitable ones for you does require:

- a good knowledge of the financial system
- a good knowledge of the broad types of product available
- an understanding of how these broad products can be matched to your needs and situation
- good information about the specific products on the market and how to compare them.

Chapters 5–19 will introduce you to tools, techniques and information sources. At one time it was very hard for you to access and use these as readily and effectively as an experienced, well-equipped professional. However, in recent years, life has become much easier for the d-i-y adviser. If you have access to the Internet, you can find an enormous amount of information, covering for example:

- **company and product details** on individual company websites and IFA sites; with many, you can even transact your business over the Internet.
- **general financial guidance** at independent websites, including regulators' sites such as that of the FSA★, or the sites of trade bodies, such as the Association of British Insurers (ABI),★ Investment Management Association (IMA)★ or the British Bankers' Association (BBA)★.
- **personal finance websites** – for example, FT Your Money, MoneyeXtra and Money Supermarket – that have a wealth of general information as well as tools to help you make decisions and organise your finances, and search facilities to help you find the best deals (see Appendix III).
- **calculators** both at company and personal finance sites, which crunch the numbers for you, helping you to work out how much to save, what your mortgage might cost, and so on. Some, like the Which? online mortgage calculator (see Appendix III), due to go live in January 2004, also take you through a series of questions to narrow the choice and produce a selection of mortgages with the features you have specified.
- **comparative information**, that lists the main features of products from different companies in a standard way so that you can readily make comparisons to help you shop around. You'll

find this information on some personal finance sites and specialist sites like Moneyfacts. The FSA★ publishes its own comparative tables. At the time of writing, these cover unit trust and OEIC ISAs, personal pensions, stakeholder pensions, pension annuities, investment bonds, savings endowments, mortgage endowments and mortgages.

• **online information booklets** produced by government departments, the FSA, trade organisations, complaints bodies and so on.

• **background information** on, for example, Budget changes, government press releases, legal information and so on.

Much of this information is available to non-Internet users, but it is a lot more cumbersome to access. The beauty of the Internet is that, even if you do not know the name of a publication or where you might get information, you can use search engines to find what you want. You don't have to be wired up at home. Increasingly, you can get on to the Internet at public libraries, cybercafés and all sorts of other public places. The Internet really is making it much easier to be your own financial adviser.

To sum up, good financial advice is the successful marrying of financial tools to personal details. At one extreme, you can simply hand your personal details to an adviser and leave him or her to do the rest. But, besides being rash, this is unlikely to be the preferred option with a good adviser, who (unless offering a discretionary service) really will see his or her role as one of advising and helping *you* to reach decisions rather than taking decisions on your behalf. At the other extreme, you can take over finding the financial tools and become, in effect, your own adviser.

There is a halfway house which has a lot to recommend it. You can learn the broad principles of financial planning and block in your own 'financial skeleton' before you seek advice. Your adviser and you will then be able to work together efficiently in partnership to choose the appropriate skin for your financial bones. This will save both of you time – and save you money, if you are using a fee-based adviser. You will also be well armed to spot rogue advisers and protect yourself against deliberate or careless mis-selling.

In practice, you are likely to find that, some of the time, your own counsel is adequate. But in new or complex areas, such as pension planning or inheritance tax, it is well worth supplementing your

How much commission?

Often an adviser selling you a product is paid commission by the product provider. Indirectly you pay this through the product's charges. The adviser might get lump sum ('initial commission') when you first buy/invest, and/or periodic instalments ('renewal' or 'trail commission') as long as you keep the product going. Often, the adviser can choose the split between initial and renewal commission. The amount may be negotiable – the lower the commission the adviser gets, the more of your money is invested or the better the deal you get. Here are a few examples of commissions.

Type of product	Commission rate	Example
Unit trust individual savings account (ISA)	3% initial plus 0.5% renewal	You invest £7,000. The adviser gets 3% × £7,000 = £210 at the time you invest. If the value of your investment did not change, he would also get 0.5% × £7,000 = £35 each year; but he will get more if your investment grows.
With-profits bond	6.75% initial	You invest £10,000. The adviser gets 6.75% × £10,000 = £675 at the time you invest.
Repayment mortgage adviser	0.35% of the advance	You borrow £50,000. The gets 0.35% × £50,000 = £175
Equity release scheme	3% of amount raised	You raise £30,000, the adviser gets 3% × £30,000 = £900
Income protection insurance	140% of the first year's premiums	You pay £30 a month, adviser gets 140% × £30 × 12 = £504

Sources: *Moneyfacts Life & Pensions, Moneyfacts*

own research with the opinion of advisers. In some provinces of financial planning, you should be especially wary of doing without professional advice: for example, if you have a farm or run your own business, are involved in family trusts or have investments abroad. Bear in mind that the more specialist your financial affairs are, the more specialist the advice you will require. Check carefully to ensure that the advisers you select have the expertise you need.

Negotiate a rebate

If you pay for advice on a commission basis, the commission earned could be more than the real cost of advice you receive. So a proportion of the commission could be given back to you. Here's an example of how much you could save:

A couple each invest £7,000 in a stocks and shares ISA

Amount invested: £7,000 × 2 = £14,000

Upfront charge at 5 per cent: 0.05 × £14,000 = £700

The adviser receives commission of 3 per cent: 0.03 × £14,000 = £420

If the adviser agrees to take 1 per cent instead of 3 per cent, the commission is: 0.01 × £14,000 = £140

The total cost drops from 5 per cent to 3 per cent, saving you £420 – £140 = £280.

Which? November 2001

Chapter 3

Protection when you buy

Buying financial products or services often involves trusting strangers to look after your money, so you want to be sure that the firms you deal with are honest, soundly run and are giving you straightforward, reliable information about their wares. The UK system of financial regulation aims to ensure this is the case.

The Financial Services and Markets Act 2000 makes it illegal to carry on most types of financial business in the UK without being either authorised by the financial regulator or specifically exempt from regulation. By mid-January 2005, this will apply to most types of financial adviser (see Chapter 2) as well as firms which provide the various products and services. Since 1 December 2001, there has been a single financial regulator responsible for authorisation, the Financial Services Authority (FSA).★

How you are protected

Provided you deal with an authorised firm, you can be confident that:

- the firm is subject to checks to ensure it is solvent, honest, prudently run and that the key people running it are 'fit and proper'
- depending on the type of business, there may be rules concerning the way the firm deals with its customers
- there are proper complaints procedures if something goes wrong, including access to an independent ombudsman (see page 56)
- there is a compensation scheme that may pay you redress if you lose money through fraud or negligence and the firm concerned has gone out of business (see page 61).

If you deal with a firm which is not authorised, you are not protected. So you should always check that a firm is authorised before you do business with it. To check authorisation, consult the FSA Register.*

The main way in which a firm is authorised is to be regulated directly by the FSA. However, firms which are based in other European Economic Area countries (see box below) can be authorised to do business in the UK while being regulated by the authorities either in their home country or, if the deal is being done at a distance (for example, by Internet) in the country in which the firm or branch is based. The protection you get when you deal with an EEA-authorised firm will be similar to – but not the same as – the protection when dealing with an FSA-authorised firm. So you should check that you are happy with the protection offered, in particular what complaints and compensation arrangements apply if things go wrong.

If you deal with a firm based in a non-EEA country, you will be outside the UK system. You will then have to rely on whatever consumer protection (if any) applies in the country in which the firm is based. Even if there is some protection, it might be difficult to make a complaint or seek redress if you have to communicate in another language and/or deal with a foreign legal system. Bear in mind that these risks may apply in particular to firms you find on the Internet. Your safest course is to avoid doing business with firms based outside the EEA.

States of the European Economic Area (EEA)*

Austria	Greece	Netherlands
Belgium	Iceland	Norway
Denmark	Ireland	Portugal
Finland	Italy	Portugal
France	Liechtenstein	Sweden
Germany	Luxembourg	United Kingdom

---

* From 1 May 2004, the following countries are also due to become part of the EEA: Cyprus, Czech Republic, Estonia, Hungary, Latvia, Lithuania, Malta, Poland, Slovakia and Slovenia. However it is likely to take several years for financial services regulation in these countries to be brought into line with European Union requirements.

Professional firms, such as accountants and solicitors, that offer financial services which are incidental to their main line of business can be regulated by their professional body (called a 'designated professional body' or 'DPB') instead of the FSA. See 'Addresses' section for a list of DPBs★.

Some financial firms do not need to be authorised because they are specifically exempt. The largest group of exempt firms is tied agents acting as appointed representatives of a firm (called the 'principal') which is itself authorised. The principal agrees to be responsible for the actions of its appointed representatives. The representative's entry on the FSA Register names the principal and you should also check the principal's entry on the Register.

By January 2005, the FSA will regulate the sale of most types of financial products, including mortgages and general insurance. Appointed representatives will be able to tie to more than one principal (though, in some cases, only one for each category of business). See page 23 for details.

The scope of regulation

Anyone engaged in a 'regulated activity' falls within the scope of the rules. The definition of regulated activities is very wide and includes the services of most types of financial firm that you are likely to deal with. However, different types of rules apply to different types of business. In some cases, regulation focuses largely on how businesses are run; in other areas, there are also rules about how firms interact with their customers. These are the main ways in which you are protected when you do business with the following types of firm:

- **banks and building societies** The regulator is responsible for seeing that banks and building societies are soundly and prudently run in order to minimise the chances of fraud or financial collapse. However, the FSA is not involved in the relationship between banks and building societies and their customers – so the FSA is not involved with setting interest rates, the cheque clearing system, and so on. However, the Banking Code Standards Board★ oversees a voluntary code of practice regulating dealings with customers.
- **credit unions** The FSA is responsible for ensuring credit unions are soundly run and for some aspects of their dealings with

customers, for example, limits on the amount they can lend and how they promote their business to members and potential members.

- **insurance companies and friendly societies** The FSA ensures that insurance companies and friendly societies are soundly and prudently run. This responsibility covers all companies and societies, not just those that offer investment-type products. In the past, the FSA has regulated these companies' relationship with their customers only in the case of investment-type products (such as endowment policies, pensions, and so on). But from 14 January 2005 (and 31 October 2004 in the case of long-term care insurance), the FSA is due to start regulating the selling process (including giving advice) of general insurance and term insurance as well. In the meantime, most insurance companies follow codes of practice drawn up by a trade body, the Association of British Insurers★.

- **investment businesses** Firms must meet strict standards on solvency, being run by fit and proper people, and so on. Authorised firms must also abide by detailed FSA rules concerning how they run their business and their relationship with customers.

- **mortgage business** Initially, the FSA did not regulating mortgages (although it is responsible for ensuring that those lenders which are banks, building societies, and so on are solvent and prudently run). However, from 31 October 2004, the FSA will take on regulating all aspects of mortgages, including the selling process and giving advice. Those equity release schemes which include a mortgage element fall within this area of regulation. (At the time of writing, the government was still considering whether other types of equity release scheme should also be regulated by the FSA.) In the meantime, selling and advice about mortgages is regulated by a voluntary code of practice overseen by the Mortgage Code Compliance Board.★

- **general insurance advisers** From 14 January 2005, the FSA is due to become responsible for regulating advice about general insurance – see Chapter 2 for details. Until then, many advisers are regulated under a voluntary code by the General Insurance Standards Council.★

The FSA, although responsible for the investment side of occupational pension schemes, does not regulate the administration and running of such schemes – for example, ensuring your employer pays in contributions on time and that scheme trustees act in the best interests of the members. This is the province of the Occupational Pensions Regulatory Authority (OPRA)* which also deals with some aspects of stakeholder pension schemes. However, the government has announced that it will replace OPRA, from a future date yet to be announced, with a new pensions regulator with tougher powers to tackle fraud, bad governance and poor administration of pension schemes.

The FSA has an extra statutory role, which is rather unusual for a regulator. This is to promote public understanding of the financial system. The thinking behind this is that investor protection is more effective, and financial markets more competitive, when consumers understand the information they are given by companies and have the necessary skills and tools to take appropriate decisions about their finances. The FSA is pursuing its role by running a consumer

Who are the regulators?

Regulator	Scope of regulation
Financial Services Authority (FSA)*	Most financial areas, except those listed below.
Banking Code Standards Board*	Oversees voluntary code of practice covering the marketing and operation of current accounts, savings products, credit cards, loans and so on.
Mortgage Code Compliance Board (MCCB)*	Oversees voluntary code of practice governing the way mortgages are sold and mortgage advice. The FSA is due to take over these areas from 31 October 2004.
General Insurance Standards Council (GISC)*	Oversees voluntary code of practice governing the way general insurance is sold and general insurance advice. The FSA is due to take over these areas from 14 January 2005.
Occupational Pensions Regulatory Authority (OPRA)*	Occupational pension schemes and some aspects of stakeholder pension schemes (but the FSA is responsible for the way stakeholder schemes are sold and advice about them).

helpline, producing information leaflets and booklets, introducing financial education into school curricula, developing a consumer website, and so on. It also publishes comparative information tables which, for selected products, list the key features of each product so that you can easily compare one with another. Tables like this are already produced by, for example, *Money Management*★ magazine and *Which?*★ but this is a first for a financial regulator.

Regulation by the FSA

All firms regulated by the FSA must observe a set of high-level principles (see Box). The principles are put into effect through detailed rules. In the case of investments, some of these rules address the way firms conduct business with their customers. From 31 October 2004 and 14 January 2005, respectively, conduct of business rules will also apply to mortgages and general insurance.

The detailed rules cover, for example, minimum levels of training and competence, financial promotion (meaning advertising and marketing), the information to be given to clients and prospective customers, safeguards for clients' money and investments, how complaints should be handled, and so on. The regulator also puts in place measures to help it to keep a check on whether

---

The FSA's high-level principles

(1) **Integrity.** A firm must conduct its business with integrity.

(2) **Skill, care and diligence.** A firm must conduct its business with due skill, care and diligence.

(3) **Management and control.** A firm must take reasonable care to organise and control its affairs responsibly and effectively, with adequate risk management systems.

(4) **Financial prudence.** A firm must maintain adequate financial resources.

(5) **Market conduct.** A firm must observe proper standards of market conduct.

(6) **Customers' interests.** A firm must pay due regard to the interests of its customers and treat them fairly.

(7) **Communications with clients.** A firm must pay due regard to the information needs of its clients and communicate information to them in a way which is clear, fair and not misleading.

---

rules are being kept and standards maintained, for example requiring reports from firms and carrying out both regular and spot checks on their businesses.

The FSA is also responsible for ensuring there are systems to deal with problems. This involves a complaints procedure for deciding what has happened in a dispute, a system for ensuring that investors who have been unfairly treated are compensated, and a system for taking disciplinary action against members who break the rules. Such action could range from warnings and fines right through to withdrawal of authorisation, in which case the firm could no longer legally carry on its financial business.

The table overleaf summarises some of the main customer safe-guards under the FSA's conduct of business rules when you buy different types of financial product – see below for a description of the documents mentioned in the table. For guidance on what to expect if you opt to receive advice, see Chapter 2.

Going it alone

If you have developed a good understanding of personal finance, you might simply want to buy products either direct from the provider or through an adviser without going to the trouble of contributing to a fact-find and receiving advice. Doing so is

---

(8) **Conflicts of interest.** A firm must manage conflicts of interest fairly, both between itself and its customers and between a customer and another client.

(9) **Customers relationships of trust.** A firm must take reasonable care to ensure the suitability of its advice and discretionary decisions for any customer who is entitled to rely upon its judgement.

(10) **Clients' assets.** A firm must arrange adequate protection for clients' assets when it is responsible for them.

(11) **Relations with regulators.** A firm must deal with its regulators in an open and cooperative way, and must disclose to the FSA appropriately anything relating to the firm of which the FSA would reasonably expect notice.

Source: FSA Handbook

Main ways you are protected when you buy FSA-regulated products

FSA rules about:	Packaged investments [1]	Other investments eg shares [2]	Mortgages and lifetime mortgages (from 31 October 2004) [3] [4]	Pure protection insurance (from 14 January 2005) [4] [5]	General insurance (from 14 January 2005) [4] [6]
Status disclosure (who the firm/individual is, what they can sell or give advice about)	On first contact: identity and contact details of firm, status of individual within firm. Also whether independent or tied. Initial disclosure document (IDD) is due to be introduced	On first contact: identity and contact details of firm, status of individual within firm.	Initial disclosure document (IDD) must be provided on first contact (unless dealing by phone in which case must be sent to you within five working days)		Usually before conclusion of contract (but may be soon after in case of phone sales). An initial disclosure document may be issued but is not mandatory unless the insurance is being issued in conjunction with a packaged investment or a mortgage
Product disclosure in a durable form, eg printed, by email etc	**Pre-sale:** Key features document (KFD) – to be replaced by Key facts document (KFD). If phone sale, adequate oral info and Key features to follow within five working days or Key facts to follow 'without delay'. If execution-only sale of unit trust, OEIC or investment trust savings scheme, similar rules but you can opt out of receiving Key facts **Post-sale:** currently some information must be re-supplied so many firms issue further KFD. Once Key facts rules start, providing post-sale information will be optional.	No special product disclosure requirements when you buy (but FSA rules govern for example what information must be supplied by companies when they issue new shares)	**Pre-sale:** Key facts illustration (KFI) **Offer:** offer document including updated KFI **Start of contract:** statement confirming the main details of the mortgage including type, whether there is a linked savings plan, your monthly payments, and so on	**Pre-sale:** (or if that is not possible – eg because deal made over the phone – as soon as possible afterwards). Should include premium, other charges, policy summary, unusual exclusions, claims procedure. **Post-sale:** policy document, claims procedure **Renewal:** notice 21 days before expiry **On request:** in addition to the above, any document should be supplier at any time (either before or after conclusion of contract) without delay if you request it	
Cancellation period (period after deal completed during which you can change your mind and cancel the deal)	**Life insurance and pensions:** at least 14 days (whether or not you received advice) **Unit trusts and OEICs:** 14 days (or can be replaced by 7 days to withdraw before deal completed if ISA) but only if you have received advice, otherwise none. **Other stocks and shares ISAs:** 7 days to withdraw before deal completed but only if you have received advice, otherwise none	**Cash ISAs:** 14 days **Other investments:** usually none	Usually none, but 7 days following supply of quotations for any tied products if not included in the offer document	30 days [7] from day contract concluded or day you receive the contract terms, whichever is later	14 days from day contract concluded or day you receive the contract terms, whichever is later

Client money	Firms may be authorised to hold client money but must be held on trust in separate account. (But this does not apply to money from a customer simply to pay for investments which have just been bought or to pay the firm's own fees.) Similarly firms may hold investments on behalf of customers but they must be kept separate from the firm's own assets, for example, in a nominee account	Firms may be authorised to hold client money (though this is rare) but must be held on trust in separate account	Firms may be authorised to hold client money but it must be held on trust in separate account, or be subject to 'risk transfer'. With risk transfer, any premiums you pay to an intermediary are treated as having been paid direct to the insurer and similarly the insurer is treated as having made any pay-out only once the money has reached you	
Complaints	Firm's procedures Financial Ombudsman Service	Firm's procedures Financial Ombudsman Service	Firm's procedures Financial Ombudsman Service	Firm's procedures Financial Ombudsman Service
Compensation scheme	Financial Services Compensation Scheme (FSCS)	FSCS may cover loss due to arranging or advising about mortgage but not lending or administration	FSCS	FSCS
Other	Best execution rules (firm must get you the best price)	Responsible lending rules (lender must be satisfied you can afford the loan payments)		

[1] Packaged investments are investment-type life insurance (such as endowment and whole-of-life policies), personal pensions (including personal stakeholder schemes), unit trusts and OEICs and investment trusts savings schemes.

[2] This includes, for example, investment trusts not bought through a savings scheme and exchange traded funds.

[3] The FSA will regulate mortgages which are a first charge on your home where the home is at least 40 per cent occupied by you or a member of your family. It does not, for example, cover buy-to-let mortgages or top-up loans that are arranged as a second charge on your home.

[4] These are the proposed rules as at July 2003 and could be altered before coming into effect.

[5] 'Pure protection insurance' is an FSA definition including for example term insurance and, unless covered by the investment rules, critical illness cover. (Long-term care insurance is also 'pure protection' but is to be subject to separate rules.)

[6] General insurance includes, for example, car, home and travel insurance and private medical insurance.

[7] Prior to these rules coming into effect, there is already a statutory 14-day cancellation period.

perfectly feasible. It is often called 'execution-only' business – in other words, the adviser or salesperson simply executes your orders without any comment or advice.

You should be aware if you decide to buy without advice that you give up some of the protection of the Financial Services and Markets Act.

If you receive advice about investments (and from 31 October 2004 and 14 January 2005 respectively, mortgages and general insurance), the adviser is required to find out about your needs and circumstances and in the light of that information recommend suitable products. If, later on, a product turns out to be unsuitable – for example, you were recommended an endowment mortgage when unwilling to expose yourself to stockmarket risk – you may have a valid complaint against the adviser which, if necessary, may be settled by going to the ombudsman and through redress from the Financial Services Compensation Scheme.

By contrast, if you buy without advice, you will usually have only yourself to blame if you end up with an unsuitable product and so you will have no cause for complaint and no means of redress. Of course, you would still be protected in other respects – for example, if you had been given incomplete or misleading information about the product or it had been badly administered.

Some companies sell products only on an execution-only basis, for example a number of discount stockbrokers. By cutting out advisers and middlemen, these businesses can often offer attractive low-cost deals. But you must be very clear that you are buying on a no-advice basis: there is no point grumbling later that you have been landed with an unsuitable investment or that the timing of your deal was wrong. By dealing on an execution-only basis, you are taking on full responsibility for your action. The provider will give you *information* about the product, but do not confuse that with advice.

The person you deal with should make clear that, if you require advice, you should either contact the firm's advisers or, if it doesn't offer advice at all, an independent adviser.

By the way, don't assume that execution-only services are always telephone-based. This is not so – you can be an execution-only customer if you are dealing with an adviser face to face. Similarly, not all telephone-only services are execution-only; it is perfectly feasible for firms to conduct fact-finds over the phone.

If you buy or invest in response to a mailshot, a prospectus for newly issued shares or through an application form included in a printed advertisement, the protection you get is restricted in much the same way as when dealing on an execution-only basis.

You should also be wary of being classified as an expert investor. If you ask to be treated as expert and the adviser has reasonable grounds for assuming that you have enough understanding and experience to make your own decisions and you have been notified in writing that you are being treated in this way, you will lose much of the protection under the Financial Services and Markets Act. However expert you are, it may still be wiser to hear the advice and keep the protection.

Information you must normally be given

When you enquire about, or apply for, a financial product, you will usually be given marketing material which inevitably presents the product in a glowing light. However, various laws and codes of practice often require that you are given at least a minimum of information needed for assessing the product.

In many cases, the FSA rules require that you are given specific information *in a set form*. The aim is to ensure that you have an easy-to-understand explanation of the core features of the product – bad as well as good – that you need to make a balanced judgement and in a form that makes it easy to compare competing products.

At the time of writing, these FSA rules were in a state of upheaval with major changes due over the period to 2006. The sections below describe the main FSA-required documents that you may get both before and after the changes take place. The 'after' information is based on the proposals as announced up to July 2003 and might change before coming into effect.

Initial disclosure document (IDD)

This is a new document that is being introduced for packaged investment products (investment-type life insurance, pensions, unit trusts, OEICs and investment trust savings schemes) – probably from mid-2004 – and mortgages (from 31 October 2004).

Firms offering general and term insurance (from 14 January 2005) can opt to provide you with an IDD but in most cases do not have to do so. They will have to if the general or term insurance is being provided in conjunction with a packaged investment product or mortgage, in which case you'll get a single combined IDD. You will also get just one combined IDD if you take out a mortgage linked to a packaged investment (for example, an endowment mortgage or ISA mortgage).

The IDD will be branded with the name 'Key facts' to alert you to the fact that this is important information that the FSA requires financial firms to tell you.

The IDD tells you about the service you will get from a firm, including:

- which providers the firm deals with – for example, the whole market in the case of an independent but a selection of named providers in the case of a tied agent
- whether or not you will be given advice
- what you will have to pay for any advice and the arrangements, if any, for refunding any fees
- what to do if you have a complaint
- whether the firm is covered by the Financial Services Compensation Scheme.

Key features document (KFD) and illustration

Since 1995, this has been the main product disclosure document for packaged investment products. As the name suggests, it summarises all the important features that you need to consider. It must normally be provided before you buy and must be included in direct offer promotions (mailshots, web pages and so on that invite you to invest based simply on the information in the advertisement). The FSA sets out in detail the information which must be given in the KFD, which includes:

- **the nature of the investment**, for example, its aims, your commitment – such as what you must invest and for how long, and the risks inherent in the investment
- **how the investment works**, including how your money is invested, what happens if you want your money back, tax treatment and so on.

As part of the KFD, you also receive an illustration. In the case of life insurance and pension investments this may be based on your own personal information (for example, how much you want to invest and for how long) and will be separate from the main text of the KFD. The illustration includes:

- **projections** showing what your investment might be worth in future based on standard growth assumptions and the provider's own charges. Usually three projections are shown using, at the time of writing, standard growth assumptions of 5, 7 and 9 per cent a year for tax-free investments like pensions and ISAs and 4, 6 and 8 per cent for other investments. Providers can use lower rates if they would be more appropriate. The illustrations are just examples and, in practice, your investment might grow by more or less.

- **a table showing the effect of charges** on your investment in the early years and later on. Again these are examples and are usually based on the middle growth-rate assumption – in other words, 7 per cent a year for tax-free investments and 6 per cent for others. This table is particularly important in showing you what might happen if you stopped the investment early. In some cases, there can be hefty early surrender charges.

- **the reduction in yield (RIY)** which sums up the effect of charges over the whole life of the investment assuming the investment grows at the mid-rate (7 or 6 per cent a year). For example, it might say that charges would reduce your return from 7 per cent to 4.8 per cent a year. Effectively, this means the investment could cost you 7 – 4.8 = 2.2 per cent a year. In other words, the bigger the gap between the two rates of return, the higher the cost of the investment. You can compare the RIY for different investments to see which are cheapest and which most expensive.

- **how much an adviser will be paid**. This states how much an adviser (if you use one) or salesperson will receive invest in this product. It is a useful figure if you want to negotiate a commission rebate (see Chapter 2) or suspect the advice you are getting is being influenced by the commission payable (see Chapter 1).

Key facts document (KFD) and example

FSA research found that the Key features document was often over-looked and not very inviting to read. So, for packaged investments the Key features document is due to be replaced with a Key facts document. The new document will be phased in over the period February 2004 to August 2006.

The Key facts document is less detailed than its predecessor, but sets out the information in a straightforward question-and-answer format and signposts you to where you can find further information if you want it. As with the Key features document, the new document draws together essential information that you need to know before buying, such as the aim of the product, your commitment, the risks involved and broad guidance on how to compare this product with others. The Key facts document should be easy to spot because it has the 'Key facts' name shown prominently on the front cover.

There is also an FSA logo and statement on the cover to remind you that this is information that the FSA requires the firm to give you. But it does not mean that the FSA in any way endorses the product. You'll need to decide whether it is good value and right for you.

Within the key facts document but separate from the main text, you'll find a Key facts example – this replaces the illustration in the Key features document. In the case of pensions, the example presents similar information but in a simpler format based on just one assumed growth rate and taking into account the effect of inflation. There is an illustration of a Key facts example in Chapter 12.

In the case of other packaged investments, the Key facts example focuses on charges and firms will no longer include projections of what you might get back. The FSA decided to drop projections from the Key facts document in order to emphasise that the return from most packaged products cannot be predicted.

In the case of unit trusts and OEICs, the key facts document will include information about how the investment has performed in the past. The FSA does not believe that past performance is a useful guide when trying to select investments, but this information must be included to comply with European legislation. For more about past performance, see Chapter 14.

The key facts logo
A document branded with this logo contains essential product information that the FSA requires a firm to give you.

Key facts illustration (KFI)

Once the sale of mortgages is regulated by the FSA (from 31 October 2004), whenever you ask for details of a particular mortgage, you should be given a Key facts illustration (KFI). You can use this to help you shop around.

The KFI summarises the main features of the mortgage. It is personalised to reflect any information you have given the salesperson or adviser, for example, about the types of loan you want, how much you want to borrow, and so on. The information is presented in a standard way so that you can use their KFIs to compare different mortgages. The information includes:

- a summary of the information you provided
- a description of the mortgage, for example, whether it is a repayment or interest-only loan, what type of interest deal applies, whether you must take out other products (such as home insurance) to qualify for this loan, and so on
- the overall cost of the mortgage
- the amount you must pay each month
- if it is an interest-only mortgage, the amount you must pay each month into a savings scheme to pay off the loan at the end of its term or, if there is no scheme attached to the mortgage, a reminder that you should think how you will repay the loan
- how your payments might change at the end of any special interest rate deal
- what fees you must pay
- what early repayment charges might apply
- if you use a mortgage adviser, how much commission the adviser will get for arranging the loan.

Similar requirements apply if you take out a lifetime mortgage, but the information in the KFI is different reflecting the different nature and purpose of a lifetime mortgage. For example, it includes the amount of income you would raise, the risks involved, how much you will owe including any rolled-up interest, and when the loan will be paid back.

Other information you might get

Suitability letter

If you take out a packaged investment as a result of advice, the adviser must give you a suitability letter setting out the reasons for his or her recommendation.

Under new rules (expected to come into effect during 2004), suitability letters will also have to state in cash the amount of commission the adviser will receive as a result of the recommendation. And the suitability letter will have to be provided as soon as possible after the recommendation is made. (At the time of writing, the letter is not usually issued until after you have invested.)

Stakeholder pension decision trees

Stakeholder pension schemes (see Chapter 12) are designed to be simple, good-value pension schemes. Their low charges mean that they will often be sold on a 'no-advice' basis, in which case you alone will be responsible for your decision to take out a scheme. To help you make this decision and to identify the situations when you may be better off seeking out some advice, the Key features documents for stakeholder schemes contain 'stakeholder decision trees'. These are flowcharts which take you step by step through the issues you need to think about. If you buy by phone or Internet, the firm selling you a stakeholder scheme must ensure you have access to a copy of the decision trees at the time of purchase.

When Key facts documents replace Key features documents (due to happen from 1 August 2004 in the case of stakeholder pensions), the decision trees will be supplied as standalone documents and not as part of the KFD.

You may be able to get help working through the decision trees – for example, from your trade union or a citizens' advice bureau. Do not confuse this type of help with financial advice. Someone helping you work through the trees is not giving you personal advice. The decision to invest is still yours alone and you will not have grounds for complaint if the scheme turns out to be unsuitable.

Minimum information about cash ISAs

Bank and building society accounts do not count as investments and so largely fall outside the scope of the FSA's investment rules. However, mini-cash ISAs and the cash component of maxi-ISAs are an exception when it comes to product information. Unless the provider is signed up to the Banking Code (which includes product disclosure requirements), you must be given at least the following information in accordance with FSA rules:

- **CAT standard** Whether the ISA meets the CAT standards (see page 310) and, if so, a table showing how its features compare with the CAT requirements.
- **mini and maxi ISAs** What they are (see page 376), the difference between them and how investing in a cash ISA affects the amount you can invest in a stocks-and-shares ISA.
- **minimum and maximum investments**
- **interest** Whether it varies and how it is calculated.
- **withdrawals** How to make them and whether any limits apply.
- **commission or remuneration** How much the adviser or sales-person will get if you take up the ISA.
- **cancellation rights and complaints procedure**
- **risk warnings and other statements** For example, that the favourable tax treatment could change in future whether the ISA is covered by a compensation scheme, and so on.

With-profits guide

If you are considering a policy or plan invested on a with-profits basis (see page 337), you can request this free guide, which tells you something about the insurer and its philosophy in setting the bonuses that make up the return on this form of investment. The information given in the guide includes:

- whether the insurer has shareholders who will want to be paid dividends, leaving less to be paid out as bonuses to policyholders
- the main types of business which will generate the with-profits returns

- the factors which influence the level of bonuses, such as how the with-profits fund is invested, the effect of inflation and tax, and the expenses of the fund
- the 'solvency margin' of the insurer. This helps you to form a view about whether current bonus levels can be sustained in the future but is not an easy figure for investors to get to grips with. Consider asking an adviser to interpret the information.

Following the problems with Equitable Life and the impact of a three-year decline in the stockmarket, the FSA has undertaken a review of with-profits policies, including the information to be supplied to policyholders. At the time of writing, the FSA had still not decided whether or not to retain with-profits guides in their present form.

What to do if things go wrong

Complain to the firm

If you are not happy with the service from, or conduct of, a financial firm, you should first complain to the firm or the branch of it with which you were dealing. If you are not happy with the response, take your complaint higher within the firm, for example to the managing director or head office. If you still do not receive a satisfactory response, the company is obliged to tell you how to take your complaint further.

All firms within the FSA's jurisdiction are required to:

- have a formal complaints system
- publish details about the system and send these to consumers as soon as a complaint is made
- publicise the availability of the system and membership of the ombudsman scheme (see below)
- give a substantive response to a complaint within eight weeks. The response might agree with your complaint, disagree or say that more time is needed to investigate the matter fully. If it disagrees, you can take your case to the ombudsman scheme. The firm should set out its final decision in writing (sometimes called a 'letter of deadlock') together with details of how you can contact the ombudsman.

The FSA Register★ contains details of who you should contact within a firm if you have a complaint.

Firms outside the scope of FSA regulations should also normally have an internal complaints procedure. In many cases, you will also have access to an independent complaints body (see page 60) if the firm does not resolve your complaint satisfactorily.

As an alternative to going to the independent complaints scheme, you could take your case to court (see page 61). However, in most cases, the complaints scheme will be much quicker and cheaper to use.

The Financial Ombudsman Service (FOS)

The FOS* is a one-stop shop for most complaints about financial firms and is the largest ombudsman scheme in the world. It started operating from 1 December 2001, when it replaced eight earlier complaints schemes:

- Office of the Banking Ombudsman
- Office of the Building Societies Ombudsman
- Office of the Investment Ombudsman
- Insurance Ombudsman Bureau
- Personal Investment Authority Ombudsman Bureau
- Personal Insurance Arbitration Service
- Securities and Futures Authority Complaints Bureau
- FSA Complaints Unit.

The FOS can deal with all the types of complaint dealt with by these former schemes, so it covers investments, bank and building society accounts, many mortgage disputes, insurance, and so on. But it does not deal with debt problems, credit cards and loans (except those offered by banks and building societies) or occupational pension schemes. From 31 October 2004, mortgage intermediaries must also be covered by FOS and, from 14 January 2005, this will also apply to general insurance intermediaries. Before then, both types of intermediary can voluntarily opt to be covered by FOS.

The FOS can look into complaints about mis-selling, unsuitable advice, unfair treatment, maladministration, misleading advertisements, delays and poor service. But the FOS does not handle complaints about a firm's commercial judgement (for example, in refusing you a loan), the way an investment has performed, or the actions of somebody else's insurance company (that you might be claiming against, say, following a car accident).

Using the FOS is free, though if you act improperly or unreasonably or cause unreasonable delays during the dispute resolution process, the ombudsman can direct that you pay something towards its costs. You can never be asked to pay anything towards the costs of the firm with which you have the dispute.

You usually have six months from receiving a firm's substantive response to your complaint within which you can take your case to the FOS. If you delay longer than this, expect your complaint to be turned away (though the FOS does have discretion to waive the time limit). Make your complaint on the form provided by the FOS.

The scheme is designed to be easy to use and you should not need the help of a solicitor. If you do use one, you'll have to pay your legal costs yourself and cannot claim them back even if the ombudsman decides the case in your favour.

Initially, the FOS tries to help you and the firm reach agreement through a process of conciliation. If this fails, the FOS can make a decision that the firm must accept.

The FOS can call for whatever evidence it needs to determine a dispute. Usually, its research into a case is paper-based, but it can call on you to give oral evidence. Its decision might involve ordering the firm to return money or assets, reinstate policies and pay compensation. The maximum award binding on the firm is £100,000. The FOS can direct a higher award, but the firm can't be forced to pay any excess over the £100,000 limit. Unlike the firm, you are not bound by the ombudsman's decision and can take your case to court if you want.

Other independent complaints schemes

Mortgage Code Arbitration Scheme (MCAS)

The MCAS★ deals with mortgage complaints that fall outside the scope of the Financial Ombudsman Service – for example, against a mortgage intermediary before 31 October 2004 – provided the firm has agreed to be regulated by the Mortgage Code Compliance Board (MCCB).★

If the firm has been unable to resolve the dispute, it should provide you with a complaints form, which both of you must complete. The firm should send the form to the MCAS for you. If it doesn't, contact the MCCB. There is no charge for using the MCAS.

The scheme is run by the Chartered Institute of Arbitrators. In agreeing to arbitration, you give up your right to take your complaint to court, so the arbitrator's decision is binding on you as well as the firm. The arbitrator can order the firm to pay you compensation up to £100,000.

General Insurance Standards Council Dispute Resolution Facility

The GISC★ Dispute Resolution Facility covers complaints about general insurance provided the firm has agreed to be regulated by the GISC (but will be replaced by FOS from 14 January 2005).

The firm should tell you how to contact the GISC scheme if you are not happy with the firm's final decision. But if the firm is slow or uncooperative, you should contact the scheme direct.

The scheme is free to use. It aims to resolve disputes through advice and conciliation. If this does not work, it can act as an independent investigator and make recommendations. However, these are not binding on the firm. They are not binding on you either, so you can choose to take your case to court if you want.

Finance and Leasing Association Arbitration Scheme

This scheme covers complaints about consumer loans, car loans, instalment credit, hire purchase, credit cards, store cards, and so on, that fall outside the scope of the FOS, provided the firm is a member of the Finance and Leasing Association (FLA).★ The FLA scheme does not deal with complaints about a firm's commercial judgement, rates of interest or other charges.

The firm should provide a complaints form which both of you complete and should send it to the arbitration scheme for you. If it does not, contact the FLA.

The scheme is run for the FLA by the Chartered Institute of Arbitrators and in accepting arbitration you give up your right to go to court. The scheme is usually free to use, but the arbitrator can order you to pay the firm's costs. The maximum award is the value of the credit advanced (or the rentals payable under a hire purchase agreement) plus up to £100 for stress or inconvenience. The arbitrator's decision is binding on both you and the firm.

Pensions Advisory Service and Pensions Ombudsman

These schemes deal with problems concerning occupational pension schemes and the way personal pensions are run. (Disputes concerning the selling of personal pensions or advice about them are dealt with by the FOS.) The schemes do not cover complaints about investment performance.

You can contact the Pensions Advisory Service (OPAS)★ at any time, though if you haven't already given the pension provider a chance to resolve the matter, OPAS will make that its first port of call. OPAS tries to help you and the provider reach agreement through conciliation. If this is not successful, OPAS may recommend that you take your case to the Pensions Ombudsman★ and will help you bring your case. Note that the ombudsman will not normally take up a case unless you have gone to OPAS first. Your case must normally come before the ombudsman within three years of the occurrence you are complaining about.

Both OPAS and the ombudsman scheme are free. Unusually for an ombudsman scheme, the Pensions Ombudsman's decision is binding on you as well as the pension provider. You do not usually have the option of going on to court.

Independent complaints schemes

Name of scheme	Types of firm covered
Financial Ombudsman Service (FOS)★	Banks, building societies, mortgage lenders, insurance companies, pension providers, investment companies (such as unit trust and investment trust managers), stockbrokers, financial advisers (but only the investment advice they give), and various other financial firms.
Mortgage Code Arbitration Scheme (MCAS)★ [1]	Mortgage intermediaries (such as mortgage brokers and estate agents), mortgage advice given by financial advisers, provided the firm has agreed to be regulated by the Mortgage Code Compliance Board (MCCB).
General Insurance Standards Council (GISC)★ Dispute Resolution Facility [1]	General insurance intermediaries (such as insurance brokers and travel agents), general insurance advice given by financial advisers, provided the firm has agreed to be regulated by GISC.
Finance and Leasing Association (FLA)★ Arbitration Scheme	Companies offering loans and credit, provided they are members of the FLA (but not banks and building societies which are covered by the FOS).
Office of the Pensions Advisory Service (OPAS)★ and the Pensions Ombudsman★	Occupational pension schemes and personal pensions providers. (But many personal pension complaints are covered by the FOS.)

[1] Due to be replaced by FOS.

Going to court

As an alternative to using an ombudsman or arbitration scheme, you could sue the firm which has caused you loss by taking it to court. However, this is more expensive than using an ombudsman or arbitration scheme, often takes a lot longer and you risk having to pay your opponent's costs or damages. An ombudsman scheme also has the advantage that it can make decisions and awards on the basis of what is fair and reasonable rather than just the strict legal position. (Arbitration schemes are more formal and work in a similar way to the courts, making decisions based on the strict legal case.)

If you have used the FOS or the GISC Dispute Resolution Facility and you are unhappy with the decision given, you can go to court and try for a different judgment. But bear in mind that, if the complaints scheme has decided against you on the basis of the evidence, it is quite likely that a judge will too. If you use an arbitration scheme or the Pensions Ombudsman, you give up your right to go to court.

If you do go to court, the case is likely to be dealt with more quickly and cheaply if you are able to use the small claims track (also called the 'small claims court'). You can do this if the amount you are claiming is no more than:

- £5,000 in England and Wales
- £2,000 in Northern Ireland
- £750 in Scotland.

To find out more, contact your local County Court* (or, in Scotland, the Sheriff's Court*).

Getting compensation

A complaints scheme or court may find in your favour, but will the firm be in a position to pay up? Many financial firms are required to have professional indemnity insurance, which might ultimately provide the compensation. The problem comes when the firm has gone out of business and does not have enough assets or insurance to pay compensation.

Provided the firm is authorised by the FSA (see page 39), you might be able to obtain redress from the Financial Services

Compensation Scheme (FSCS).* The FSCS replaces five earlier compensation schemes:

- Deposit Protection Scheme (which covered bank deposits)
- Building Societies Investor Protection Scheme
- Investors' Compensation Scheme
- Policyholders' Protection Board (which covered life and general insurance)
- Friendly Societies Protection Scheme.

The FSCS can pay compensation in cases where you have lost money due to an authorised firm's fraud or negligence and the firm has ceased trading. The maximum compensation you can get depends on the type of financial product involved – see the table. For more information, contact the FSCS.*

Summary of the Financial Services Compensation Scheme

Type of financial product	Amount of your loss covered by compensation	Maximum compensation
Deposits (e.g. bank and building society accounts)	100% of the first £2,000 90% of the next £33,000	£31,700
Investments (e.g. unit trusts, shares)	100% of the first £30,000 90% of the next £20,000	£48,000
Long-term insurance (e.g. life insurance)	100% of the first £2,000 At least 90% of the remainder (including future benefits already declared)	Unlimited
General insurance (e.g. car insurance, home insurance)	*Compulsory insurance* (e.g. third-party motor insurance, employer's liability insurance): 100% of claim *Non-compulsory insurance* 100% of first £2,000 90% of remainder	Unlimited

Unlimited |
| Mortgages and lifetime mortgages (but only advice about and arranging them) [1] | 100% of the first £30,000 90% of the next £20,000 | £48,000 |

[1] Due to be covered by the scheme from 31 October 2004.

A separate compensation scheme covers occupational pension schemes which may pay out in some, fairly limited circumstances. These circumstances are: the funds in the occupational scheme are found to fall short by more than 10 per cent of the amount needed to pay the members' pension rights, the shortfall has arisen because of fraud, theft or some other dishonesty, the employer has gone bust so can't be made to make good the shortfall, and it is judged reasonable to pay compensation. Any compensation is paid to the scheme, not direct to the members.

However, at the time of writing, the government had proposed setting up a new Pensions Protection Fund which could pay out whenever an employer became insolvent and there was a shortfall in the pension fund, regardless of whether or not there had been any dishonesty or fraud. The government is to consult on the proposals but expects the fund would guarantee 100 per cent of pensions which had already started to be paid and 90 per cent of pension rights built up by members still working, but subject to an overall maximum.

The Pensions Protection Fund is unlikely to be established before Spring 2005. More immediately, employers who are still in business will be required, probably from Summer 2003 onwards, to make good any shortfall in the pension fund if they decide to wind up a pension scheme.

Firms which break the rules

In addition to pursuing your complaint, if you are concerned that the firm acted dishonestly or has broken the rules in some other way, you should report the firm to the FSA★ or, if the firm is not regulated by the FSA, to the appropriate alternative regulator – see the table on page 43.

Self-defence

Although the financial system is designed to protect consumers, it cannot shield you from every eventuality. It pays to protect yourself as well. Follow these 12 steps when you buy financial products:

1. Think twice before buying without advice – you lose some of the legal protection.
2. For investment advice, go only to authorised advisers. Check that an adviser is authorised by consulting the FSA Register.★ Make

sure that the individual or subsidiary you deal with actually is part of the authorised firm and is not some other related business which is not itself authorised. Visit at least two advisers.

3. For mortgage advice, stick to advisers that subscribe to the Mortgage Code. You can check this by contacting the MCCB.* Similarly, for general insurance advice, stick to GISC members – contact GISC* to check this out. Bear in mind that completely unregulated advisers are allowed to sell term insurance, so make sure you understand what you are being sold and agree that it is suitable for you. Don't be afraid to use the cooling-off period (see page 46) to cancel the deal if you have second thoughts.

4. Know your adviser. Is the adviser tied or independent? If tied, are you especially interested in the products of that company, or do you particularly value the convenience, say, of using that provider? Consider getting advice from an independent adviser who can look at the full range of companies' products.

5. How can the adviser help you? Is the adviser authorised for the type of investment business you are interested in? Does the adviser have expertise in the financial areas you need help with? If independent, how does the adviser keep track of the available products? Nowadays, you should be wary of advisers who do not have access to regularly updated computerised systems (but don't assume that you will be guaranteed good advice just because an adviser has a computer).

6. Be prepared. Be clear about your financial objectives and the priority you attach to them – see Chapter 4. To comply with the 'know your customer' rule, an adviser or salesperson must find out a lot about you. Make sure you have the information to hand, for example in the form of the checklist in Appendix I.

7. Be informed. Know what literature to expect, read it all – especially documents labelled 'key features' or 'key facts'. Ask questions if there are gaps in your knowledge.

8. Be sceptical. If a deal sounds too good to be true, then it is probably suspect. High returns always go hand in hand with high risk. Don't take terms like 'free' and 'guaranteed' at face value – check exactly what is on offer. And always remember that any guarantee is only as good as the company making it. Query the appropriateness of a deal if the adviser stands to get an unexpectedly large commission.

9. Never be pressurised into making a deal on the spot. Take your time and make sure that the product on offer fits in with your financial plans. Discounts and special offers are poor compensation for bad, hasty decisions.

10. Most independent advisers are not authorised to handle their clients' money. The firm's entry on the FSA Register⋆ will say if they are. If not, never hand money over to the adviser. Instead, make payments to the company or companies you are investing in or buying from. Even if the adviser is authorised to handle your money, there is nothing wrong in insisting that you make your payments direct to the provider.

11. If the adviser looks after investments on behalf of clients, check exactly what safeguards there are to protect the clients. If you are not happy with them, insist on looking after your own investments.

12. Always get, and keep in a safe place, receipts, documents, records of interviews and telephone conversations, and so on. If anything does go wrong, it is essential that you have this information.

Chapter 4

Your financial skeleton

It is very easy to respond to *ad hoc* needs and opportunities as they arise without thinking about how they contribute to your overall financial situation: for example, starting a savings plan because the salesman said it was a good idea, buying newly issued shares on a whim, or finding yourself unexpectedly shelling out for school fees. Such decisions might turn out to be good ones, but, equally, with hindsight they might look like white elephants or could prove to be unnecessarily heavy burdens. The key to financial planning is to have a comprehensive overview of your circumstances, your needs, your wants, and the priority which you attach to each of your financial objectives. This gives a framework on which to base your decisions.

To draw out your skeleton, you need to work through the following stages:

- identify and prioritise your financial targets
- assess what resources you have available to commit towards meeting those targets
- if necessary, revise your targets in the light of available resources
- consider the personal factors which will influence how you meet your targets.

This will give you a strong, coherent structure on which to build. You can then go on to identify the appropriate financial tools for meeting your targets, given your priorities, resources and personal factors. The final step – deciding which particular companies' products to choose – is perhaps the hardest for the d-i-y financial planner. You need to keep a close eye on the various financial markets, being aware of new product launches, changes to existing products, special promotions, and the impact of external events, such as changes in the law or economic crises, on the various types of product. This used to be very laborious and time-consuming and *Which?* used to suggest that, at this stage, it might be sensible to seek professional help. However, the Internet is fast changing all that. Most product providers now have a website or are in the process of setting one up. You can rapidly get product information from these and, if you want to, make your purchase over the Net too. (This is generally secure, but for tips on buying safely over the Internet, see Appendix III.) There are also many websites – including Switch with Which? and the FSA's site – that compare products from different providers, letting you easily pick out ones with the features you need. (See Appendix III for these web addresses.)

Finally, be aware that your financial skeleton and the choice of products to meet your needs should be reviewed regularly. Certain events in life – such as marriage, separation or divorce, having children, promotion at work, receiving an inheritance, being made redundant, reaching retirement – clearly signal that it is time for a review. Even apart from these events, there are changes over time to the economic and social climate and to the opportunities available, so it makes sense to review your financial skeleton every year or so. The review is also a time to assess how well on track you are for your longer-term objectives and to decide whether you need to make any adjustments, such as increasing the amount you are saving.

The whole process of drawing up your financial skeleton and fitting a financial plan around it is summarised in the chart overleaf.

Identifying and prioritising your targets

Just as the body's skeleton grows and alters as you grow up, so your financial skeleton should adapt to the changing phases of your life. To some extent, these phases vary from person to person, but it is possible to map out a typical sequence – see the chart on page 69. You personally might not pass through all these phases, but some will certainly apply.

Each phase is characterised by a different set of opportunities and demands which will tend to determine the financial priorities you choose. Possible priorities are outlined in the descriptions that follow. These are not set in stone, and what is right for one person may be quite wrong for another. Their aim is to set you thinking about your own phase of life and your own financial aims.

How to build your financial plan

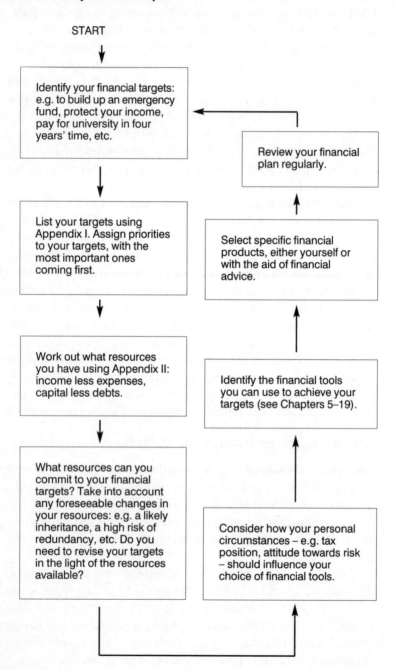

START

Identify your financial targets:
e.g. to build up an emergency
fund, protect your income,
pay for university in four
years' time, etc.

Review your financial
plan regularly.

List your targets using
Appendix I. Assign priorities
to your targets, with the
most important ones
coming first.

Select specific financial
products, either yourself or
with the aid of financial
advice.

Work out what resources
you have using Appendix II:
income less expenses,
capital less debts.

Identify the financial tools
you can use to achieve your
targets (see Chapters 5–19).

What resources can you
commit to your financial
targets? Take into account
any foreseeable changes in
your resources: e.g. a likely
inheritance, a high risk of
redundancy, etc. Do you
need to revise your targets
in the light of the resources
available?

Consider how your personal
circumstances – e.g. tax
position, attitude towards risk
– should influence your
choice of financial tools.

Typical phases of life

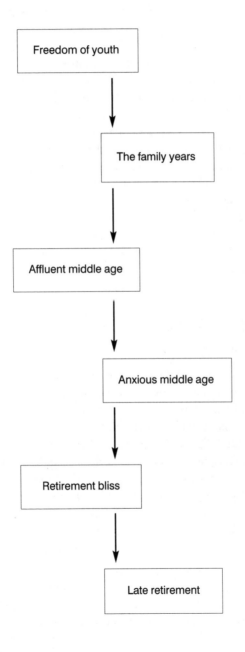

To the targets dictated by the life phase you need to add your own personal hopes and ambitions: for example, maybe you want to retire when you are 50, in which case pension planning will need to be a much higher priority in the early phases of life than is shown in the outlines below; or you might want to take a year off work to sail around the world, which would probably influence your savings targets.

Your objectives and the way you prioritise them should reflect not just what you would *like* to achieve financially, but also what you *need* to do given your family commitments, what the state provides, and so on. For example, though you might prefer not to dwell on the risks of life, if you have dependants you should consider how they would cope if you were no longer there. Similarly, it is very easy to ignore pension planning until it is too late to build up the level of income you would ideally like to enjoy when you retire.

You might be surprised to see that throughout many of the life phases described below, protecting your income should you fall ill is given higher priority than life insurance. Yet this is perfectly logical, given that you are roughly 20 times more likely to be off work sick for a prolonged period than you are to die during your working years.

Typical phases of life

Freedom of youth

This is the early phase of life, when you cease to rely on your parents and, all being well, start to earn your own living. Typically, no one is dependent on you, and your main priority is having a roof over your head. Quite possibly, rented accommodation fits in with your desire for mobility. Other commitments are likely to be few, but might include, say, paying off loans taken out during student days (though see pages 395 for suggestions on how a student loan can be part of your financial planning). The net result is likely to be a surplus of income over necessary expenditure. The temptation of youth is probably to spend the excess, but there are some bones you can build into your skeleton even now. In a realistic order of priority, these are:

- emergency fund to draw on if you face unexpected expenses
- protecting your income in the event of your falling ill
- pension planning: it takes a lot of investment to build up an adequate pension, so the earlier you start the better

- short-term saving, for example for a car, holidays, and so on
- medium- to long-term non-pension saving for eventual house purchase plus other, non-specific reasons.

The family years

At some stage, most people find a partner whom they either live with or marry. This immediately creates a changed situation. Even if your partner is financially independent, you are likely to develop some joint commitments. These may be major items, such as sharing the costs of buying and running a home. In this case, you have to consider what would be the financial impact on your partner if, say, you fell ill or died, and similarly what the impact on you would be if your partner became ill or died. For those with children, the shared commitments are even more demanding and complex, requiring financial fore-thought and planning. Children are likely to exert greater pressures on your resources than will occur at any other stage of your life. If you or your partner stop working or cut back your work in order to care for the children, these resources will be further depleted.

In this situation, it is essential to decide what your financial prior-ities are. They are likely to take on this sort of shape:

- emergency fund
- protecting your own and your partner's income in the event of illness, at least to the extent that joint expenses would be covered
- life insurance on your own and your partner's life
- borrowing to buy a home
- planning for education, for example school fees if you opt for private-sector schooling, or the cost of maintaining your child(ren) at university
- pension planning: ideally, this should have higher priority but this might not be possible if funds are tight
- short-term saving for family events, for example presents, holidays, and so on
- medium- to long-term saving, if you have surplus funds.

Many couples separate or divorce, and, if children are involved, the financial pressures can become particularly severe. Often the same overall resources must be stretched to finance two households, extra childcare costs, solicitors' bills, and so on. Although money may be tighter, the overall needs and priorities associated with the family years are likely to be much the same as shown above. In particular, bear in mind that if you are relying on maintenance from a former husband or wife for part of your income, you probably still have a need for life insurance which would pay out if he or she were to die. Don't overlook pension planning both when negotiating the divorce settlement and afterwards, since often it will be appropriate to transfer some pension rights from one spouse to another.

The Which? Guide to Divorce and The Which? Guide to Living Together, both available from Which? Books,★ contain further advice on the financial implications of separation and divorce.

Affluent middle age

When eventually the financial demands of a family subside, you may enter a phase of relative wealth. This would be a good time to anticipate future events. But if you choose simply to concentrate on the present, increased spending and personal ambitions are likely to dominate your priorities after basic needs have been met. Typically, your priorities might look like this:

- emergency fund
- protecting income against illness
- life insurance if you have a partner or other dependants
- fun targets – more holidays, hobbies, a second home and so on
- pension planning
- other saving.

Anxious middle age

Unfortunately, the relaxed feeling of early middle age tends to give way as you enter your fifties. Realisation grows that retirement is just around the corner, and perhaps you should be doing more to prepare for it. Pension planning should now move up your priorities and, for the first time, your thoughts might turn to the health problems of old age. At this phase of life, you might also find elderly parents becoming more dependent on you, though, equally, your resources might be boosted through inheritance.

The following profile of priorities is possible:

- emergency fund
- protecting income against illness

- life insurance if you have a partner or other dependants
- pension planning
- long-term care planning, if you are not confident of adequate state provision
- serious investment.

Retirement bliss

By the time retirement arrives, your earlier planning should be bearing fruit. With luck, this should be another relaxed phase of life. But it pays to have a weather eye on the future, making sure that your income will be sustained as retirement progresses and that you will be able to cope with increased costs due to health problems. At retirement, you are likely to receive a lump sum which you may want, at least partly, to invest rather than spend.

Priorities could be:

- emergency fund
- continuing income if you or your partner were to die
- replacing perks that went with your job, for example a car, medical insurance, and spending on capital items expected to see you through retirement
- fun targets, for example increased travel, new hobbies, indulging grandchildren
- investment for income either now or later on (which also usually includes investing partly for growth in order to maintain the future buying power of the income)
- long-term care planning, if you are not confident that the state will provide
- inheritance planning – taking steps to reduce a potential inheritance tax bill at your death.

Late retirement

The last phase of life. Your priorities now depend very much on how well your earlier financial planning succeeded. For some, a shortage of income might be the top concern; for others, how to pass on their assets. Very loosely, then, priorities might be:

- emergency fund
- continuing income if you or your partner were to die

- investing for income/boosting income
- paying for care if the health of you or your partner fails
- inheritance planning.

The impact of other factors on your targets

As well as responding to your life phase and personal ambitions, you will also have needs that arise because of the risk of outside shocks upsetting your financial plans. These shocks range from near-certain events, such as changes in interest rates and periodic changes to the tax system, to others that might not come to pass at all, such as being made redundant. Whether or not you respond to the threat of these shocks depends on how likely you think they are to happen to you and the severity of the impact they would have. You can gather statistics about the probability of certain events happening – how likely you are to have a fatal heart attack at age 40, how likely you are to be off work sick, how likely you are to live to a hundred, and so on. These may help to frame your perception, but different people will come to a different conclusion about the risks they think they personally face, coloured by their own temperament (optimistic or not) and circumstances (for example, a family history of illness). Likewise, the impact of a shock on your finances will vary from person to person depending on the resources you have, the expenses you have, how important it is to you to protect a particular lifestyle, and so on.

Changes in government policy can have a big impact on how you perceive risks. For example, the reduction in support for mortgage payments in the event of having to claim state benefits prompted more people to consider taking out insurance to cover their mortgage payments in case of unemployment. Presumably, they did not think it more likely that they would face unemployment, but the damage unemployment could cause to their finances is now expected to be greater. Similarly, debate on whether the health service can continue to provide free (at the point of use) treatment for all indefinitely does not increase your likelihood of falling ill. However, it might encourage you to take out insurance to pay for private treatment, because you perceive a potentially worse impact on your finances if you were to need treatment.

Your perception of the risks posed by outside shocks will tend to vary according to the general economic climate. For example, in a recession people tend to save more because they perceive a higher risk of becoming unemployed and want the means to keep going financially if their main income is lost. Inflation can have a complex influence on financial planning. In the early stages of high inflation, people often save more to cope with rising prices but, if inflation persists, they may save less as they become aware that the value of their savings is being eroded.

In a climate of low inflation, the headline rates of return from investments may seem very low. Even though the real return – in other words the amount they get over and above inflation – might still be reasonable, people may decide to take higher risks as they seek higher headline returns.

All in all, the way you arrive at your list of financial targets and the priority you give to each one is a subtle and complex process. Although some targets should be built into everyone's financial skeleton, there can be no single rule which universally applies. In Appendix I is a checklist prompting you to clarify your own targets and priorities – this is the essential first step in financial planning.

Assessing your resources

If you had unlimited resources, you could meet all your financial objectives without problem and would have little need for financial planning. For most of us, life is not so straightforward. Usually, it is impossible to achieve instantly all we would wish; hard choices have to be made and targets have to be approached step by step.

The second stage in your planning has to be a frank assessment of what resources you have, what claims there are on them, to what extent resources are already being used to meet your targets and what surplus (if any) is available to further your plans. Appendix II contains Resources Calculators to guide you through this process.

It is important that you are as accurate as possible when filling in these Calculators. If you have doubts about any entries, check back to any relevant documents, such as pay slips, mortgage statements, bills and so on.

Once you have completed this stage, you should have a reasonably clear idea of what resources – both assets and money set aside out of income – are currently available for meeting your targets. You are also invited to consider how your resources might change in the foreseeable future, since this could influence your choice of financial tools, for example borrowing (that is, committing future resources to current spending), insurances with the option to increase payments later on, and so on.

Revising your targets

At this point, you might come to the conclusion that your targets are too ambitious in the light of the resources you have available. Something will have to give. You have several choices:

- boost your resources: for example by taking on extra work to increase your income
- alter one or more targets: for example if you had pencilled in a tour of India for next year, defer the trip for a year or two; if you had planned to retire at 55, consider retiring at 60 instead
- abandon one or more targets at least temporarily. If you have prioritised the targets realistically, the ones you abandon should be those to which you have given the lowest priority.

Alternatively, you might find that you have more resources than you had anticipated. This opens the way to increasing the scale of one or more targets, accelerating the timescale over which you plan to meet the targets or adding further targets to your plan. Once again, if you have allocated your priorities correctly, any new targets should be added after existing targets and would be the first to go if resources became tighter.

As you can see from the chart opposite, your financial targets are like a ladder, with your most fundamental priorities at the base and less important objectives on the higher rungs. The more resources you have, the higher up the ladder you can climb. A temporary fall in resources would mean retreating down the ladder a little; a windfall inheritance or unexpected pay rise would let you climb a bit higher.

Personal factors

In practice, measuring up your targets against available resources can be done only in a broad-brush fashion, if you have not thought about what financial tools could be used. After all, you need to know how quickly an investment might grow, or how much it might cost to buy a particular type of insurance. But there is another important stage to go through before you can pick the tools: you need to consider the personal factors that will tend to make some financial tools more appropriate than others for you. There are four key factors: tax, your attitude towards risk, your timescale for investment and your state of health.

Your tax position

It is essential that you consider the impact of tax on your financial planning, especially when choosing investments, because the way the proceeds are taxed will have a big impact on the return you get. Throughout Chapters 5–19, your attention is drawn to the tax treatment of the various financial tools, and guidance is given on how this should influence your planning.

A ladder of targets

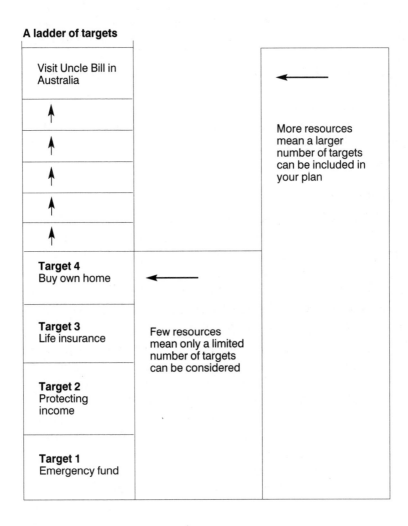

Visit Uncle Bill in Australia

More resources mean a larger number of targets can be included in your plan

Target 4
Buy own home

Target 3
Life insurance

Few resources mean only a limited number of targets can be considered

Target 2
Protecting income

Target 1
Emergency fund

The main taxes that concern you will be income tax and capital gains tax. An outline of these – and also tax credits – is given below.

Inheritance tax, which may be due on what you leave when you die and on some lifetime gifts, is also important. Chapter 19 provides a brief introduction. For more information, see *The Which? Guide to Giving and Inheriting* published by Which? Books*.

These taxes are all administered by the Inland Revenue* which produces a wide range of explanatory booklets, some of which are mentioned in this book. You can obtain them from any tax enquiry centre, your own tax office or the Inland Revenue website (see Appendix III).

The tax system is reviewed each spring in the annual Budget and other changes are often announced in the November Pre-Budget Reports. These are usually broadcast live and full details can be downloaded from the HM Treasury website (see Appendix III). Summaries are published in the next day's newspapers, in personal finance magazines and on many personal finance websites (see Appendix III). Make sure you keep abreast of these changes as they will often have a major impact on your financial planning.

Income tax

Income tax is charged on most types of income, including earnings as an employee, profits from self-employment, interest and dividends from most investments, pensions, and so on. It is charged at one of three main rates – the starting, basic and higher rates. In the 2003–4 tax year, these are 10 per cent on the first £1,960 of income, 22 per cent on the next £28,540 and 40 per cent on anything over £30,500. However, you do not pay tax on all your income because:

- some types of income are specifically tax-free, for example the return from National Savings & Investments certificates and, until 5 April 2004, dividends on shares held in individual savings accounts (ISAs) and personal equity plans (PEPs)
- certain expenses qualify for income tax relief, for example dona-tions to charity under gift aid or Give As You Earn, and amounts you pay into a pension scheme or plan
- you get an allowance which lets you have your first slice of income tax-free. You might get other allowances too.

The main tax allowances for 2003–4 are shown in the table on page 80. The personal allowance is deducted from your income before tax is worked out and so gives you tax relief up to your top rate of tax. The personal allowance is higher if you are aged 65 or over, and higher again if you are aged 75 or over.

If you are a married man and you or your wife were born before 6 April 1935, you can get married couple's allowance. (This allowance was abolished for younger couples from April 2000 onwards.) This allowance gives tax relief at a rate of 10 per cent as a reduction in your tax bill.

People aged 65 or over lose some of their allowances if their income exceeds a certain limit (£18,300 in 2003–4). They lose £1 of allowance for every £2 by which their income exceeds the income limit. The personal allowance is reduced before any married couple's allowance. However, the allowances are never reduced below a certain level. You stop losing your allowances when:

- **your personal allowance** has been reduced to the amount someone under age 65 gets – in other words, £4,615 in 2003–4
- **your married couple's allowance** has been reduced to £2,150 in 2003–4.

The lower table opposite shows the range of income for which someone over 65 will be losing age allowance. If your income is within this range, in effect your top rate of tax is 33 per cent, rather than just the basic rate of 22 per cent. Therefore, choosing tax-free income will often be particularly worthwhile for you.

The tax bands and allowances are normally increased each year in line with inflation. However, in 2003–4 the under-65s' personal allowance was frozen at £4,615.

Example: age allowance

In 2003–4, Jack is 72 and his wife is 76. Because of his age, Jack qualifies for a higher personal allowance of £6,610. But Jack's income is £18,900. This is £600 above the limit at which age allowance starts to be lost. Therefore, his age allowance is reduced by £600 ÷ 2 = £300, to £6,310.

Jack also qualifies for married couple's allowance. He gets the higher rate of £5,635 because his wife is over age 74. Jack's income is not so high that this allowance has to be reduced.

Main income tax allowances in 2003–4

Allowance	Amount	Saves you up to this much tax if you pay tax at:		
		Starting rate	Basic rate	Higher rate
Personal allowance – under age 65	£4,615	£196.00[1]	£1,015.30	£1,846.00
Personal allowance – age 65 to 74	£6,610	£196.00[1]	£1,454.20	£2,644.00
Personal allowance – age 75 and over	£6,720	£196.00[1]	£1,478.40	£2,688.00
Blind person's allowance	£1,510	£151.00	£332.20	£604.00
Married couple's allowance – age 67 to 74	£5,565	£556.50	£556.50	£215.00[2]
Married couple's allowance – age 75 and over	£5,635	£563.50	£563.50	£215.00[2]

[1] Income too low to use whole allowance
[2] Income too high to get age-related addition; allowance restricted to £2,150

Tax rates	Rate	On this much taxable income
Starting rate	10%	first £1,960
Basic rate	22%	£1,961 to £30,500
Higher rate	40%	over £30,500

Range of income where you are losing age allowance in 2003–4

Your status	Income range
Single person or wife aged 65 to 74	£18,300 to £22,290
Single person or wife aged 75+	£18,300 to £22,510
Married man under 65 with wife aged 68 to 74	£18,300 to £25,130
Married man under 65 with wife aged 75+	£18,300 to £25,270
Married man aged 65 to 67 with wife under 68	£18,300 to £22,290
Married man aged 65 to 67 with wife aged 68 to 74	£18,300 to £29,120
Married man aged 65 to 67 with wife aged 75+	£18,300 to £29,260
Married man aged 68 to 74 with wife under 75	£18,300 to £29,120
Married man aged 68 to 74 with wife aged 75+	£18,300 to £29,260
Married man aged 75+ with wife any age	£18,300 to £29,480

Tax credits

When considering your income tax position, you should also take into account tax credits. Despite the name, these are state benefits (not a reduction in your tax bill), but the amount you get is based broadly on your household's taxable income. Usually, you qualify for state benefits only if your income is fairly low , but, if you have children, you can qualify for tax credits even if your income is as high as £66,350 in 2003–4 and the amounts can be substantial – see Example on page 82.

The rules are tortuous, but here is a broad outline. You can claim working tax credit if you work at least 30 hours a week, or 16 hours if you have children or a disability. There are eight elements – see the table – and you add up each element that applies to you. But the total is then reduced by 37p for each £1 by which your income exceeds the 'first threshold', which is £5,060 in 2003–4. This means, if you have no children, you usually get no working tax credit if your income is more than £10,857 (single person) or £14,911 (couple). But, if you have children and claim the childcare element, you can get working tax credit at very much higher income levels.

If you have children up to age 16, or under 19 and in full-time education, you can also claim child tax credit. This has two elements: an individual element for each child plus a family element. The family element is higher for the first year if you have a new baby. The individual elements are added to your working tax credit (if any) and also reduced by 37p for each £1 of income over the threshold. If you get only child tax credit (and no working tax credit), the individual elements are reduced only if your household income exceeds £13,230 in 2003–4.

Every household with children can also get the full family element of child tax credit if their income is no more than the 'second threshold', which is £50,000 in 2003–4. Above this, the family element is reduced by £1 for each £15 of excess income, so the family element is entirely lost only if your income exceeds £58,175, or £66,350 if you have a child under the age of one.

Tip

If your income is in the region where you risk losing the extra age allowance (see the table opposite), be very wary of increasing the taxable income you get: for example, by cashing in a single-premium life insurance bond (see pages 337 and 363). Avoid the problem by choosing investments which give a tax-free return.

Tax credit elements in 2003-4

Element	Who can get it [1]	Amount
WORKING TAX CREDIT		
Basic	Everyone eligible for this credit	£1,525
Lone parent	Single parent caring for child(ren)	£1,500
Second adult	Most couples	£1,500
30-hour	Working at least 30 hours a week	£620
Disability	Disabled person	£2,040
Severe disability	Severely disabled person	£865
50-plus	Aged 50-plus and returning to work	£1,045 [2]
Childcare	Paying eligible childcare costs	70% of costs but ignoring costs over £135 a week (one child) or £200 a week (two or more children)
CHILD TAX CREDIT		
Individual element	For each child in your care	£1,445 [3]
Family element	Each family	£545 [4]

[1] Broad indication only – the rules are complicated.
[2] £1,565 if you work at least 30 hours a week.
[3] £3,600 or £4,465 if child is disabled or severely disabled.
[4] £1,090 if child under age one.

Example: tax credits
Arif and Julia have four children. They both work full-time, the household taxable income is £40,000 a year and they spend £220 a week on childcare. The couple can claim the following elements of working tax credit: basic, second adult, 30-hour, childcare; plus 4 × the individual element of child tax credit. In 2003–4, this comes to £16,705 but is reduced by 37p for every £1 by which their income exceeds £5,060. The credits are reduced to £16,705 − 0.37 × (£40,000 – £5,060) = £3,777. In addition they can get the full family element of child tax credit of £545. So, in total, they can claim £3,777 + £545 = £4,322 in tax credits in 2003–4.

> **Tip**
> Tax credits are not paid automatically – you must claim them. The government reckons that nine out of ten families with children are eligible. Because the amount you get is based broadly on your household's taxable income, you can increase the credits you get by, for example, switching to tax-free investment such as individual savings accounts and making payments, such as pension contributions and gift aid donations, that qualify for tax relief.

Capital gains tax

Capital gains tax (CGT) is charged on profits you make from selling or disposing of assets, such as investments, second homes, antiques, and so on. Chargeable gains are added to your taxable income for a given tax year and, in 2003–4, CGT is levied at 10 per cent on any part of the gain falling within the starting-rate band, 20 per cent on any part within the basic-rate band and 40 per cent on any part falling within the higher-rate band. However, some or all of your capital gains escape tax because:

- gains on some assets are tax-free: for example, your main home
- some transactions are tax-free: for example, gifts of assets to your husband or wife
- expenses associated with buying and selling the asset can be deducted before tax is worked out
- gains due purely to inflation up to March 1998 are not taxed
- losses on other assets can usually be deducted
- gains built up from April 1998 onwards may be reduced by 'taper relief' if you have held the asset for long enough
- the first slice of otherwise taxable gains each year (£7,900 in 2003–4) is tax-free.

Your attitude towards risk

Everyone's temperament is different. Some people give high priority to security and predictability. Others are relaxed with, or even crave, a high degree of uncertainty. The degree of uncertainty – or risk – with which you are comfortable will shape your financial planning and the financial tools you select, especially in relation to saving and investing.

Your attitude towards risk is not simply a reflection of temperament. It depends also on such factors as:

- **your income** If you have little cash to spare, you might quite rightly be reluctant to take risks with it; the more 'surplus' income you have, the more adventurous you can afford to be financially.
- **your age** In later years, especially after retirement, it may be difficult or impossible to replace any money you lose, which will tend to make you cautious; when you are young and earning, you can usually make good your losses.
- **your responsibilities** If, for example, you have a young family dependent on you, it might be unacceptable to risk their financial security; with only yourself to consider, the consequences of a gamble going wrong may not seem as important.

Starting out

The targets

Jason is 27 and works as a research chemist. He's been in full-time work since 1991 but joined his present company only in 1998. He's single and living in shared rented accommodation. He is considering buying his own house but there have been redundancies at work recently, so he has some concerns about job security. Jason is also thinking about a career break to travel or work abroad for a few years. Finally, Jason wants to make sure he'll eventually have a good pension.

The resources

Jason has an after-tax income of £1,200 a month. He pays £255 a month in rent and £100 on other bills. Food and household expenses account for £200. The other big expense for Jason is running a car. Repaying a car loan costs him £120 a month. Tax, insurance and petrol come to £100. Jason usually has £30 to £50 a month outstanding on his credit card. He estimates that leisure spending comes to about £100 a month. This leaves spare cash of around £200 to £300 a month which he currently puts in a savings account. Having recently paid the deposit on his car, Jason has just £500 in that account. His only other assets are £4,000 worth of shares which he'll receive in four years' time from a previous employer's share option scheme. Jason joined his current employer's pension scheme in

---

Throughout, this book highlights the areas where risk is a key element in your choice of financial tools and suggests ways in which you can attempt to match risk to your own attitude.

Your timescale for investment

This factor is in many cases intrinsic to your financial targets. For example, if you are saving for a holiday or to pay for a wedding, you generally have a set date in mind by which you need the proceeds of your investment. Some financial tools are completely inappropriate for such financial targets, either because they tie up your money for too long a period or because their capital value fluctuates and you cannot be sure of getting back the amount you need at a precise point in time. On the other hand, some financial aims are either long-term or open-ended and give you scope to choose from a much wider range of investments.

1999 and contributes £80 a month. He'll get a pension of 1/60 of his final salary for each year he's in the scheme.

The financial plan

- Save £100 a month out of surplus income to build up an emergency fund of at least £3,000 in an instant access cash ISA.
- Jason's savings account offers a poor rate of interest. Shop around for a better one.
- Compare the cost of a mortgage with the current rent. If – as is likely – a mortgage would cost no more, Jason should buy a home sooner rather than later. In the meantime, he should save towards the cost of house purchase using a savings account or the cash ISA.
- Jason should check what protection he has through work if he is off sick for a prolonged period. If the cover looks inadequate, he should consider taking out income protection insurance.
- Jason should put any remaining spare cash in a unit trust, OEIC or investment trust savings plan, investing through an ISA for tax-efficiency.
- The employer's pension scheme is a good one. Making more pension payments is not a high priority for now.

Which? January 2000

Your health

Health is a factor you need to consider when you take out many types of insurance and when you buy some types of annuity (a form of investment which is basically an educated gamble on how long you will live). Poor health can push up the cost of many insurances or even bar you from having them. The chapters that follow discuss the health factor wherever appropriate.

Chapter 5

Protecting your family

Your top priority if you have dependants is to ensure that they are protected financially if you were to die or be unable to work for a prolonged period. Chapter 6 looks at replacing income when you are ill. This chapter concentrates on the role that life insurance can play in your financial plan.

The chart overleaf summarises who needs life cover. Bear in mind that not only the loss of a breadwinner's salary could cause financial hardship: if you are caring for children, your spouse or partner might need to pay for professional childcare and/or babysitters if you were to die. Similarly, you should take into account any extra costs of running the house, maintaining the garden, and so on. A government survey found that, nationwide, housework – which even today is still done mainly by women – takes up more hours each day than paid work. If all the cooking, cleaning, childcare, gardening, and so on had to be paid for at the market rates for each activity, they would be worth some £340 billion – about half of the whole national income.

If you have identified that you need some life insurance, the next step is to work out how much. You might require a lump sum, for example to pay off the mortgage, as well as replacement income, which could be provided either by income-paying life insurance (known as family income benefit) or by insurance which pays out a lump sum which you could invest to produce the required income. This is discussed further on page 100. To find out the basic cash and income your family would need in the event of your death, work through the Calculator (see page 89). If you are married or live with a partner, you should each work through the Calculator separately. The notes following the Calculator will help you to fill it in.

Who needs life insurance?

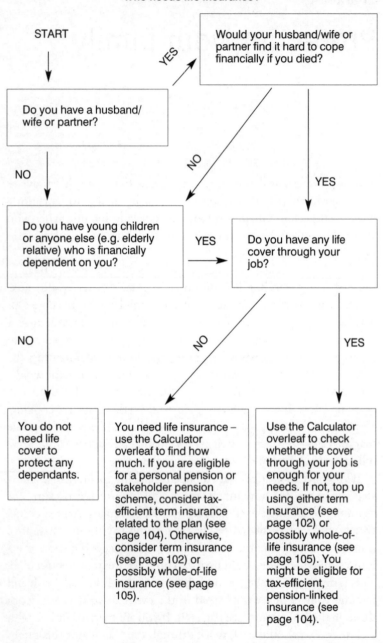

START

Do you have a husband/wife or partner?

Would your husband/wife or partner find it hard to cope financially if you died?

YES

NO

NO

Do you have young children or anyone else (e.g. elderly relative) who is financially dependent on you?

YES

Do you have any life cover through your job?

YES

NO

NO

YES

You do not need life cover to protect any dependants.

You need life insurance – use the Calculator overleaf to find how much. If you are eligible for a personal pension or stakeholder pension scheme, consider tax-efficient term insurance related to the plan (see page 104). Otherwise, consider term insurance (see page 102) or possibly whole-of-life insurance (see page 105).

Use the Calculator overleaf to check whether the cover through your job is enough for your needs. If not, top up using either term insurance (see page 102) or possibly whole-of-life insurance (see page 105). You might be eligible for tax-efficient, pension-linked insurance (see page 104).

Life insurance Calculator

Part 1: Cash required and cash available	£
Funeral expenses	a
Emergency fund to cover household expenses for, say, two months	b
Repayment of mortgage	c
Repayment of other loans	d
Inheritance tax	e
Bequests in will to people other than dependants	f
Other lump-sum expenses	g
TOTAL CASH NEEDED =a+b+c+d+e+f+g	A
Payout from existing insurance to cover mortgage	h
Lump-sum payout from any other existing insurance policies	i
Savings and investments which would be cashed in	j
Capital raised from sale of assets	k
Bereavement payment from state	l
Other lump sums available	m
TOTAL CASH AVAILABLE = h+i+j+k+l+m	B
NET LUMP SUM NEEDED Work out A – B. If the answer is zero or less, set C equal to zero Otherwise C = A – B	C

Part 2: Change in income and expenses   £/month

I: Reduction in income

Your earnings after tax and other deductions	n
Your pension	o
Your state benefits	p
Your spouse's/partner's earnings if he or she would give up work or work fewer hours	q
Income from investments which would be sold	r
Other income lost	s
TOTAL REDUCTION IN INCOME =n+o+p+q+r+s	D

II: Increase in income

Widowed parent's allowance or bereavement allowance from the state	t
Other state benefits	u
Other pensions	v
Income from any existing life insurance policies	w
Earnings if your spouse/partner would start work or work longer hours	x
Other	y
TOTAL INCREASE IN INCOME = t+u+v+w+x+y	E

III: Reduction in expenses

Mortgage and other loan repayments paid off	z
Living expenses saved	aa
Life insurance premiums and pension contributions	bb
Other	cc
TOTAL REDUCTION IN EXPENSES = z+aa+bb+cc	F

	£/month
IV: Increase in expenses	
Cost of childcare	dd
Cost of home help/odd-job person/gardener, etc.	ee
Cost of replacing fringe benefits of job, e.g. running a car, private medical insurance premiums	ff
Other	gg
TOTAL INCREASE IN EXPENSES = dd+ee+ff+gg	G

Part 3: Amount of cover required	£
Work out $D + G - E - F$. If the answer is zero or less, set H equal to zero. Otherwise $H = D + G - E - F$	H
Extra income needed each year $= H \times 12$	I
Lump-sum insurance needed to produce income I (see the table on page 101)	J
TOTAL LUMP-SUM INSURANCE REQUIRED $= C+J$	K

Part 1: Cash required and cash available
Funeral expenses (a)

Death is a costly affair. Among other items, there could be funeral director's fees to pay, including the cost of a coffin and hearse, minister's fees, charges for crematorium and/or burial plot, gravediggers' fees, flowers, and so on. Marking a grave with a headstone is another optional but expensive item to consider. A survey by Oddfellows Friendly Society found that the average cost of a UK burial service in 2000 was £2,048, and that of a cremation £1,215, but your survivors could easily spend a lot more. During your lifetime, you can pay either a lump sum or regular savings over, say, five years for a prepaid funeral plan (see page 108) which guarantees to cover the cost of your chosen funeral. If you have such a plan, amount 'a' will be reduced and could be zero.

Emergency fund (b)

In the event of death, there is likely to be a period of confusion and coming to terms with the new situation. Your family is likely to need a financial breathing space in which to sort out long-term money affairs. There might also be delays in distributing your possessions and turning them into cash if necessary. An emergency fund will tide your dependants over during this period. It need not be provided by life insurance. It could, for example, be money which you have in a joint account with your spouse or partner. Since there could be a delay before a life insurance policy pays out, it is a good idea to have at least part of the emergency fund in an instantly available form (see Chapter 18).

Repayment of mortgage (c)

If you have a mortgage, you might also have some life cover which will automatically pay off the mortgage in the event of your death (see Chapter 9). In this case, any value you put under 'c' will be balanced by the same amount under 'h' below. With a repayment mortgage or ISA mortgage (which are not necessarily sold in a package with insurance), you might not have matching life cover. You will have to decide whether you would want to pay off the mortgage. In general, this is a good idea, especially now there is no tax relief to reduce the cost of mortgage borrowing (see Chapter 9).

Repayment of other loans (d)

This covers things like the debt outstanding on your credit card(s). If you have taken out credit insurance to pay off, for example, a bank or car loan in the event of death, then the amount of loans covered by insurance will be balanced by an identical amount under 'i' below. (Note that credit insurance linked to loans does not necessarily pay the loan in the event of death; it might be limited to meeting the repayments if you are unable to work because of illness or redundancy. Check the policy to see what is covered.)

Inheritance tax (e)

Chapter 19 considers whether there is likely to be any inheritance tax to pay on your estate (your assets less your debts) when you die.

If your estate is worth less than £255,000 (in 2003–4) or you leave everything to your husband or wife, there will be no tax to pay.

Bequests to people other than dependants (f)

Your will, or the rules of intestacy if you did not make a will, may require some of your assets to be given away. See Chapter 19 for more information.

Other lump-sum expenses (g)

These might include, for example, buying a car to replace a company car which you had through your job (but not the expenses of running it – see 'ff' below).

Payout from existing insurance to cover mortgage (h)

This could be an endowment policy to repay an endowment mortgage or a mortgage protection policy to pay off a repayment or ISA mortgage. See Chapter 9.

Lump-sum payout from any other existing insurance policies (i)

This would include insurance taken out with a loan other than a mortgage. It would also include any other life insurance which you already have either through your work or policies you have taken out yourself.

Savings and investments which would be cashed in (j)

These could range from cash in a bank account to a portfolio of shares. If the investment had been producing an income, the effect of cashing it in will have to be taken into account at 'r' below.

Capital raised from the sale of other assets (k)

This could be the sale of valuable possessions, such as a car, boat, jewellery, and so on. You might consider trading down to a smaller home and so releasing some capital, but bear in mind that there could be a long delay before you manage to sell.

Bereavement payment from the state (l)

Bereavement payment is a state benefit your husband or wife should get if you paid the required National Insurance contributions during your working life (see page 98) and either you are or your husband or wife is under state pension age at the time of death. The payment is a tax-free lump sum of £2,000.

Bereavement payment is payable only to husbands and wives, not to unmarried partners. Your spouse can't get it if you were divorced or if you were still married but your spouse was living with someone else.

Other lump sums (m)

If your income and capital are very low, you might qualify for an emergency payment from the Social Fund. Other possible sources of help are gifts or loans from relatives.

Part 2: Change in income and expenses

Your earnings after tax and other deductions (n)

This is the amount of take-home pay which your household would lose if you are working. If you are an employee, enter your monthly pay after deducting income tax, National Insurance, contributions to an employer's pension scheme and any other deductions. If you run your own business, it is the amount of money which you draw out of your business for personal use.

Your pension (o)

Put here the amount of any pensions which would cease to be paid if you were to die. This could be state pension, pension from an employer's scheme or from a personal plan. If your spouse or other dependants would receive another pension, for example bereavement allowance from the state or a widow(er)'s pension from a pension scheme, enter this at 't' or 'v' below.

Your state benefits (p)

If you receive any state benefits, for example jobseeker's allowance or incapacity benefit, enter here the amount which would be lost. If your spouse or other dependants would receive other benefits instead, enter these at 'u' below.

Your spouse's/partner's earnings (q)

You are most likely to enter an amount here if you have children. Would your spouse or partner have to cut back on or stop work to look after them?

Income from investments which would be sold (r)

If you entered an amount under 'j' above, then put here any income which would be lost as a result.

Other income lost (s)

This might include, say, maintenance payments from a former spouse.

Bereavement benefits from the state (t)

If your husband or wife is under state pension age at the time of your death, they might qualify for either of the following benefits. They are available only to husbands and wives, not unmarried partners. Your spouse can't qualify if you were divorced or if, although still married, he or she was living with another partner. A widow or widower under age 45 with no children cannot qualify for either of these benefits.

Widowed parent's allowance

This is payable where your spouse is caring for a child or children (and entitled to claim child benefit) or expecting your unborn child and you have paid enough National Insurance contributions during your working life (see page 98). The allowance is made up of:

- a basic amount (£77.45 a week in 2003–4); plus
- part of any SERPS pension you had built up – see table on page 97 – and half of any state second pension (S2P) you had built up. SERPS and S2P are both state additional pensions – see Chapter 10 for details.

Your husband or wife might also qualify for an increase in child tax credit or become newly eligible to claim it – see page 80. This has replaced the child additions that are now payable with widowed parent's allowance only where claims were made before 6 April 2003.

The basic amount of widowed parent's allowance and any additional pension are taxable. The allowance stops when your spouse ceases to be entitled to receive child benefit or, if earlier, reaches state pension age, or remarries.

Bereavement allowance

If your widow or widower is not caring for children, he or she can obtain bereavement allowance provided he or she is over the age of 45 at the time of your death and you had paid enough National Insurance contributions during your working life (see page 98). If he or she is aged 55 or over, the full allowance (£77.45 a week in 2003–4) is paid. But for each year by which your spouse's age at your death falls short of 55, the allowance is reduced by £5.42 a week in 2003–4. The allowance is taxable. Bereavement allowance is paid for a maximum of 52 weeks. The allowance stops even earlier if your spouse reaches state pension age, remarries or starts to live with another partner.

Other state benefits (u)

If your spouse or partner would be left on a very low income, he or she might qualify for income support, housing benefit, working tax credit and various other means-tested benefits.

Regardless of whether you were married, your partner may be able to claim child tax credit (or an increased amount) if he or she will be caring for one or more children – see page 80.

If your widow or widower will already be over retirement age at the time of your death and does not qualify for the full state basic retirement pension based on their own National Insurance record (see Chapter 10), they may be able to increase their basic pension using your record.

They can also inherit part of any SERPS pension to which you were entitled – see table opposite – and half of any state second pension (S2P) (see Chapter 10).

Inherited SERPS pension

Date you reached (or would reach) state pension age	Proportion of SERPS pension your widow(er) can inherit[1]
5 Oct 2002 or earlier	up to 100%
6 Oct 2002 to 5 Oct 2004	up to 90%
6 Oct 2004 to 5 Oct 2006	up to 80%
6 Oct 2006 to 5 Oct 2008	up to 70%
6 Oct 2008 to 5 Oct 2010	up to 60%
6 Oct 2010 or later	up to 50%

[1] When added to any SERPS pension your widow(er) has built up in his or her own right, the total including the part inherited from you must not come to more than the maximum amount of SERPS pension that a single person could have (£138 a week in 2003–4).

Other pensions (v)

Enter here pensions your widow(er), partner and/or children would receive from occupational pension schemes which you belong to or personal pensions or stakeholder schemes you have. If these schemes or plans would pay out a lump sum, include it under 'i' or 'm' above.

Income from any existing life insurance policies (w)

If you already have life insurance which would pay out a regular income (that is, a family income benefit policy), record the monthly payout here.

Your spouse's/partner's earnings (x)

Would your spouse or partner take up a job, increase their hours or take up higher-paid work? Enter the likely increase.

Other (y)

Include here any other increases in income, such as rent from letting out a room in the family home. Enter the amount accordingly.

Mortgage and other loan repayments (z)

If the mortgage and/or other loans would be repaid ('c' and 'd' above), your family would no longer have to make repayments. Record the monthly amount saved here.

Help from the state for your widow or widower

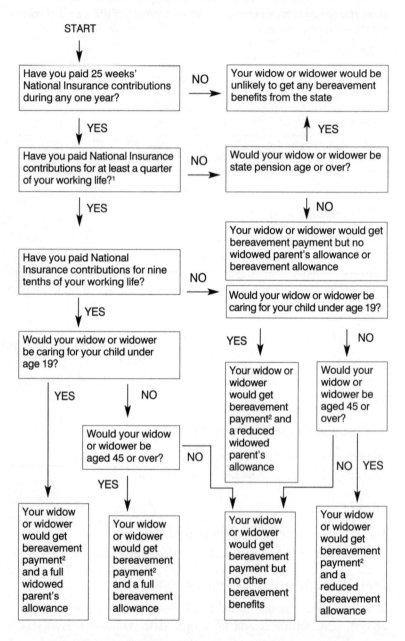

[1] Working life is officially defined to start with the tax year in which you reach age 16.
[2] Provided your widow or widower is under state pension age at the time of your death.

Living expenses (aa)

There is likely to be some reduction in food bills, travelling expenses, entertainment, and so on. Enter the amount accordingly.

Life insurance premiums and pension contributions (bb)

If you are paying for life insurance or into a pension plan, these amounts would be saved. Don't include deductions from your pay, for example for 'superannuation', as these are already accounted for under 'n'.

Other (cc)

Any other reductions in expenses, for example maintenance payments which no longer have to be paid to a former spouse.

Cost of childcare (dd)

Record here any increase in the amount the family would pay for childcare. If both you and your spouse or partner work anyway, there might not be much change from the current position. But if you stay at home to look after the children, your spouse or partner would face a hefty bill for a nanny, childminder or nursery, unless you have relatives or friends who would be willing to help. Bear in mind too that if you are the main breadwinner, your spouse or partner might have to take up work (increasing the family income under 'x') but might need to incur childcare costs in order to do so. They might qualify for state help with childcare costs through the working tax credit (see page 80).

Cost of home help, etc. (ee)

Would your dependants pay for other people to do jobs around the home which you had carried out?

Cost of replacing fringe benefits of your job (ff)

Your survivors might want to carry on enjoying some or all of the perks of your job. Replacing some fringe benefits, such as a company car, might mean paying out a lump sum and should be entered under 'g' above. But with others, regular expenditure might be required: for example, paying premiums for private medical insurance to cover hospital bills (see Chapter 7) or petrol and insurance for your car. Bear in mind, though, that any tax on such benefits will be saved.

Other (gg)

Enter here any other extra expenses not covered elsewhere.

Part 3: Amount of cover required

Do the sums shown in the Calculator. If amount 'I' is greater than zero, you need life insurance to provide the extra income shown. Either choose a family income benefit policy (see page 104) to provide the required amount, or lump-sum insurance which could be invested to provide the income. If you opt for the latter, consider who would manage the investments. To work out what size lump sum would be necessary, you could just multiply the yearly income by the number of years for which it will be required. But this is only a rough guide and will tend to overstate the amount of cover you need. To make a more accurate estimate, you should take into account the fact that an invested lump sum will earn some return which can also be put towards providing the income you need. To do this you'll have to take a view about future investment returns. The second column of the table opposite shows the lump sum you would need (to the nearest £100), assuming investment returns of 4 per cent a year, to provide *each* £1,000 of income – so if you would need £10,000 a year to be paid out for 15 years, you will need lump-sum cover of 10 × £11,600 = £116,000. The third column of the table shows how much you would need, assuming 4 per cent a year investment returns, if you wanted the income to grow by 2 per cent each year as some protection against rising prices. Bear in mind that 4 per cent investment growth and 2 per cent income growth are just assumptions. If you think investments might grow by less or your survivors would want larger income increases, you will need more life cover.

Add the lump sum required to produce the income your dependants would need to the cash sum (if any) worked out at 'C'. This tells you the total amount of lump-sum life insurance you ideally require. The next section describes the types of policy you could choose.

Which type of insurance?

There are two broad types of life insurance: **protection-only ('term insurance')** and **investment-type**. If your main need is for protection, there are two schools of thought:

Lump sum needed to provide each £1,000 of income a year

Period for which income is to be paid	Assuming invested lump sum grows by 4% a year	Assuming invested lump sum grows by 4% a year and income is increased by 2% each year
5 years	£4,600	£4,800
10 years	£8,400	£9,200
15 years	£11,600	£13,100
20 years	£14,100	£16,700
25 years	£16,200	£20,000

- The first recommends that you choose protection-only insurance, which is called 'term insurance'. In its simplest form, it pays out a specified amount if you die within a selected period of years. If you survive, it pays out nothing. It is the cheapest way overall of buying the cover you need. The numerous variations on this basic theme are described below.
- The second recommends that you choose a whole-of-life policy which is one form of investment-type policy. As the name suggests, this provides cover for as long as you live. Since the policy must eventually pay out, it builds up an investment value which you can cash in by surrendering the policy. But it takes many years for a surrender value to build up and, in general, whole-of-life policies are an expensive buy if your main need is protection. However, a variation called a 'maximum protection policy' lets you buy a high level of cover at a premium which is initially very low. This type of policy is discussed in more detail on page 105.

You should definitely avoid taking out an endowment policy if your primary need is protection. Endowment policies are investment-type life insurance which pay out if you die within a specified period (the endowment period) and also pay out if you survive. On the face of it this may seem appealing – something to gain whether you die or not – but such policies are an expensive way of buying life cover. Endowment policies can have a role to play in your financial planning, and this is considered in Chapters 9 and 16, but they are not a good tool for straightforward protection of your dependants.

Variations on the term insurance theme

Level term insurance

The standard policy pays out a set lump sum on death. You choose what level of cover you need and the period for which you require it – for example, until the children have finished their education, or beyond the period when Great Aunt Florence can reasonably be expected to be relying on your support. The lump sum is paid out tax-free if you die within that term.

The premiums you pay are set at the time you take out the policy and depend largely on the level of cover, the term you choose, your age at the start and your state of health. You will normally be charged more – or even refused cover – if your work, hobbies or lifestyle are deemed to be particularly risky. Some insurance companies reserve the right to increase the premiums – often substantially – if they experience unusually high levels of claims against their term insurance policies. This is a device which was adopted in response to the problem of deaths through AIDS.

Increasing term insurance

This works much like the basic term insurance, except that the level of cover increases – and usually the premiums too – for example by 5 per cent a year or in line with inflation. It is worth considering this type of policy, especially if you are insuring for a long term, because increasing prices eat away at the value of a fixed level of cover as the years go by.

Increasable term insurance

This variant gives you the option to increase the level of cover either at set intervals – such as on each anniversary of taking out the policy – or when particular events occur – for example, marriage or the

> **Warning**
> Investment-type life insurances, such as endowment policies, are an expensive way to buy life cover.

> **Tip**
> Overall, term insurance is the cheapest way to buy large sums of life cover to protect your family. A maximum protection plan might be cheaper in the early years, but watch out for premium increases later on.

birth of a child. You pay extra in premiums for any increase in cover, but the premiums are worked out on the basis of your health at the time you first took out the original policy, even if your health has subsequently deteriorated.

Decreasing term insurance

With this variant, the amount of cover reduces year by year. The two main uses for this type of insurance are to repay loans, such as a mortgage (see Chapter 9), or to cover a potential inheritance tax bill on a lifetime gift (see Chapter 19).

Renewable term insurance

This version allows you to extend the insurance term when it comes to an end. The premium you then pay is based on your health at the time you took out the original policy, even if your health has subsequently deteriorated. This can be a useful variation for dealing with the unexpected, for example a child who stays in full-time education for longer than you had expected.

It is also a good option if you cannot, at present, afford the level of cover you need for the period you want. Instead, you could take out the cover you need but for a shorter period. At the end of the period, you could take up your option for a further period. Premiums would then be higher because you would be older, but there would be no additional charge even if you had developed health problems.

Convertible term insurance

With this type of term insurance, you have the option at specified dates to convert your protection-only policy into an investment-type insurance policy based on your health at the time you took out the original term insurance. This option is of limited use. See Chapter 16 for more about investment-type policies.

Family income benefit insurance

Instead of paying out a single lump sum, this type of term insurance pays out a series of regular tax-free lump sums which you can use as income. The income starts to be paid at the time of death and continues until the end of the policy term. Since the policy pays out less overall the longer you survive, this is generally the cheapest form of term insurance and can be a good choice for families. A useful variation allows the regular income to increase over time to counteract the effects of inflation.

Pension-linked term insurance

If you are eligible to contribute to a personal pension or stake-holder scheme (other than one simply used for contracting out of part of the state pension scheme), you are also eligible to take out pension-linked term insurance. Chapter 12 explains who is eligible. If you are newly starting pension-linked term insurance, from April 2001 onwards, you can use up to 10 per cent of whatever you actually contribute to your personal pension or stakeholder scheme to buy pension-linked term insurance. This means you must be paying towards a pension to be eligible for the related term insurance.

If you started a policy before 6 April 2001, the rules are different. You can pay up to 5 per cent of your 'net relevant earnings' (basically your earnings if you are an employee or your profits if you are self-employed) towards the pension-linked term insurance. You can do this even if you are not making any contributions towards your pension.

The big advantage of taking out this type of term insurance is that you get tax relief on your premiums at your highest rate of income tax. The drawback is that what you pay towards any term insurance reduces the amount you can put towards a pension. But sometimes

Tips
- If you cannot afford the amount of life insurance cover you need, you do not necessarily have to insure for less. Consider taking out the full cover but for a shorter time, using renewable term insurance, which guarantees that you can take out a further policy at the end of the original term when perhaps you can afford to pay more.
- If you are eligible for a personal pension or stakeholder pension scheme, you can get tax relief on what you pay for term insurance.
- Don't assume that pension-linked term insurance will always be the cheapest cover; compare it with the premiums payable for ordinary term insurance too.

companies use this as an excuse to charge higher premiums for pension-linked policies than for their ordinary term insurance.

If you are in an occupational pension scheme, you will often get some life cover through the scheme. Usually, the most this can be is four times your salary. If your scheme offers less than the maximum cover, you may be able to increase it by paying additional voluntary contributions (AVCs) either to an in-house AVC scheme or a free-standing scheme. In either case, what you pay qualifies for tax relief at your highest rate, but does reduce the maximum you can pay towards your pension. See Chapter 11 for more about AVCs.

Maximum protection policies

Over the years, *Which?* has generally advised that you keep your protection and investment arrangements quite separate, independently choosing the best options to meet each need. However, there is one type of investment-type life insurance which does need to be considered within the context of protection: flexible whole-of-life policies which give the option of choosing maximum protection.

These are unit-linked policies (see page 363). The premiums you pay go into an investment fund which is divided up into units. The value of your policy depends on how the price of these units moves and that, in turn, depends on the value of the underlying investments in the fund. You decide how much life cover you want within limits:

- **minimum cover** Most of your premiums remain in the investment fund and hopefully build up a good cash-in value to give you a return on your investment. Alternatively, you might use the fund which has built up to pay for insurance later on: for example, to cover a potential inheritance tax bill (see Chapter 19).
- **maximum cover** Your units in the investment are cashed in each month to pay for the life cover. At this highest level of cover, and assuming a given return on the investment fund, it is expected that cover can be maintained at the same premium for, say, five or ten years. After that, it is likely that premiums would have to rise to maintain the same level of cover.

The policy is reviewed regularly, usually after the first ten years and after that every five years. At the review, the balance of premiums, investment fund and cover are checked. If your current premiums and fund are insufficient to maintain the chosen level of cover, either the premiums must increase or you must reduce your cover.

A maximum protection policy can be cheaper than term insurance in the early years and is, therefore, an option to consider if you need a lot of cover now for the lowest possible premium. But you must bear in mind that, at the policy review, your premiums are likely to rise or the cover reduce.

Other things to consider

Joint life policies

Instead of you and your spouse or partner taking out separate insurance policies, you could take out a joint life policy. A 'first death' policy covers both your lives and pays out once on the death of the first of you to die. A 'last survivor' policy pays out once on the death of the second of you to die. For protecting dependants, the 'first death' option is usually the more appropriate. A joint life policy will be suitable only if you both need to insure for the same amount. For example, a joint life policy may be ideal for paying off a mortgage in the event of one of you dying, but less suitable as a means of replacing lost income since the income needs will vary depending on which of you has died.

Writing life insurance in trust

If the proceeds of a life policy are paid to your estate on death, there can be a long delay before the money becomes available to your dependants and there could be inheritance tax to pay on the proceeds (see Chapter 19). Writing an insurance policy in trust avoids these problems by ensuring that the policy pays out direct to your dependants, bypassing your estate altogether.

Many insurance companies give you the option of writing a policy in trust at no extra charge and have standard forms for doing this. Policies on your life (but not joint life policies) which are to benefit your husband, wife or children can be very simply and easily written in trust using the Married Women's Property Act 1882. The form of trust set up under the terms of this Act cannot be altered later, so you need to make sure that it really does suit your requirements.

Life-of-another policies

So far, this chapter has considered life insurance policies you take out based on your own life, which pay out either to your estate or indirectly to someone else via a trust. An alternative is a policy which pays out direct to someone else if you die. This is called a life-of-another policy. For example, your husband, wife or partner takes out life insurance based on your life. If you die, the policy pays out direct to him or her, so there is no need to write the policy in trust.

With all types of life insurance, at the time the policy is taken out you must have an insurable interest in the life of the person covered. This means that you must stand to lose financially if he or she were to

---

Tip

In the vast majority of cases, it makes sense to have your life insurance policy written in trust. Make a point of asking the insurer's advice about arranging your policy this way.

---

die. You are assumed automatically to have an unlimited insurable interest in your own life and in that of your husband or wife. When it comes to other people, your insurable interest is limited to the amount that you would lose if they died. Therefore, a life-of-another policy cannot be taken out on someone with whom you have no financial connection. The main disadvantage of a life-of-another policy is if your relationship breaks down: your former spouse or partner owns the policy and has the absolute right to the proceeds if you were to die, so you may need to take out your own policy to ensure that any children would be financially provided for. On the other hand, where a relationship has already broken down, a life-of-another policy taken out by a parent with care of the children on the life of the absent parent can be useful as a way of protecting the family against the loss of maintenance payments in the event of the absent parent dying.

Waiver of premium

Both term insurance and whole-of-life policies may include 'waiver of premium'. This lets you suspend your premiums for a certain period in specified circumstances: for example if you are unable to work because of illness. You need to check the policy wording carefully to see precisely what conditions apply. Not all policies offer the waiver. With those that do, the waiver is sometimes automatically included and sometimes an optional extra. As an option, it could increase your premiums by around 6 per cent, say. Waiver of premium is a relatively cheap and straightforward way of making sure that your life cover would continue even if your finances were temporarily straitened.

Prepaid funeral plans

Even the simplest funeral is not cheap, and the idea of paying for your own funeral *in advance* is catching on in the UK. The advantages of a prepaid funeral are that you can choose the type of funeral you want and you don't have to feel a burden to relatives by leaving them to pick up the tab. Also it's easier to shop around for the best deal when you are planning ahead. Very few people feel inclined to shop around different funeral directors immediately following a death in the family.

Typically, a prepaid plan works like this. You choose a funeral and pay for it at today's prices – either by handing over a lump sum or by making instalments spread over, say, five years. The idea is that the plan will pay for your funeral whatever the increase in funeral costs between now and then.

In practice, you can't always rely on all the funeral costs being met. You can divide the cost into two parts:

- the funeral director's fees and expenses which the plan normally guarantees to pay; and
- 'disbursements' – things like doctor's fees, church fees, the cost of a minister, cremation fees, the burial fee, the gravedigging fee and the cost of a burial plot. Often a plan will guarantee to pay only the current cost of these plus any increase in line with general price inflation. But, in recent years, these costs have tended to increase much faster than inflation. If this continues to be the case, your estate or relatives could face a bill for, say, £200 or £300, despite your having a prepaid funeral plan.

You need to check the small print carefully to see just which costs are guaranteed and which are not. A survey by *Which?* found that although the literature usually made this clear, funeral directors and middlemen selling the plans often gave confusing and even misleading verbal guidance on this point.

You should also check what is included as part of the funeral. For example, a simple funeral might not include a church service – your estate or relatives would have to pay extra if this was to be part of your funeral. So be wary if you are attracted to a prepaid funeral plan. If a plan does not guarantee to cover all the costs, it might be better to earmark some of your savings or investments to cover eventual funeral expenses (see Chapters 14–17).

The money you pay for the plan is invested. It builds up a fund which the funeral director uses eventually to finance your funeral.

This raises concerns about what happens to the money you pay in. For example, in 1993, £35,000 disappeared from a prepaid scheme in Huddersfield and 30 elderly people's funeral arrangements were jeopardised. Fortunately, another company stepped in to help.

On the back of this and similar incidents, prepaid funerals plans were brought within the scope of the Financial Services and Markets Act 2000 (see Chapter 3). The Financial Services Authority (FSA)* has the powers, if necessary, to make rules governing the way such plans are run. However FSA regulation does not apply to plans where the money you pay in is used to buy whole-of-life insurance policy (which is already within the scope of the FSA's regulations) or the money is held in a trust fund that meets certain conditions. In a trust fund, the money should be safe from misuse by the funeral director and safe from the director's creditors if the firm goes bust.

The funeral industry has set up its own self-regulatory body called the Funeral Planning Authority (FPA)* to ensure that its members do meet the conditions which exempt plans from FSA regulation. FPA members observe a code of conduct which includes requirements to provide adequate information about what is covered in a contract, charges and so on. Members must have proper complaints procedures. Consumers also have access to the FPA's conciliation service and independent arbitration. If a member goes out of business, there is a commitment that the FPA will try to arrange for other members to take over the contract. Membership of the FPA is voluntary, so make sure any firm you deal with does belong.

Do not confuse prepaid plans with funeral expenses insurance. The latter is life insurance which on death pays out an amount which is intended to be enough to cover your funeral costs. However, the insurance is not linked to any particular funeral and there is no guarantee that it will be enough to cover the costs. Funeral expenses insurance is often poor value – because you are usually elderly when

---

Expensive funeral

Brendan took out a funeral expenses life insurance plan in 1990 when he was 69. It is designed to pay out £1,808 for a monthly premium of £16.95. However, he realised that by March 1999, he had paid more than the policy will ever pay out. He asked the company what he should do. It said he could surrender the policy and receive £422.36 now; stop paying the premiums but keep the policy – it would then pay out the paid-up value of just £578.96 when he dies; or keep up the premiums to ensure his family receives the full £1,808. Whatever he does, Brendan will lose money.

Which? January 1999

---

you start the plan, the premiums are high, and if you live a long time, you can end up paying more for the plan than it will pay out.

Prepaid funeral plans are sold through funeral directors and often advertised in magazines aimed at older people. If you do take out a prepaid funeral plan, don't forget to let your relatives know about it – otherwise they may arrange and pay for a funeral elsewhere, in which case your plan will be wasted. When choosing a prepaid funeral plan, be sure to ask: whether the firm belongs to the FPA; whether the proceeds are paid into a trust fund and who administers it; whether all disbursements are covered, regardless of inflation (and if this applies equally to burial and cremation); whether all incidental expenses are covered; what happens if you choose to pay by instalments and die before completion; and whether you can choose your funeral director without restriction.

More information

To find out more about most of the state benefits for which your dependants might qualify, see the relevant leaflets published by the Department for Work and Pensions (DWP)*. Leaflets are available from your local Jobcentre Plus*, social security office* or pension

Leaflets about state benefits you might claim following a death

NP45	A guide to bereavement benefits
GL14	Widowed?
CA09	National Insurance contributions for widows or widowers
D49	What to do after a death in England and Wales
D49S	What to do after a death in Scotland
IS20	A guide to income support
RR2	A guide to housing benefit and council tax benefit
GL16	Help with your rent
GL17	Help with your council tax
GL18	Help from the social fund
GL23	Social security benefit rates
SB16	A guide to the social fund
CH2	Child benefit claim form and notes
SERPSL1	Inheritance of SERPS: Important information for married people
WTC2	Child tax credit and working tax credit – a guide

For information on what to do after a death in Northern Ireland, see the website www.ssani.gov.uk

centre★, many public libraries, some post offices, by post and from the DWP website.

Child benefit and tax credits are administered by the Inland Revenue★, from where you can obtain explanatory leaflets and claim forms.

Got it covered

Andrea, 38, and Steven, 40, have two children, aged six and three. Andrea works part time and her employer provides her with life cover of four times her salary. Steven, who is self-employed, has no life cover but pays into a personal pension. Both salaries are needed to cover the family's costs.

If Steven died ... Because Steven is the higher earner and has no life cover, the family would be particularly vulnerable if anything happened to him. Andrea would receive the fund that has built up in his personal pension but that's all. Andrea needs a regular income while the children are growing up. She would like to keep working but would want to be flexible about her hours, particularly while the children are very young. If Steven's income was lost, Andrea thinks she would need about £2,500 extra each month. However, she also needs to think about retirement. She is a member of her pension scheme at work, but if she continues to work part time and reduces her hours further, this might not produce enough pension to live on so it might need topping up. A family income benefit policy on Steven's life which pays out an income of £30,000 a year for 18 years would provide Andrea with the income she needs until their youngest child is 21. A level term insurance policy for £50,000 would give her a nest egg for retirement and emergencies.

If Andrea died ... If Andrea's income was lost, Steven estimates he would need about £1,000 a month to cover extra childcare costs and to allow him to reduce his hours slightly to have more time with the children. He would have a lump sum of about £60,000 paid from Andrea's employers, so Steven does not need further capital. He needs a buffer to top up his earnings until the children are independent. A family income benefit policy on Andrea's life paying an income of £12,000 a year for 18 years would meet his needs.

Which? November 2000

To find out which insurance companies offer the best-value protection insurance, see the regular surveys in *Which?*★ and specialist personal finance magazines. If you have a fax machine, you can get rates from the *Moneyfacts* service (see Fax services★). Having narrowed down your choice to a few companies, contact those companies direct and ask them to send you literature about the policies you are interested in and to give you a quotation of how much you'll have to pay for the cover you want. (Some may refer you to an independent adviser.)

Chapter 6

Protecting your income

It is estimated that you are 20 times more likely to be off work for six months because of sickness or injury than you are to die before reaching retirement. Few people question the need for life insurance to protect their dependants if they were to die, but only one working person in ten has any specific long-term financial protection if they are unable to work because of sickness.

Government figures show that about one in six people report having an illness or disability which limits their activities and over two million people each year claim benefits for long-term sickness or disability. As the chart on page 117 suggests, few people would find it easy to cope with the financial impact of a prolonged illness. So why is this area of financial planning so often neglected? There are three main reasons:

- a mistaken belief that the state and employers will provide. A survey by Norwich Union Healthcare found that a quarter of the UK workforce believes they would receive their full salary from their employer or be supported by the state if they fell ill
- a lack of understanding about how you can arrange protection privately. This is not helped by the somewhat obscure name 'permanent health insurance' that used to be given to the main tool for protecting your income
- the relatively high cost and complexity of this form of protection.

What help can you expect if you fall ill?

The table on page 118 summarises the main types of health crisis that might damage your income. The two middle columns tell you broadly what help you might get from the state and from your employer. The final column suggests ways in which you can provide for yourself. The various sources of protection are described more fully starting on page 122.

Warning

Do not rely on the state to provide you with a reasonable income if you were unable to work for a long period due to illness or disability. You have to pass strict medical tests to qualify for incapacity benefit, and even then the average long-term payment was only £86 a week in 2002.

Protection from the state

Most people assume that the state provides a safety net to catch anyone who is unable to earn a living and has no other income to rely on. After all, is that not why we pay National Insurance? But you might be surprised at how little the state would provide if you could not work because of a long-term illness or disability. Since April 1995, the core help you can expect if you are off work sick is incapacity benefit; the main rules for this are described below. In the case of disability, you might also qualify for other state benefits – see page 119.

For the first 28 weeks

No benefits are payable for the first three days of illness. After that, most employees qualify for Statutory Sick Pay (SSP) which is paid by your employer – see page 121.

If you are self-employed or you are an employee who does not get SSP, and provided you have paid enough National Insurance contributions (see the chart on page 120), you can claim the lower rate of short-term incapacity benefit. In 2003–4 this is a tax-free £54.40 a week. There is no extra if you have children but you can claim child tax credit (see page 80). You can claim an increase for your husband, wife or partner, but only if:

- they are caring for dependent children of the family (an increase of £33.65 a week in 2003–4), or
- your spouse or partner is aged 60 or over (an increase of £41.50 a week in 2003–4), and
- if working, your spouse or partner earns no more than the amount of the increase.

During this first stage, you can qualify for incapacity benefit because you are unable to do your normal job – you will need sick notes from your doctor. However, you may be required to attend a 'work-focused interview', the purpose of which is to identify work you could do and to help you draw up a plan for training, getting a job or starting a business if appropriate. If you refuse to attend the interview, your benefit may be cut or lost completely. From week 29 onwards, you must pass a strict medical test called the 'personal capability assessment'. It looks at your ability to perform certain functions, such as standing, seeing and reaching. You'll have to be found incapable of doing *any* work, not simply your normal job, in order to continue getting benefit. The personal capability assessment also focuses on what work you could undertake, despite your illness or disability.

From week 29 to week 52

Provided they satisfy the medical assessment, both employees and the self-employed switch to higher-rate short-term incapacity benefit (£64.35 a week in 2003–4). Although the amount is higher, it is now taxable. This means that, if you have taxable income from other sources, you could actually receive less than you did during the first 28 weeks. If applicable, you still get the increase for your partner and child tax credit in respect of any children – see above. The increase for your partner is now also taxable, but child tax credits are tax-free (though the amount you get is dependent on your income).

After a year

You switch to long-term incapacity benefit (£72.15 a week in 2003–4). If you are terminally ill or you are very severely disabled, you can get this rate of incapacity benefit from the twenty-ninth week onwards.

Do you need to protect your income in case of illness?

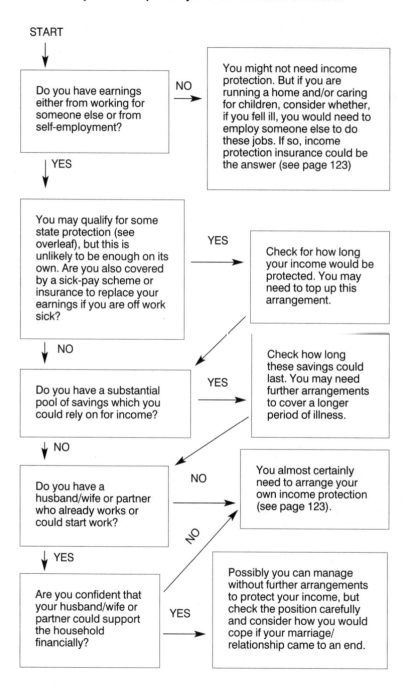

START

Do you have earnings either from working for someone else or from self-employment?

NO → You might not need income protection. But if you are running a home and/or caring for children, consider whether, if you fell ill, you would need to employ someone else to do these jobs. If so, income protection insurance could be the answer (see page 123)

YES

You may qualify for some state protection (see overleaf), but this is unlikely to be enough on its own. Are you also covered by a sick-pay scheme or insurance to replace your earnings if you are off work sick?

YES → Check for how long your income would be protected. You may need to top up this arrangement.

NO

Do you have a substantial pool of savings which you could rely on for income?

YES → Check how long these savings could last. You may need further arrangements to cover a longer period of illness.

NO

Do you have a husband/wife or partner who already works or could start work?

NO → You almost certainly need to arrange your own income protection (see page 123).

YES

Are you confident that your husband/wife or partner could support the household financially?

NO (to income protection box)

YES → Possibly you can manage without further arrangements to protect your income, but check the position carefully and consider how you would cope if your marriage/relationship came to an end.

117

How your income might be protected if you fall ill

What can go wrong	Help from the state [1]	Help from your employer	Possible private health insurances
You are off work sick for between 4 days and 28 weeks	• Incapacity benefit (lower rate) if you don't qualify for Statutory Sick Pay • Child tax credit if you have dependent children	• Statutory Sick Pay (unless your earnings are very low) *or* • Employer's own sick pay, if more generous than statutory scheme	• Sickness and accident insurance • Income protection insurance
You are off work sick for more than 28 weeks	• Incapacity benefit (higher rate/long-term rate) but you must pass a strict medical assessment • Disability benefits • Child tax credit if you have dependent children	• Sick pay if your employer runs a long-term scheme • Pension through early retirement on ill-health grounds	• Sickness and accident insurance – unlikely to extend beyond two years • Income protection insurance • Personal pension or stakeholder pension scheme – benefits can be paid from any age if you retire because ill, but the pension could be very low, especially if you are young
You have an accident which seriously maims you	• Benefits as above if you cannot work • Industrial injuries benefit if accident is work-related and you are an employee	• Protection as above if you cannot work • Lump sum if your employer has taken out accident insurance for employees	• Accident insurance • Critical illness insurance – some policies • Insurances as above if you are unable to work
You are diagnosed with a life-threatening illness	• Benefits as above if you cannot work	• Protection as above if you cannot work • Retirement pension might be replaced by a lump sum if you are not expected to live long	• Critical illness insurance

[1] In addition to the benefits listed, you might also qualify for income support, housing benefit and council tax benefit if your income is very low.

There is also an increase if you are under age 45 at the start of the illness. If you are under 35, you get an extra £15.15 a week in 2003–4. Between the ages of 35 and 44, you get less – £7.60 a week in 2003–4.

If you have children, you still get extra for your husband, wife or partner caring for your children, though this is paid at a higher rate than previously (£43.15 a week in 2003–4) provided he or she earns no more than £54.65 a week. This is taxable. You continue to claim child tax credit if you have dependent children (see page 80).

Long-term incapacity benefit is not payable if you are over state pension age, but you will usually qualify for state retirement pension instead (see Chapter 10).

Reductions in incapacity benefit

Since 6 April 2001, any incapacity benefit you qualify for will be reduced if you have income from pension schemes (which could be personal pensions, stakeholder schemes or occupational schemes) or income protection insurance (either your own policy or cover provided by an employer) and this income exceeds a given threshold. In 2003–4, the threshold is £85 a week (unchanged since its introduction). For every £1 of such income above £85 a week, you will lose 50p of benefit.

Other help from the state

Various benefits are available if you are deemed to be long-term disabled.

For example, you might get disability living allowance if you need help with your personal care or have mobility problems. Where an injury was due to an accident at work or you suffer from an industrial disease, you might get industrial injuries disablement benefit. If you work at least 16 hours a week and qualify for certain disability benefits, you might also get disabled person's tax credit which tops up your earnings.

Whether or not you get illness- or disability-related benefits, if your income is low, you might qualify for means-tested benefits to top up your income. If you are available for work, this will usually be non-contributory jobseeker's allowance. If you are not able to work, you might be able to claim income support. You might also qualify

Who can get incapacity benefit?

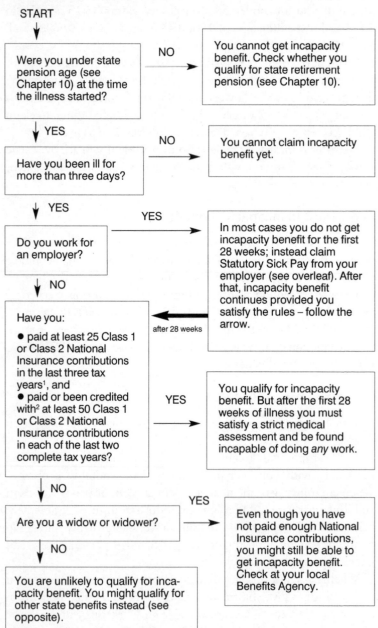

START

Were you under state pension age (see Chapter 10) at the time the illness started? — **NO** → You cannot get incapacity benefit. Check whether you qualify for state retirement pension (see Chapter 10).

↓ YES

Have you been ill for more than three days? — **NO** → You cannot claim incapacity benefit yet.

↓ YES

Do you work for an employer? — **YES** → In most cases you do not get incapacity benefit for the first 28 weeks; instead claim Statutory Sick Pay from your employer (see overleaf). After that, incapacity benefit continues provided you satisfy the rules – follow the arrow.

↓ NO

Have you:
● paid at least 25 Class 1 or Class 2 National Insurance contributions in the last three tax years[1], and
● paid or been credited with[2] at least 50 Class 1 or Class 2 National Insurance contributions in each of the last two complete tax years? — **YES** → You qualify for incapacity benefit. But after the first 28 weeks of illness you must satisfy a strict medical assessment and be found incapable of doing *any* work.

after 28 weeks ← (arrow pointing back to the 28 weeks box)

↓ NO

Are you a widow or widower? — **YES** → Even though you have not paid enough National Insurance contributions, you might still be able to get incapacity benefit. Check at your local Benefits Agency.

↓ NO

You are unlikely to qualify for incapacity benefit. You might qualify for other state benefits instead (see opposite).

[1] Before 6 April 2001, this condition was satisfied if you had paid the contributions in any one tax year (rather than the last three).
[2] You may have been credited with contributions if you were out of work because of, say, illness or unemployment.

for help paying rent and council tax. You will not normally be able to get means-tested benefits if you have savings of more than £8,000. The benefit you get will be scaled down if your savings are less than this but still more than £3,000. Higher capital limits apply to people over age 60 and people living in residential and nursing homes.

If you have a disability but work at least 16 hours a week, you may be able to claim working tax credit including a disability element (see page 80).

How much help from the state?

Precisely what benefits you will qualify for and how much help you get will depend on your particular circumstances. See below for an example of how much a single-earner family with two children might get.

Example: how much state help?

Joe is self-employed and was earning £28,000 a year after tax, but has been off work for over a year with back problems. His wife Delia does not go out to work but looks after their two children, aged 2 and 3. In 2003–4, Joe is getting long-term incapacity benefit for himself of £72.15 a week plus an increase for Delia of £43.15, making a total of £115.30 a week or £5,995.60 a year. After tax, this is reduced to £5,857. The couple also claim child tax credit (see page 81) made up of two individual elements (2 x £1,445 = £2,890) and the family element of £545. In total, the couple's income is £5,857 + £2,890 + £545 = £9,292 a year, in other words just a third of their previous income.

Protection through your job

By law, your employer must usually pay you at least a minimum amount if you are off work sick for more than three days; this is called Statutory Sick Pay (SSP). In 2003–4, SSP is set at £64.35 a week. It is taxable just like ordinary pay, so income tax and National Insurance may be deducted from it if you also have some other income. SSP is payable for up to 28 weeks.

If you earn less than the 'lower earnings limit' – a figure set by the government each year, equal to £77 a week in 2003–4 – your employer does not have to pay you SSP. A few other groups of employees are not covered by the scheme, including workers over state pension age, anyone on a contract lasting less than three months and people working for overseas employers. If your employer does not pay you SSP, he or she must give you a claim pack SSP1. This includes a claim form for incapacity benefit, which you might be able to get instead.

Your employer may run a sick-pay scheme which is more generous than the minimum SSP: for example, maintaining your full pay for several months and then perhaps half-pay for a few more. Some employers take out insurance to provide income for sick employees over a longer period; this is called 'group income protection insurance'. The insurance works in a similar way to the private insurance you can arrange for yourself (see below), except the income it pays out is taxable. Income protection insurance through your job usually counts as a tax-free fringe benefit.

If you are unlikely to be able to return to work at all, you may qualify for early retirement on the grounds of ill health. This could trigger an immediate pension from your employer's pension scheme if it runs one – see Chapter 11.

Check your contract of employment to see what arrangements apply to you.

Arranging your own protection

The main way in which you can make sure that you would still have enough to live on if you could not work because of illness is by taking out insurance. There are three types of policy to consider, which are described below.

Warning

Whenever you apply for insurance, you are under a duty to disclose all 'material facts', in other words information that might affect an insurer's decision to cover you or the premium that will be charged. This is especially important with health insurances, where a subsequent claim may be refused if you have failed to disclose information about symptoms or treatment you have had for a health problem you already had before applying for cover (called a 'pre-existing condition').

Income protection insurance

Income protection insurance (IPI) replaces part of your income if you are unable to work because of illness or disability. IPI has been available for around 50 years but in the past has been known by an array of different and often confusing names, including permanent health insurance (PHI), long-term disability insurance and income replacement insurance.

Since 6 April 1996, income from IPI has been tax-free. Typically, the maximum income you are allowed to replace is 50 to 65 per cent of your income before tax (your gross salary if you are an employee or your taxable profits if you are self-employed). Usually this limit includes replacement income from all IPI policies, pension schemes and so on. Often it also includes benefits you are entitled to claim from the state. You won't be able to claim more than the permitted maximum, so it's important to work out the limit which applies to you and make sure you don't pay extra for cover you wouldn't be able to have.

The replacement income is normally paid until retirement or until you recover, whichever comes first. But some budget policies limit the maximum payout period to, say, two or five years. This makes the plans cheaper, but would leave you unprotected if you suffered a prolonged illness or permanent disability.

There's no doubt that IPI is expensive, but there are various steps you can take to cut the cost.

You choose how soon after the onset of an illness you want the policy to start paying out. This is called the 'waiting period' or 'deferred period' and can normally be 4, 13, 26, 52 or even 104 weeks. Choosing a longer waiting period reduces the premiums you pay. You can fit the waiting period to your other resources, for example a sick-pay scheme at work, or savings.

When choosing the amount of income you want the policy to provide, you do not have to opt for the maximum allowed under the policy rules. You can choose a lower amount. Work out what level of spending you need to cover.

The payout can be at a flat rate. Alternatively, you can opt for an increasing income – worth considering, since otherwise inflation will erode the value of the income. There are two aspects to this: first, you want to know that the amount you would start to get if you made a claim is being increased each year; secondly, once an income is being paid, you want to be sure that it will be increased. The drawback is that the premium increases each year along with the cover.

Watch out for the definition of 'inability to work' used by the policy. There are three possibilities:

- inability to do your own job
- inability to do a job for which you are suited by training and experience
- inability to do any job.

The last definition is the broadest, reducing the likelihood of your having a valid claim, so you should expect to pay less for a policy using this definition. The first definition is the narrowest and usually the most expensive. Some policies change the definition after, say, two years. For example, you might be covered for the first two years if you can't do your normal job, but then payouts cease unless you are so ill or disabled that you can't do any job.

Premiums are set on one of three bases. Most common and generally cheapest are *reviewable premiums*. These are set for an initial period – usually five years – after which they can be increased if the insurance company finds that claims by its policyholders are higher than it had expected. But any increase in premiums as a result of a review will apply to *all* policyholders as a group, not just to selected individuals.

Renewable policies have a fixed term, typically five years, after which you can take out a further fixed-term policy but based on your age at renewal and, with some companies, a reassessment of your health and other factors at that time.

The most expensive policies have *guaranteed premiums*, which are set for the full duration of the policy and do not increase (except with increases in cover).

How premiums are set at the start of the policy depends on a wide range of factors:

- **your sex** Usually, women have to pay substantially more (for example, around half as much again) as men for the same cover. This is because, as a group, they tend to make more claims and for longer periods.

- **your age** at the time you first take out the policy. IPI is more expensive the older you are, because older people tend to have more health problems.
- **your job** Some jobs carry bigger risks to health than others. For example, your premiums will be lower if you have a relatively 'safe' job, such as a bank manager, civil servant, computer programmer, or secretary, than if you are a manual worker or driver, say. Some workers, for example bar staff and divers, might find it hard to get cover at all. Some plans offer cover to housewives and househusbands, deeming the value of their work to be equivalent to earnings of, say, £10,000 a year. The insurance providers set their job categories according to their own experience of claims. A job treated as high risk by one insurer might be assigned a lower risk by another, so it is definitely worth shopping around.
- **your state of health** Expect to pay higher premiums or be refused cover altogether if you already have health problems. However, with most policies, once you have been accepted for cover you will not be turned down or have your premiums loaded because you *subsequently* claim on the policy. But while all IPI insurers refuse claims related to AIDS or HIV, a few will not continue your cover at all if, having taken out a policy, you are subsequently diagnosed as HIV-positive.
- **your hobbies** Expect additional premiums or restrictions on cover if you enjoy flying, racing or other sports which insurers consider dangerous.
- **your lifestyle** Smokers are often charged more, you'll usually have to give details of how much alcohol you drink regularly, and insurance companies want to find out whether there's a risk of your contracting HIV.
- **the chosen level of payout** The higher the income you choose, the higher the premiums.
- **the waiting period** The sooner you want the payout to start, the higher the premiums.
- **other policy options** For example, you pay more for increasing policies than ones paying out a level benefit.

Income protection policies can either be pure insurance, in which case your monthly premiums go directly to buy the cover you've selected, or they can be investment-linked. With the latter, your monthly payments are invested and the cost of the insurance is paid from your investment fund. Your plan is reviewed, typically, every five years. If the investments have grown by a target rate or more, cover continues at the standard price (and you might receive a cash sum when the policy comes to an end). But if the investments have not grown as well as expected, your premiums are increased or the cover might finish earlier than you had originally intended.

Payment protection insurance

Don't confuse payment protection insurance with full IPI (see above). The former is taken out in conjunction with, say, a mortgage (see page 179) or some other type of loan. It is a type of accident and sickness insurance (see below) and often also includes cover if you are unemployed. But in general, the payouts just cover the interest or repayments on the loan and do not provide the extra replacement income you would need to cover other expenses.

On the other hand, it is common for mortgage-linked payment protection insurance to give you the option of adding extra cover. For example, in the event of illness or unemployment, the policy would cover your monthly mortgage payments and also give you extra cash equal to, say, £3 a month for each £1,000 of your initial mortgage. It would be up to you how you used the extra cash, so it could be put towards covering your household costs. However, you should be wary of looking on this type of insurance as a substitute for full IPI, since the amount of extra cash is not directly linked to your spending needs. And a major disadvantage of payment protection insurance policies compared with full IPI is that typical payment protection insurance pays out for a maximum of one or at most two years, so you are not protected in the event of a long-term illness.

Sickness and accident insurance

Accident insurance pays out a tax-free lump sum if you suffer a specified injury or die: for example, you might get £5,000 for the loss of a finger or a big toe, £10,000 for the loss of hearing, £100,000 for permanent disability. Although this type of insurance is very cheap – sometimes it is even offered free as an enticement to you to take up some other financial product – the probability of your suffering the particular injuries which are covered is very low. On the whole, accident insurance on its own is not worth buying.

However, accident insurance is often included with other insurances, such as travel policies and car insurance. It is also sometimes combined with sickness insurance (the latter is not offered on its own). The sickness insurance element of the policy typically pays out a limited income, usually from the first week you are ill, for a maximum of two years, if you cannot work because of illness or an accident. As with IPI, the income has been tax-free since 6 April 1996. Unlike IPI, there is no ongoing cover with sickness insurance; you simply take out the policy for a year at a time. At renewal, the premiums can be increased or cover refused if you have built up a record of claims or suffered a deterioration in your health. For this reason and because of the limited period for which the benefits are payable, sickness insurance is a poor substitute for IPI.

Critical illness insurance

Critical illness cover (CIC) pays out a sizeable tax-free lump sum if you are diagnosed with a specified life-threatening condition or have to undergo certain types of surgery. Over the last ten years or so, CIC has become increasingly popular due to its relative cheapness and seeming simplicity

CIC policies are often sold as part of a mortgage package and are also sold as stand-alone policies. CIC is also commonly combined with life insurance, with some policies paying out either on diagnosis of a specific illness or on death and others paying out in both events.

When you first take out the policy, you may be able to opt for 'buy-back CIC' or 'buy-back life insurance' which lets you take out further CIC or life cover, often at a nominal cost, after you have claimed on a CIC policy. This is certainly worth considering. Survival rates from a critical illness are often good and it is usually impossible to get new cover in the years immediately following such an illness. Typically, buy-back CIC covers the major three critical illnesses – heart attack, stroke and cancer – from which you are most likely to recover but also risk a further attack.

There is often a waiting period between diagnosis and payout: for example, 28 days or even as long as six months or a year for certain conditions, such as total permanent disability. However, if the diagnosis is clear-cut, the insurer might be prepared to waive the waiting period.

The maximum payout varies from policy to policy, with £500,000 or £1 million being common, though cover for higher amounts might be available on request. Where the policy is linked to your mortgage, the lump sum is obviously designed to pay off the mortgage but, with other policies, there are no restrictions on how you use the money. For example, you might use it in the same way as an income protection policy to cover living expenses while you are off work, but equally you could pay for private medical treatment, buy the services of a carer, adapt your home, put it towards retraining for a less stressful career, help your dependants or even take a holiday.

Nearly all policies cover seven core conditions: cancer, heart attack, stroke, kidney failure, coronary artery bypass, multiple sclerosis and major organ transplant. Insurers who are members of the Association of British Insurers (ABI) – and most are – agree to use standard definitions of both these core conditions and many of the additional conditions that policies typically cover, such as blindness, motor neurone disease, Parkinson's disease and third degree burns. The ABI reviews these definitions usually once every three years.

Although CIC seems on the surface to be a fairly straightforward type of insurance, medical advances make it increasingly complex. Health conditions that a few years ago were unequivocally 'critical' may no longer be life-threatening or disabling. For example, prostate cancer can now be detected at a much earlier stage when the chances of successful treatment are greatly increased. This has led the ABI to change its standard definition of cover to: *'all tumours of the prostate unless histologically classified as having a Gleason score greater than 6 or having progressed to at least TNM classification T2N0M0'*. While this clarifies the validity of claims for insurers, it is total gobble-de-gook for the average consumer. But the alternative would be to have simpler, broader definitions that would allow increasingly more claims for non-critical conditions with a commensurate increase in premiums – perhaps to the stage where CIC is no longer affordable at all.

Beware of policy exclusions: for example, some policies do not cover Alzheimer's or Parkinson's disease if it is first diagnosed after the age of 60, which is very likely to be the case. Also, do not be overly impressed by long lists of ailments; often another policy will cover the same conditions but under one of its broader headings. For example, in recent years some insurers have added Creutzfeldt

Jakob Disease (CJD) as a specified condition, but this would almost certainly be covered under another section, such as coma, terminal illness or total permanent disability.

Cancer, heart attacks, stroke, total permanent disability and multiple sclerosis account for nine-tenths of all claims, with cancer topping the list by a wide margin (54 per cent of all claims). Government statistics show that about one person in three develops cancer and around a fifth of the population have a cardiovascular disease, ranging from angina and high blood pressure through to heart attacks and stroke. Overall, nearly two-thirds of the population suffer a critical illness at some stage in their lives. In the past they would often have died, but survival rates are now reasonably good. For example, 40 per cent of cancer sufferers survive for five years or longer, and over half of heart attack victims are alive ten years later.

CIC is substantially cheaper than IPI, which makes it look a tempting substitute. However, although a large lump sum from a critical illness policy could be used to provide a replacement income for an extended period, the range of conditions it covers is by definition limited. If you are unable to work because of, say, a back injury or stress (both common conditions), a critical illness policy will not be any help.

Warning

Some policies combine CIC with life insurance but pay out just once – either on diagnosis of a life-threatening condition or on death, whichever happens first.

Be wary of these policies. They make sense if you intend to use the payout to, say, pay off your mortgage. But, if you would use the payout to cover care costs while you were ill but also want to protect your family if you die, this type of policy is not suitable unless it includes a life cover buy-back (see page 127). Without a buy-back, using the payout during your lifetime would leave your survivors unprotected in the event of death.

More information

To find out more about the state benefits you might qualify for if you are ill, contact your local Jobcentre Plus★ or, if you are over pension age, The Pension Service★ or check out the website of the Department for Work and Pensions (DWP).★

See the table below for a list of useful leaflets about state benefits. Most are published by the DWP, but tax credit leaflets are produced by and available from the Inland Revenue★.

Free leaflets about the main state benefits if you are ill or disabled

Leaflet number	Title
DWP leaflets	
SD1	Sick or disabled
SD2	Sick and unable to work?
SD3	Long-term ill or disabled?
IB1	A guide to incapacity benefit
IB214	Incapacity benefit: the personal capability assessment
GL23	Social security benefit rates
Inland Revenue leaflet	
WTC2	Child tax credit and working tax credit – a guide

Check your contract of employment or talk to your Human Resources department to find out what arrangements your employer has for paying sick employees.

Magazines such as *Money Management*★ publish regular surveys of income protection policies and critical illness insurance. Having identified suitable policies, you can contact most companies direct. However, because of the complex nature of income protection insurance and the many factors influencing premiums, this is an area where it is probably worth visiting an independent financial adviser. A good adviser will have access to a database of most or all of the policies available and can arrange quotations of those which would be most suitable for you.

Don't underestimate homework

Melanie, 28, and Peter, 31, have recently had their first baby, which started them thinking about their finances. In particular they were worried about what would happen if either one of them died or couldn't work. Which? drafted in the help of two independent financial advisers to give them advice.

Peter is a children's worker and Melanie is a full-time mother. The couple have a monthly income of £1,350 but, because of some fairly strict budgeting, still manage to save £100 each month and have around £150 left over.

As well as life insurance – a real priority – the advisers look at income protection. Neither of the experts recommend critical illness cover – it isn't as helpful as income protection and should be seen as an extra rather than an alternative.

The risk of being off work for six months is considerably higher than the risk of dying before the age of 60. As Peter is the only earner, it's important that the family could cope financially if he couldn't work. But forking out for income protection insurance is unnecessary. Because his income is reasonably low, the total amount of state benefits he could claim would actually be greater than the maximum amount he could insure himself for. That's because insurers don't want claimants to be better off sick than when working. The maximum benefit Peter could get under a policy would be around £200 tax-free a week. The couple will need to review the situation if Peter's salary increases and/or the benefits he could claim change.

They also need to think about what would happen if Melanie became too ill to look after the baby. They might need to pay for childcare or help around the house. It could be worth taking out insurance to cover these expenses, as Melanie would not be entitled to state benefits or sick pay. Most income protection policies allow you to take out houseperson's cover. You're usually limited to a maximum yearly benefit of around £15,000. The family could expect to pay between £20 and £25 a month for a policy that would start to pay out after six months of illness. The cost would be higher if they wanted the policy to start paying out earlier.

Which? September 2002

Duty to tell all

When Val learnt that she had multiple sclerosis (MS), one small comfort was that she had taken out insurance that would pay out a £50,000 lump sum if she contracted a serious illness and would pay her an income if she was unable to work. However, Val was shocked when the insurer refused to pay out because of 'non-disclosure'. The term means that the company can refuse your claim if it believes you didn't disclose all relevant information when you applied for cover. When she claimed, the insurer asked to see Val's medical records. These showed some visits to her GP which she hadn't put on the application form. Two incidents – of blurred vision and pain in one eye – were diagnosed as eye strain. Another two related to tingling in her thigh and backache, for which no diagnosis was made. Val explained that these incidents were temporary and didn't require any time off work. Her doctor clearly didn't feel they were significant and consequently neither did Val. MS was not diagnosed until two years after the last incident. But the insurer said that had Val disclosed the problems, its underwriter would have recognised the early symptoms of MS and would not have offered cover.

The insurer's adviser who helped Val complete the application forms did not mention the importance of disclosing medical incidents, even seemingly trivial ones. Val took her case to the ombudsman, but her claim was rejected. The non-disclosure rules mean that the customer alone must bear the responsibility of deciding what is or is not a relevant fact.

Which? July 2001

Chapter 7

Insuring against illness

Unlike most of the other areas described in this book, insuring against illness does not meet an *essential* need – after all, the National Health Service (NHS) provides cradle to grave care, doesn't it? Well, up to a point. The promise of a huge increase in funding for the NHS over the period to 2008 has not stemmed a steady increase in the number of people willing to 'go private'. Their decision reflects actual or perceived shortcomings in NHS provision.

Over 1 million surgical procedures every year are carried out privately. A survey by Which? found that the most common reasons for choosing private treatment are:

- to see a consultant more rapidly
- to avoid NHS waiting lists for operations, and
- to choose a convenient time to be treated.

Private treatment is not cheap and one way to cover the cost is to plan ahead by taking out private medical insurance (PMI). PMI covers some 6.7 million people with nearly three-quarters getting cover through work. But PMI itself can be costly, especially as you get older, and, according to the Independent Healthcare Association (IHA), the number of people choosing to fund their own private treatment has almost doubled over the last five years to over 250,000.

Who needs private treatment?

Traditionally, the NHS provides cradle-to-grave care largely free at the point of use. Like any service which is free to users, there is a built-in tendency for demand to mushroom. Resources are limited, so some form of rationing or queuing is inevitable. For example, in March 2003, in England alone, there were just under a million people waiting to be admitted to hospital (for inpatient or day-patient treatment).

In the past, many such patients could expect to wait a year or more, but government efforts to reduce inpatient waiting lists mean that very few patients now have to wait quite that long. However, waiting to be admitted to hospital is only part of the story. The usual pattern of treatment is that first you visit your GP, who then refers you to a consultant as an outpatient, who in turn may recommend that you be admitted. The government target is that you should wait no longer than 26 weeks for your first outpatient appointment with a consultant, but – as the table below shows – thousands of people have to wait longer.

Clearly, waiting months for treatment is likely to be unpleasant, especially if you are in pain. But in some cases it can be a financial disaster as well. For example, if you run your own business, you simply may not be able to afford to be off work for months pending treatment. The same thinking is behind the increase in the number of employers offering cover for private treatment as a fringe benefit to employees.

More controversially, going private might sometimes give you access to better treatment. For example, a case in the news in April 2000 involved a woman suffering from breast cancer. Her consultant explained that one drug existed which would almost certainly cure

NHS waiting lists

	Patients waiting more than 12 months to be admitted (as inpatient or day patient)	Patients waiting more than 26 weeks to see a consultant (as an outpatient)
England	229	9,655
Northern Ireland	11,543	n/a[†]
Scotland	1	44,850
Wales	12,382	76,399

[†] not available: statistics differ in presentation

Source: Government figures 1st quarter 2003 (2nd quarter 2003 for Northern Ireland)

her while a second was good but less reliable. Because the first drug was considered too expensive, the district health authority would not allow it to be prescribed on the NHS. However, the drug, which had been in use for many years, was available to patients who could pay for private treatment.

Going private lets you choose a time to go into hospital which is convenient for you, given your family, work and other commitments. You can expect quality treatment because you will be seen by a consultant rather than a more junior doctor, as is often the case on the NHS. Going private also lets you enjoy hotel-style facilities, such as your own room, TV and private bathroom.

On the minus side, most private hospitals do not have on-site emergency facilities, so even if you opt for the private route you will still be treated on the NHS in a crisis. This means you might have to be moved to another hospital if your condition became critical.

Who needs medical insurance?

A major drawback of private treatment is its high cost (see the table on page 137). However, it is estimated that only four out of every 100 procedures cost more than £5,000. So one option is to set aside some of your savings and simply pay for private treatment as and when you need it (called the 'self-pay' option). The IHA estimates that around a fifth of the cost of private treatment comes out of the patient's own pocket. The most common operations done on a self-pay basis are hip replacements, cataract removal and knee replacements, reflecting the fact that older people make up a high proportion of self-payers. Shopping around for a hospital is often worthwhile. Some hospitals run special deals, such as a fixed price for selected operations, particularly at times of the year when demand for beds tends to be lower. There are even specialist advisers, Health Care Navigator★ and Go Private★, which for an annual fee take customers through the process of getting private treatment at an affordable price.

Given that medical insurance is costly, especially as you get older, the self-pay route may be a good option for many people. But it is not without drawbacks. The first is that a need for treatment might arise soon after you had started saving and before you had built up a large enough fund. The second is that, however much you saved, there would always be an outside chance that you would need very costly treatment – for example, a series of operations – that would require more than you had set aside. You could resign yourself to falling back on the NHS if your savings are not enough.

Or you could take out a loan to cover the shortfall. Many private hospitals offer their own loan arrangements. Alternatively, you can plan ahead by taking out appropriate insurance.

The most direct way to insure yourself is to take out private medical insurance (PMI) – see below. In the past, this was an alternative to using the NHS or paying yourself for private treatment. But, increasingly these days, you can use PMI in conjunction with the self-pay option largely due to the growing use of PMI policies with a large 'excess' (see page 140).

Hospital cash plans (see page 142) are sometimes erroneously viewed as an alternative to PMI. While these cash plans in no way fully fund private treatment, they can help you to meet the cost in part or cover some of the incidental costs of being in hospital. According to the IHA, over 6 million people are covered by these plans.

The plans you make for coping financially with hospital treatment depend in part on how likely you feel it is that you would need such treatment. The table opposite shows the proportion of people in Britain receiving hospital treatment in a year. It shows that at younger ages women are slightly more likely than men to go into hospital but less likely at older ages, and that as you might expect hospital treatment tends to increase with age.

The chart on page 138 summarises who needs medical insurance.

Private medical insurance (PMI)
What is PMI?

PMI is insurance to cover the costs of receiving private hospital treatment. It has a long history, dating from pre-NHS days, when people paid into friendly societies which then helped members financially in times of need. Some PMI providers, such as BUPA, are still non-profit-distributing bodies. But many commercial insurance companies also offer PMI nowadays.

Guide prices to some common private treatments

Treatment	Cost
Varicose vein treatment	£1,050–£1,850
Hernia	£1,050–£2,025
Cataract removal	£1,275–£2,560
Hip replacement	£5,500–£9,750
Heart bypass	£9,500–£12,500

Source: Health Care Navigator as published in Which? May 2002

Proportion of people receiving hospital treatment and time spent in hospital

Receiving treatment as:	Men aged:				Women aged:			
	16-44	45-64	65-74	75+	16-44	45-64	65-74	75+
Inpatient in 12 month period	5%	8%	12%	19%	9%	8%	10%	15%
Average number of nights as inpatient in 12 month period	6	10	11	13	3	8	13	20
Day patient in 12 month period	7%	8%	8%	10%	8%	8%	8%	8%
Average number of separate days as day patient in 12 month period	2	2	2	4	2	2	3	3
Outpatient or casualty patient in 3 month period	11%	16%	22%	31%	12%	18%	21%	23%

Source: National Statistics, Living in Britain: Results from the 2001 General Household Survey, The Stationery Office, 2003

It is important to realise that no PMI policy covers every possible private treatment cost. PMI is designed to cover only 'acute illnesses', that is, conditions which can be cured or substantially alleviated by treatment. In particular, 'chronic illnesses', such as arthritis or multiple sclerosis, which would require long-term treatment, are excluded. However, treatment for an acute problem related to a long-term illness might be covered: for example, a hip replacement to ease pain and immobility caused by arthritis. Cover for mental conditions – which in one form or another affect one person in four in Britain – is generally very restricted or excluded altogether.

Other common exclusions are cosmetic surgery, treatment for alcoholism or drug abuse, treatment for infertility or normal pregnancy, and AIDS. Most standard policies also do not cover seeing a GP privately, routine check-ups and dental work (unless carried out in a hospital), although some of the more comprehensive policies do.

Who needs medical insurance?

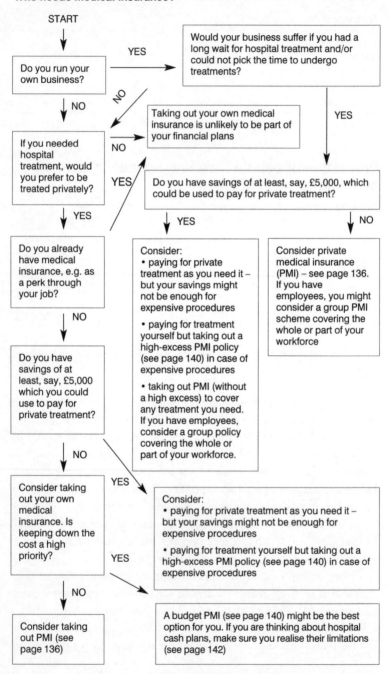

One other important exclusion is so-called 'pre-existing conditions', that is, health problems you already have at the time you apply for insurance. All PMI providers are willing to 'underwrite' these conditions. That means that they look at the likelihood of such conditions causing a claim and either charge you a higher premium or put special rules into your policy, such as refusing to cover any treatment related to the condition. Some providers offer a 'moratorium' approach. How this typically works is that the PMI provider refuses to pay for any treatment relating to the condition until two full years have gone by without your needing treatment for it. After that, the health problem is covered just like any other.

Warning

If you have a health problem which is covered by an existing PMI policy, you should be very wary about switching to another policy because you would lose cover for that health problem.

What does PMI cover?

PMI covers the cost of treatment as an inpatient or daypatient in a private hospital or a private ward or pay bed in an NHS hospital. Outpatient treatment might also be included.

Top-of-the-range plans – sometimes called 'comprehensive' – cover treatment, whether as an inpatient or an outpatient, in most or all private hospitals and wards, and the full cost of treatment is paid by the insurance. These plans usually include extras such as complementary medicine (for example, osteopathy and chiropractic) and home nursing. Some add in the cost of seeing GPs privately and dentists' and opticians' charges. Cover may extend abroad. A top-of-the-range plan can easily cost you hundreds of pounds a month. Not surprisingly, then, there is a whole spectrum of policies offering less cover in exchange for lower premiums.

What might be dubbed 'standard plans' cover fewer extras than the top-notch plans, and outpatient treatment is often covered only if related to a spell as an inpatient. But a major way of keeping down cost is to restrict the range of hospitals you can use. A common way plans do this is to offer you a choice between three lists (or more) of hospitals. One list covers most or all private hospitals and wards, the next excludes the most costly of these (generally the more expensive London hospitals) and the third is limited to the hospitals and wards which are least expensive. If you use a hospital which is not on the selected list, there is no guarantee that the full cost will be met; instead, you get an 'out-of-band' benefit of a specified cash sum for each night in hospital. The more restricted the hospital list you choose, the lower your premiums. If you live outside London, you are unlikely to need the most comprehensive list. The important point to check is that the list you choose includes the private facilities that you would want to use – because they are convenient to your home, for example.

'Budget plans' keep down costs by limiting cover further still. This can be done in one or a combination of the following ways:

- capping the amount which the policy will pay out overall each year
- capping the amount which the policy will pay out for certain areas of cover: for example, surgeons' fees, outpatient costs
- excluding cover altogether for some treatments: for example, physiotherapy, outpatient care
- restricting you to a single and fairly limited list of private hospitals and wards
- 'six-week waiting plans'. These cover private treatment only if the waiting list for NHS treatment is longer than six weeks.

At least one insurer has contained cost by introducing a new type of PMI that covers treatment only for two specific, albeit relatively common conditions: heart problems and cancer.

High-excess PMI plans

The traditional breakdown between comprehensive, standard and budget plans is being broken through the emergence of a relatively new type of PMI: the 'high-excess plan'. Instead of cutting cover, these plans offer standard or comprehensive coverage but keep the cost down by requiring you to pay a large 'excess'. An excess is the first part of a claim which you agree to pay yourself. The insurance kicks in to pay any amount over and above the excess. The amount of excess and impact on price vary from one company to another but, for example, agreeing to pay the first £1,000 could cut the premium by around a quarter and a £2,000 excess could knock as much as 60 per cent off the price. You should check carefully the basis used to work out the excess. A few policies apply the excess to every claim, so if you claimed several times you would have to pay the excess several times over. Most policies apply the excess to each policy year, so even if you claimed twice in the year you would still only pay one excess – but you need to watch out where a claim straddles two policy years as you could then be charged two lots of the excess. At least one company charges just one excess a year but sets the clock ticking at the start of the claim, so you have a full 12 months within which to settle the claim or make further claims without a second excess being incurred. Also watch out if there are cash limits on the payout – check if the cash limits include any excess you pay (in which case, the policy may in fact pay out very little). It is better if the limits apply over and above any excess.

High-excess plans are a good idea if you have some savings which you are happy to use towards the cost of private treatment but you want to be protected against larger bills. Some experts suggest that budget PMI should be approached in the same way – in other words, be prepared to pay to fill in the gaps in cover, particularly the cost of initial private outpatient consultations.

What does PMI cost?

With PMI, you get very much what you pay for. If you want a comprehensive plan, you pay a high price or a high excess. If you want to pay less, you must accept restrictions or be prepared to meet part of the cost of treatment yourself.

Apart from the type of cover you choose, age is the other major influence on price. This reflects the fact that the older you are the more likely it is that you will need hospital treatment. Figures from the Association of British Insurers suggest that someone aged 65 will generally pay more than twice as much as someone aged 45 who will typically pay around a quarter more than someone aged 35. Some PMI insurers have also started to take your postcode into account on the basis that people in some areas tend to experience more health problems than people living in other districts.

Some companies offer numerous discounts on premiums under certain circumstances: for example, if you belong to a particular profession, have a certain credit card, belong to a particular motoring organisation, and so on. There is often a discount (5 per cent, say) if you agree to pay annually rather than monthly. A few plans have a no-claims discount, so that the next year's premium is reduced if you don't make any claims. One of the most effective ways to cut the cost is to choose a high-excess plan (see page 140) or agree a voluntary excess with other types of plan.

The cost of medical insurance can rise rapidly from one year to the next, reflecting overall claims experience and increases in the cost of private treatment.

Hospital cash plans

What is a hospital cash plan and what does it cover?

This pays out a tax-free cash sum for each day you are treated as an inpatient or daypatient in either an NHS or a private hospital. This type of insurance may be combined with a range of other cash benefits: cash payments if you need dental treatment or chiropody, for example, or become pregnant.

Hospital cash plans are not a substitute for PMI: the cash payments are typically small – for example, one leading plan pays from £10 up to £80 a night, depending on the premium level you choose – and they are not enough to cover the cost of private treatment. Usually, they are marketed as useful for covering the incidental costs of being in hospital: childcare or relatives travelling to visit you, for example. It is sometimes suggested that they are also useful as a way of replacing earnings lost because of being off work, but once again the low payments and the fact that the size of the sum paid out is totally unrelated to the income you may need to replace mean that such plans are a poor substitute for proper income protection insurance (see Chapter 6).

How worthwhile a hospital cash plan will be depends crucially on the amounts it pays out and the probability that the events which trigger the payments will occur. Particular points to note are as follows:

- There is often a waiting period before any benefits become available. Often this will be, say, six months, but it may be longer for some types of claim.

- Usually, claims connected with health problems you had before taking out the plan or before the expiry of the waiting period are not covered at all.
- You get a cash sum for each night you spend in hospital. According to a government survey, the 8 per cent of people who had been an inpatient one or more times during a 12 month period, on average spent eight nights in hospital during the course of the year.
- Plans sometimes cover a wide range of medical situations – for example, dental treatment, physiotherapy, staying in a convalescent home, having a baby, and so on. But payouts for some claims – for example, for dental treatment or getting a hearing aid – are restricted by an upper cash limit and may also be restricted to just half the actual cost you incur.
- Cover will often be for a whole family rather than just an individual, but bear in mind that children are unlikely to give rise to claims under some sections - for example, children receive free NHS dental treatment and sight tests and are far less likely than older people to need chiropody or hearing aids.

Research by Which? found that the average premium for a hospital cash plan in 1999 was £100, but the average amount claimed was only £75. But, of course, experience will differ from person to person.

All in all, cash plans are not a good tool for meeting specific financial targets, such as paying for private treatment or income protection. Nevertheless, they can provide handy lump sums from time to time and the outlay is relatively small. But carefully consider which benefits are likely to be relevant to you and check the small print for restrictions.

What a hospital cash plan costs

This depends on the level of benefits you choose but, in general, you could expect to pay from under £100 a year up to, say, £750 a

---

Warning
Hospital cash plans appear to be fairly cheap but can be poor value for money when you look at the restrictions and the low probability of claiming some of the benefits.

---

year for a family. At these higher levels, you might be able to afford a budget PMI policy instead.

Critical illness insurance

Critical illness cover (CIC) is described in Chapter 6. It pays out a tax-free lump sum if you are diagnosed with a life-threatening condition or you have to undergo certain specified types of surgery. Since there is no restriction on how you use the money, it could fund private treatment. However, you should not view CIC as an alternative to PMI. The latter pays out when you suffer an acute illness which can be cured or relieved by hospital treatment. CIC pays out mainly in the case of chronic or terminal illness. There is some potential overlap – for example, both policies might be triggered if you had a heart attack – but, on the whole, PMI and CIC are best viewed as complements of, rather than substitutes for, each other.

More information

There are many variations on the PMI theme, so you need to check carefully what's on offer. Consult the regular surveys of private medical insurance in magazines such as *Which?*★ and *Money Management*★. The Association of British Insurers★ can provide details of companies offering particular types of insurance. You can also gather this information from business directories kept in the reference sections of most public libraries. Several PMI providers have websites where you can get details of their products.

Switching dilemma

Richard has, with a few breaks, had PMI through the same company since the early 1950s. He has claimed about a dozen times on his policy and overall is satisfied with it. He has thought about switching company but says: 'I always come up against the same stumbling block – the waiting period before a new insurer will cover existing medical conditions.' Once you have a health problem, a new policy normally excludes claims related to it either for two years or permanently.

Which? June 1998

Self-pay reduces delay

When Karen found a lump in her breast, it was all too horribly familiar. Her mother had had breast cancer and both of her sisters-in-law were receiving chemotherapy. On top of all this, the timing was terrible – she and her husband were due to go on holiday in just ten days time.

Understandably, Karen wanted the lump diagnosed as soon as possible. Her GP referred her to the weekly breast clinic at her local hospital in the hope that she'd be treated as a priority case because of her family history. Karen was optimistic that she'd get an appointment for the following week and was very disappointed when she found out that the clinic was already fully booked.

Faced with the prospect of either spending her holiday miserable with worry or cancelling it altogether, Karen decided she couldn't face either option and contacted a local independent (ie private) hospital. She couldn't easily afford the £240 fee for a private consultation, but felt it was her only choice.

Karen saw a consultant that day and a simple needle aspiration revealed that the lump was actually a cyst. The results of a mammogram and ultrasound the following day confirmed there was nothing to worry about. Karen's relief was immense. In the end, she was given an NHS appointment four weeks after she had seen her GP.

Which? May 2002

Chapter 8

Care in your old age

The twentieth century saw great improvements in life expectancy. The table below shows how in recent times life expectancy at birth has been increasing by around one year every four or so. At the same time, healthy life expectancy has also been increasing, but more slowly. So, as we live longer, we can still expect more health problems and, as you might expect, the older we get, the greater the likelihood of failing health – see the table opposite. Many of us will

Life expectancy and healthy life expectancy

Year of measurement	Life expectancy at birth	Healthy life expectancy at birth	Expected number of years of ill health
Men			
1981	70.9	64.4	6.5
1985	71.8	65.3	6.5
1990	72.9	66.1	6.8
1995	74.2	66.4	7.8
1997	74.6	66.9	7.7
1999	75.1	66.6	8.5
Women			
1981	76.8	66.7	10.1
1985	77.6	67.6	10.0
1990	78.5	68.3	10.2
1995	79.4	68.7	10.7
1997	79.6	68.7	10.9
1999	80.0	68.9	10.9

Source: Government statistics

eventually become unable to cope on our own with normal daily activities and will require help and support from others.

This support might come from members of the family, though some experts predict that, as more women are now working, they will abandon their traditional role as carers of elderly parents and other relatives. And families are often geographically fragmented, making it harder for relatives to provide the regular support that might help an elderly person to stay in his or her own home. Some people need to move into a residential or nursing home, particularly in later life. In 2001, there were just under 237,000 places for elderly people in residential care homes in England (and, for example, 22,300 in Scotland). Statistics for occupancy by age are scant but a survey in 1995 found that just over one person in 100 aged 65 to 74 was living in a residential or nursing home. By age 75 to 84, nearly one person in 20 was living in a home. For people aged 85 and over, the proportion rose to one person in five.

Many people imagine that if they did need to move into a home, the state would look after them. In fact, this is not so, unless your

Proportion of people reporting health problems in 2001

	16–44	45–64	65–74	75–79	80–84	85+
				Age		
Men						
People reporting a longstanding illness	22%	44%	58%		64%	
People reporting a longstanding illness that limits activities in any way	10%	28%	36%		47%	
People reporting permanent mobility difficulties		4%	13%	21%	25%	50%
Women						
People reporting a longstanding illness	21%	42%	56%		63%	
People reporting a longstanding illness that limits activities in any way	12%	26%	37%		45%	
People reporting permanent mobility difficulties		4%	15%	30%	37%	65%

Source: National Statistics *Living in Britain: Results from the 2001 General Household Survey*, The Stationery Office, 2003

income and savings are very low. In the main, you would have to foot the bill yourself – and the bill is high.

According to health research specialists Laing & Buisson, the average fees for a nursing home are £422 a week (£22,000 a year) and £302 (£16,000 a year) for a residential home. Laing & Buisson estimate that the average stay in a nursing home is from 18 to 30 months. This means that an average person could get through £33,000 to £55,000 – and that ignores fee increases, which tend to outstrip inflation. In your own particular case, the figure could range from nothing (if you did not need to move to a home at all) to a sum far in excess of £55,000.

The number of residential care home places has been tending to fall and government policy currently is to try to support people in their own homes for as long as possible. In 2001, some 381,000 households in England were receiving care services in their own home. Again, the state will not normally pick up the cost unless your income and capital are low, so over the years, you could run up substantial bills. On the other hand, you might remain healthy throughout and never need to use any on these services. So how do you plan sensibly for this phase of life?

One tool available is long-term care insurance. In return for a series of regular premiums or a lump sum, the insurance company pays out if you become too disabled to cope alone. The snag with this type of insurance is its high cost. Given this fact and the present rules about state provision of long-term care (see below), it is hard to view long-term care insurance as an essential player in the majority of people's financial plans.

Help from the state

Local authorities are largely responsible for providing state support for elderly people whose physical or mental health is failing. The system works as follows.

Types of care

If you can no longer cope alone at home or your carer needs help, you can contact the social services department of your local authority. If you need financial help from the state, social services will carry out an 'assessment of needs'; they will also carry out an assessment of needs on request from people who do have enough money to pay for care themselves. Based on this assessment, a care plan will be drawn up. This sets out the level of care which social services reckon you need and the ways in which your needs can be met. There are three main options:

- **staying in your own home** Social services might suggest special equipment to make life easier – for example, grab rails and bathroom aids – and services such as a home help, meals-on-wheels, care assistance (such as someone calling each morning to help you get washed and dressed), home visits from the community nurse and a place at a day centre. The cost of services varies but, for example, personal care typically costs around £10 an hour.

- **moving to a more suitable home** Social services cannot force you to move, but they might suggest it as something worth considering. For example, you could move to sheltered housing with a resident warden available to give emergency assistance, or to a bungalow, say, if you have trouble with stairs, or somewhere closer to relatives who can help.

- **going into a care home** Again, you cannot be forced to go into a home, and social services will generally try to help you stay in your own home for as long as possible. If their recommendation is that you move into a residential or nursing home, you will need to be realistic about your ability to carry on if you are determined to stay in your own home. Where possible, you will be offered a choice of homes, although if the local authority is paying in full for you cost will be a constraint.

Who pays?

Disability benefits

If you are aged 65 or over and need frequent care or supervision, you may qualify for attendance allowance. This is a tax-free state benefit paid at one of two rates depending on the degree of care you need (£38.30 or £57.20 a week in 2003-4).

People under age 65 might instead qualify for an alternative benefit called disability living allowance.

You can spend your attendance allowance in any way you want, but it is intended to help you cope with the additional costs you incur as a result of your disability, such as paying for carers or buying special equipment. Not surprisingly, therefore, if you have to move into a care home and the state picks up part or all of the cost of the home fees (see below), you lose the attendance allowance. However, if you move into a home and pay all of the fees yourself, you keep the attendance allowance.

Care in your own home
You can, of course, organise whatever help you need independently. But you have the right to ask your local authority to carry out an assessment of your needs (regardless of whether you or the state will be paying for your care). The local authority will then draw up a care plan and can arrange for you to receive whatever equipment and/or services are deemed necessary.

Some equipment and services provided by your local authority may be free or offered at a minimal charge. But usually you will be expected to pay for personal carers, domestic help, and so on unless your income and savings are low.

Nursing care that you receive in your own home is funded by the National Health Service (NHS) and so free from your point of view.

Living in a care home
If you move into a nursing home, perhaps after a hospital stay, in order to receive ongoing medical care, the NHS may pick up the tab. In other cases, who pays depends on the type of care you receive and what financial resources you have.

Nursing care provided in hospital, your own home or a residential home has always been an NHS service free at the point of use. However, this used not to be true of nursing care you received in a nursing home, where typically the fees would be much higher to cover this additional cost. This anomaly has now been addressed and, where you receive care from a registered nurse, this is free up to certain limits (figures as for mid-2003):

- £40, £75 or £120 a week in England depending on whether your nursing needs are assessed as low, medium or high
- £65 a week in Scotland
- £100 a week in Wales.

In Scotland, personal care (for example, help with washing, dressing, going to the toilet and so on) up to £145 a week is also free if you are aged 65 or over regardless of your financial situation. This does not apply in the rest of the UK where you will get help with the cost of personal care only if you pass a means test.

Throughout the UK, you are expected to pay the living costs (bed and board and so on) of living in a care home unless you pass the means test.

Local authorities set a 'standard rate' which is the amount they will pay for a place in a care home. Different authorities can set different rates, reflecting the varying costs around the country. The means test (see below) determines whether you have to pay part or all of that cost yourself.

In general, the means test is based just on your own income and savings. If you are married, it can't be based on your husband's or wife's income and savings as well (although joint amounts are apportioned between you). However, the local authority can ask your husband or wife to help with the cost of your care home fees. It cannot demand any information about your spouse's financial situation and the amount your husband or wife might pay is a matter initially for negotiation. If no agreement is reached, the local authority can refer the matter to court. Only a court can order your husband or wife to help with your care home costs.

No-one else – for example, an unmarried partner, son or daughter, other relative – can be asked to pay towards your care home fees. However, they can volunteer to help – this is called a 'third party contribution'. This could be useful if you have chosen a home with fees which are higher than the standard rate, in which case the local authority might not agree to pay the extra.

The means test

The rules for assessing your income and savings are set nationally. Local authorities have some limited discretion, but broadly speaking the same rules apply wherever you live.

In working out whether or not you have enough income to pay for long-term care yourself, all your income will be taken into account, including pensions and any state benefits, but not the actual income you get from your savings (see below). If someone else is dependent on your income, the assessment will allow enough to cover that person's reasonable living costs. There is an exception to this approach: if you get a pension from a former employer's occupational scheme, half of it will be disregarded as belonging to your husband or wife (but not an unmarried partner) provided you normally share your pension with them.

This means an unmarried partner in particular could be left with too little to live on, so you should plan how they might cope in this situation – for example, by putting extra savings into either joint names or your partner's name and considering what state benefits, such as income support, might be claimed.

A small personal expenses allowance (£17.50 a week in mid-2003) will be deducted from your income for the purpose of the means test. This is intended to cover your incidental and personal expenses while living in a home. The local authority has discretion to increase this allowance, for example, to enable you to pay something towards the ongoing costs at home that an unmarried partner might be struggling to cope with.

If your capital (i.e. your savings and other assets) come to no more than a lower capital limit, it is ignored altogether. If it comes to more than an upper limit, then regardless of your income, you get no help with the means-tested part of the care home fees (but would still qualify, for example, for free nursing). Once your savings had run down to below the upper limit, state help could kick in. See the table below for the capital limits that applied in mid-2003.

Capital limits in mid-2003 used to determine whether you must pay towards care home fees

	Lower limit	Upper limit
England	£12,000	£19,500
Scotland	£11,500	£18,500
Wales	£12,250	£20,000
Northern Ireland	£12,000	£19,500

If your capital is more than the lower limit but less than the upper one, you are deemed to receive £1 a week of income from each £250 (or part) of your capital. This is added to your other income to determine whether you can afford to contribute something towards the fees.

Who needs long-term care insurance?

START

Are you aged 40 or more? — NO →

Planning ahead for care in your old age is sensible even from a relatively young age, but it is unlikely to be a high priority at this stage of your life

↓ YES

Have you reached retirement age? — NO →

Ideally, you should have started to consider how you will cope when you are older

↓ YES

If you have not done so already, you should decide now what provision, if any, you will make for care in later life.
Do you own your own home and/or have you built up a reasonable pool of assets?

— YES →

Are you anxious that your children or others should inherit your home and/or other assets?

YES ↓ · ↓ NO

Would you want the freedom to choose any care home, even the most expensive, rather than be limited to a local authority's preferred list?

YES ↓ · ↓ NO

↓ NO

You could rely on the state to foot the bill for long-term care if you needed it (see page 148) but make sure that your spouse or partner would be financially secure if you moved to a home, and vice versa (see page 152)

Would having to pay residential/nursing home fees of £16,000 a year or more seriously eat into your assets?

Consider:

• using your home and/or assets to pay for the cost of care, if required, and
• relying on the state once those assets are largely gone (see page 148).
But make sure that your spouse or partner would be financially secure if you moved to a home, and vice versa (see page 152)

Consider long-term care insurance (see page 157) ← YES

NO ↓

It is unlikely that you need long-term care insurance under the current rules

The value of your home is included as part of your capital unless your stay in the care home is only temporary or one of the following people will still be living in the home:

- your husband or wife or a partner who lives with you as husband or wife
- a relative who is aged 60 or more or is incapacitated
- a relative under the age of 16 for whom you are legally responsible.

The local authority has discretion to ignore the value of your home in other circumstances: for example, if a younger relative or friend lives with you and would face hardship if they had to move. Under current rules, you would have to rely on this discretion if your same-sex partner lived with you. However, the government has proposed that same-sex couples who register their relationship as a 'civil partnership' might gain many of the same rights as married couples. If the proposals go ahead, this is an area where the rules might change.

If none of these exceptions applies, the value of your home (or if applicable your part-share of the home) counts as part of your capital. However, its value is ignored for the first 12 weeks to give you a breathing space while you find out whether moving into care is the right solution for you. After the 12-week period, you may find that you need to sell your home in order to meet the fees. However, there are other options. You might be able to rent out your home and use the rental income towards the fees. And you can ask the local authority to pay your fees for now but to take a 'charge' on your home so that it recoups the money it is in effect lending you when the home is eventually sold. The local authority cannot charge you interest on this loan.

You might be tempted to give away some of your capital or make some expensive purchases before being assessed, but if the social services department thinks you've done this deliberately to manipulate the rules, it can treat you as still owning the capital.

Concern for the future

Much concern has been expressed about our ageing population and whether the state can continue to provide the present level of support. The table below shows how the proportion of retired people to people of working age is expected to change over the next 50 years or so. Some forecasters suggest that this falling ratio means that either the workers of the future will have to bear much higher taxes than at present or that state help for the elderly will have to be reduced. This is, however, too simple an analysis. More important is the ratio of non-working elderly to active participants in the workforce: that is, after allowing for those of working age not actually in work and those of pension age who continue to work. It is also alarmist to assume that future workers would not be prepared to pay tax at higher rates, since the wealth of the nation might be considerably greater than at present and forms of distributing part of that wealth to non-workers, other than transfers through taxes, might have been devised.

Expected number of people of working age for each pensioner

Year	Number
2000	3.4
2010	3.2
2030	2.7
2050	2.5

Source: Government Actuary's Department, 1999

In the past, all political parties had indicated they might support some form of compulsory system, requiring people of working age to take out insurance or make savings to pay for their own care in old age should they need it. But the Labour government has not taken any action on this. The previous Conservative government had suggested two possible approaches:

- introducing partnership schemes for long-term care. These would work by letting people who take out insurance up to a given amount keep more of their wealth – on top of the normal capital limits – at the point where state funding kicks in.
- giving members of employers' pension schemes (see Chapter 11) the option of taking a pension once they retire which increases in the later years of retirement, thus giving them more income at those times when they are most likely to face long-term care costs.

The wisdom of this latter option has to be questioned – in most cases, people do not invest enough in their pension schemes to provide an adequate standard of living in retirement, let alone to fund long-term care needs as well. Until the government makes the next step clear, the key question for the present remains: how anxious are you to pass on your wealth to your heirs? In the longer term, it seems possible either that it will become compulsory to make at least some advance provision for yourself or that a two-tier system might develop where those who are forced to rely on the state have less choice and enjoy lower standards than those who can directly buy the care they need.

Helping yourself

If your income and/or capital are above the limits for state help, you will have no choice but to rely on your own resources. Family members can be an important source of private care. Currently, one in five men and one in four women aged 45 to 64 is caring for a relative, friend or neighbour; over a third of these are looking after a parent.

However, as already noted, the outlook for the future is uncertain. There is a strong possibility that, if you do need long-term care later in life, you will have to pay for professional care either in your own home or in an institutional setting. This could quickly run down your assets, but that should not necessarily be viewed as a problem. There are two main questions to consider:

- If you have a husband, wife or unmarried partner, would he or she be financially insecure if you had to move into a residential or nursing home? Similarly, would you have too little to live on if he or she went into a home?
- Are you particularly keen to preserve your assets, for example to hand on to your children? (This is an issue which perhaps you should discuss with your family. In a poll by Mintel, eight out of ten adults said that their parents should spend their money on looking after themselves in old age rather than storing it up to be passed on in inheritance.)

If your answer to either of these questions is 'yes', long-term care insurance could be worth looking at.

Long-term care insurance
What is long-term care insurance?

This type of insurance pays out an income – often after a waiting period, such as 90 days – if you become unable to cope on your own. The income can be used to pay fees to a nursing or residential care home or to provide help in your own home. The income is tax-free. Typically, you'll have a valid claim if you are unable to carry out two or three out of five 'activities of daily living' (ADLs) – such as personal hygiene, dressing, feeding yourself, mobility and continence.

Although aimed mainly at paying for care in old age, this type of plan pays out whatever your age if you meet the disability test. But bear in mind that you might need care even though you are not so disabled as to qualify under the long-term care insurance tests, in which case the policy would not pay out.

There are two main types of long-term care insurance: pure insurance plans and investment-based plans. Pure insurance simply pays out if you have a valid claim and otherwise returns nothing. Investment-based plans combine an investment bond with the insurance. Provided the investment grows at a target rate, it provides enough to pay the premiums for the insurance and hopefully to return your original investment when you die. Investment-based insurance generally costs more but could be reassuring if your main concern is to preserve assets to hand on to your heirs.

What long-term care insurance costs

Premiums vary with your age, sex and health, the payout you choose and the number of ADLs you must fail to have a claim (the fewer the ADLs, the more expensive the policy). There is huge variation from one company to another, so you should shop around. For example, in 2001, a 60-year-old woman might pay anything from £30 to £170 a month or a single premium from £7,500 to £29,000 for a pure insurance policy providing cover of £1,000 a month. An investment-backed policy could cost her from £14,500 up to £34,000. Rather than paying the full cost of care, the payout is used typically to top up your other resources to the required level. So £1,000 a month would not be enough on its own to cover nursing home fees, but could be when combined with pension income, say.

Alternative strategies

Insurance-based long-term care plans are a tool for planning ahead for your possible care needs. Other types of long-term care plan aim to meet an immediate need for care. Essentially, they require you to use a lump sum to buy an annuity (in other words an income for life). The annuity rate may be particularly favourable taking into account the fact that your illness or disability may be shortening your life expectancy. Unlike ordinary annuities, the monthly payout is usually tax-free provided it is paid direct to the care provider.

Immediate-need plans may take the form of an equity release scheme under which you sell all or part of your home (while keeping the right of your spouse, say, to live there) and use the capital raised to buy an annuity to pay for care. You could arrange your own equity release scheme (see Chapter 18) and use the money raised for any purpose including paying for care, but immediate care plans have advantages in that the annuity rate may be higher and the income should be tax-free if paid direct to the care home.

The advantage of immediate-need plans over simply paying for care out of whatever savings you have to hand is that, for a cost which is fixed at the outset, you can be confident that the monthly payments will continue however long you live. Therefore, you reduce the risk of running down your capital completely.

More information

You can find out what help is available from your local authority by contacting its social services department (look in the local telephone directory under the entry for your local authority). You can also get information from a wide range of voluntary bodies, such as Citizens' Advice Bureaux,* Age Concern* and Help the Aged.* Check *Yellow Pages* and leaflets in your library for locally based organisations that signpost enquirers to support services.

For details of the income and capital assessment rules, see *Charging for residential accommodation*, a manual which you can inspect at any social services department and many local advice centres (such as a Citizens' Advice Bureau). Long-term care insurance is developing only slowly in the UK and there are as yet relatively few plans on offer. *Which?*★ and money magazines, such as *Money Management*★, publish regular surveys of the long-term care plans available.

Insuring for a secure future

Mr X is 74 years old and recently widowed. He owns his own house and has no children. Taking out a long-term care insurance policy is not likely to be the best bet for Mr X – he has no dependants so is probably less worried than he might otherwise be about protecting his assets. Also, if he takes out a policy at his age, the premiums will be extremely high. If he does want to take precautions, Mr X would be better off with an equity release scheme. Otherwise, he may as well just pay for any care he ends up needing from his assets.

Mr and Mrs Y are retired, in their 60s, in good health and own their own house. They have three children and are keen to be able to leave them their house and savings. The best bet for the Ys would be to apply together for long-term care insurance policies. They could end up paying over £100 a month to be guaranteed of covering average care costs outside London. But at least they'll know that the policy will pay out for as long as required, and that their remaining assets will be protected.

Which? February 1997

Help from the state

John went into a nursing home because he needs constant care for Alzheimer's disease. His savings are modest and he has never owned a house. Because he needs day and night care and because he's funding his own place in an independent home, he is able to claim the higher rate of attendance allowance (£57.20 a week in 2003–4). This, together with his teacher's pension and state pension, is enough for him to meet the cost of the home without dipping into his savings.

Which? November 1999

Chapter 9

Mortgages

In one form or another, borrowing plays some part in most people's lives, whether it be a mortgage to buy a home or credit cards as a convenient way to shop. Borrowing enables you to bring forward the time at which a financial target can be met and is worth considering if there is not enough time available to use the savings route or if the cost of borrowing is lower than the return you would get on saving.

Few people can afford to buy a home outright, and it would be totally impractical to save up the full cost of your home before you bought it; after all, you need somewhere to live in the meantime. Therefore, the usual practice is to take out a mortgage – a loan secured against the property you are buying. This practice has been encouraged by past governments through the giving of tax relief on the interest paid on a mortgage to buy your only or main home. However, this tax incentive was abolished from 6 April 2000 onwards (except for some mortgages linked to home income plans – see page 400). Without any tax incentive, it makes sense to pay off your mortgage as soon as you can – in contrast to the position in earlier years. The removal of the incentive has had a dramatic impact on the types of mortgage which are suitable for most people. In particular, endowment mortgages (see page 165) – which were a popular choice in the past – should now have no place in the financial plan of most people choosing a mortgage for the first time. And, for many people, some form of flexible mortgage (see page 176) will often be a good choice.

There is a wide range of mortgages to choose from, though they fall into two main groups:

- **repayment mortgages,** where you gradually pay off the amount you have borrowed over the term of the loan, together with interest
- **interest-only mortgages,** where you pay only the interest on the loan during its term. Usually, you simultaneously make other arrangements for paying back the capital at the end of the term. In the past, the most common type of interest-only mortgage was the endowment mortgage. Other variations are ISA (formerly PEP) mortgages – see page 169 – and pension mortgages – see page 171.

If you were moving home today, which type of mortgage would you end up choosing? Back at their peak in 1988, more than 80 per cent of mortgage customers were choosing endowment mortgages. This is despite the fact that endowment mortgages had by then lost most of the advantages which made them a good buy back in the early 1980s. However, a consistent bad press and warnings from the financial regulators about the unsuitability of modern endowment mortgages for most people has finally taken effect. By 2003, only 3 per cent of new mortgages were endowment mortgages. Far and away the most popular type of mortgage taken out nowadays is the repayment mortgage.

Most popular types of mortgage

Type of mortgage	Percentage of first mortgages on a home	
	All buyers	First-time buyers
Repayment	78	85
Endowment	3	4
Interest-only	13	11
Pension	0	0
PEP/ISA	0	0
Other	6	1

Source: Council of Mortgage Lenders, data for first quarter of 2003

Repayment mortgage

This is the most straightforward type of mortgage. Your monthly payments pay off both interest and capital, which, provided you keep up the payments, ensures that the whole loan is paid off by the end of the term – see the table on page 172.

A further advantage of repayment mortgages is that they are very flexible and can easily be adapted if you run into temporary difficulties in making the repayments. For example, the most common mortgage term is 25 years at the outset, but, if you ran into problems, your lender might agree to extend the term. This would have the effect of reducing the monthly payments, making them more manageable. Another option might be to add arrears to the amount of the loan outstanding and then adjust the monthly payments, so that the arrears as well as the original loan are repaid by the end of the term.

The way these repayment mortgages are structured means that your payments in the early years are almost completely devoted to paying interest, and very little goes towards reducing the outstanding loan. Critics point out that a move in the early years of the mortgage leaves you back at square one with no reduction in the amount you need to borrow.

A point also to bear in mind is that, unlike some other types of mortgage, there is no built-in life cover to pay off the mortgage in the event of your death. If you have dependants, you will need to arrange separate life insurance, though this is easily done through a relatively cheap mortgage protection policy (a type of decreasing term insurance; see page 103).

Two factors stand out to make repayment mortgages a good choice for many people. The first is their low risk. If on a one-to-ten scale (one being the lowest risk and ten being the highest) you feel most comfortable with a risk of, say, four or less, a repayment mortgage would be most suitable for you. The second factor is their flexibility. In the current climate of unstable work patterns and no tax incentives for mortgages, it makes sense to have the flexibility both to cope with possible hiccups in your earnings and to pay off your mortgage early if you can. You can build in even more flexibility by opting for a specially designed flexible mortgage (see page 176).

Interest-only mortgages

These are the alternative to a repayment mortgage. You do not pay off the loan during the mortgage term. Instead, you pay just the interest and, in most cases, simultaneously pay into an investment to build up a lump sum which you will use to pay off the mortgage at the end of the term. The investment might be an endowment policy, ISAs (or, before April 1999, PEPs), a pension scheme, or indeed any other investment.

In effect, you are gambling that you can use the money you would otherwise have paid back to invest for a profit over and above the cost of borrowing that money. If your gamble pays off, you will either have an extra lump sum for your own use at the end of the mortgage term or you will have saved money during the mortgage term by paying out less each month than you would have paid for a repayment mortgage. If the gamble does not pay off, you either face a shortfall when you come to pay off your mortgage or you have to pay more over the mortgage term than you would have done with a repayment mortgage.

In the past, there were some good reasons why this gamble was likely to pay off. There are now some equally good reasons why the gamble may not work:

- **tax relief on your investment** Up to 1984, if you took out an endowment mortgage, you got tax relief (called 'life assurance premium relief') on the amount you paid into an endowment policy. This was abolished for new or altered policies from 1984. Now, only a pension mortgage (see page 171) offers you tax relief on the amount you pay each month in savings to repay the mortgage.
- **tax relief on the mortgage** The table overleaf shows how tax relief on mortgage interest has changed over the years. Up to April 1991, you got relief at your highest rate of tax on interest on up to £30,000 of a loan to buy your only or main home. In April 2000, tax relief was abolished altogether. This makes borrowing much more expensive and reduces the likelihood that you will be able to invest the borrowed money at a profit.
- **inflation** People who had mortgages in the late 1970s and early 1980s experienced periods when inflation was very high and interest rates were lower than inflation. In effect, people were being

paid to borrow (instead of paid to save, as is more usual). The cost of paying their mortgages fell and the value of their outstanding loans also fell dramatically in real terms. However, stock market returns kept ahead of inflation. So as mortgage loans plummeted, the value of investments soared, making handsome profits for people with endowment and similar mortgages. The economic climate is now entirely different: inflation is low and interest rates are considerably higher than inflation. Worse still, a three-year slide in the stock market between 2000 and 2003 has been a brutal reminder of the risks involved in the gamble. However, taking a longer-term view, stock-market investments might still be expected to outpace inflation over the whole lifetime of a mortgage.

So, although people who have had endowment mortgages in the past may tell you that in their experience they are a great deal, be aware that today's endowment mortgage is a very different product. Some interest-only mortgages – such as ISA mortgages – do still have tax benefits which might make them worth the gamble, but endowment mortgages do not have that advantage.

Tax relief on mortgage interest

Tax year	Tax relief (available on interest on first £30,000 borrowed)	Effective cost of each £100 of gross mortgage interest if you were a:	
		Basic-rate taxpayer	Higher-rate taxpayer
1990–1	At your highest rate	£75	£60
1991–2	At the basic rate	£75	£75
1992–3	At the basic rate	£75	£75
1993–4	At the basic rate	£75	£75
1994–5	20%	£80	£80
1995–6	15%	£85	£85
1996–7	15%	£85	£85
1997–8	15%	£85	£85
1998–9	10%	£90	£90
1999–2000	10%	£90	£90
2000–1 onwards	None	£100	£100

The risk attached to interest-only mortgages depends heavily on the type of investment to which they are linked. But you don't need to have an investment link at all. Some lenders are prepared to make interest-only loans and leave entirely up to you how you will repay the capital at the end of the term. This might be suitable if, say, you expect to be able to sell the property at that time and repay the loan out of the proceeds, or you already have substantial investments which can be used eventually to repay the loan, or you run a business and anticipate using the proceeds of selling your interest in it. However, in 1997 it came to light that some people had been sold interest-only mortgages with no corresponding investment, thinking that they had taken out endowment mortgages. Make sure that you understand what type of mortgage you have and that, if there is no investment linked to it, you are comfortable with the situation.

The main types of interest-only mortgages are discussed in the next few sections. The table on page 172 summarises their key characteristics.

Low-cost endowment mortgage

This comprises an interest-only mortgage linked to an endowment policy, which can work either on a with-profits or a unit-linked basis (see below for more about this). If the investment in the endowment policy grows at a reasonable rate, it is anticipated that the policy will produce enough to pay off the loan at the end of the mortgage term and even leave you a bit of extra cash as well. But there is no guarantee that this will happen.

In September 1999, the Association of British Insurers (ABI)* introduced a code of practice to ensure that endowment mortgage holders were given regular information about the progress of their endowment policy towards paying off the mortgage. Under that original code, it was envisaged that information would be needed only in the later years of the mortgage and then only at five-yearly intervals. The inadequacy of this approach became clear as the stock market started its long slide at the start of 2000 and, from July 2001, a new code came into force requiring endowment providers to send out review letters much more frequently:

- the first review should be no later than three years after the start of the endowment mortgage
- subsequent reviews should be sent to you at least every two years throughout the term of the endowment

165

- you can ask for more frequent reviews (but not more often than once every 12 months).

These reviews have since become known as 'reprojection letters'. They recalculate the return you might get from your endowment policy taking into account growth so far and standard growth assumptions and compare this with the mortgage loan to be paid off. The letters are colour coded. A 'red letter' signifies there is a high risk that the amount you'll get back from the endowment policy at the end of its term will fall short of the amount needed to repay your mortgage in full. An 'amber letter' indicates there is a significant risk of a shortfall. A 'green letter' means you are currently on track to repay your mortgage.

Stock-market performance affects any shortfall. So, you could have a green reprojection letter at one review but, if the stock market falls, get an amber or red letter next time. Similarly, if you have an amber letter at one review, a rise in the stock market might mean you get a green letter next time. But, if you get a red letter, there would normally have to be a very substantial rise in the stock market before you returned to green, so you should usually consider other action to put your mortgage back on track.

The most obvious action is to increase the amount you save each month. You may be able to do this by increasing the premium you pay into the endowment policy, although you don't have to do that. You could pay extra savings into another, quite separate investment – for example, an ISA. If you already have other savings and invest-ments, you might simply choose to earmark some of these to meet the forecast shortfall.

Other options involve altering your mortgage by, for example, replacing part or all of the endowment loan with a repayment mortgage or repaying a lump sum early. If you feel you were mis-sold an endowment mortgage – for example, you would not have been comfortable with the risk of a stock market investment and your adviser did not check this – you may have grounds to complain and seek compensation, but normally you should do this within the sooner of:

- six years of receiving the bad advice, or
- three years of the date you became aware there was a problem (usually the date you were first told your endowment would fall short of the amount needed to repay your mortgage), or
- six months of receiving the second letter warning you that you have an endowment shortfall.

A useful aspect of linking your mortgage to an insurance policy, if you have dependants, is that the policy automatically gives you life cover, which would pay off the loan if you were to die during the term.

There are two major drawbacks with an endowment mortgage. As already discussed, there is a very real possibility that the endowment policy will not grow enough to produce a profit over and above the cost of borrowing. This means the endowment mortgage can end up costing you more than a repayment mortgage.

The second drawback is the very low cash-in value of the endowment policy if you stop paying the premiums in the early years. The costs associated with selling the policy (which include any commission paid to an adviser or salesperson) are intended to be spread over the full term of the policy. But if the policy stops early, these charges are set against the policy in full, even though the policy has had little time in which to build up much investment value. The result is that stopping the policy early can mean that you get back far less than you have paid in premiums, or even nothing at all. This makes endowment mortgages particularly inflexible if you run into problems keeping up the mortgage repayments. You may be able to alter the interest payments on the mortgage loan itself, but reducing or missing payments into the endowment policy might bring the policy to an end. A waiver of premium option (see page 108) might be at least a partial solution to this problem.

These drawbacks mean that endowment mortgages are not usually a good choice for anyone newly taking out a mortgage. But, if you already have an endowment mortgage, be wary of changing it. Stopping the endowment policy or cashing it in may crystallise the heavy charges discussed above. Your best option may be to carry on with the endowment mortgage. If you move house or remortgage without moving, it may be sensible to use the existing endowment policy to back a further interest-only mortgage, but you could look at taking out any top-up mortgage on a different basis. For example, if you are taking out a bigger loan, consider a repayment mortgage for the extra amount, or linking ISAs to the extra loan if it is on an interest-only basis.

With-profits version of low-cost endowment mortgage

This is the traditional form of low-cost endowment mortgage. At the start of the mortgage, the endowment policy has a guaranteed value (payable at the end of the term or on earlier death), which is far smaller than the amount of your mortgage loan. But bonuses are added to this guaranteed sum. There are regular bonuses, usually credited each year, called 'reversionary bonuses', and normally a 'terminal bonus' added when the policy reaches the end of its term. Once added, the bonuses cannot normally be taken away (but can be clawed back through a market value reduction if you cash in early – see page 342) and so the value of the policy grows and is intended by the end of the term to be worth at least as much as the amount of the mortgage loan. The aim of a with-profits policy is to produce steady growth protected from the thrills and spills of the stock market. Bonuses are smoothed, with money being kept back from good years to keep up bonus levels in the lean years. However, if the stock market turns in poor returns over a prolonged period, bonus levels will slide and the return from a low-cost endowment may then fall short of earlier expectations. This has been the experience in recent years, causing many people to be disappointed with the performance of their endowment policy, especially where they were misled into thinking when they took it out that the policy would definitely pay off the whole mortgage.

Despite this disappointment, provided you keep a with-profits policy going for its full term, it is a lower-risk investment than the direct exposure to the stock market that you would experience with, for example, a unit-linked policy. This makes with-profits investments compatible with people who would rate their attitude to risk at around five on a ten-point scale of risk. However, if you would be likely to cash in your policy early, due to the impact of a possible market value reduction (see page 342), the risk is greater – say, around six upwards. For more information about with-profits insurance, see Chapter 16.

Unit-linked version of low-cost endowment mortgage

With a unit-linked endowment mortgage, instead of the value of the policy depending on bonuses, it is linked directly to one or more funds of investments managed by the insurance company. The fund typically will be invested in shares, and you can often switch between the funds (see Chapter 17). The value of your policy will go up – and down – with the value of the underlying investments. Although share prices tend to grow over the long term, at any point in time stock markets can be riding high or in the doldrums. If share prices happen to be low at the time your mortgage comes to an end, the value of your policy will reflect this and might not be enough to pay off the loan. This makes the unit-linked version of endowment mortgages generally more risky than its with-profits cousin, and on a ten-point risk scale it scores around six upwards.

Even if you are happy with this level of risk, a unit-linked endowment mortgage is still unlikely to be the best choice, because an ISA mortgage will give you a very similar level of risk but has three important advantages:

- ISA mortgages benefit from favourable tax treatment; endowment mortgages do not
- the charges (even allowing for the cost of buying life insurance if you need it) for an ISA mortgage are usually much lower than the charges for an endowment mortgage
- there are usually no, or only low, surrender penalties if you cash in an ISA before the end of the mortgage term.

Given these differences, it is very difficult to justify choosing a unit-linked endowment mortgage nowadays. If you want a share-linked investment to pay off your interest-only mortgage, choose a broadly invested ISA.

Individual savings account (ISA) mortgage

With this type of interest-only mortgage, you pay into an individual savings account (ISA) to build up enough to pay off the mortgage at the end of its term. ISAs – which are described in detail in Chapters 16 and 17 – are a tax-efficient way in which to invest in shares, unit trusts and many other investments: tax-efficient, because all the income and growth from the underlying investments is – for now – completely tax-free.

ISAs replaced personal equity plans (PEPs) from April 1999 onwards. From that date no new PEPs could be started but old PEPs can continue. You can earmark any PEPs you already hold, as well as any ISAs you now take out, to repay your mortgage. With both PEPs and ISAs, dividends from shares are tax-free only until April 2004, but from then on they are due to become taxable. Other income and gains will continue to be tax-free.

Despite the tax advantages which ISA mortgages, and in the past PEP mortgages, have over endowment mortgages, borrowers have been slow to switch to them.

Cynics suggest that this is because the commission paid to mortgage advisers is lower on an ISA or PEP mortgage than on a traditional low-cost endowment mortgage, but there is more to it than that. People are cautious by nature about new ideas and, until the introduction of bond-based PEPs and ISAs, this type of mortgage was always a higher-risk option than a with-profits endowment mortgage. Unlike the with-profits endowment, where the addition of bonuses gives you an increasing value over the years, the investments in a share-linked ISA or PEP can fall in value as well as rise. Over the long term, shares, unit trusts and investment trusts are likely to show good returns and might be expected to beat the more broadly based investment funds underlying with-profits endowment policies. But, at any point in time, stock markets may fall, and the value of your ISA or PEP along with them. So although your payments into an ISA (and in the past to PEPs) will be pitched at the level expected to produce a fund large enough to pay off the

---

Tip

ISA mortgages are tax-efficient and flexible. They can be a good choice provided the annual investment limit (£7,000 until 2005–6 and £5,000 a year thereafter) is sufficient given the size of your mortgage. But they are a much higher risk choice than a repayment mortgage.

mortgage at the end of the term, there is a significant element of uncertainty about the future. However, since there are no restrictions on withdrawing money from your ISA or PEP, as the end of the mortgage term approaches you could make a practice of cashing in part or all of your investment when share prices are high and reinvesting in a lower-risk alternative. Share-linked ISA mortgages are suitable only for people who would place themselves around six or more on a ten-point risk scale.

You can use ISAs – and, since 6 April 2001, PEPs also – to invest in medium-risk investments such as corporate bonds, gilts and preference shares. But it is doubtful that these investments would produce a high enough return over the mortgage term to make this type of mortgage worthwhile, bearing in mind the relatively high cost of borrowing now that mortgage tax relief has been abolished.

There is no built-in life cover with an ISA mortgage. If you have dependants, consider taking out term insurance – see Chapter 5.

Payments into an ISA are generally very flexible. This has the advantage that, if you run into temporary difficulties, it is easy to cut down or suspend payments into the ISA for a while. The flipside of this is that you need the self-discipline to ensure that you pay steadily into the ISA enough to build up the sum needed to repay the mortgage at the end of the day.

This flexibility is particularly valuable since the abolition of tax relief on mortgage interest. There is no longer any tax advantage in keeping a mortgage for the long term. If you can afford to, it makes sense to pay off your mortgage as rapidly as possible. An ISA mortgage gives you the necessary flexibility to completely repay your mortgage before the original term is up.

Pension mortgage

A pension mortgage is the most tax-efficient mortgage of all, but is inflexible and does not suit everyone. You take out an interest-only loan and simultaneously pay into a personal pension (which can be a stakeholder pension scheme). The idea is that the tax-free lump sum payable at retirement – see page 267 – will be used to pay off the mortgage. This gives you a number of tax advantages:

- your payments into the pension plan qualify for tax relief at your top rate; no other type of mortgage has this advantage

How different mortgages compare

	Repayment	Low-cost with-profit endowment	Unit-linked endowment	Pension	PEP/ISA
Guarantees to pay off loan	YES	NO	NO	NO	NO
May give you extra lump sum at maturity	NO	YES	YES	YES	YES
Tax advantages	NO	NO[1]	NO[1]	YES	YES
Life insurance built in	NO	YES	YES	NO[2]	NO
Monthly payments can be reduced easily	NO[3]	NO	NO	MAYBE	YES
Monthly payments can be increased easily	YES	NOT USUALLY	NOT USUALLY	YES	YES
Mortgage can be completely paid off whenever you choose without penalty[4]	YES	LOAN: YES POLICY: NO	LOAN: YES POLICY: NO	LOAN: YES PLAN: NO	YES

[1] Unless you are a higher-rate taxpayer. The proceeds of an endowment policy have already had tax deducted at the equivalent of the basic rate, but usually there is no higher-rate tax to pay.
[2] But can be added tax-efficiently.
[3] Unless the loan is designed as a 'flexible mortgage' (see page 176).
[4] With some loans, there is an early redemption charge if you pay off in the early years.

- if you need life cover, you can use a term insurance policy linked to the pension plan, which means you get tax relief at the top rate on your premiums
- your investment in the pension plan builds up largely tax-free
- the lump sum used to pay off the mortgage is tax-free.

Against this, you must set the following disadvantages. First, if you no longer want to pay into the personal pension – because you decide to join a pension scheme at work, for example – you will have to find some other method of building up the sum needed to pay off your mortgage. Secondly, using a pension plan in this way reduces your scope for building up retirement income. Trying to use one financial tool to meet two targets inevitably causes a conflict.

Be particularly wary of taking out a pension mortgage if you are relatively young. If you are only, say, 25, but plan not to retire until age 65, do you really want a 40-year-term mortgage? Alternatively, will you really be happy to start taking at least some of your pension from age 50, say – long before your intended retirement age?

What sort of interest rate to choose

As well as choosing between the basic types of mortgage, there is a wealth of interest rate options too:

- **variable rate** The 'standard' option in the UK. The interest you pay rises and falls with interest rates generally in the economy, making it hard to know from one year to another what your payments will be. Interestingly, this is not the norm in some other countries, where the uncertainty of variable rates is considered too risky.
- **base rate tracker** A variable rate that moves up and down in line with changes in some reference interest rate, such as the Bank of England base rate.
- **fixed rate** You lock into a set interest rate for a fixed period of time, which could be just a year or two or as long as ten years. At the end of the term, you usually revert to the normal variable rate. Usually an arrangement fee has to be paid when you take out this type of mortgage, and there will be hefty penalties if you want to pay off the mortgage: for example, to switch to a cheaper lender. The penalty period sometimes extends beyond the fixed-rate term: for example, you might fix the rate for three years but face early redemption penalties for five years in all. This means that you are not only locked into the fixed rate but also into whatever variable rate that lender subsequently charges. However, this practice is widely considered to be unfair. In response to consumer and regulatory pressure, many providers now offer fixed-rate mortgages where there is no 'penalty overhang' – in other words, penalties for paying off the mortgage are not charged once the fixed-rate period ends. In general, you should not accept a fixed-rate loan with a penalty overhang. Choosing a fixed rate can be a speculative move – you choose a fixed rate if you expect interest rates generally to rise. If you are right, you will be quids in; if you are wrong and variable

rates fall, you will have lost the gamble and be stuck with the higher fixed rate. But fixed rates also have the advantage that you know what your payments will be, which helps you to plan your budgeting.

- **discounted rates** Some mortgages, particularly those aimed at first-time buyers, have a lower rate of interest in the early years. This is useful if money is tight at present but you expect the situation to improve, for example as you work your way up the promotions ladder at work. But make sure that what is on offer is a genuine discount. Beware of deals where the interest saved in the early years is simply deferred and added to the outstanding loan – this is an expensive way to cut costs in the early years and can cause problems when you come to move house if the outstanding loan has become larger than the value of your home. As with fixed-rate deals, there are early redemption penalties if you pay off a discounted-rate mortgage in the early years, and usually the penalty period extends beyond the discount period. For example, even a discount for just one year may go hand in hand with redemption penalties in the first five years. This means that you may be locked into the lender's standard variable rate for some time.

- **capped rates** A capped rate varies in line with general interest rates but is subject to a limit: the rate is guaranteed not to rise above the interest rate cap. There might also be a floor below which the interest rate will not fall, even if general rates go lower; this is called an interest rate 'collar'. The deal runs for a fixed period of time, after which you revert to the normal variable rate. Capped rates give you some of the certainty of fixed rates, helping you to plan your budgets, without so much risk of being locked into a punishingly high rate. As with fixed-rate mortgages, expect to pay an arrangement fee for a capped mortgage and to face hefty early redemption penalties if you try to get out of a collared deal in the first few years.

- **cashback deals** With some standard variable-rate mortgages, you get a cash sum when you take out the mortgage. This can be a sizeable sum: for example, 5 or 6 per cent of the amount you are borrowing. You can use the cash however you like, so it can be handy to put towards the costs of moving, decorating your new home, and so on. Although a cashback is not strictly

---

Warning

Capped and discounted rates are usually linked to the lender's standard variable rate. Some lenders have tried introducing a new, lower standard variable rate for some customers while leaving existing capped- and discounted-rate borrowers linked to the old, higher variable rate. This meant the capped- and discounted-rate borrowers could be paying more for their mortgage than they would have done had the new variable rate also applied to them. Based on the particular terms of their mortgage contracts, some discounted- and capped-rate borrowers have successfully challenged the practice before the Financial Services Ombudsman. As a result, other borrowers in a similar situation might be entitled to claim compensation from their lender. If you think this might apply to you, contact your lender.

---

speaking an interest-rate option, it is useful to look at it here because one use for the cashback would be to invest it to give you a sum to call on if your mortgage rate rises. For example, if you borrowed £50,000 and the mortgage rate rose by 2 per cent over the first year of your mortgage, you could pay up to an extra £910 interest that year. This would be well covered by a 5 per cent cashback deal, giving you a £2,500 lump sum. After paying the extra interest you would still be in profit to the tune of £1,590. This looks a better option than, say, a one-year fixed-rate mortgage taken out at the same initial interest rate with an arrangement fee of £250, which would have saved you £910 – £250 = £660. This is a very simplified example; real life is more complex and your sums will need to take into account the difference in interest rates between deals and longer time periods than one year. With cashback deals, there is usually an early redemption penalty period of five years or so. If you pay part or all of the mortgage during that time, you generally have to pay back the cashback you received.

Some mortgage lenders let you mix-and-match different interest-rate options. For example, you could borrow part of your mortgage at a variable rate and part at a fixed rate. Compared with taking out the whole mortgage on a fixed-interest basis, you would gain some benefit if interest rates fall, though, conversely, you would suffer some increase if interest rates rose. Compared with taking out the whole mortgage at a variable rate, you would face a smaller increase in payments if interest rates rose but also a smaller decrease if interest rates fell. So mixing-and-matching is a way of hedging your bets.

Warning

Be very wary of taking out a mortgage which keeps interest payments low in the early years by deferring the interest and adding it to the outstanding loan. The amount you owe can grow alarmingly, increasing future costs and causing particular problems if the value of your property is falling.

Flexible mortgages

Many lenders now offer flexible mortgages. These are particularly suited to today's lifestyles, since jobs for life are now virtually unknown and your income may fluctuate widely during your working life, especially if you take career breaks to raise a family, say. Flexible mortgages offer some or all of three types of flexibility:

- **overpayments** You can pay off your mortgage more rapidly by making regular overpayments or by paying off ad hoc lump sums without incurring any redemption penalties. Flexible mortgages recalculate your outstanding mortgage balance on either a daily or a monthly basis, so your interest payments immediately adjust to any overpayment.
- **underpayments** You can reduce your regular mortgage payment or even take a complete payment holiday without being in default. There will be conditions attached to this option. For example, you might have to have built up a reserve of overpayments before being allowed to underpay. Also, underpaying increases your outstanding mortgage balance, and there will usually be a ceiling on the overall amount you can borrow (for example, 90 per cent of the value of your home).

- **further loans** You can withdraw extra lump sums from your mortgage account to be used for any purpose, without going through the formality of applying for a new loan. Once again, there are usually conditions. For example, you may have to have built up a reserve of overpayments against which you can borrow. And there will be a ceiling on the overall amount you can borrow through the original mortgage plus any subsequent loans.

Not all flexible mortgages offer all of these features, so you will have to shop around.

In response to the advent of flexible mortgages, many lenders have either stressed or improved the flexibility of their traditional mortgages. For example, at least one lender now waives the normal redemption penalties where borrowers pay off up to 10 per cent of their mortgage balance a year. So before switching to a flexible mortgage, it could be worth checking what flexibility your existing lender can offer.

All-in-one mortgages

An increasing number of lenders offer all-in-one mortgages that combine a flexible loan with a current account and, in some cases, savings accounts and a credit card as well. In its simplest form, called a 'current account mortgage' (CAM), you pay your salary direct into the mortgage account where it immediately reduces your mortgage balance. You then draw against the account for your normal spending as you would with an ordinary current account. The mortgage balance and interest on it is calculated daily, so even money left in the account for only a short period of time has some impact on the cost of your mortgage. In the more sophisticated versions (called 'offset mortgages'), you have several accounts – one each for the mortgage, your current account, savings account and so on – running alongside each other. Each day the net balance for all the accounts is calculated and interest worked out on the overall total.

On the face of it, all-in-one mortgages are very efficient. Any positive balance in your current or savings account reduces your mortgage balance and so saves you interest. In effect then, your current account balance and savings are earning the mortgage rate of interest. Not only is that typically higher than the rates available on savings, but you are not charged any tax on the interest saved.

In effect, an offset mortgage puts you in a position where you are devoting the bulk of your savings to reducing your mortgage. This can save thousands of pounds off the cost of your mortgage and could mean you pay off the loan early. You still have the flexibility to divert your savings instead to other uses, in which case you give up some of the mortgage cost savings.

Of course, you don't need an offset mortgage to pay off your loan early. You could have an ordinary mortgage and a completely separate savings account. From time to time, you could use your savings to pay off a chunk of your mortgage. That too would save you thousands of pounds in mortgage costs and could mean paying off the loan early. But, unlike the all-in-one mortgage, your savings would not earn the mortgage rate of interest, you would have to pay tax on the savings interest and, having paid off part of the mortgage, it would be more difficult to change your mind and use your savings for some other purpose after all (because you would need to take out a new mortgage to 'get back' your savings).

The drawback of all-in-one mortgages is that the mortgage rate of interest is often higher than deals you could get elsewhere and, in particular, there are often no special deals, such as a low discounted rate for the first few years. If you have only a low balance in your current account and little in savings, the benefits you get from combining the accounts may be too small to outweigh the extra cost of the mortgage. And combining your finances in this way could be confusing, especially in the case of a CAM where you have just a single account for both your mortgage and current account. You need to be the sort of person who can efficiently keep track of their money.

If you are good with your finances, generally have a high current account balance, have reasonably high savings and you are a taxpayer (particularly a higher rate taxpayer), an all-in-one mortgage could be a good choice. But check the mortgage is reasonably priced and has all the features you want.

Mortgage packages

As if deciding the type of mortgage and the nature of the interest rate were not enough, mortgages often come packaged with other products, some of which may be worth having, others not.

Mortgage protection insurance

This is term insurance to pay off your mortgage if you die during the term. (It is not required with endowment mortgages, which have built-in life cover.) If anyone is financially dependent on you – your wife, husband, partner, children, elderly relative – this type of insurance is usually well worth having. However, if you have no dependants, there is no need for this cover and you might prefer to do without it (in which case your home would be sold on your death and the mortgage paid off out of the proceeds).

Be aware that a traditional mortgage protection policy may not be the most suitable type of life cover to protect a flexible mortgage. Mortgage protection policies are a type of decreasing term insurance (see Chapter 5) designed to track a mortgage balance that falls steadily over the years. Particularly if you use the flexibility to pay off your mortgage more slowly than a normal repayment loan, you could be underinsured. Consider taking out level term insurance instead.

Mortgage payment protection insurance

One of the biggest problems, if you lose your job or fall ill for a prolonged period, is how to pay the mortgage, because failing to keep up the payments could end in your losing your home. Until October 1995, if you became unemployed and your income and savings were low enough, you could qualify for income support to cover half your mortgage interest payments during the first 16 weeks and the full amount thereafter on up to £100,000 of loan. Since then, anyone taking out a mortgage on or after 1 October 1995 is excluded from this safety net for the first nine months of claiming benefit. For existing borrowers, there is no cover at all for the first two months, and there-after only half of the interest payments is covered for the next four months. To plug this hole in the state safety net, the government expects people taking out new mortgages simultaneously to take out mortgage payment protection insurance, which pays out if you are unable to work because of sickness, disability or unemployment. You can also take out this insurance to cover a mortgage you already have.

Mortgage payment protection insurance has been around for some time, though in the past it had limited appeal because of the many restrictions, often including a waiting period of, say, three months after taking out the policy before claims could be met, no cover for claims related to medical problems you had at the time you took out the policy, pregnancy, drugs or alcohol, HIV, and so on. Even more of a problem has been the list of people who are not normally welcomed by insurers for this type of policy, for example:

- part-time workers, meaning those who work fewer than 16 hours a week
- fixed contract workers
- people with no fixed income
- newly self-employed who haven't yet built up a track record
- people with risky jobs, for example divers
- people who already know that they are likely to lose their job.

Since the restriction on state support, insurers have been experimenting with less restrictive policies. However, you should take special care to read the terms of this type of policy to ensure that it provides cover which is suitable for you. The Association of British Insurers (ABI)★ has drawn up a code of practice requiring its members to make sure that customers understand what they are buying and that policies recommended to them are suitable. However, policies are often sold through lenders or mortgage intermediaries who have little knowledge of the details of these policies. In this situation, you should normally be given a written summary of the cover. It is very important that you read it and check that the policy is suitable for you.

Whether or not you need mortgage payment protection insurance depends on what arrangements are already in place to protect your income in case of illness (see Chapter 6) or unemployment. In general, it is probably a wise precaution to take out this cover. A few lenders offer it free as part of the mortgage package. Usually the premium you pay is linked to the size of your mortgage. If you do pay off part of your mortgage early, don't forget to tell the insurer and get the premium revised.

House insurance

Insurance companies pay commission to agencies which arrange the sale of their policies. Banks and building societies have found this to be a useful source of extra income, so you may well find that you are expected to take out house buildings and even house contents insurance through the society or bank as part of the mortgage package. But check both the cost and cover carefully: you may be able to get better value insurance elsewhere, especially if you qualify for discounts with some companies because of your job. In the past, it was common for lenders to insist that you took out their insurance as part of the particular mortgage deal, so you had little choice. But a change in the law outlawed this practice. Another ruse is where the bank or building society makes an administration charge if you choose to buy your house insurance elsewhere – you will have to weigh up the impact of the charge against the amount you stand to save by insuring elsewhere. Check whether the new insurer will pay the administration charge for you – at least one company does this.

Switching your mortgage

Having taken out a mortgage, you are not locked into that particular loan for the full mortgage term. Lenders compete fiercely for your custom and you may be able to reduce the cost of your mortgage by switching to a new lender. Against this you must set the costs of making the switch. These might include: valuation, legal and land registry fees; arrangement fee and mortgage indemnity insurance premium charged by the new lender; discharge fee, deeds fee and any early redemption charge levied by the old lender. The costs can easily come to £1,000 or more, but the savings can be substantial too. For example, each 1 per cent cut in the mortgage rate on a 25-year £50,000 loan could save you around £360 in interest each year. Although this is not widely advertised, rather than losing you to another lender, your existing mortgage lender might be willing to give you a better deal: for example, by extending to you discounted rates normally available only to first-time buyers. It is certainly worth talking to your existing lender before going ahead with any switch, since it will cost you less to stay put.

If you are interested in switching mortgage, check what deals are currently on offer (see 'More information' on page 190). Get quotes for the loans you are interested in, including the associated charges. Check what fees your existing lender might charge and check out whether your existing lender might be prepared to offer you a better deal than your current loan in order to keep your custom.

Bear in mind that switching mortgage counts as taking out a new loan, so you could be entitled to less help from the state if you ran into problems keeping up the payments – see page 179.

Deciding how much to borrow

When you take out a mortgage, the amount you borrow is driven by three main factors:

- **the price of the home you want to buy** The amount you can borrow will generally restrict your choice of properties. But, often, if you need to live in a particular area – for work, say – there will also be a minimum amount you must borrow if you are to buy anything at all.
- **the value of the home you buy** The lender will have the property valued. Usually, they will not be prepared to lend you the full value of the property. Commonly, the maximum will be 90 per cent or 95 per cent of the property's value – called a 90 per cent or 95 per cent loan-to-value (LTV) proportion. Bear in mind the value of the property for this purpose may be less than the price you are required to pay for it.
- **what you can afford to pay** Lenders often work on the basis of crude income multiples. For example, you might be able to borrow three times your gross salary. If you are a couple, you might get, say, two-and-a-half times your joint salaries. But you should never take out the maximum loan offered unless you have worked out that this is an amount you can afford to pay.

What you can afford

Write down your monthly budget:

- Look at the money you have coming in each month – your pay after tax and other deductions, income from investments, any child benefit or other state benefits, maintenance payments from a former partner, and so on.
- Deduct your monthly expenses for, say, council tax, water, heating and lighting, food, travel to work, telephone, and so on. Apportion annual and quarterly bills as if they were spread out

monthly. Do not include rent or current mortgage payments if these will be saved once you have bought your new home.

• In the first instance, deduct non-essential spending – for example on holidays, meals out, cinema trips and so on. But, if it looks unlikely that you can afford the size of mortgage you want, go back and consider what non-essential spending you could do without. Be realistic – you must not count on savings which in practice you will not really make.

• Deduct your total spending from your income to see how much you can afford to pay each month for a mortgage. If you plan to choose a variable-rate mortgage, bear in mind that your mortgage costs will increase if interest rates rise. Similarly, if you choose a discounted mortgage, make sure you have allowed for the increase in payments once the discount period has finished.

Once you know how much you can afford to pay each month, compare this with the cost of a mortgage to find out the maximum loan you can afford to borrow – see below.

How much your mortgage might cost

The table overleaf shows how much you can expect to pay each month for each £1,000 of mortgage loan depending on the term of your mortgage and the interest rate. Find the interest rate you will pay in the left-hand column and your chosen mortgage term across the top, or go straight to the last column if you plan to have an interest-only mortgage. The corresponding figure in the table tells you broadly how much you will have to pay for each £1,000 of loan. Divide the amount you can afford to pay each month by this figure, to find out the maximum loan you can afford – see Example.

Different lenders use different methods to work out your payments, so the amount you pay might not be exactly the same as the amount from the table but it should be close.

In the table, payments for repayment mortgages assume that the interest you must pay is recalculated daily using the latest mortgage balance. Some lenders calculate the interest only monthly or even once a year. This means that there is a delay before loan repayments work through to reduce the interest charge. Overall, you will pay more for a mortgage if the interest is recalculated infrequently.

Monthly mortgage payments for each £1,000 of mortgage loan*

Interest rate % pa	Repayment mortgage with term of:						Interest-only mortgage
	5	10	15	20	25	30	Any term
1%	£17.09	£8.76	£5.98	£4.60	£3.77	£3.22	£0.83
2%	£17.51	£9.19	£6.43	£5.06	£4.24	£3.69	£1.67
3%	£17.95	£9.65	£6.90	£5.54	£4.74	£4.21	£2.50
4%	£18.39	£10.11	£7.39	£6.05	£5.27	£4.77	£3.33
5%	£18.84	£10.59	£7.90	£6.59	£5.84	£5.36	£4.17
6%	£19.29	£11.08	£8.43	£7.16	£6.44	£5.99	£5.00
7%	£19.75	£11.59	£8.97	£7.74	£7.06	£6.65	£5.83
8%	£20.22	£12.11	£9.54	£8.35	£7.71	£7.33	£6.67
9%	£20.70	£12.64	£10.13	£8.99	£8.38	£8.04	£7.50
10%	£21.18	£13.18	£10.73	£9.64	£9.08	£8.77	£8.33
11%	£21.67	£13.74	£11.35	£10.31	£9.79	£9.52	£9.17
12%	£22.17	£14.31	£11.98	£11.00	£10.52	£10.28	£10.00

* Interest calculated daily

The column for interest-only mortgages shows just the interest you would pay for the mortgage. To this you must add whatever you would pay each month to any investment you will use to pay off the mortgage.

Example

Rachel and Ben are thinking about taking out a repayment mortgage. Ben earns £36,000 a year and Rachel, who has just had a baby, currently earns just £10,000 a year. They've been told by one lender that they can borrow up to three times Ben's salary plus Rachel's earnings – a total of (3 × £36,000) + £10,000 = £118,000.

Rachel and Ben work out their monthly budget. They reckon they can afford to spend £400 a month on a mortgage. They are thinking about a 25-year-term repayment mortgage and expect to borrow at 5 per cent a year.

They find 5% in the left-hand column of the table and read across to the 25-year column. This tells them that they'll have to pay about £5.84 a month for each £1,000 they borrow. Dividing this into the £400 they can afford gives a figure of £400 ÷ £5.84 = 68.5. This suggests that the maximum loan they can afford is £68,500 – considerably less than the maximum they can get according to the lender's formula.

If Ben and Rachel borrowed £118,000 at an interest rate of 5 per cent a year for 25 years, it would cost them 118 × £5.84 = £689 a month. This is much more than the amount they feel they can afford.

As interest rates are low at the time Rachel and Ben are looking for their mortgage, they should also consider whether they would cope financially if there was an increase in the mortgage rate.

Information you will get when shopping for a mortgage

At the time of writing, a hotchpotch of rules – some statutory and some voluntary – governs the information you will be given when shopping around for a mortgage.

Mortgages come within the scope of parts of the Consumer Credit Act 1974. Under this Act, if you ask for a written quotation you must be given one. This sets out the main terms of the mortgage loan, the interest you will pay expressed as an annual percentage rate (APR – see overleaf) and what you will have to pay each month. Many lenders can produce a computerised quote within minutes.

Under the Mortgage Code (see Chapter 2) which covers most – but not all – lenders and advisers, you should be given information to help you choose your mortgage. This includes a general description of any charges and fees, an explanation of charges if you pay off your mortgage early, a description of the interest-rate options, an explanation and illustration of what happens to your mortgage payments once any fixed-rate or discounted-rate period ends, an explanation of the effect on any special terms if you move house, and so on. There is no prescribed format for this information, but most lenders will have printed brochures giving summaries and perhaps even the full mortgage terms.

When you take out the mortgage, under the Consumer Credit Act, you must be given a written loan agreement, which you must sign. This sets out the salient features of the loan – its type, interest rate, type of interest, mortgage term, your monthly payments – together with all the detailed small print.

Annual percentage rate (APR)

An APR is a standardised way of stating the total cost of a loan. It takes into account not just the interest rate, but also the timing of the interest payments, the timing of any capital repayments and other charges, such as arrangement fees. You do not have to know how to work out an APR. All you need to know is that one APR can be compared directly with any other APR. A loan with a lower APR is cheaper overall than a loan with a higher APR.

Mortgages sometimes start with a period during which the interest rate is fixed or discounted. After that period, the interest rate usually reverts to the lender's standard variable rate. In the past, some lenders quoted the APR as if the lower interest rate applied for the full mortgage term, giving a misleadingly low impression of the cost of the loan. The government changed the law to ensure that the APR reflects the actual rates of interest charged over the full period of the loan.

Faced with all these different pieces of paper, consumers have often found it hard to compare one mortgage deal with another. There has been no standard format for the information and important features – such as redemption penalties – are often tucked away in the small print. However, life is set to become easier.

From 31 October 2004, the FSA is due to bring in rules to govern the advertising of mortgages and the disclosure of their main features to customers in a key features illustration (KFI). This will have a set format, enabling one loan to be easily compared with another (See Chapter 3).

In April 2000, the government published 'CAT standards' for mortgages. 'CAT' stands for Charges, Access and Terms. CAT standards are benchmarks. You can be sure that a product which meets the CAT standard offers reasonable value and has no hidden charges or terms. But a CAT-standard product will not necessarily be suitable for everyone. A product which does not meet the CAT standard is not necessarily a bad product, but it is different and you should normally check what the differences are, what extra you have to pay and whether the differences you get are worth the extra cost or any extra restrictions.

There are two CAT standards for mortgages – one for variable-rate mortgages, the other for fixed-rate or capped loans. CAT standards can apply to repayment loans and interest-only mortgages. The standards are set out in the tables overleaf.

CAT-standard mortgages are voluntary, so lenders do not have to offer them (and, in practice, few do so). Where a lender does offer a CAT-standard mortgage it must be available to existing borrowers (who can switch to it) as well as new borrowers. However, you can be refused a CAT-standard mortgage on commercial grounds – for example, if your credit standing is not good enough or the property you want to buy is substandard.

Mortgage problems

Payment difficulties

According to official figures, as a nation we owe nearly £671 billion in mortgages. For a minority of people this debt becomes a problem. Usually this happens because of some unforeseen crisis, such as redundancy or divorce. It can be very tempting to close your eyes to mounting bills and simply hope the problem will go away. But debt problems nearly always get worse the longer you leave them. It's essential that you take action as soon as you can.

Your mortgage is a priority debt, because failing to tackle the problem could mean losing your home. Contact your lender immediately and let them know that you are having problems. They are as anxious to find a solution as you, and in most cases will take drastic action only as the very last resort. Some building societies and banks run in-house debt counselling services or will refer you to the Consumer Credit Counselling Service,* an independent debt management service to which some lenders subscribe. These services will help you to prioritise your debts, advise on any state benefits for which you might qualify and will try to set a realistic target for clearing your mortgage arrears, taking into account your whole financial position. Most mortgage lenders stress that repossessing your home is the last thing they want to do. Extending the term of the loan and thus reducing the monthly payments is a possible solution. Where repossession is unavoidable, a few societies have successfully used mortgage-to-

CAT standards for mortgages

CHARGES   All mortgages

- Interest must be calculated daily
- Every regular payment and overpayment you make must be credited immediately
- You must not be charged separately for a mortgage indemnity guarantee (see page 189)
- All fees must be disclosed in cash upfront before you take out the loan
- A broker arranging a CAT-standard mortgage for you must not charge a fee

Variable-rate mortgage	Fixed-rate or capped mortgage
<ul><li>There must be no arrangement fee</li><li>The interest rate must be no more than 2 per cent above the Bank of England base rate</li><li>When the base rate falls, your mortgage payments must be adjusted within one calendar month</li><li>You must be able to pay off part or all of the mortgage at any time without penalty</li></ul>	<ul><li>The maximum arrangement fee is £150</li><li>The maximum redemption charge is 1 per cent of the amount you owe for each year of the fixed period, reducing monthly</li><li>There must be no redemption charge once the fixed-rate or capped period has come to an end</li><li>There must be no redemption charge if you stay with the same mortgage lender when you move home</li></ul>

ACCESS   All mortgages

- Maximum arrangement fee is £150 (but not variable-rate loans)
- Maximum redemption charge is 1% of the amount you owe for each remaining year of a fixed period, reducing monthly. No redemption charge after a fixed or capped rate period ends
- No redemption charge if you stay with the same mortgage lender when you move house

TERMS   All mortgages

- All advertising and paperwork must be straightforward, clear and fair
- You do not have to buy any other product to get a CAT-standard mortgage
- You must be given at least six months' notice if your lender can no longer offer you a mortgage on CAT-standard terms
- If you fall into arrears, you should pay interest only on the outstanding debt at the normal rate

rent schemes to allow people to stay in their old home but as tenants of a housing association.

You can get independent help with your debt problems from your local Citizens' Advice Bureau,★ National Debtline,★ Consumer Credit Counselling Service★ and independent money advice centres.★

Negative equity – where the mortgage on your home is greater than the value of your home – can be a problem, because even if your home is repossessed, there may still be a big mortgage debt outstanding. Your lender may insist on your paying for a 'mortgage indemnity guarantee' when you first take out your mortgage. This is insurance to ensure that your lender can recover their money if you default on the mortgage, but it does not protect you. The insurance company which reimburses the lender can still chase you for the outstanding mortgage debt.

Mortgage complaints

If you are unhappy about the actions of your mortgage lender, you should complain initially to the branch where you took out the loan. If you are not satisfied with the response, take your complaint to the lender's head office. If this still fails to produce a satisfactory resolution to the problem, you can go to the Financial Ombudsman Service (FOS)★ or (until replaced by FOS from 31 October 2004) Mortgage Code Arbitration Scheme,★ who can examine the evidence, make a judgement and, if appropriate, recommend that the lender pay you compensation up to £100,000 – See Chapter 3 for more details.

If you are unhappy about any dealings with an independent mortgage adviser, complain to the firm. If this is unsuccessful, and provided the adviser is covered by the Mortgage Code (see Chapter 2), you can take your complaint to the Mortgage Code Arbitration Scheme. If the adviser is not covered by the code, there is at present

---

Warning
If you run into difficulties in paying your mortgage, contact the lender immediately. Debt problems have a nasty habit of getting worse if you ignore them.

---

no independent complaints scheme to turn to. You could take your case to court, but this could be expensive and slow. All in all, you would be wise to deal only through lenders and intermediaries who are covered by the code – their stationery should make this clear. From 31 October 2004, all mortgage advisers will be covered by FOS.

More information

You can get information about mortgages direct from lenders but that is a laborious way of shopping around. If you have access to the Internet, there are some useful sites that do the shopping around for you and have handy calculators to help you work out how much you can borrow and to filter the huge number of mortgages available (estimated to be about 4,000) down to a selection that is particularly suited to you. Sites worth looking at include Switch with Which?, CharcolOnline, The Mortgage and Loan Group, FT Your Money, MoneyeXtra, Money Net and Money Supermarket (see Appendix III). The Financial Services Authority (FSA)★ comparative tables cover both mortgages and mortgage endowment policies. These are available on the FSA website, and you can also order paper versions of the tables from its consumer helpline.

See also the regular surveys of mortgages in *Which?*★ and specialist personal finance magazines. *What mortgage*★ gives listings of mortgages on offer, as does *Moneyfacts*★ magazine. Moneyfacts also operates a website and a fax information service.

The FSA publishes a number of useful booklets and factsheets about mortgages, including information about what to do if you have an endowment mortgage and the policy looks unlikely to repay your full mortgage. These include *The FSA guide to repaying your mortgage*, and FSA factsheets *Your endowment mortgage – time to decide*.

If you don't ask, you don't get

Mona saved £900 by making a single phone call to her mortgage lender. Three years earlier, she had taken out a 25-year mortgage with a fixed interest rate of 6.59 per cent for three years. In August, the lender wrote to Mona to tell her the fixed deal was coming to an end and her new rate would be its standard variable rate of 5.99 per cent. Mona used a couple of mortgage-search websites to see what else was available. She phoned her existing lender to see if it would match a better deal she had found. The lender agreed that instead of paying its standard variable rate, Mona could switch to one of its new fixed-rate deals. This gives her a rate of 4.95 per cent fixed for 12 months, saving her just over £900 over the year. It will cost her nothing to switch and she will be free to switch again without penalty at the end of the 12 months.

Which? November 2001

Tied insurance comes at a price

Barrie and Tracey took out a five-year fixed-rate mortgage in 1998. As part of the deal, they had to take out the lender's buildings and contents insurance for five years. If they had chosen to buy the insurance from another insurer, the lender would have increased the fixed rate by 0.35 per cent. After phoning a few insurance companies, Barrie and Tracey realised they could cut the cost of their insurance by more than half if they were not tied to their lender. The cost of the lender's insurance has risen to £643 a year. A similar *Which?* Best Buy policy would cost just £245. The extra cost of the lender's policy effectively wipes out the savings on the cost of the mortgage.

Which? January 2000

Chapter 10

Pensions

One of your highest financial priorities should be ensuring that you will have an adequate income in retirement. In many areas of personal finance, the aim is to protect yourself against the *possibility* that certain events will happen. But with pension planning you are dealing with the very near *certainty* that you will retire and you will need an income.

Virtually everyone will need a pension. A few people are rich enough not to worry too much about where their retirement income will come from, but even they should take advantage of the tax incentives available for pension planning. If you run your own business, you might think that you do not need to make special plans for retirement. After all, you'll sell the business and live off the proceeds, won't you? But this is a very risky strategy: your business might fail before you reach retirement, or you might be unable to sell it at the time you want to retire or for enough to provide a comfortable income.

Do not underestimate the financial resources you will need for retirement. This is a phase of your life which can span two or three decades: see the table on page overleaf. To build up the resources you need, you should start your retirement saving as soon as possible.

This chapter looks at the basic strategy of planning how much retirement income you will need, what part of it might come from the state and how this is changing. Chapter 11 looks at pensions which might be available through your job if you work for an employer. Chapter 12 considers your pension options if you are self-employed or don't work.

How much retirement income will you need?

One of the difficulties in looking ahead to what income you might need in retirement is that price levels are likely to be very different. But as a first step you should consider what income you might need in terms of today's prices. Your income needs are likely to be substantially different from your current needs. For example, in retirement you might no longer be paying out on a mortgage, and you will not have work-related expenses (although you might need to replace, say, running costs of a car previously met by your employer, out of your own pocket); on the other hand, you might spend more on travelling and holidays (being able to go away at off-peak times could reduce the outlay). Health problems tend to be more prevalent the older you are, so you might spend more in that area too, and so on. You should also consider how you will meet capital outlays once you are retired – for example, the cost of replacing a company car, the washing machine or the fridge. You may need to set aside a little of your income each month to meet such capital needs. Try to envisage what your expenditure patterns might be in retirement and fill in the Calculator starting on page 197, estimating how much you might spend each month, assuming *today*'s prices, on each type of expenditure. Fill in the figures up to amount B on page 199, then follow the instructions overleaf.

Average length of retirement

If you retire at this age:	On average, you can expect this many years of retirement:	
	women	men
50	32	28
55	27	24
60	23	19
65	19	16
70	15	12
75	12	9
80	9	7
85	6	5

Source: Government Actuary's Department

The impact of tax

Amount B in the Calculator gives the total of your expected yearly spending in retirement. However, this makes no allowance for income tax. Both state pensions and pensions you build up for yourself are taxable, though you may enjoy higher age-related allowances once you reach 65 (see page 80). It is fairly pointless going into detailed calculations at this stage to estimate how much extra income you might need to foot the tax bills. After all, the tax system could be wildly different by the time you retire. As a very rough rule of thumb, you might adjust the value at B in the Calculator by the amount suggested in the table below. Follow the instructions in the Calculator to find amount D (the before-tax income you'll need). If you are a couple, decide how the income at B is likely to be split between you and work out the tax on each share.

Rough guide to tax on your future retirement income

If the after-tax income you need (B in the Calculator) is about:	This is the factor you enter as amount C in the Calculator:
£5,000	1
£10,000	1.1
£15,000	1.1
£20,000	1.2
£25,000	1.2
£30,000	1.2
£35,000	1.3
£40,000	1.3
£50,000	1.4

Example
Holly and Dan use the Calculator to estimate that they will need a starting income of about £21,000 at today's prices to cover their retirement spending (figure B).

Although Holly has a well-paid job now, she took a career break when their children were younger, so the couple expect that Dan's pension savings are likely to bring in about two-thirds of their retirement income (say, £14,000) and Holly's the remaining third (say, £7,000).

To check up how much extra they will need to cover their tax bills, Dan looks in the table above for an income of around £14,000 The table tells him to multiply value B by 1.1 to cover tax. This comes to 1.1 × £14,000 = £15,400.

Holly goes through the same procedure. But with an after-tax income of only £7,000, she needs to multiply value B by 1 – in other words, no increase

Holly and Dan work out the before-tax retirement income they will need (at today's prices): £15,400 + £7,000 = £22,400 (figure D in the Calculator).

The impact of inflation

When planning for retirement, it is essential that you do not overlook the effects of inflation. Even relatively low rates of inflation can eat heavily into the spending power of your income. For example, if prices were to rise by just 2.5 per cent a year over the next 20 years, a loaf of bread costing 60 pence would then cost 98p and you would need an income of nearly £16,400 to be able to buy the same things that you can today with just £10,000.

Taking account of inflation

Multiply by the appropriate factor below to turn a sum in terms of today's money into an equivalent sum in terms of future prices

Number of years until retirement	Rate of inflation you expect between now and retirement			
	2.50%	5%	7.50%	10%
5	1.13	1.28	1.44	1.61
10	1.28	1.63	2.06	2.59
15	1.45	2.08	2.96	4.18
20	1.64	2.65	4.25	6.73
25	1.85	3.39	6.10	10.83
30	2.10	4.32	8.75	17.45
35	2.37	5.52	12.57	28.10
40	2.69	7.04	18.04	45.26
45	3.04	8.99	25.90	72.89
50	3.44	11.47	37.19	117.39
55	3.89	14.64	53.39	189.06
60	4.40	18.68	76.65	304.48

The effect of inflation is important in pension planning for two reasons:

- **making sure you save enough in the years before retirement** Suppose you reckon that a pension of £20,000 a year would give you a reasonable standard of living if you retired today. But, if you'll be retiring many years hence, it would be foolish to set £20,000 a year as your target. Inflation between now and retirement could mean that £20,000 buys only, say, two-thirds or a half or even a quarter of what it would today. So it's important to think of your pension target in terms of future money. For example, if you want the standard of living £20,000 can buy today and you think future inflation will average, say, 2.5 per cent a year, your pension target for 20 years' time should be £33,000.

- **maintaining your living standards throughout retirement** On the day you retire, you might have a perfectly adequate income. But, unless that income increases over the years, its buying power will almost certainly fall as time goes by. The fall could be substantial, making it impossible to maintain a comfortable lifestyle.

Throughout Chapters 11–13, we consider the protection different

---

Example

Holly and Dan work out they will need £22,400 retirement income in today's money. They expect between them to get about £8,500 of this from state pensions. Their state pension entitlement is automatically increased each year in line with inflation, so they don't need to make any adjustments to this amount. They deduct it from their pension target, leaving £13,900 (amount F in the Calculator).

On the face of it, £13,900 is the amount of pension they need to save for. But inflation will swell this figure as time goes by. Holly and Dan think inflation might run at 2.5 per cent a year on average between now and when they retire. They hope to retire in 25 years' time. Using the table opposite they look up the inflation factor corresponding to 25 years and 2.5 per cent inflation – this is 1.85. They put 1.85 in the Calculator as amount G.

Holly and Dan work out £13,900 × 1.85 = £25,715 (amount H). This is their target retirement income on top of what they can expect from the state.

---

pension arrangements can give you against inflation. In the Retirement Income Calculator, amount F is your pension target in today's money. You can convert this to the income which buys the same standard of living at the start of retirement by multiplying by an inflation factor. But first you can deduct any pensions – like the state pension – which automatically increase with inflation.

Now follow the instructions in the Calculator to find amount H (the yearly before-tax income you'll need after allowing for inflation).

Retirement Income Calculator

Write down how much you might spend on:		£/month
Household expenses		
Food shopping and household basics	a	
Buying and repairing household equipment	b	
Newspapers/magazines/books	c	
TV licence/videos/music	d	
Dog/cat/other pets	e	
Clothes/shoes/cosmetics/hairdressing	f	
Other home-related expenses		
Mortgage/rent	g	
Repairs/service charge/decoration/furnishing	h	
Building and contents insurance	i	
Council Tax/water charges	j	
Gas/electricity/heating oil/solid fuel	k	
Home help/window cleaner/other paid help	l	
Gardening	m	
Telephone	n	
Leisure and treats		
Sports and hobbies: materials/lessons/other	o	
Dining out/theatre/cinema/concerts/exhibitions	p	
Holidays/holiday home/second home	q	
Other (e.g. smoking, drinking)	r	

	£/month
Transport	
Owning a car: tax/insurance/servicing/repairs/ breakdown insurance	s
Renting a car: rental charges/insurance	t
Running a car: petrol/oil/diesel	u
Train fares/bus fares/coach fares	v
Other	w
Health-related	
Dentist	x
Optician	y
Private medical insurance/hospital cash plan	z
Long-term care insurance	aa
Other health-related expenses	bb
Caring for others	
Spending on children and grandchildren	cc
Financial help for elderly relatives	dd
Christmas/birthday/other presents	ee
Gifts to charity/church collections	ff
Protection-type life insurance	gg
Other	hh
Saving and borrowing	
Saving to replace car/major household equipment	ii
Saving to finance home improvements	jj
Saving to cover higher health spending later on	kk
Other regular saving	ll
Loan repayments (other than mortgage)	mm
Other spending	
Postage/stationery, etc.	nn
Other	oo

		£/month
TOTAL (Add items a to oo)	A	
Multiply A by 12 to give yearly amount. This is the yearly after-tax income you need to cover your retirement spending at today's prices	B	
Find the factor that corresponds to B, in the table on page 194	C	
Multiply B by C to find the before-tax (gross) income you need	D	
Yearly pension you can expect from the state – see page 203	E	
Subtract E from D. This is the yearly retirement income (at today's prices) which you need to build up for yourself, through schemes at work or your own pension savings	F	
Choose an inflation factor – see page 195	G	
Multiply F by G. This is the yearly retirement income you need to build up for yourself, taking into account rising prices between now and retirement	H	

Minimum income for pensioners

A difficulty with planning a pension when retirement is many years ahead is deciding how much attention to pay to current laws and regulations that might well have changed by the time you retire. It seems reasonable to assume that the state basic pension (see page 203) in broadly its current form might continue because this has been a fairly stable feature of state support for many decades and attempts to change it are politically very sensitive. But other areas of governments' pension policies have been subject to frequent change and so you should perhaps be wary of assuming that they will still apply many years ahead.

The latest change to state pensions is the introduction of the pension credit from October 2003. The credit has two elements:

- a guarantee that everyone aged 60 or over will have at least a minimum amount of income to live on. (This replaces the earlier

minimum income guarantee – MIG – which was a fancy name for the income support that pensioners could claim)
- a savings credit to 'reward' people over 65 on modest incomes who have made their own savings for retirement over and above their state basic pension.

A brief outline of the pension credit is given below and, as you plan your pension savings, you might bear these arrangements in mind because, if you were to qualify for the credit, it could reduce the amount you need to save. However, it is impossible to predict whether the pension credit will still be available when you retire and, even if it is, it will be relevant only if your target retirement pension is fairly low (around £7,200 a year if you are single or £10,600 a year if you are a couple at 2003-4 rates).

The income guarantee

In 2003-4, people aged 60 and over whose income is less than a certain amount (£102.10 a week for a single person and £155.80 for a couple) can receive a state top up to bring their income to that level.

Income includes state pensions, other pensions, some state benefits, earnings from any work, and so on. It does not include actual income from savings (such as interest and dividends). Instead, you are deemed to receive a 'tariff income' of £1 a week from each £500 of savings you have over a capital threshold (£6,000 in 2003-4). If your savings are less than £6,000, they are ignored completely.

Example

In 2003-4, Kitty is 62 and has a state pension of £77.45 a week and savings of £8,200. For the purpose of pension credit, she is treated as receiving a tariff income of £5 a week from these savings (because £8,200 – £6,000 = £2,200 which can be divided into five lots and part-lot of £500). This brings her income up to £82.45 a week which is less than the income guarantee of £102.10. Therefore she qualifies for pension credit of £102.10 – £82.45 = £19.65 a week to bring her income up to the minimum level (she will also qualify for some savings credit too).

The savings credit

The savings credit tops up your pension credit by 60p for each £1 of income you have, over and above the level of the state basic pension up to the level of the income guarantee, as a result of your own savings for retirement. But you lose 40p of this credit for every £1 by which your income exceeds the income guarantee.

The income from your own savings includes any state additional pension scheme (see page 203), occupational pension, personal pensions and the tariff income from any other savings and investments.

At the rates for 2003-4, this means that single pensioners with an income of £140 a week or more and couples on an income of £204 a week or more would not usually get any pension credit. And the closer your income is to these levels, the smaller the amount of pension credit you would get – see the tables below.

Examples of pension credit in 2003-4 for a single person

Income before pension credit		Income less level of state basic pension	Guaranteed income top up	Savings credit	Income including pension credit
£77.45	[1]	£0.00	£24.65	£0.00	£102.10
£80.00		£2.55	£22.10	£1.53	£103.63
£90.00		£12.55	£12.10	£7.53	£109.63
£100.00		£22.55	£2.10	£13.53	£115.63
£102.10	[2]	£24.65	£0.00	£14.79	£116.89
£110.00		£32.55	£0.00	£11.63	£121.63
£120.00		£42.55	£0.00	£7.63	£127.63
£130.00		£52.55	£0.00	£3.63	£133.63
£139.10	[3]	£61.65	£0.00	£0.00	£139.10

[1] Level of state basic pension
[2] Income guarantee
[3] No pension credit

Examples of pension credit in 2003-4 for a couple

Income before pension credit	Income less level of state basic pension	Guaranteed income top up	Savings credit	Income including pension credit
£123.80 [1]	£0.00	£32.00	£0.00	£155.80
£130.00	£6.20	£25.80	£3.72	£159.52
£140.00	£16.20	£15.80	£9.72	£165.52
£150.00	£26.20	£5.80	£15.72	£171.52
£155.80 [2]	£32.00	£0.00	£19.20	£175.00
£160.00	£36.20	£0.00	£17.52	£177.52
£170.00	£46.20	£0.00	£13.52	£183.52
£180.00	£56.20	£0.00	£9.52	£189.52
£190.00	£66.20	£0.00	£5.52	£195.52
£200.00	£76.20	£0.00	£1.52	£201.52
£203.80 [3]	£80.00	£0.00	£0.00	£203.80

[1] Level of state basic pension
[2] Income guarantee
[3] No pension credit

Example

Jo, 66, and his wife Amy have a state basic pension of £154.90 a week in 2003-4 and an occupational pension of £22 a week bringing their total income to £176.90 a week. This is more than the income guarantee so they do not qualify for that part of the pension credit but they can claim the savings credit. The amount they get is worked out as follows. Their own savings for retirement give them an income which is £155.80 − £123.80 = £32 more per week than the amount of the state basic pension for a couple, ignoring income above the level of the guarantee. Initially, this qualifies them for a savings credit of 32 x 60p = £19.20. But this is reduced by 40p for every £1 by which their income exceeds the income guarantee. So the reduction is (£176.90 − £155.80) x 40p = £8.44. Therefore, Jo and Amy get pension credit of £19.20 − £8.44 = £10.76, bringing their total weekly income to £176.90 + £10.76 = £187.66.

A pension from the state

You would be very unwise to rely on the state pension alone for your retirement income; on its own – even with the pension credit – it is too low to support a comfortable standard of living. However, it does provide a useful core to your retirement planning, and it is worth making sure that you maintain your entitlement to it.

How much pension?

State retirement pensions become payable when you reach state pension age (see page 205), regardless of whether you have stopped work. You can, however, choose to delay the start of your pension for a time, in which case the amount payable is increased.

State pensions have three components:

- **basic pension** This is payable to everyone who has paid enough National Insurance contributions throughout their working life – see page 207. In 2003–4 the full basic pension for a single person is £77.45 a week (£4,027 a year). A couple who both qualify for their own basic pension could get double this. Alternatively, a wife over state pension age can have a basic pension of up to £46.35 a week (£2,410 a year) based on her husband's contribution record, provided he is receiving his state pension. If the wife is under pension age, the husband gets the extra sum, but only if his wife earns no more than a given limit (£54.65 a week in 2003–4).
- **additional pension** Until April 2002, this was limited to employees who earn above a lower earnings limit (£77 a week in 2003–4) and who are not 'contracted out' of this part of the state scheme – see page 206. But, from April 2002, it has been extended to people who are caring for young children, certain other carers and some people who are unable to work because of illness or disability. If you are unemployed for any other reason, if you are self-employed or your earnings are below the lower earnings limit, you cannot build up additional pension. Until April 2002, additional pension was built up through the State Earnings-Related Pension Scheme (SERPS); from April 2002 onwards, additional pension was built up through the State Second Pension (S2P). See the box overleaf for guidance on the amount of additional pension you might get.

How much additional pension?

The State Earnings-Related Pension Scheme (SERPS) was designed to provide pensions linked to your earnings. So if you have a well-paid job you could expect a bigger pension than if you were in a low-paid job. In 2003–4, the maximum SERPS pension a high earner could get was £138 a week. In practice, most people get a lot less than this. Government figures show that for people retiring in 2002, the average was £21.63 a week for men and just £9.58 a week for women.

The amounts actually paid out are low partly because breaks from work – for example, to care for children – reduce the pension and partly because the people who stay in SERPS tend to be in low-paid jobs. Higher-paid employees are often 'contracted out' – see page 000.

The State Second Pension (S2P), which has replaced SERPS from April 2002, is designed to improve your additional pension if your income is low or if you have to take breaks from work because of certain caring duties or health problems.

Initially, S2P gives you twice as much as you would have got under SERPS if you earn up to the low earnings threshold (£11,200 in 2003–4). If you earn less, you are treated as if your earnings are £11,200. If your income is between £11,200 and £25,592, you initially get more than you would have done under SERPS with the extra declining as earnings rise. Over £25,592, you initially get broadly the same as you would have done under SERPS.

From a date yet to be announced (possibly April 2006), S2P may change to a flat-rate pension for everyone under a certain age – probably then aged 45. People earning above the low earnings threshold would be encouraged to contract out – see page 206.

- **graduated pension** This is an older, simpler but much less generous earnings-related scheme for employees which ran from 1961 to 1975. If you belonged to the scheme, the National Insurance contributions you paid were related to your earnings. The contributions you paid are divided into 'units'. You now get so much pension for each unit (9.37 pence per unit in 2003–4). In 2003–4 the most graduated pension you can get is £6.76 a week (£351 a year) if you are a woman and £8.07 a week (£420 a year) if you are a man. You could have been contracted out of the graduated scheme, in which case your employer's scheme took over responsibility for paying you a pension instead and you gave up your rights under the state graduated scheme.

All the state pensions are increased each year in line with inflation, and they are taxable.

Working life and state pension age

In general, your entitlement to state pensions depends on the National Insurance contributions paid during your working life. 'Working life' is an official definition which, for most people, means the tax years from the start of the one in which you reach age 16 to the last complete tax year before you reach state pension age.

At present, state pension age is 65 for men and 60 for women. But for women born after 5 March 1955, their pension age is 65. There is a transitional period during which women's pension age gradually rises from the old level of 60 to the new level of 65. Women who were born between 6 April 1950 and 5 March 1955 are affected by the transitional rules. If they apply to you, your state pension age is calculated according to the following rule: pension age is 60 plus one month for each month (or part-month) that your birth date falls after 5 April 1950. For this purpose, a month runs from the sixth day of one month to the fifth day of the next. If you have access to the Internet, you'll find a calculator to work out your state pension date and age on The Pension Service website (see Appendix III).

If your state pension age is 65, you normally have a working life of 49 years. If your state pension age is 60, your working life is normally 44 years.

National Insurance contributions

Not all National Insurance contributions count for the purpose of building up state pensions: the table on page 207 specifies those that do and don't.

To qualify for the full basic state pension, you must have paid the right type of National Insurance contributions for at least nine-tenths of your working life. If you have paid these contributions for less than a quarter of your working life, you will get no basic pension at all. Contributions paid between a quarter and nine-tenths of working life qualify you for a reduced-rate basic pension.

If you do not pay contributions for a time because you are at home caring for children or a dependent relative, you can claim Home Responsibilities Protection (HRP). This, in effect, reduces the length of your working life, so that you need fewer years in order to qualify for a given rate of basic pension.

Warning

Home Responsibilities Protection is given only for full tax years (running from 6 April to the following 5 April). You cannot claim it for part of a year during which you stopped work to care for children or an elderly relative.

Tip

If you have gaps in your National Insurance record during the last six years (whether for full tax years or just part of any tax year), check whether filling the gaps would increase your entitlement to the state basic pension. If it would, consider paying voluntary Class 3 contributions. Contact your local Inland Revenue* office for details.

Contracting out

'Contracting out' means opting out of the additional state pension (now S2P) and instead building up a private pension either through a pension scheme run by an employer or through a scheme you arrange for yourself.

If you contract out of a state scheme, the state will eventually save money because it will have to pay you less pension. In return, you get a rebate of the National Insurance contributions you are paying now. The rebate is given in different ways depending on how you contract out:

- if you are contracted out through an occupational pension scheme run by your employer, you (and your employer) get the rebate as a cut in the rate of National Insurance you pay

Do your National Insurance contributions count towards your pension?

Type of contribution	Description	What do you pay in 2003–4?	Do they count towards your state pension?
Class 1: standard rate on earnings up to lower earnings limit (LEL)	Paid by most employees including company directors	0% on earnings up to £77 a week	YES, towards basic pension. (If you earn less than the LEL, you are not building up any pension)
Class 1: standard rate on earnings above the LEL up to the primary threshold	Paid by most employees including company directors	0% on earnings from £77 a week up to £89 a week	YES, towards S2P pension, but NO, if you are contracted out
Class 1: standard rate on earnings above the primary threshold up to the upper earnings limit (UEL)	Paid by some employees including company directors	11% on earnings above £89 a week up to £595 a week	YES towards S2P pension
Class 1: contracted-out rate on earnings above the primary threshold up to the UEL	Paid by some employees including company directors	9.4% on earnings above £89 a week up to £595 a week	NO
Class 1: additional rate on earnings above the UEL	Paid by most employees including company directors	1% on earnings above £595 a week	NO
Class 1: reduced rate	Paid by some married women and widows	4.85% on earnings above £89 a week up to £595 a week	NO
Class 2	Paid by the self-employed. (Optional for people with profits below a given level and for some married women and widows)	£2 a week	YES towards basic pension but NO if you opt not to pay them
Class 3	Voluntary contributions	£6.95 a week	YES, towards basic pension
Class 4	Paid by the self-employed	8% of profits from £4,615 a year up to £30,940 a year	NO
National Insurance credits	You may get these if you are not working because, say, you are unemployed, ill or having a baby	You pay nothing	YES towards basic pension

- if you contract out through a personal arrangement – a personal pension or a personal stakeholder pension scheme (see Chapter 12) – you pay the standard National Insurance rate and the rebate is paid direct to your pension scheme.

While you are contracted out, you are building up either less or no state additional pension. Instead you build up a pension through the private scheme. There are rules setting out what pension (and other benefits) must be provided by the private scheme. The rules vary depending on the type of scheme concerned and are explained in Chapters 11 and 12.

In general, there is no guarantee that the pension you will get from the private scheme will be as much as the state pension you give up. This will depend on various factors including the amount of the rebate and the rate at which you expect investments to grow. At the time of writing, most advisers thought the decision was at best finely balanced and, for many people, tilted towards the state scheme. So, general advice was that, on the whole, it would be better to stay in, or contract back into, the state scheme. However, if S2P becomes a flat-rate scheme, higher earners are likely then to be better off contracting out. Bear in mind that if your employer runs an occupational pension scheme, it is usually a good idea to join whether or not it is contracted out and whether or not contracting out would be best for you personally. This is because occupational schemes have advantages (see Chapter 11) which outweigh any gains or losses from contracting out.

If you can join an occupational pension scheme through work, ask your pension scheme administrator about the contracting out position. If you are saving through a personal pension or a personal stakeholder scheme, get advice from the salesperson providing the scheme or an independent financial adviser (IFA).★

What state pension(s) will you get?

The state pension system is complicated and thankfully you do not need to work out for yourself what your state pension entitlement will be; instead, you can ask the Department for Work and Pensions (DWP)★ to provide you with a retirement forecast. This states what rights to pension you have built up so far and projects what your state pensions might be by state pension age if your circumstances continue unchanged. Note that the projection is in terms of today's money. The forecast also gives guidance on steps you might take to boost your entitlement: for example, by paying voluntary National Insurance contributions to fill any gaps in your record.

To obtain a retirement forecast, get form BR19 from The Pension Service★ or the DWP website (see Appendix IV). Complete it and send it to the address given on the form. You should receive your forecast within a few weeks.

The government has stated that in future it intends to send out regular state pension forecasts automatically to all people of working age instead of your having to request them. It plans to start with self-employed people.

Increasingly, the annual statements you receive from any occupational pensions scheme you belong to or personal pension you have will be in the form of 'combined benefit statements'. These include a forecast of your state pension based on your actual National Insurance record. (Do not confuse this with other benefit statements that simply indicate the state pension that anyone might get but not based on your specific details.) If you receive a combined benefit statement, you will not need to use form BR19. The government wants to encourage more schemes and providers to issue combined statements and has said, if necessary, it will legislate to make them compulsory.

At retirement

State pensions become payable from state pension age but you can earn extra (either as income or a lump sum) by putting off the start of your pension. This will be viable only if you have other resources, for example, because you carry on doing some work. At the time of writing, the government was proposing improvements from 2006 to the amount of extra state pension you could earn. However, you'll need to weigh up the terms on offer when you reach retirement and consider, for example, whether a better option would be to start your pension at the normal age and invest it.

Action list for state pensions

- Check what your state pension entitlement will be by getting a retirement forecast from The Pension Service★ or DWP website or by checking your combined benefit statement if you receive one.

- If you have any gaps in your National Insurance record during the last six years, consider filling them by paying voluntary Class 3 National Insurance.
- If you are paying Class 1 National Insurance at the married women's reduced rate, you are not building up your own pension entitlement, though you will be able to claim a pension based on your husband's record. Check whether you would get a higher pension by switching to standard-rate Class 1 contributions.
- If you have chosen not to pay National Insurance – for example, you are self-employed and your profits are low – you are not building up a state pension entitlement. Consider paying the contributions for the sake of your future pension (Class 2 contributions also qualify you for other state benefits such as incapacity benefits – see Chapter 6 – so are good value at just £2 a week.)
- If you are out of work, check whether you are getting National Insurance credits. If not, can you do so? For example, is it worth signing on for unemployment benefit in order to get credits? If you are caring for someone at home, are you getting Home Responsibilities Protection? (It is given automatically if you are getting child benefit.) If not, make sure you claim it.
- If you have the choice, consider whether you would be better off staying in the state additional pension scheme or contracting out (see page 206). Review this decision every year.

More information

Your main source of information about state pensions – both in general terms and concerning your own entitlement – is The Department for Work and Pensions★. If you have access to the Internet, you'll find a lot of useful information on its websites www.dwp.gov.uk and www.pensionguide.gov.uk. The DWP's services are delivered by two agencies: Jobcentre Plus★ for people of working age and The Pension Service★ for people of retirement age and for matters to do with pension planning. The Pension Service website, www.thepensionservice.gov.uk is a useful source of further information and, from there, you can download form BR19 in order to request a state pension forecast. DWP publications, forms and services are also available locally through your social security office★.

Check whether any occupational scheme you belong to or personal pension you have provides combined benefit statements showing a forecast of your state pension. If so, you will not need to use form BR19.

The payment of National Insurance contributions is dealt with by the Inland Revenue.★ Contact your local tax office for information about the types and amounts you should be paying and to arrange voluntary contributions. General information and leaflets are available from tax offices and the Inland Revenue website.

If you want to read more about state pensions see *The Which? Guide to Planning Your Pension*, and for a detailed guide to working out how much to save for retirement see *Take Control of Your Pension. An Action Pack*, both from Which? Books★.

Useful leaflets about state pensions and National Insurance

Leaflet code	Leaflet name
NP46	A guide to retirement pensions
PM1	A guide to your pension options
PM2	State pensions – your guide
PM5	Pensions for the self-employed – your guide
PM6	Pensions for women – your guide
PM7	Contracted-out pensions – your guide
CA01	National Insurance for employees
CWL2	National Insurance contributions for self-employed people. Class 2 and Class 4
CA02	National Insurance contributions for self-employed people with small earnings
CA04	National Insurance contributions Class 2 and Class 3. Direct debit – the easier way to pay
CA08	Voluntary National Insurance contributions
CA09	National Insurance for widows or widowers
CA10	National Insurance for divorcees
CA12	Training for further employment and your National Insurance record
CA13	National Insurance contributions for women with reduced elections
CA17	Employees' guide to minimum contributions
CA25	Agencies and people working through agencies
CA44	National Insurance for company directors
GL23	Social security benefits rates

Filling the gaps

Clare left school at 18 and went to university for a three-year course. She is now 25 and earning a good salary. She has National Insurance credits for the tax years when she reached 16, 17 and 18 and was in school. But the years at university are gaps in her contribution record and could eventually mean she'll get less basic pension.

Clare can fill this three-year gap by making Class 3 contributions. But she should not delay too long: after this year, she will no longer be able to pay contributions for the year in which she reached 19 because it will be more than six years ago. Clare has longer on which to make good the contributions for the years in which she reached 20 and 21.

Small pay rise, big pension increase

Julia's pay is just below the lower earnings limit (£4,004 in 2003–4), so she does not build up any state second pension (S2P). If she increased her hours slightly to bring her pay up to £4,004, she would start to build up S2P. She would then be treated as if she had earnings equal to the low earnings threshold (£11,200 in 2003–4) and this would qualify her for £1.13 S2P a week at 2003–4 prices. Over a whole working life and assuming earnings equal to the lower earnings limit each year, this could build up a pension payable at age 65 of around £55 a week (at 2003–4 price levels).

Which? Guide to Planning Your Pension

Chapter 11

Pensions through your workplace

If you have filled in the Retirement Income Calculator in Chapter 10, it is almost certain that any state pension you expect falls far short of the income you would ideally like to enjoy in retirement. A key part of financial planning is ensuring that the shortfall is made good.

Any long-term saving could help you do this. But, in practice, there are worthwhile tax advantages to using a dedicated pension scheme or plan:

- **tax relief on contributions** You get tax relief at your highest rate on contributions you pay into the scheme.
- **tax-free fringe benefit** If your employer pays into the scheme on your behalf, this normally counts as a tax-free fringe benefit.
- **tax-free gains** Any capital gain on the money invested in your pension fund is tax-free.
- **some tax-free income** Income earned by the investments in your pension fund is tax-free unless it is dividends on shares (and similar income, such as distributions from unit trusts) in which case it is taxed at 10 per cent.
- **tax-free lump sum** At retirement, you can take part of the proceeds of most pension arrangements as a tax-free lump sum. The rest of your pension fund must be used to provide an income (your pension) which is taxable.

Pension schemes run by your employer

Many employers, especially larger ones, have set up their own 'occupational pension schemes' (also called 'superannuation schemes' especially in the public sector). If you are eligible to join one, this is usually the best way to save for retirement because an occupational scheme has the following additional advantages:

- **employer contributions** In most cases, your employer must pay into the scheme on your behalf. Some schemes are even 'non-contributory' which means that the employer meets the full cost of the scheme and you don't have to pay anything at all.
- **package of benefits** Usually, the scheme provides more than just a pension at retirement. Common extra benefits are an early pension if you have to stop work because of illness, lump-sum life insurance, pensions for your spouse and sometimes other dependants if you die before or after retirement.
- **charges** The costs of the scheme may be lower than for pension schemes you arrange yourself and your employer might pay the charges direct instead of the costs being deducted from the pension fund.

There are two main types of occupational pension scheme: salary-related schemes and money purchase schemes – see pages 215 and 219.

Other pension schemes available through work

Not all pension schemes available through work are occupational schemes. Instead of running its own scheme, your employer might instead give you access at work to one or more pension schemes run by other organisations – often insurance companies, but also banks, unit trusts and so on.

Often these alternative schemes are group personal pension schemes (GPPS). These are simply personal pensions – which are described in detail in Chapter 12 – but they may have advantages over a personal pension you arrange for yourself, for example:

- **employer contributions** Your employer does not have to pay into a GPPS on your behalf, but some do.
- **special features** Your employer may have negotiated special terms with the pension provider. For example, charges may be lower or contributions might be more flexible, allowing you to vary your payments or stop them altogether without penalty.

Normally, when you leave your employer, you lose the special advantages of the GPPS, though the personal pension itself continues if you are still eligible to have one (see Chapter 12).

Since April 2001, if your employer does not offer you membership of an occupational scheme, and does not offer you a GPPS to which it makes a contribution of at least 3 per cent of your pay, then your employer must usually give you access through work to one or more 'stakeholder pension schemes'. This does not apply if your employer has fewer than five employees.

Personal stakeholder schemes are described in Chapter 12. To earn the title 'stakeholder' these schemes must be low-charging and flexible. But your employer does not have to pay into a stakeholder scheme on your behalf. This means that, in general, you will still be better off joining an occupational pension scheme if you can.

Tip

An occupational pension scheme is usually hard to beat as a way of saving for retirement. Not only does it benefit from favourable tax treatment, but your employer puts in money on your behalf and will often pay separately the major costs of administering the scheme instead of the costs being charged to the pension fund.

Salary-related occupational pension schemes
How much pension?

Occupational salary-related schemes promise you a given amount of pension worked out according to a formula. The pension you get depends on your pay before retirement and the number of years you have belonged to the scheme. Typically, you might get one-sixtieth or one-eightieth of your pre-retirement salary for each year in the scheme – see Example.

Your pension must be increased once it starts to be paid. The rules are complicated, but for pensions you build up now increases must usually be in line with inflation up to 5 per cent a year. However, the government has proposed that the upper limit be reduced to 2.5 per cent with this change likely to take effect from 2005.

In an occupational salary-related scheme, other benefits – such as widow's pension and the tax-free lump sum at retirement – are worked out in a similar way, according to a formula.

Example

Harry's employer runs an occupational salary-related pension scheme. The scheme offers one-sixtieth of pre-retirement salary for each year of membership. By retirement, Harry expects to have clocked up 15 years in the scheme. If his earnings just before retirement are £30,000, he can expect a pension of:

$1/60 \times £30{,}000 \times 15 = £7{,}500$ a year.

On past experience the scheme usually increases pensions each year in line with inflation once they start to be paid. If that policy continues, the buying power of Harry's pension should be protected.

Your employer must ensure that enough is paid into the pension scheme to provide the promised benefits. If the scheme is contributory, you will have to pay part of the cost.

The Inland Revenue (a government department) sets a ceiling on the pension and other benefits you can have from an occupational pension scheme – see page 224. Most schemes provide benefits which are well within the ceiling.

Contracted-out salary-related schemes

For periods when you belong to a contracted-out occupational scheme, you build up pension through the scheme in place of part or all of the pension you would have had through the state additional pension scheme (see page 203).

It is up to your employer to ensure that enough is paid into the pension scheme to provide the contracted-out benefits. In a contributory scheme, you are required to pay part of the cost.

You build up different benefits depending on the period for which you were contracted out. In the case of a salary-related scheme:

- **for periods up to April 1997:** You built up guaranteed minimum pension (GMP) payable from state pension age and GMP for your widow or widower should you die. Your GMP was broadly the same amount as the SERPS pension you were giving up (see page 189). A contracted-out scheme could offer benefits greater than just the GMPs.

- **for periods from April 1997 onwards:** To qualify as contracted-out, the scheme must provide most employees with benefits which are at least as good as those specified for a benchmark 'reference scheme'. In the reference scheme, pension equals one-eightieth of 90 per cent of earnings between a lower and upper earnings limit (£77 and £595 a week in 2003-4) for each year of membership plus a widow's or widower's pension of half that amount.

How much do you pay?

The government is proposing to radically alter the rules concerning the limits on contributions to pension schemes. The proposals which are due to come into effect from 6 April 2005, are outlined on page 237. Until then, the rules described below apply in the case of occupational schemes.

The Inland Revenue limits the amount you can pay into an occupational pension scheme, but there is no limit on the amount your employer can pay in on your behalf.

The maximum you can pay is generally 15 per cent of your earnings – see Example below. If you joined your scheme on or after 1 June 1989, or if you joined earlier but the scheme was set up on or after 14 March 1989 (or you opt to be treated under these rules), there is also a cap on the earnings which can count towards this limit. The cap usually increases each year – in 2003–4 it is £99,000.

In practice, your regular contributions to the scheme will generally be much lower than the maximum. Typically, you might pay, say, 5 or 6 per cent of your earnings. This will automatically be deducted from your pay before income tax is worked out, thereby giving you relief at your top rate.

Example

Harry currently earns £20,000 a year before tax. He pays 6 per cent of this into the occupational pension scheme:

6% × £20,000 = £1,200 a year.

In 2003-4, income tax on earnings of £20,000 would normally come to £3,149.50. When Harry's pension contributions are deducted, tax on the remaining income is £2,885.50. So paying £1,200 into the pension scheme saves Harry £264 in tax (in other words, 22 per cent of £1,200).

Pros and cons of salary-related schemes

A major advantage of salary-related pension schemes is that your employer, rather than you, takes on most of the risk of providing your pension. With most other types of pension scheme, the amount of pension you get depends heavily on the returns you can get from investments, particularly the stock market. With a salary-related scheme, you are promised a set amount of pension, expressed as a percentage of your pre-retirement pay. Whatever the stock market does, you are – in theory – promised the same amount of pension. If the stock market slumps, it's up to your employer, not you, to find the means to provide the expected pension.

However, your protection from stock market volatility is not complete. As a result of the long fall in share prices between 2000 and 2003, employers have been called upon to pay very large extra sums into their final salary schemes to ensure that the promised benefits are being adequately funded. Many employers have decided they can no longer afford this open-ended commitment and have closed their schemes to new members, in some cases closed them also to further contributions from existing members and even in the most drastic cases wound up the final salary pension scheme. When a scheme is wound up, the members are usually entitled to much lower benefits than they would have received at retirement. Moreover, if the pension fund does not have enough money to fund all the benefits, the pensions and other benefits may be scaled down. The government has proposed new legislation to come into effect during 2003 to help protect members' pension rights in these situations. Despite some risk of your employer abandoning the scheme when the going gets tough, the advantages of final salary schemes mean that in general if you can join one it is usually a good idea.

Because your pension is linked to your pay, the amount of pension you will get automatically increases as your earnings increase. This gives in-built protection against inflation during the period that your pension is building up.

Once the pension starts to be paid, schemes must by law give you protection against inflation up to 5 per cent a year (to be reduced to a maximum of 2.5 per cent a year assuming government proposals go ahead). In practice, larger schemes often give more protection than this. Public sector schemes (covering, say, teachers, the police and local authority workers) generally give full protection against inflation.

Salary-related schemes make pension planning fairly easy, because you can frame both your target retirement income and your expected retirement income as proportions of your pre-retirement income.

These schemes are less useful if you change jobs often. Your pension is then linked to your pay before you left the scheme – which might be low compared with what you will be earning by retirement. However, this 'preserved pension' as it is called must be increased up to retirement in line with inflation up to 5 per cent a year. (The government has yet to say whether this maximum will also be reduced to 2.5 per cent a year in line with proposals for pensions in payment) You can opt to transfer the value of your preserved pension to another pension arrangement – see page 233.

Warning

Salary-related occupational schemes are an extremely good way to save for a pension. As well as benefiting from your employer's contributions, you are sheltered from the investment risks inherent in most other types of retirement saving (as long as your employer is not considering closing the final salary schemes). When changing jobs, think carefully about the impact on your eventual pension if you will be losing the security of a salary-related pension scheme.

Money purchase occupational schemes

How much pension?

Occupational money purchase schemes are a type of 'defined contribution' (DC) scheme. All defined contribution schemes provide you with your own savings pot, and the pension you get depends on:

- the amount paid into the scheme
- how well the invested payments grow
- how much is deducted in charges

- the amount of pension you can buy with your fund when you reach retirement.

Typically, the contributions made by your employer and you are invested in the stock market. Over the long term, shares and share-based investments tend to produce good levels of growth and more than is needed to compensate for inflation. However, share prices can fall as well as rise. If the stock market slumped in the months leading up to retirement, your pension pot might fall in value. To guard against this, it is common to switch to less volatile investments, such as gilts, other bonds and money market deposits, as retirement approaches.

The amount of pension you can buy at retirement depends on 'annuity rates'. An annuity is a special investment where you swap a lump sum (in this case your pension fund) for a regular income – your pension. Once the annuity is bought, you can't get your money back as a lump sum. The annuity rate tells you how much income you will get for your lump sum and is expressed either as a percentage or as so many £s for each £10,000 lump sum. For example, an annuity rate of 6 per cent is the same as £600 for each £10,000 invested.

Annuity rates are changing all the time. But the rate at which you convert your pension fund to income sets the pattern of your pension for the whole of your retirement, regardless of any subsequent changes in annuity rates. For more information about annuities, see Chapter 13.

Your pension must be increased once it starts to be paid. The rules are complicated, but for pensions you build up now increases must usually be at least in line with inflation up to 5 per cent a year (to be reduced to a maximum of 2.5 per cent a year assuming government proposals go ahead).

Instead of using your pension fund to buy an annuity straight away, you can put this off as late as age 75 and, in the meantime, draw an income straight from your pension fund – for more on this, see Chapter 13.

The Inland Revenue puts a ceiling on the pension and other benefits you can get from occupational pension schemes – see page 224. In general, these limits apply regardless of whether schemes are salary-related or money purchase.

However, since April 2001, occupational money purchase schemes have been able to opt into the 'DC regime' described in Chapter 12. So far, few if any, schemes have done so, but if they do opt into this regime, there will no longer be limits on the amount of pension (and other benefits) you can get from the scheme – only limits on the amount you can pay in.

Example

At retirement, Gill has built up a fund of £52,000 in her occupational money purchase scheme. The annuity rate at that time is 7.5 per cent or £750 for each £10,000 invested. Her pension will be:

£52,000 / £10,000 × £750 = £3,900 a year.

Contracted-out money purchase schemes

For periods when you belong to a contracted-out occupational scheme, you build up pension through the scheme in place of part or all of the pension you would have had through the state additional pension scheme (see page 203).

In the case of a money purchase scheme, your employer must pay into the scheme an amount equal to the National Insurance rebate you and your employer receive as a result of being contracted out (see page 206); in a contributory scheme, your employer will require you to hand over some or all of your share of the rebate. The rebate is invested and must be used to provide 'protected rights' which are:

- **a pension for you** This is payable from retirement but not before age 60. The whole fund must be used for pensions – none can be taken as a tax-free lump sum.
- **a widow's or widower's pension** This is whatever pension the fund will buy if death occurs before retirement or half your pension in the case of death after retirement.
- **pension increases** once the pension is being paid, at least up to inflation or 5 per cent a year (whichever is lower).

A contracted-out money purchase scheme can provide extra pension and other benefits in addition to protected rights.

How much do you pay?

The government is proposing to radically alter the rules concerning the limits on contributions to pension schemes. The proposals, which are due to come into effect from 6 April 2005, outlined on page 237. Until then, the rules described below apply in the case of occupational schemes.

The Inland Revenue puts limits on the amount you can pay into an occupational money purchase scheme. In general, these are the same as the limits already described for occupational salary-related schemes, see page 224.

However, since April 2001, occupational money purchase schemes have been able to opt to join the 'DC regime' described in Chapter 12. Few, if any, have so far done so, but if they do opt into this regime, the limit on contributions will be as follows:

- Contributions up to £3,600 a year (before tax relief) are allowed, regardless of earnings.
- Contributions in excess of £3,600 a year are allowed but depend on your earnings.
- Anyone can pay these contributions – you, your employer, a relative, and so on.
- The limit applies to your total contributions to all pension arrangements within the DC regime – in other words, occupational money purchase schemes which have opted in, personal pensions and the new stakeholder schemes.
- Contributions are paid after deducting income tax relief at the basic rate – you keep the tax relief even if your income is too low to pay that much tax.

The rules for the DC regime are described more fully in Chapter 12.

In practice, your regular contributions to an occupational money purchase scheme are usually much lower than the maximum allowed. Typically, you might pay in about 5 to 6 per cent of your earnings.

Pros and cons of money purchase schemes

Occupational money purchase schemes are reasonably simple to understand. They work much like any other type of saving or investment – money is paid in, it is invested and whatever fund builds up is yours to use for your pension.

But these schemes are unpredictable. You don't know how well your investment will grow or what annuity rates will be when you retire. This makes it more difficult to plan ahead for retirement and you directly bear the risk of your pension turning out to be less than expected.

There's no guarantee that investment growth will be enough to compensate for the effects of inflation in the period up to retirement. However, shares and share-based investments do tend over the long term to outstrip inflation. In the past, planning ahead used to be particularly difficult because benefit statements typically did not take into account the effect that inflation might have on your pension between now and retirement. But benefit statements issued from April 2003 onwards must include a forecast of your possible pension shown in today's money – see the example below. The forecast in today's money is worked out using standard assumptions, including that inflation will average 2.5 per cent a year. Of course, reality may turn out to be very different from the assumptions but, even so, having a forecast in today's money makes it very much easier to judge whether or not your pension savings are on track for the retirement income you want.

Since April 2001, occupational money purchase schemes have been able to opt into the new 'DC regime'. If such a scheme meets the conditions, it will be able to register as a stakeholder scheme. An occupational stakeholder scheme must by definition be low-

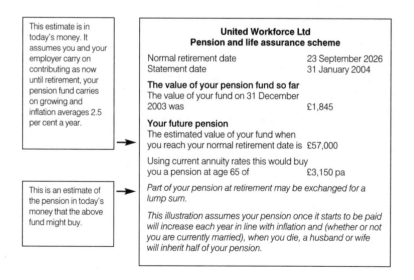

This estimate is in today's money. It assumes you and your employer carry on contributing as now until retirement, your pension fund carries on growing and inflation averages 2.5 per cent a year.

This is an estimate of the pension in today's money that the above fund might buy.

United Workforce Ltd
Pension and life assurance scheme

Normal retirement date	23 September 2026
Statement date	31 January 2004

The value of your pension fund so far
The value of your fund on 31 December 2003 was £1,845

Your future pension
The estimated value of your fund when you reach your normal retirement date is £57,000

Using current annuity rates this would buy you a pension at age 65 of £3,150 pa

Part of your pension at retirement may be exchanged for a lump sum.

This illustration assumes your pension once it starts to be paid will increase each year in line with inflation and (whether or not you are currently married), when you die, a husband or wife will inherit half of your pension.

Main Inland Revenue limits on pensions and tax-free cash [1]

Description of scheme	Limit on pension payable at retirement[2]	Limit on lump sum at retirement
Post-April 2001 Occupational money purchase schemes which opt into the new DC regime	No limit	No limit
Post-1989 regime a) Scheme set up on or after 14 March 1989, or b) Scheme set up before 14 March 1989 but you joined it on or after 1 June 1989, or c) Scheme set up before 14 March 1989 which you joined before 1 June 1989, if you elect to be treated under post-1989 regime rules	Two-thirds of final pay up to a maximum cash limit (£66,000 in 2003–4)[3]	One and a half times final pay up to a maximum cash limit (£148,500 in 2003–4)[3]
1987–9 regime Scheme set up before 14 March 1989 which you joined on or after 17 March 1987 and before 1 June 1989 (unless you have opted to be covered by the post-1989 regime)	Two-thirds of final pay (without cash limit)	One and a half times final pay up to a maximum of £150,000
Pre-1987 regime Scheme you joined before 17 March 1987 (unless you have opted to be covered by the post-1989 regime)	Two-thirds of final pay (without cash limit)	One and a half times final pay (without cash limit)

[1] These limits apply to nearly all employers' schemes, regardless of whether they work on a final pay basis, money purchase basis, or some other basis. Under the 1987–9 regime and pre-1987 regime, the limits shown apply at the normal retirement age for the scheme. Under the post-1989 regime, limits shown apply at any age within the range 60–75.

[2] This is the maximum pension you can have if you do not take any of the proceeds as a tax-free lump sum. If you take tax-free cash, the maximum pension is reduced to less than the amounts shown in this column.

[3] The limit is based on an 'earnings cap' which puts a ceiling on the amount of final pay which can be used in the formula. The earnings cap is usually increased each year in line with the Retail Prices Index and is set at £99,000 for 2003–4.

charging and flexible. See Chapter 12 for more details of stake-holder scheme features.

In general, money purchase occupational schemes are not quite such a good way to save for retirement as salary-related schemes because you, rather than your employer, bear the risk of poor investment returns affecting your savings. In addition, although in theory your employer could pay just as much into either type of scheme, in practice employers' contributions to money purchase schemes tend to be substantially lower than to salary-related schemes.

Hybrid occupational schemes

Hybrid schemes provide a mix of benefits worked out on both a salary-related and a money purchase basis. For example, your pension might be worked out on both bases with you receiving the greater of the two.

Keeping track of your pension target

When your pension is paid

Inland Revenue rules currently allow you to start your pension at any age between 50 and 75.

However, the government has proposed raising the earliest age to 55 by 2010 (phasing in the increase over the period 2005 to 2010).

Presently, most schemes have a normal retirement date at which your pension usually starts. You can start your pension earlier but it will normally be reduced. If you start your pension later it may be increased. GMPs (see page 216) may not be paid before state pension age.

But these rules are also due to change. New laws from 2006 to outlaw age discrimination are likely to prevent employers from setting a compulsory retirement age, though the concept of a 'normal' age at which your full pension first becomes payable is likely to continue. Flexible retirement will also be encouraged in future, with the government changing the rules probably from spring 2005 so that you can start to draw your pension but carry on working for the same employer – perhaps using this as an oppor-tunity to ease back from full-time into part-time work. The rules are also set to change to allow GMPs to start from the same date as other elements of your occupational pension.

Checking how much pension you'll get

While it is essential that you know what type of occupational scheme you belong to and the nature of the pension you are being offered, you do not have to wade through a mass of complicated sums to find out how much pension you should expect. Final salary schemes must provide you with a 'benefit statement' if you ask for one and will under new legislation due from 2005 have to provide these statements automatically each year. By law, you already automatically get a benefit statement each year if you belong to a money purchase scheme.

As described on page 223, from April 2003 onwards benefit statements from money purchase schemes must include a forecast of the pension you might get expressed in today's money. Benefit statements from final salary schemes already generally give you a forecast in terms of today's money (by expressing your possible pension as a fraction of your current salary).

If you have used the calculator in Chapter 10 to work out how much retirement income you might need in today's money (amount F on page 199), you can subtract the amount shown on your benefit statement (or statements if you belong to more than one scheme) together with the forecast of any state pension (this may be shown on the benefit statement from your occupational scheme if it is a combined pension forecast – see page 209) to find out whether you are on track for the retirement income you want.

In all probability, you will belong to more than one pension scheme during your working years. You might transfer your pension rights from a former employer's scheme to another pension arrangement (see page 233). But if you leave pension rights in an old scheme, you can request a benefit statement to keep you up to date on the amount of pension you can expect at retirement.

Boosting your occupational pension

If you belong to an occupational pension scheme but your expected retirement income still falls short of the desired amount, you can usually boost your pension by paying in extra to one or more other

How you can boost your pension

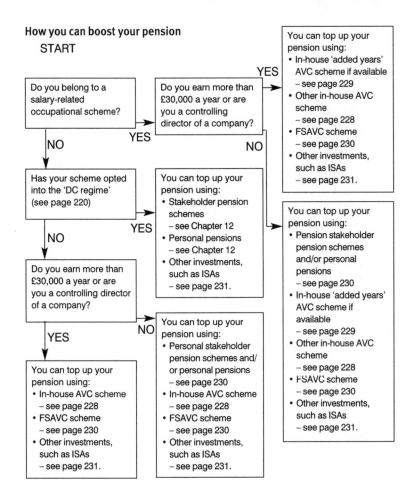

pension arrangements. The arrangements you can choose depend on your pay and the type of occupational pension scheme you belong to and are shown in the chart above. The table on pages 235–6 summarises the pros and cons of each option.

Who can boost their pension?

If you belong to a money purchase occupational scheme that has opted into the DC regime, see Chapter 12 for the limits on contributions you can pay into the occupational scheme, stakeholder schemes and personal pensions.

In other cases, everyone can boost their pension savings provided:

- total contributions to the occupational scheme and any AVC scheme (added years, other in-house or FSAVC) come to no more than the maximum allowed for your type of scheme. See 'How much do you pay?' on pages 217 and 221. The Calculator on page 232 will help you work out how much you are allowed to pay in AVCs under the current rules
- the total benefits you will get do not exceed the Inland Revenue limits set out in the table on page 224.

In addition, provided that, in any one of the past five years, you have earned £30,000 a year or less and you have not during any of those years been a controlling director of a company, you can pay up to £3,600 a year into stakeholder pension schemes and/or personal pensions. During the transition while these rules come into effect, no account is made of your earnings and director-status in any year earlier than 2000–1. See Chapter 12 for information about stakeholder schemes and personal plans.

Your occupational pension scheme administrators can tell you whether you have scope to make extra contributions. But they usually can't advise on which is the best way to boost your pension. If you are uncomfortable making this choice yourself, consult an independent financial adviser (IFA).★

The rules described here applied in 2003-4. However, the government has proposed sweeping changes to the restrictions on how much you can pay into pension schemes and the benefits you can take out – see page 237. It is expected that these new rules will come into effect from 6 April 2005 onwards.

Additional voluntary contributions (AVCs)

AVCs and salary-related schemes

All employers which offer an occupational scheme must under current rules also offer an in-house additional voluntary contribution (AVC) scheme. However, the government has proposed that in future it will be optional for employers to offer an in-house scheme. If your employer decides not to offer one, you will have to make your own arrangements to top up your pension – see the other options below.

Contributions to the in-house scheme boost the pension and possibly other benefits you will get from the main occupational scheme.

An in-house AVC scheme works in one of two ways:

- **added years scheme** Remember that your pension and other benefits depend on your earnings before retirement and the number of years you have been in the scheme. Your AVCs are used to buy extra years, so you are credited with more years than you have really been a member for – see Example below. Those AVCs which are made to an added years scheme boost all the benefits you get from the main occupational scheme, including the tax-free lump sum. Added years schemes are most commonly found in the public sector.
- **defined contribution schemes** See page 219 for a full description of how defined contribution schemes work. Your AVCs are invested to build up a pension fund which is then used to buy extra pension and/or other benefits. But where you started to pay the AVCs on or after 8 April 1987, they can't be used to create or increase the tax-free lump sum.

Example

By retirement, Harry (see previous Examples) will have belonged to his pension scheme for 15 years, which would qualify him for a pension of £7,500 a year. By paying AVCs into the in-house added years scheme, Harry 'buys' an extra three years' membership. This means he is credited with 18 years in the scheme, which increases his pension to:

$1/60 \times £30,000 \times 18 = £9,000$ a year.

Instead of, or as well as, paying into the in-house AVC scheme, you can instead pay into a free-standing AVC (FSAVC) scheme. This is not organised by your employer. You go to a separate pension provider – usually an insurance company. All FSAVC schemes work on a defined contribution basis (see page 219).

Your money builds up a fund which is used to buy extra pension and possibly other benefits. But FSAVCs cannot be used to create or increase a tax-free lump sum.

Unlike an in-house AVC scheme, an FSAVC scheme is not tied to a particular occupational scheme. When you change jobs, your

FSAVC scheme stays with you and can be used to boost benefits from your new employer's scheme if it has one.

Tip

From 30 June 1999 onwards, benefits from in-house AVC schemes (other than added years schemes) and FSAVC schemes can be taken at any time between ages 50 and 75, regardless of whether you have retired. This makes AVCs and FSAVCs useful if you will want to partially retire on a small pension ahead of your main retirement or if you want to boost your pension part-way into retirement.

AVCs and money purchase schemes

As with salary-related schemes, employers that offer an occupational money purchase scheme must also currently offer an in-house AVC scheme (but will not have to do so in future). This will always work on a defined contribution basis. Your AVCs are invested to build up a pension fund which is then used to buy extra pension and/or other benefits. But where you started to pay the AVCs on or after 8 April 1987, they can't be used to create or increase the tax-free lump sum.

Instead of, or as well as, paying into the in-house AVC scheme, you can pay into a free-standing AVC (FSAVC) scheme. This is not organised by your employer. You go to a separate pension provider – usually an insurance company. All FSAVC schemes work on a defined contribution basis (see page 219).

Your money builds up a fund which is used to buy extra pension and possibly other benefits. But FSAVCs cannot be used to create or increase a tax-free lump sum.

Unlike an in-house AVC scheme, an FSAVC scheme is not tied to a particular occupational scheme. When you change jobs, your FSAVC scheme stays with you and can be used to boost benefits from your new employer's scheme if it has one.

Stakeholder pensions if you belong to an occupational scheme

Provided you are not a higher earner (defined for this purpose as

> **In-house AVC scheme versus FSAVC scheme**
>
> Your in-house AVC scheme is often a better choice than an FSAVC scheme because:
>
> - charges may be lower for the in-house scheme
> - your employer might be prepared to match your AVCs and pay in extra contributions on your behalf.
>
> Inland Revenue rules do not allow employers to contribute to FSAVC schemes, but FSAVC schemes may offer you a wider choice of investments and are not tied to a particular pension scheme.

someone who earns more than £30,000 a year) and you are not a controlling director of a company, you are allowed to pay up to £3,600 a year into stakeholder schemes and/or personal pensions. This is in addition to any contributions to your occupational pension scheme and AVC schemes.

Using a stakeholder scheme to top up your pension savings has some clear advantages over AVC schemes other than added years schemes:

- A condition for stakeholder status is that charges must be no more than 1 per cent a year of the value of your investment. This means charges for the stakeholder scheme are likely to be lower than charges for an AVC scheme.
- You can take part of the proceeds of a stakeholder scheme as a tax-free lump sum. Most AVC schemes cannot be used to provide a lump sum.

Other ways to boost your retirement income

You do not have to use a special pension arrangement to boost your retirement income. Instead you could use ordinary savings and investments.

As described on page 213, pension arrangements have tax advantages over most other forms of saving and investment, but one form – the individual savings account (ISA) – also benefits from comparable tax treatment. Compared with most in-house AVC schemes (other than added year schemes) and all FSAVC schemes, the tax treatment of ISAs is different but nearly as good:

How much can you pay in AVCs and/or FSAVCs?

	£ a year
Your earnings	A
Include salary, commission, bonuses, overtime payments, the taxable value of fringe benefits, etc.	
Earnings cap	B
If the 'post-1989' rules apply (see the table on page 000), enter the *lower* of your earnings or £99,000 for 2003–4	
The most you can contribute	C
Multiply B by 15 and divide by 100	
Your current contributions	D
How much are you paying each year in regular contributions and AVCs? Your pay slips will tell you this. Also deduct any FSAVCs which you are already paying	
How much you can pay in AVCs and/or FSAVCs	E
Subtract D from C. What is left is the amount you can pay to top up benefits from your pension scheme (assuming your benefits do not exceed the Inland Revenue limits – see page 000)	

- **the amount you invest** There is no tax relief on what you pay into an ISA. You get tax relief at your highest rate on AVCs and FSAVCs.
- **investment growth** Gains made by your invested money are tax-free with ISAs, and also with AVC and FSAVC schemes.
- **investment income** Until April 2004, all income from investments in an ISA is tax-free. With AVC and FSAVC schemes, all income is tax-free apart from share dividends and similar income which is taxed at 10 per cent. From April 2004 onwards, the treatment of ISAs is due to be brought into line with that of pension schemes.

- **taking your money out** There is no tax on money withdrawn from an ISA. Money withdrawn from most in-house AVC schemes and all FSAVC schemes is taxable.

ISAs do not compare so well, on tax grounds, with personal pensions and stakeholder schemes because the latter allow you to take part of your pension fund as a tax-free lump sum. That part of your money will have had tax relief on the way into the scheme *and* tax relief as it comes out.

However, set against all the different pension arrangements, ISAs have the advantage of flexibility. You can withdraw your money at any time without losing the tax benefits. With pensions, your money is tied up until a minimum age – at present, this is usually 50 (due to rise to 55 by 2010) or 60 depending on the type of scheme. In addition, you can take your ISA proceeds in any form you like – for example, a single lump sum, several lump sums or regular withdrawals. With pension schemes, all or the bulk of your money must be taken as pension and many schemes require you to buy an annuity by age 75 even if annuity rates are very poor.

Leaving a scheme before retirement

Under the current rules, if you leave an occupational pension scheme after being a member for less than two years, the scheme does not have to give you any pension rights. Instead, it can refund your contributions (but not any paid by your employer) less income tax at a special 20 per cent rate. The government has proposed to amend the above rule, so that if you leave within the two years (or other shorter period specified by your scheme) but you have been a member for at least three months, you must be offered a choice of your contributions back or a transfer value which can be switched to another pension arrangement such as a new employer's scheme or stakeholder pension scheme. In a money purchase scheme, the transfer

---

Tip
Very few people can expect a pension which is as good as the maximum allowed under Inland Revenue limits, so there is plenty of scope for making extra contributions as a tax-efficient way of boosting your retirement savings.

---

value is the value of the pension fund you have built up so far. In a final salary scheme, the transfer value is a lump sum which, based on various assumptions, would if invested be enough to provide the pension you are giving up. Either way, the transfer value will be more valuable than a contribution refund because it includes the benefit of contributions made by your employer.

If you leave a pension scheme after two years' membership but before you have reached retirement, you must by law be given rights to a pension. You have a variety of choices about what to do with these rights. No general rule states which choice is best. Each situation has to be looked at on its own merits. To make a rational choice, you will probably need the help of an expert to evaluate the relative benefits of each choice. If a large sum is involved, it would be worth seeking help from an actuary (see 'More information', on page 239). If the cost of consulting an actuary cannot be justified, you could get advice from a couple of independent financial advisers (IFAs)* who specialise in pensions.

Although the decisions facing early leavers cannot be generalised, there are some points worth considering:

- If you belong to a public-sector scheme, there may be a 'transfer club' which lets you transfer your pension, without loss, to another scheme within the public sector.
- Many public-sector schemes offer exceptional benefits, even to early leavers. Be wary of transferring your pension rights to a private-sector scheme; it is very unlikely that the new scheme could match the benefits you would give up.
- It may make sense to transfer your pension rights from one private-sector scheme to another as you switch jobs. It can be easier to keep track of your pension entitlements if they are not spread too widely across many schemes. But you might lose out each time you transfer.
- Be wary of transferring pension rights from an employer's scheme to a personal pension other than a stakeholder scheme. The charges for personal pensions are often a lot higher than for an employer's scheme (where the employer, rather than the pension fund, might be meeting the costs separately).
- When considering the relative merits of a possible transfer, make sure you look at the whole package of benefits under each option.

Comparison of ways to boost your pension

Feature	Type of scheme					
	In-house added years AVC scheme	In-house defined contribution AVC scheme	FSAVC scheme	Stakeholder pension scheme	Personal pension	Individual savings account (ISA)
Payments into the scheme						
Tax relief on amount you pay in	YES	YES	YES	YES	YES	NO
You keep the tax relief even if your income is too low to pay that much tax	NO	NO	YES	YES	YES	N/A
Your investment						
Wide choice of investments	N/A	Often NO	YES	Often NO	YES	YES
Gains on investments are tax-free	N/A	YES	YES	YES	YES	YES
Income from investments is tax-free	N/A	Partly NO	Partly NO	Partly NO	Partly NO	YES until April 2004 then partly NO
Charges						
Charges are low	N/A	Maybe	Often NO	YES	Often NO	Often NO

	In-house added years AVC scheme	In-house defined contribution AVC scheme	FSAVC scheme	Stakeholder pension scheme	Personal pension	Individual savings account (ISA)
You may face penalties if you switch to another scheme	NO	Often YES	Often YES	NO	Often YES	Often YES
Withdrawing your money						
You can make withdrawals at any time	NO	NO	NO	NO	NO	YES
Part of your money can be taken as a tax-free lump sum	YES	Usually NO	NO	YES	YES	YES
All your money can be taken in tax-free lump form	NO	NO	NO	NO	NO	YES
Most or all of your money must be taken as a regular income	YES	YES	YES	YES	YES	NO

Pension choices if you run your own company

If you run your own business, you could use personal pensions or stakeholder schemes (see Chapter 12) to build up your retirement income. But if your business is set up as a company, you could instead set up your own occupational pension scheme. There are two broad types of occupational scheme which are particularly suited to your situation: executive pension plans and small self-administered schemes. A detailed discussion of these schemes is outside the scope of this book. But they enable very flexible retirement planning as well as having business and tax advantages. Before setting up such a scheme, you would be wise to get advice from a pensions consultant, your accountant or an IFA experienced in this area. Be warned that the Inland Revenue takes a close interest in how these schemes are used and has severe penalties if the rules are breached, even accidentally.

Proposed changes to the tax rules for pensions

Pension savings attract various tax reliefs (see page 213) to encourage you to save for retirement. But to contain the cost to the government of these incentives, there have always been rules limiting the amount you can save this way and/or the pension and other benefits you can receive.

If you have read this far, you'll have realised that the rules are complicated and have changed several times. In general changes have not affected pension rights that had already built up and so you can find yourself covered by several sets of rules for different tranches of your pension.

The government has set forward proposals to clear away this complexity. Further details were due to be announced in autumn 2003, but here is an outline of the new proposals as they stood at the time of writing. It is expected that the new rules will be introduced from spring 2005 onwards.

The new regime will apply to pensions from all sources, including occupational schemes (this chapter), personal pensions and retirement annuity contracts (see Chapter 12).

The present limits on contributions and benefits will be swept away and replaced by a single lifetime limit on the retirement savings you can have in tax-advantaged pension schemes and plans. The limit will apply to the size of your pension fund at retirement, adding together the amounts you have in all your pension schemes and plans. The government proposes to set the limit initially at £1.4 million and this will be increased each year in line with inflation.

In addition there may also be a yearly limit on the 'inflows' to your pension schemes. 'Inflows' would include contributions paid in (by you, your employer and anyone else) and the growth of your investments in a money purchase scheme or increase in your pension rights in a final salary scheme. It is suggested that this limit be set initially at £200,000 and be increased yearly in line with inflation.

Provided you do not breach the two limits, you would be free to save any amount you like and your savings would still benefit from the present tax reliefs (in other words, tax relief on contributions and pension fund building up largely tax free).

At retirement, you would be able to take up to quarter of your pension savings as a tax-free lump sum. The rest must be drawn as taxable pension. If your pension funds at retirement breached the lifetime limit, the excess would be paid back to you but as taxed income and after a 33 per cent tax deduction to claw back the tax reliefs you've had. This means the excess could effectively be taxed at up to 60 per cent – a strong incentive not to breach the limit.

There will be no other controls on contributions and no other benefit limits.

Action list for occupational pension schemes

Bear in mind the following considerations:

- If you are not a member of an occupational pension scheme, check whether there is a scheme you can join. Your personnel or human resources department can tell you this.
- If you do belong to an occupational scheme, find out what sort of scheme it is and what benefits it provides. You should have a scheme booklet. If you have lost it or have questions, contact your occupational pension scheme administrator.
- Get a benefit statement and check whether your expected pension will bring your retirement income up the level you will

need. If you haven't been sent a statement recently, ask your pension scheme administrator for one

- If there is a shortfall between your expected retirement income and the amount you will need, find out what options you have for topping up your occupational pension. Your pension scheme administrator can tell you if you have the scope to pay extra contributions and what types of scheme you can use.

More information

The operation of your particular employer's occupational pension scheme is summarised in a scheme booklet which you should have been given before or shortly after you joined the scheme. Read the booklet: your pension is a major asset which will come into its own in the years ahead, so it makes sense to understand how it is being built up. If you do not have a booklet or you have queries which the booklet cannot answer, contact your pensions administrator and/or personnel department at work. Private-sector pension schemes are set up as special legal arrangements called 'trusts'. Trustees are appointed to ensure that the pension fund is used properly according to the rules of the scheme. The trustees are also a good source of information and advice about the scheme.

The pensions administrator (usually based in your personnel or human resources department) is also the place to address requests for a benefit statement, whether from your current pension scheme or one in which you have left benefits built up during an earlier job. The same source can tell you what arrangement the scheme has for making AVCs and how the scheme treats transfers from a previous employer's scheme. To find out about free-standing AVCs or, if you can top up your pension in these ways, stakeholder schemes and personal pensions, either contact the companies which offer them direct – see regular surveys in magazines such as *Money Management*,★ and *Pensions Management*★ – or consult an independent financial adviser (IFA).★

If you have lost track of a scheme in which you had benefits – for example because you have lost the address or the company has merged with another – contact the Pension Schemes Registry.★

If you change jobs and are wondering whether or not to transfer your pension rights, consider getting the advice of a pensions expert.

Early retirement comes at a cost

Barbara, 36, and Bruce, 41, are members of the local government pension scheme which is salary-related. They each pay the standard 6 per cent of their income in contributions to the scheme. To fulfil their wish to retire early, they both need to save more now. Under the local government scheme rules, to retire without losing pension benefits Bruce will have to work through to 56 and Barbara to 55. Their combined pension income at today's levels will then be just over £16,000 a year. They will also receive lump sums totalling £48,000 between them. If they invest these, they could receive a further £1,500 a year. But Barbara and Bruce will need just over £23,000 a year to maintain their current standard of living – a gap of around £6,000 a year. With inflation this rises to a shortfall of £10,000 a year by Barbara's retirement. To provide the additional income, they need to build up a fund of around £200,000 between them. To achieve this, they'll have to invest an extra £300 to £350 a month until they retire (and increase it by 3 per cent each year for inflation). This assumes their investment grows by at least 7 per cent a year; if growth is less, they'll have to invest more.

There are a number of ways in which they can build up this extra fund. The local government scheme allows employees to make AVCs which when invested boost the pension fund. The AVCs buy pension income but no tax-free lump sum. Another option is stakeholder pensions (for those earning no more than £30,000 a year) which allow a quarter of the built-up fund to be taken as tax-free cash. A further option is stocks and shares ISAs. The major advantage of these is that Bruce and Barbara would have complete control of their money and would not have to buy an annuity at retirement.

Whichever of these options they go for, Bruce and Barbara should also provide part of the extra income by buying 'added years' in their local government scheme. Under the rules, Barbara can buy one year and Bruce six. The cost of doing this between them would be £128 a month and would provide an extra £1,300 a year plus a lump sum of £3,900 at today's prices. This might seem expensive but it provides a guaranteed income not dependent on investment returns.

Which? December 2001

The Association of Consulting Actuaries★ can put you in touch with an actuary. The Society of Pension Consultants★ can refer you to members who are either actuaries or specialist IFAs. Actuaries charge fairly high fees. A cheaper option is to consult an IFA. Under rules put in place since the scandal over the mis-selling of personal pension plans to people transferring their pensions, only IFAs who are specially authorised to deal with pension transfer business can give advice in that area, and they must now use proper transfer analysis systems before giving you advice about your options.

If you have a problem with your scheme – for example, long delays in sorting out a transfer payment – and the scheme does not respond satisfactorily to your queries or complaints, you can ask the Pensions Advisory Service (OPAS)★ for help. OPAS is an independent body which will try to clarify and conciliate. If this is not enough to resolve the problem, you can take your case to the Pensions Ombudsman,★ who can make what is known as a determination and an award, if necessary.

If you suspect there is something badly wrong with your scheme – dishonesty or maladministration, say – you might take your doubts to the trustees or your trade union if you have one. You can also take your suspicions to the Occupational Pensions Regulatory Authority (OPRA),★ which was set up under the Pensions Act 1995 to police employers' pensions (The government is proposing to replace OPRA in due course with a new, more proactive pensions regulator).

To help you check whether you are on track for the retirement income you want, see *Take Control of Your Pension. An Action Pack* from Which? Books★.

Chapter 12

Stakeholder pensions, personal pensions and the 'DC regime'

If you can't join an occupational pension scheme (see Chapter 11), you will need to build up your retirement savings in some other way. This will apply to you if, for example, you are an employee whose employer does not offer an occupational scheme, you are self-employed, or you are not working.

Any long-term savings or investment schemes would be suitable. But there are tax advantages to using a personal pension (an individual pension which typically you take out with an insurance company). These advantages are:

- **tax relief on contributions** You get tax relief at your highest rate on contributions you pay into the scheme.
- **tax bonus** From April 2001 onwards, you keep the tax relief on your contributions even if your income is too low for you to pay that much tax. Before then, you got this bonus only if you were an employee.
- **tax-free fringe benefit** If you have an employer which pays into the scheme on your behalf, this normally counts as a tax-free fringe benefit.
- **tax-free gains** Any capital gain on the money invested in your pension fund is tax-free.
- **some tax-free income** Income earned by the investments in your pension fund is tax-free, unless it is dividends on shares (and similar income, such as distributions from unit trusts) in which case it is taxed at 10 per cent.
- **tax-free lump sum** At retirement, you can take part of the proceeds of most pension arrangements as a tax-free lump sum. The rest of your pension fund must be used to provide an income (your pension) which is taxable.

Warning

If you can join an occupational pension scheme (see Chapter 11), that will usually be a better way of saving for retirement than a stakeholder scheme or personal pension.

Stakeholder pension schemes

Stakeholder pension schemes are low-charging, flexible pension schemes available since 6 April 2001. There are two types of stakeholder scheme:

- **personal stakeholder schemes** These are simply personal pensions which meet the conditions set out below and have been registered as stakeholder schemes. You can have one or more personal stakeholder schemes whether you work or not and independently of any particular job.
- **occupational stakeholder schemes** These are occupational money purchase schemes (see Chapter 11) which meet the conditions set out below and have been registered as stakeholder schemes. You can belong to this type of stakeholder scheme only if you work for the employer who runs it and you are eligible to join according to the rules for that particular scheme.

Schemes are registered by the Occupational Pensions Regulatory Authority (OPRA)★ which is responsible for ensuring that schemes meet, and will continue to meet, the stakeholder conditions. OPRA keeps a public register of stakeholder schemes open to inspection by anyone.

The main conditions which distinguish stakeholder schemes from other pension arrangements are set out below.

Stakeholder condition 1: low charges

Charges must total no more than one per cent a year of the value of your pension fund. This must cover all the costs of running the scheme and managing your investments.

The cost must include information and basic advice. If there is a fee for more detailed advice, this must be set out in a separate contract and charged separately.

Stakeholder condition 2: low and flexible contributions

The minimum contribution must be no higher than £20, whether it is a one-off payment or a regular contribution.

You can't be required to make contributions at regular intervals. It is up to you when or how often you pay.

Stakeholder condition 3: portability

You must be able to transfer out of a stakeholder scheme into another stakeholder scheme or another pension arrangement without penalty.

Stakeholder schemes must accept transfers from other stakeholder schemes and other pension arrangements.

Stakeholder condition 4: simplicity

The scheme must include a default investment option which determines how your money is invested if you don't want to choose an investment fund for yourself (see 'How your money is invested').

Stakeholder condition 5: keeping you informed

The scheme provider must give you an annual benefit statement at least once a year showing you in straightforward terms the value of your rights under the scheme.

If the scheme's charges alter, you must be informed within one month of the change.

Stakeholder schemes and personal pensions if you belong to an occupational scheme

If you can't join an occupational pension scheme, stakeholder schemes and personal pensions are useful as your main way of saving for retirement. But, even if you have joined an occupational pension scheme, there are some circumstances in which you might also take out a personal pension or stakeholder scheme:

- **to contract out of the state additional pension scheme** If your occupational scheme is not contracted-out of the state additional pension (see page 203), you can use a personal pension or, from April 2001, a stakeholder scheme to contract out. See below for more about this.
- **to top up your occupational money purchase scheme** See Chapter 11.

- **where you have earnings from another source which are not covered by your occupational scheme** For example, these might be earnings for doing freelance work or from a second job.

Contracted-out stakeholder schemes and personal pensions

For periods when you have a contracted-out stakeholder scheme or personal pension, you build up pension through the scheme in place of part or all of the pension you would have had through the state additional pension scheme (see page 203).

Part of the National Insurance contributions you and your employer have paid is rebated and paid direct to your pension scheme. The rebate is invested and must be used to provide 'protected rights' which are:

- **a pension for you** This is payable from retirement but not before age 60. The whole fund must be used for pensions – none can be taken as a tax-free lump sum.
- **a widow's or widower's pension** This is whatever pension the fund will buy if death is before retirement and half your pension in the case of death after retirement.
- **pension increases** once the pension starts to be paid, at least up to inflation or 5 per cent a year, whichever is lower. (Although the government has proposed to reduce the maximum to 2.5 per cent in the case of occupational pension schemes, it had not at the time of writing said whether this limit would also be reduced.)

A contracted-out stakeholder scheme or personal pension will not on its own provide much retirement income. Make sure you make other pension savings, for example through an occupational scheme if one is open to you or through further stakeholder schemes or personal pensions.

The 'DC regime'

From April 2001, there were big changes to the way you can save for retirement. One change was the introduction of stakeholder pension schemes. Another was the 'DC regime'.

The DC regime is a single system for making payments to all the following 'defined contribution' (DC) pension arrangements:

- stakeholder schemes
- personal pensions
- occupational money purchase schemes (see Chapter 11) – but only those schemes which opt into the new regime. You must work for the employer running the scheme to be eligible.

The DC regime does not cover old-style personal pensions (called retirement annuities contracts). They continue to be covered by earlier rules. For details, see *The Which? Guide to Planning Your Pension* available from Which? Books.★

The DC regime sets limits on the amount you can pay into the pension schemes and plans covered by the regime. The sections below describe the limits that applied in 2003–4. However the government has proposed to sweep away all these rules, from 6 April 2005 onwards, and replace them with a simpler system applying to all types of pension scheme and plan. For details, see page 237.

Limits on what you can pay

Under the DC regime, you can pay up to £3,600 a year (before taking into account any tax relief) in total into any of the above pensions, regardless of your earnings. Even if you have no earnings at all, you can still pay up to £3,600 in pension savings.

If you want to pay in more than £3,600 in a year, you can do this provided the contributions do not breach a limit based on your age and earnings – see opposite.

In fact, contributions do not have to be paid by you – they can be paid by you, your employer, a relative or anyone else. For example, if you are a woman off work caring for children, your husband or partner could pay into your pension scheme for you. A parent, say, can pay contributions for a child.

If you are an employee who receives shares under an approved employee share scheme at work, you can transfer these shares into your pension scheme, provided you stay within the contribution limit.

You can use up to 10 per cent of the amount you contribute to pay premiums for life cover.

Any National Insurance rebates paid in because you are contracted out of the state additional pension scheme do not count towards the limit.

Any amount you pay for a 'waiver of contribution' option does not qualify for tax relief and does not affect your contribution limit. This option is often available with plans where you contract to make regular payments – every month, say. The waiver pays your contributions for you if you lose your income because of illness or disability. Contributions paid under the waiver qualify for basic-rate tax relief in the normal way.

All contributions under the DC regime are paid after deducting tax relief at the basic rate. The scheme provider then claims the relief back from the Inland Revenue and adds it to your scheme. You keep the relief you have deducted, even if your income is too low to pay that much tax. This means that, if you have no earnings or are on a low income, the government effectively adds a bonus to your pension savings – see Example.

If you are a higher-rate taxpayer, you can claim extra tax relief, which you receive through either the self-assessment system or PAYE.

Example

Rebecca works part time while her children are at school. She earns £5,000 a year on which she pays £38.50 tax in 2003–4.

Rebecca was left some money when her mother died and she is using this to pay the maximum allowed into a stakeholder pension scheme. The maximum is a before-tax amount of £3,600. After deducting tax relief at the basic rate (22 per cent in 2003–4), Rebecca hands over 78% × £3,600 = £2,808 to the pension provider.

The pension provider claims £792 from the Inland Revenue and adds it to Rebecca's scheme. This means that £2,808 + £792 = £3,600 goes into the plan at a cost to Rebecca of just £2,808.

Rebecca gets the full £792 of basic-rate tax relief even though she actually pays tax of only £38.50. The additional £753.50 is pure bonus.

Breaking the £3,600 limit

If you want to contribute more than £3,600 in any year to the pensions in the DC regime, you can, provided your total contributions come to no more than the percentage limit shown in the second column of the table overleaf.

The earnings on which your percentage contribution is based are your earnings for a basis tax year. You choose the basis year and are then deemed to have earnings at that level for the next five years, regardless of any change in your actual earnings. If you want to change the basis year – for example, because your earnings have subsequently increased – you can (see Example opposite).

The basis-year system enables you to continue paying contributions in excess of the £3,600 limit for five years if your earnings stop. After five years, the maximum you could pay would drop back to £3,600 a year.

Maximum contributions to DC pension schemes

Your age at the start of the tax year	Contribution limit as a percentage of your earnings or profits	Overall cash limit on contributions if 2003–4 cap had applied[1]
Up to 35	17.5%	£17,325
36–45	20%	£19,800
46–50	25%	£24,750
51–55	30%	£29,700
56–60	35%	£34,650
61-74	40%	£39,600
75 and over	You can no longer contribute	

[1] Percentage limit multiplied by earnings cap. The cap is usually increased each year in line with inflation. In 2003–4 it was £99,000.

Carrying back contributions

If you have not used up your contribution limit for the previous tax year, you can pay a contribution and claim to have it treated as if it had been paid in the previous tax year.

The contribution must be paid on or before 31 January following the end of the year to which you want to carry back the contribution. For example, a contribution paid on or before 31 January 2005 can be carried back to the 2003–4 tax year. You must elect to carry it back either before or when you make the payment.

Tax relief is given at the rates for the year to which the contribution is carried back (not the year in which it is paid).

If you run your own business and want to make contributions above the £3,600 threshold, the carry-back provision could be useful if you will not know what your taxable profits will be until after the end of the tax year. It could also be useful if you normally do not use your whole contribution limit but occasionally have extra money to invest – for example, due to an inheritance or a bonus payment from work.

Example

In the 2003–4 tax year, George, who is self-employed, has taxable profits of £80,000. He wants to pay as much as he can into his stakeholder pension scheme. He can choose either this year or any of the last five tax years as his basis year. His profits over the last five years have been:

1998–99	£64,000
1999–2000	£71,000
2000–1	£82,000
2001–2	£79,000
2002–3	£80,000
2003-4	£78,000

George chooses 2000–1 as his basis year. This sets his earnings for pension contribution purposes at £82,000. As George is aged 52, he can contribute up to 30 per cent of his earnings, making a maximum contribution for 2003–4 of:

30% × £82,000 = £24,600.

George can continue to use his 2000–1 earnings as the basis of his contributions for up to five years – in other words, until 2005–6. But he can change the basis year if he wants to and this would be worth doing if his profits rise above £82,000.

How much pension?

Stakeholder schemes and personal pensions are types of defined contribution scheme. Your pension depends on the factors described in the box. You can use stakeholder schemes and personal plans to provide other benefits too, such as a widow's or widower's pension and increases to pension once they start to be paid, but in general this reduces the standard amount of pension you will get.

How your money is invested

With all defined contribution schemes – stakeholder schemes, personal pensions, retirement annuity contracts and occupational money purchase schemes – what you and anyone else pays into the scheme is invested. With most schemes, you invest in one or more funds run by professional fund managers.

How well the invested contributions grow is the single most important factor determining how much pension you will get. Unfortunately it is also the factor which you cannot predict. You might be tempted to put your money in funds that have done well in the past. But countless studies show that past performance is not a good guide. Especially when considering long-term investments such as pensions, there is no correlation between the star funds of the past and the funds which do well today. Similarly, there is no evidence that the funds which do well today will be the stars of the future. So what can guide your choice of how to invest your pension fund?

- **Risk** If asked: 'Are you happy taking risks with your money?' your answer would probably be: 'No'. But it is a fundamental law of investment that to get higher returns you must take on extra risk. So you must ask yourself: 'How much extra risk am I happy to take to get a better return?' Different funds expose you to different levels of risk.
- **Charges** Although, at the end of the day, investment performance will far outweigh the effect of charges, a fund with high charges will obviously have to perform better to beat a fund with low charges. If you choose a high-charging fund, satisfy yourself that the extra costs are justified.

- **Consistent performance** There is no good evidence that even the funds which perform consistently well now will do so in the future, but common sense suggests that you might do well to avoid consistently bad performers.

The main types of investment fund you can choose from are outlined below. Not all schemes will offer all choices, so if you want a wide choice you will need to shop around.

Most pension schemes let you invest in more than one fund if you want to and let you switch your contributions and the fund you have built up so far from one fund to another. But watch out for minimum investment levels for some funds and for charges if you switch.

Actively managed funds

Fund managers select the shares and/or other investments which they expect to do well. As market conditions change, they sell and buy other investments. Usually, they are aiming to beat some benchmark stock market index, such as the FTSE All Share. There is no evidence that they are consistently able to do this.

All of the funds below, apart from tracker funds, are actively managed.

Tracker funds

These invest in a range of shares which are selected to mimic the performance of a particular stock market index, such as the FTSE-100 index. There is relatively little buying and selling of shares once the fund has been set up so costs are a lot lower than for an actively managed fund. For this reason, tracker funds are likely to be a popular default fund for stakeholder pension schemes.

Tracker funds are generally considered suitable for people who don't like to take too much risk. But you do need to look carefully at the index being tracked. Provided the index covers a broad spread of companies and sectors (for example, industries), risk should not be high. But if the index becomes dominated by a few large companies or one or two particular sectors, you could end up with too many eggs in one basket. In general, a tracker fund is slightly less risky than an actively managed fund invested in a similar range of shares. The manager chooses the timing of sales and purchases in the hope of increasing returns, but some of the time the manager will get the timing wrong. Tracker funds do not have this timing risk.

Deposit-based funds

These invest in money market accounts – which are rather like bank and building society accounts but paying higher interest rates. Your money is very safe in the sense that you can't lose any of your capital, but over the long term, the return on your money would tend to be low compared with funds investing in shares. Deposit-based funds are useful when you are approaching retirement. By switching from shares into deposits, you can lock in past stock-market gains and protect yourself from any falls in share prices in the run-up to retirement.

With-profits funds

Your return is linked mainly to the performance of a wide range of investments such as shares, gilts, bonds and property but also depends on other factors connected with the provider's business. The key difference from other types of funds is that your investment grows steadily as bonuses are added year-by-year and can't usually fall in value. This generally makes with-profits funds less risky than funds linked directly to shares or bonds.

However, you are only protected from stock-market falls as long as you keep your pension with the same provider. If you decide to transfer your fund before retirement to another provider, the amount you can transfer may be reduced by the amount of a 'market value reduction' (MVR). The purpose of the MVR is to ensure that you do not take away more of the with-profits fund than would be fair to all the other policyholders who are staying with the old provider. When the stock market is rising, the MVR will often be zero. But when the stock market is falling, a high MVR might be imposed. This could reduce the transfer value of your pension fund by, say, a tenth or a fifth. For more information about investing on a with-profits basis, see Chapter 16.

Bond-based funds

These invest in gilts, corporate bonds and so on. They tend to be lower-risk than shares but, over the long term, generally do not perform as well. If you are young and a long way from retirement, bonds might not be for you, but as you get nearer to retirement it generally makes sense to spread your risks by putting some of your fund into bonds, increasing the proportion as retirement approaches. For more about gilts and bonds, see Chapter 16.

Share-based funds

The fund invests mainly in a spread of shares but sometimes other investments too. The value of your investment rises and falls with the value of the underlying investments. Provided you choose a fund with a broad spread of shares – typically going by names such as 'UK managed', 'UK growth', 'International growth' and so on – this is a medium-risk way to invest that is suitable for many people.

Specialist funds

These invest in the shares and/or other investments of a particular country or particular sector. Examples include Japanese funds, smaller companies and recovery stocks. Specialist funds tend to be high-risk – sometimes they turn in spectacular growth but equally there have been spectacular nose-dives too. Generally, these are not the place for the core of your retirement savings, but could be useful if you can afford to invest extra.

Self-investment

Some providers offer pension schemes where you yourself select the individual shares and other investments which make up your pension fund. Charges for self-invested schemes are usually higher than for managed schemes and to manage risk you will need a good spread of investments, so this is generally an option only if you have a reasonably large sum to invest (say, £100,000 or more). Needless to say, you must be confident about your abilities to select investments which will perform well.

Information about stakeholder schemes, personal pensions and other schemes

Before you agree to take out a stakeholder scheme or personal pension, or to start paying into an FSAVC scheme, you will get a Key features document (due to be replaced by a Key facts document – see Chapter 3). If you are considering joining an occupational money purchase scheme or AVC (other than 'added years') scheme, the trustees of the scheme will have received a Key features/ Key facts document and can pass you relevant information from it.

If you don't get a Key features/Key facts document before you sign up – say, because you've taken the scheme out by phone – the main details must be given to you orally and the full document sent to you within five working days.

The Key features/Key facts document gives you all the important information about the scheme which you need to make a decision about whether to take it out or not and to compare it with other schemes. It includes: the nature of the scheme, its aims, what you must invest or your commitment to make regular payments and the risks involved (for example, whether your capital can fall in value, whether you have a right to cancel the scheme, and so on).

With the Key facts document, you will also get a Key facts example. This shows how much pension your savings might produce based on various assumptions. The document is quite long, but the example overleaf shows extracts and explains how you can use the information given. The earlier Key features document included an illustration which performed the same function but the Key facts example aims to be clearer. An important difference is that the Key facts example includes an estimate of your projected pension in today's money (ie after taking into account the effects of inflation).

The projected pension and information about charges tell you what might happen based on various assumptions. The Financial Services Authority (FSA)* (the investment regulator – see Chapter 3) sets the rules about what assumptions must be used. *Bear in mind that assumptions are just guesses – reality may turn out to be better or worse.*

The example helps you to plan how much you need to save to get the retirement pension you need and to compare different pension plans.

When taking out a stakeholder pension scheme, you must aalso be given a set of stakeholder decision trees. If you are buying by phone, the firm you are dealing with must ensure that you have the decision trees in front of you at the time you make the purchase. The decision trees are produced by the FSA and provide guidance on whether a stakeholder pension is suitable for you. But the trees give only general guidance and fall short of advice specific to you and your circumstances. Even if someone – for example, a union

What a Key Facts example might look like

 example

Personal Pension Plan
Prepared for Mr. J. Brown on 30th May 2004
Age 40 next birthday
Chosen pension age: 65
What do I pay in this example?
You pay £39 a month
Basic tax rebate £11 a month
Total payment £50 a month
…

(A)

Let's assume:
you decide to invest 100% of your payments in the balanced managed fund;
we do not change the level of charges we take and the tax rebate remains the same (not guaranteed); and
the investments in your plan grow at a steady rate of 7% each year (not guaranteed).

The early years

(B)

At the end of year in:	You would have paid (inc tax rebate) £	What your plan would be worth without charges £	after charges £
1	600	622	588
2	1,200	1,280	1,210
3	1,800	2,000	1,900
4	2,400	2,760	2,630
5	3,000	3,570	3,400

(C)

The later years

At the end of year in:	You would have paid (inc tax rebate) £	What your plan would be worth without charges £	after charges £
10	6,000	8,598	8,030
15	9,000	15,620	14,200
20	12,000	25,490	22,500
25	15,000	39,280	33,600
…			

Put another way: at age 65, our charges would have reduced the assumed growth of your plan from 7% to 5.9%.
…

(D)

What would a fund of £33,600 give me if I retire at age 65?
Let's assume:
_ you choose to have your income paid monthly from the day you retire;
_ you choose to have the same income paid out each year;
_ inflation from now until you are 65 averages at 2.5% a year (not guaranteed); and
_ at age 65, annuity rates are based on an interest rate of 5.4% (not guaranteed);

(E)

You could use this to get:

A tax-free lump sum of:	**£8,410**	A yearly income of: *(before tax)*	**£2,000**	What this income would be worth in today's money:	**£1,080**

OR

A tax-free lump sum of:	**£Nil**	A yearly income of: *(before tax)*	**£2,660**	What this income would be worth in today's money:	**£1,440**

(F)

Notes to the Key Facts example:

(A) You deduct tax relief from what you pay in. The plan provider claims the relief from the Inland Revenue and adds it to your plan.

(B) A table summarises the amount you have paid in and how it might grow based on a standard assumption about how your investment might grow and assuming the provider continues to levy the same charges as now.

(C) The last column of the table tells you what your plan might be worth. This is the amount you would be able to transfer if you decided to switch to another plan, so this column gives you an idea of how portable your plan is. The lower the figure in the last column compared with the figure in the column before the more you would lose in charges if you transferred.

The last figure in the column (£33,600 in this example) tells you what your pension fund might be worth by retirement. But this is in terms of future money, so it is not very useful in this form.

(D) This sentence summarises the last line of the table in a different way. It is comparing the final figure (£33,600) with the figure in the previous column (£39,280). The difference between them is the effect of the charges you've had to pay throughout the life of your plan. In cash terms, charges have reduced your return by £39,280 - £33,600 = £5,680. This is equivalent to your investment growth having been reduced from 7% to 5.9%, i.e. a reduction of 1.1% a year in this example. The bigger the reduction (called the 'reduction in yield' or 'RIY'), the higher the charges for the plan. The RIY is a useful figure when comparing one plan with another. A plan with a lower RIY is cheaper than a plan with a higher RIY.

(E) The middle column of this section shows you how much pension you could buy with your pension fund at retirement, and assuming the pension increases in line with inflation after retirement. It is based on assumptions, so is only a rough guide – in practice you might get more or less. Again, this is not a very useful figure because £2,000 might buy a lot less than today due to inflation between now and retirement.

(F) The final column of the table converts the pension you might get into a figure that is useful and can help you plan how much you need to save for retirement. It does this by adjusting the pension for the effects of inflation to give you an idea of what your pension might be worth in today's money. So, in this example, the £2,000 pension at retirement would buy only the same as £1,080 today. The adjustment is made using an assumption about how prices might rise between now and retirement.

representative at work or a Citizens Advice Bureau worker – helps you work through the trees, they are not deemed to be giving you financial advice and you remain responsible for your decision to take out the stakeholder scheme. If you want advice personal to you, you should consult an independent financial adviser (IFA)*or ask the firm providing the scheme if it is able to give financial advice.

After you have taken out the scheme, you should get annual statements summarising the amount you have invested and the growth of your pension fund to date. From April 2003 onwards, these statements must include a forecast of how much pension you might get at retirement in today's money. The government is also encouraging providers to give you a combined pension statement which tells you both how much pension your personal or stakeholder scheme might provide and also what you might get from the state.

Why choose a personal pension rather than a stakeholder scheme?

The government developed stakeholder pension schemes in response to the lack of good-value pension plans available to people who could not join an occupational pension scheme through their work.

In the past, the only alternative if there was no scheme at work or if you were self-employed was a personal pension. *Which?* consistently found personal pensions to be inflexible and expensive. Charges were complicated and those for the worst plans would eat up 40 per cent of your pension fund by the time you retired. Typically, if you switched to another provider, you would face hefty penalties for stopping your old plan.

In the run-up to April 2001 when stakeholder pension schemes first went on sale, personal pension providers were cleaning up their act. Increasingly, they offered stakeholder-friendly personal pensions which have some or all of the features of stakeholder schemes. Some of these have subsequently been registered as stakeholder schemes.

So the personal pensions which are left in the main are those which do not meet the stakeholder conditions. Why would anyone want to take out a personal pension once they can have a lower-charging, more flexible stakeholder scheme? There are four likely reasons:

- **minor differences only** The personal pension might be essentially the same as a stakeholder scheme but have only a minor difference – typically, a higher minimum contribution limit – that you find perfectly acceptable.
- **investment choice** Low stakeholder charges will limit providers' scope to pay expensive investment managers to run the pension funds. As a result, some stakeholder schemes offer only a limited choice of investments, focusing in particular on tracker funds (see page 251). If you want a big choice of different investment funds, a personal pension might be the better option. If you want a self-invested scheme, personal pensions are the only option.
- **investment advice** Some – though by no means all – stakeholder providers are not able to offer individual pensions advice within the low stakeholder charges. If your affairs are complex or you have large sums to invest or transfer, you might look at personal pensions instead. But a better option could be to choose a stakeholder scheme and pay separately for fee-based advice (see Chapter 1).
- **group personal pension schemes (GPPS)** If you have a personal pension taken out through a GPPS at work (see Chapter 11), your employer may be contributing to the plan on your behalf and/or you may get special terms. These could outweigh any disadvantages *vis-à-vis* stakeholder schemes.

Already have a personal pension?

If you already have a personal pension which you started some years ago, it might not be a good idea to switch to a stakeholder scheme, even though the latter offers a better deal to new investors. This is because you typically paid a big chunk of the costs of a personal pension upfront when you first took out the scheme. If you stop your personal pension now, those upfront costs crystallise as early surrender charges which will reduce the value of your pension fund – perhaps even to less than you have invested in it.

Before you take any action, ask your provider for a statement showing the value of your plan if you stop or transfer it now and an illustration of the pension you might get if you carry on with the personal pension until retirement. Also get an illustration for the stakeholder scheme you are interested in. Does the extra you can expect from the stakeholder scheme outweigh any loss you will make for stopping the personal pension?

Check, too, the ongoing charges you are now paying for your personal pension. Charges are often tiered with reduced levels as your pension funds grows. If you have already built up a reasonably large pension fund, you may find that the charges you are now paying are even less than the maximum 1 per cent you would pay in a stakeholder scheme.

If you took out a personal pension after March 1999, the provider is required to make sure you can switch to a stakeholder scheme without 'material disadvantage' once stakeholder schemes became available. 'Material disadvantage' is not defined but is generally taken to mean that there should be no penalty for stopping the personal plan and that you should not pay a second lot of setting-up charges when you make the switch to the stakeholder scheme. Some providers apply this rule when you switch to any provider's stakeholder scheme; others may apply it only when you switch to their own stakeholder scheme. Check the situation before you make a switch.

Alternatives to stakeholder schemes and personal pensions

Any form of long-term investment is suitable for retirement saving. But stakeholder schemes and personal pensions have the edge because of their tax advantages.

However, all pension arrangements tie up your savings until at least age 50 (due to increase to 55 by 2010) and restrict the way you can take the benefits. So, if you want more flexibility, it might make sense to choose alternative investments, such as individual savings accounts (ISAs) which combine flexibility with tax advantages. See the table on page 235 for a summary of the pros and cons of ISAs compared with other pension arrangements. For more about ISAs as a long-term investment, see Chapter 13.

Action list for stakeholder schemes and personal plans

Consider the following before choosing a scheme or plan.

- Don't delay the start of your pension savings – it can cause a big reduction in your eventual pension.

- Work out how much pension you'll need and how much you can afford to save towards your pension (see Chapter 10).
- Look at surveys of different schemes – see 'More information', below – to help you select several schemes to look at in more detail.
- Get literature about the schemes which interest you. Pay particular attention to the Key Features and illustration/Key Facts and example (see page 255).
- Compare the schemes on the basis of investment choice, risk, charges, flexibility (to vary your contributions and retirement age, say), portability (being able to transfer to another scheme without loss), and other features. The illustration/example and Key Features/Key Facts will help you to make this comparison.
- Select a scheme. You may be able to invest direct with the provider. Some providers only sell their plans through IFAs.
- Don't confuse help taking you through decision trees with advice. If you need advice, you will need to consult an IFA or a provider's own advisers.
- Make sure you get regular statements. Keep them in a safe place.
- Review your pension planning regularly. How well is your scheme performing? Do you need to increase your contributions to meet your pension target? Can you get a better deal by switching to another scheme?

More information

There are literally hundreds of different personal pensions, though only a fairly limited choice of stakeholder schemes. Independent surveys are a useful shortcut to screening out unsuitable plans and homing in on those which are likely to suit you best.

The FSA publishes comparative tables of stakeholder schemes and personal pensions. You can view the tables on the FSA website or get a copy from the FSA consumer helpline.★ The FSA tables summarise features and let you shortlist suitable schemes. They do not include any data on past investment performance. Regular surveys are published by magazines such as *Which?*,★ *Money Management*,★ and *Pensions Management*.★ These usually summarise the main features of schemes, give details of past performance and often pick out best buys. The best buys will be based on particular features or scenarios, so check carefully whether they would be best for you given your own particular circumstances.

If you are not confident selecting, say, half a dozen possible schemes from a survey, consider enlisting the help of one or two independent financial advisers (IFAs).* Choose ones who specialise in pensions and have access to computer databases comparing the pension plans on offer. Ask the IFA to arrange for you to receive information about the plans which look best for you. Do not commit yourself to anything until you have been able to study and compare the information at leisure in your own home.

If you are considering transferring rights from a previous employer's occupational scheme to a personal pension or stakeholder scheme, you are recommended to get advice from an IFA or specialist pensions adviser. The IFA must be specially authorised for this type of business and is required to use a proper transfer analysis system to

---

Switching schemes

Malcolm, who is 26, left university in 1993. His first job was with a small research company. It didn't operate a company-wide pension scheme for employees, so Malcolm decided to ask a financial adviser for advice on what to do about getting a pension. He knew that the sooner he started paying towards a pension, the more it would be worth in years to come. After seeing the adviser, Malcolm took out a personal pension.

Two years later he joined Consumers' Association (CA), where he had the chance to join a hybrid-type employer's pension scheme (see page 225). Malcolm decided to join CA's scheme. He stopped making contributions to his personal pension and is letting the money he paid in grow until he retires. However, he has to pay extra charges on top of the usual monthly ones because he won't be making any more contributions. He could have transferred the money from his personal pension to CA's pension scheme, but after finding out the transfer penalties that would be imposed by his personal pension provider, Malcolm decided not to do so.

Which? October 1996

---

compare the options open to you. Pay particular attention to the assumptions used to make the comparison. Follow similar steps if you are considering opting out of your current employer's occupational scheme in favour of a personal pension or stakeholder scheme. Bear in mind that the occupational scheme will nearly always be your best option.

To check that an IFA or company salesperson is authorised and registered to conduct pensions business, call the FSA Register.*

To help you check whether you are on track for the retirement income you want, see *Take Control of Your Pension. An Action Pack* from Which? Books*. The FSA and Association of British Insurers have jointly produced an online calculator which you can use to check how much pension a monthly contribution of a given size might produce by retirement – see Appendix III.

Staking a claim

Nusheen is 27. She doesn't already have a pension and won't have access to an employer's stakeholder scheme. Nusheen told *Which?* 'I know nothing at all about pensions – except that I probably should have one.' Nusheen could pick out a stakeholder plan for herself, for example, from *Which?* Best Buy tables. But if she'd like help choosing which funds to invest in and how much to pay in, she should see an independent adviser.

Which? August 2001

Chapter 13

Planning at the point of retirement

Whatever type of pension scheme you have, your first decision is when to start drawing your pension – see below.

With many schemes, you can choose whether to take part of your benefits as tax-free cash – see page 267.

If you have been saving for retirement using any defined contribution (DC) pension schemes, you will face some or all of the choices from page 272 onwards when you decide to start taking your pension. You are affected if you save using:

- an occupational money purchase scheme
- an in-house money purchase AVC scheme
- an FSAVC scheme
- a stakeholder pension scheme
- a personal pension (including one taken out through a group personal pension scheme, GPPS, at work – see Chapter 11).

When is your pension payable?

Occupational schemes
The normal pension age for an occupational scheme is usually between ages 60 and 75 inclusive. Inland Revenue rules prohibit a later age. But earlier ages can be approved for certain occupations – for example, professional footballers can have a normal pension age of 35. However, the government has proposed raising the minimum pension age to 55 by 2010 and this would apply to all professions.

You can usually start your pension earlier than the normal pension age for your scheme if you have reached at least age 50 (rising to 55 by 2010) but the maximum pension you are allowed to have under the Inland Revenue rules (see the table on page 000) must usually be scaled down.

You can start your pension at any age if you can no longer work because of illness or disability.

In a contracted-out salary-related scheme, contracted-out pension built up from 6 April 1997 onwards is paid at the normal age for your scheme. Guaranteed minimum pensions (see page 216) built up before that date can't be paid until you reach state pension age (though the government is proposing to abolish this rule so that this part of your pension can be paid at the same time as the rest).

In a contracted-out money purchase scheme, contracted-out pension can't be paid before age 60 (though, again, this age limit may be abolished under government proposals).

At the time of writing, the normal pension age for an occupational scheme is also the normal retirement age for the firm (i.e. the age at which you stop work). Moreover, the Inland Revenue rules prohibit you from drawing a pension from your current employer while carrying on working for that employer (though you could carry on working for another employer or as a self-employed person). However, this is all set to change.

Probably from spring 2005, you will be able to carry on working for your present employer while starting to draw your pension from that employer's scheme. This could make it possible, for example, to switch to part-time work while drawing part of your pension to top up your income. And, from October 2006, new anti-age discrimination laws are due to take effect. It is likely that employers will then no longer be able to set a compulsory retirement age (unless there are exceptional circumstances to justify it), though a normal pension age at which the full pension first starts to become available is likely to continue. The government is consulting on whether employers should nevertheless be able to set a default age of 70 or above after which workers could be dismissed without it breaching the age discrimination laws.

AVC and FSAVC schemes
It used to be the case that you had to take the benefits of an AVC or FSAVC scheme at the same time you took benefits from your main

occupational scheme. But, since 30 June 1999, benefits can be taken at any age between 50 (due to rise to 55 by 2010) and 75, regardless of whether you have started to take a pension from your main scheme. You do not have to retire from work to start taking benefits from your AVC or FSAVC schemes.

Stakeholder schemes and personal pensions

With stakeholder schemes and personal pensions started on or after 1 July 1988, you can start to take your pension at any age from 50 (due to rise to 55) to 75 and you do not have to stop working.

If you have a retirement annuity contract (the type of personal pension on sale before 1 July 1988), the earliest age at which you can start your pension is 60. You could transfer to a personal pension, in which case the lower age of 50 (55) would apply. However, this would also affect the size of tax-free lump sum you can have – see below.

As with occupational schemes, lower pension ages currently apply to some professions, and anyone can start their pension early if they have to stop work because of ill health or disability.

Pension from a contracted-out scheme currently can't be paid before age 60.

Since April 2001, if you have a personal pension or stakeholder scheme the scheme is allowed to have multiple pension ages. This means that you can convert part of your pension fund into pension on one date, a further part on a later date, and so on. This is a particularly useful option if you want to ease gradually out of work.

Choosing early retirement

Retiring from age 50 (55), say, may seem attractive but it is also expensive. If you want to retire early, you need to plan ahead and save extra.

In an occupational salary-related scheme, your pension is worked out according to a formula depending on the years you have been in the scheme and your pre-retirement salary. If you retire early, your pension will be lower for several reasons:

- You have been in the scheme for fewer years. This feeds through the formula, reducing your pension – see Example.

- Your salary may be lower than it would have been had you waited and retired later on. Again this feeds through the formula to reduce your pension – see Example.
- Your pension will be payable for more years. This means providing your pension will cost the scheme extra. It may recoup part of this cost by adjusting your pension (called an 'actuarial reduction'). The adjustment might, for example, be a reduction of 6 per cent for each year you retire early.

Example

Jay belongs to an occupational salary-related pension scheme. The normal pension age for the scheme is 65. By that age, Jay will have been in the scheme for 12 years and, although he can't know this, his pre-retirement salary would have been £30,000. It is a 'sixtieths scheme' and Jay's pension at age 65 would have been:

$12 \times £30,000 \times 1/60 = £6,000$ a year.

However, Jay decides to retire at age 60 – in other words, five years early. His salary then is £26,000. His formula pension is:

$(12 - 5) \times £26,000 \times 1/60 = £3,033$ a year.

To make matters worse, the scheme reduces his pension by 6 per cent for each of the five years he is retiring early – a total reduction of $5 \times 6\% = 30\%$. Jay's pension is reduced to:

$70\% \times £3,033 = £2,123$ a year.

Retiring five years early has cost Jay nearly £4,000 a year in pension.

You may be offered a more attractive early retirement pension, if your employer is looking for volunteers to take redundancy.

And, in some public sector schemes, there is no actuarial reduction provided you have been in the scheme enough years and have reached a high enough age – for example, the 'rule of 85' says that your pension is not reduced provided the sum of your age and your years of membership equals 85 or more.

If you have any of the defined contribution (DC) pensions, your pension depends on the fund built up by retirement and the amount of pension you can buy with it. Retiring early will reduce your pension because:

- payments will have been made to the scheme for fewer years. Your pension fund is therefore reduced not just by the contributions lost, but also the investment growth they would have produced.
- the pension will have to be paid out for more years. This will cost the firm which provides your pension extra. It recoups the extra cost by offering lower annuity rates (see page 272) the younger you are when the pension starts.

Tax-free cash at retirement

Occupational pension schemes

Under current Inland Revenue rules, the maximum tax-free lump sum you can have from an occupational pension scheme is normally 3/80th of your pre-retirement salary for each year you've been in the scheme, up to a maximum 1½ times salary after 40 years' membership. In some circumstances, you can build up entitlement to the lump sum at a faster rate than 3/80ths a year – your occupational pension scheme administrator* can tell you if this applies to you.

Under current Inland Revenue rules, the maximum pension you can have – 1/60th of pre-retirement salary for each year you've been in the scheme, rising to two-thirds of pre-retirement salary after 40 years – is before taking account of any lump sum. In effect, you swap some of this pension for lump sum, so the maximum pension is reduced. As a rough guide, if you are entitled to the maximum two-thirds pension and you opt to take the maximum lump sum, your pension will be reduced to about one-half of your pre-retirement salary.

See the box on page 269 for how the above limits are due to be abolished.

AVC and FSAVC schemes

With an in-house added years AVC scheme, your AVCs automatically increase all benefits from your occupational scheme, including the tax-free cash sum – see Chapter 11.

With an in-house money purchase AVC scheme started before 8 April 1987, you can use your AVCs to increase the tax-free cash from your occupational scheme, provided the lump sum remains within the limits outlined above under 'Occupational pension schemes'.

In the case of all FSAVC schemes, and in-house money purchase AVCs which you started to pay on or after 8 April 1987, you cannot use the proceeds of the scheme to provide or increase the tax-free cash sum.

See the box opposite for how the above rules are due to be abolished.

Stakeholder schemes and personal pensions

You do not have to use your whole pension fund to provide retirement income.

You can swap part of your pension at retirement for a tax-free lump sum. The table on page 271 sets out the maximum amount of cash you can have under the present rules.

If your personal pension plan includes any amounts which were transferred to it from an occupational pension scheme, there may be a restriction on your cash lump sum from the personal pension or stakeholder scheme if any of the following applies:

- The transfer was from an AVC scheme started on or after 8 April 1987 or an FSAVC scheme, neither of which can be used to provide a tax-free lump sum. The amount transferred cannot itself be taken as a lump sum, although it can still be counted as part of the pension fund when you calculate the maximum cash as a proportion of the fund.
- At any time in the ten years up to the date of transfer being made, you were a controlling director of the company whose occupational pension scheme you belonged to, or you counted as a high earner (that is if your earnings exceeded the earnings cap – see page 217 – which applied in the year the transfer was made). The scheme you left must provide you with a certificate saying how much of the transfer value can be taken as a lump sum from the personal pension plan; this amount can be increased in line with price inflation up to the date on which the lump sum is paid out.
- The transfer was from a scheme with a normal retirement date of 45 or less, or certain old schemes which you contributed to

before April 1980, in which case none of the transfer value may be taken as a lump sum.

See the box below for how the above rules are due to be abolished.

Proposed changes to the rules for tax-free lump sums

All the above rules concerning tax-free lump sums are due to be replaced probably as described on page 237 from 6 April 2005 onwards, assuming government proposals go ahead.

At retirement you will be able to take a quarter of your pension savings from all sources as a tax-free lump sum. To work out the total value of your pension savings, any final salary pensions will have to be converted into an equivalent cash sum. The government has said that it will publish tables setting out the conversion rates that must be used.

Under the new rules, if the value of all your pension savings is £10,000 or less, you will be able to take the whole lot as a lump sum. A quarter of this lump sum would be tax free and the rest taxed in the same way as income.

Example

Mick retires at age 65. He has a pension fund of £10,000 built up in an old personal pension and qualifies for a maximum pension of £15,000 from his employer's final salary scheme. Government tables value his final salary pension rights at £165,000*. So Mick's pension savings at retirement are £165,000 + £10,000 = £175,000. This is well within the lifetime limit of £1.4 million. He can have a tax-free lump sum equal to ¼ × £175,000 = £43,750. The rest of his pension rights must be drawn as taxable pension.

* At the time of writing, conversion tables had not been published, so this is just an example of the possible value put on the pension.

Should you take the tax-free cash?

In some occupational schemes, the tax-free lump sum is automatically part of your benefit package. But in other occupational schemes and with personal pensions and stakeholder schemes, you choose whether or not to take the tax-free cash.

Taking cash reduces your pension. But, in general, taking cash from a personal pension or stakeholder scheme is a good idea, even if you need the maximum possible income. This is because the pension you give up is taxable income. The lump sum, itself tax-free, can be used to buy a 'purchased life annuity' (see page 331). The income from a purchased life annuity is only partly taxable. So, if you are a taxpayer, by taking the cash you could end up with a higher after-tax income than if you had kept the full pension and turned down the lump sum.

The decision is more complicated if you belong to an occupational pension scheme. The pension you give up must usually by law be increased each year once it starts to be paid, so you will be giving up not just pension but also pension increases, which could be costly to replace. You also need to check how other benefits are worked out. For example, will any widow's or widower's pension payable on death after retirement be based on the pension you would have had before taking into account any lump sum, or the pension you actually receive after reduction for the lump sum?

Tip

At retirement, it is nearly always worth taking the maximum tax-free lump sum from your personal pension or stakeholder scheme even if you then use it to buy an annuity to provide an income. Different tax rules mean you should usually get a higher after-tax income from the annuity than the pension you give up.

How much tax-free cash?[1]

Type of plan and when you started it	Maximum amount of tax-free cash
Retirement annuity contracts	
Started before 17 March 1987	Three times the remaining pension, e.g. if, after taking the lump sum, you would have a pension of £5,000, then the maximum lump sum would be $3 \times £5,000 = £15,000$
Started on or after 17 March 1987 and before 1 July 1988	Three times the remaining pension up to an overall maximum of £150,000 per plan[2]
Personal pension plans	
Started on or after 1 July 1988 and before 27 July 1989	A quarter of the pension fund (excluding amounts to be used to provide dependants' pensions)[3]
Started on or after 27 July 1989	A quarter of the pension fund (except amounts to be used to provide contracted-out pensions)
Stakeholder pension schemes	
Started on or after 6 April 2001	A quarter of the pension fund (except amounts to be used to provide contracted-out pensions)

[1] All the rules in this table are due to be replaced, from 6 April 2005. See box on page 269.
[2] In practice, the limit was often avoided by taking out a cluster of several smaller plans instead of just one.
[3] Strictly speaking, an overall limit of £150,000 per plan applies. In practice, the limit is easily avoided by taking out a cluster of plans or switching to a later plan without the cash limit using the open-market option.

Pension choices

If your pension will come from a defined contribution scheme, your pension at retirement will normally be provided by using your pension fund to buy an annuity. An annuity is an investment where you swap a lump sum – in this case your pension fund (after deduction of any tax-free lump sum) – for an income, in this case a pension payable for the rest of your life.

There are different types of annuity. Which you choose depends on the type of pension you want for yourself and for anyone who is dependent on you.

As an alternative to buying an annuity, you could leave your pension fund invested and take an income direct from it. This option is described on page 282.

Annuity choices

Most pension schemes give you what is called an 'open-market option'. This means you do not have to buy your annuity from the provider with whom you have built up your pension fund. Instead you can shop around for the providers offering the best rate. Under FSA rules, the provider should draw your attention to the open-market option. Annuities are sold by insurance companies.

Usually, it will be worth exercising your open-market option. The difference between the best and worst providers can be hundreds of pounds of yearly pension – see Example A overleaf. If you are in poor health or a smoker, some companies are particularly worth looking at because they offer preferential rates (since you are not expected to live as long as someone in good health or a non-smoker).

You should be wary of exercising your open-market option if the company with which you have built up your fund offers a guaranteed annuity rate which is higher than the rates generally available now, or would levy a hefty penalty charge if you switched. If you have built up your pension fund on a with-profits basis, there should not normally be any market value reduction (MVR) when you use the fund to buy an annuity even if you use your open-market option to switch to another company.

You may be tempted just to choose the maximum possible pension from day one. But this is not such a good idea. You need to look at how well your pension will continue to support you as retirement progresses and how to protect anyone who depends on you financially. Different types of annuity offer different features which can help you to meet these needs.

Example A

Doug, 65, has been paying FSAVCs into a scheme with XYZ insurance company and has built up a fund of £33,000. XYZ offers him an annuity of £635 a year for every £10,000 of fund. This would give him a pension of:

£635 / £10,000 × £33,000 = £2,096 a year.

But, if Doug shops around, he could get an annuity of £807 a year for every £10,000 of fund from ABC Insurers. This would give him a pension of:

£807 / £10,000 × £33,000 = £2,663 a year.

By shopping around, Doug has increased his yearly pension by £567 a year.

Level annuities

This is the most basic type of annuity. It provides a level income which does not change from one year to the next. It pays you this income for the whole of your life and stops when you die.

A major problem with a level annuity is that there is no protection against inflation. If prices rise, your pension buys less and less as time goes on – see Example B. This might not be a drawback if the bulk of your retirement income is from another source – an occupational scheme, say – which does have built-in increases to counter the effects of inflation. But, if a level annuity is to be your main source of retirement income, you should be prepared to save some of your income now to use later on in retirement.

Example B

Doug (see Example A) opts for the annuity from ABC Insurers and retires at age 65 on a pension of £2,663 a year. However, this is a level pension, so its buying power will fall if prices rise. How much the buying power falls depends on inflation.

For example, if prices rise by 2.5 per cent a year on average, by age 75, Doug's £2,663 will buy only the same as £2,080 today and Doug will have to go without a few luxuries.

If price increases averaged 5 per cent a year, the £2,663 would buy only the same as £1,635 today. That is a substantial cut in Doug's buying power and he will have to go without quite a few things he would have hoped to enjoy in retirement.

If inflation averaged 10 per cent a year, the £2,663 would buy only the same as £1,027 today. Doug will now have to be very careful with his money just to pay for necessities.

Increasing annuities

You can protect yourself either partially or fully from inflation by choosing an increasing annuity. There are three main options:

- **escalating annuity** Your income increases by a fixed percentage each year. For example, you might choose increases of 5 per cent a year. This protects you from rising prices, provided inflation does not rise above 5 per cent a year. If inflation is greater, the buying power of your pension still falls but not by as much as it would do without the increases. If inflation is consistently lower than 5 per cent, the buying power of your pension will gradually rise over the years.

- **RPI-linked annuity** Your income changes each year to keep pace with inflation as measured by the Retail Prices Index (RPI – the main measure of inflation used by the government). This means that your pension maintains exactly the same buying power throughout retirement. At the time of writing, inflation is running at less than 5 per cent a year and is expected to remain fairly low in the longer term. Therefore, the starting pension you can get from an RPI-linked annuity is currently higher than from an annuity escalating at 5 per cent a year.

- **limited price indexation (LPI) annuity** Your income changes each year to keep pace with inflation but only up to a maximum of 5 per cent a year. If inflation is less than 5 per cent, your pension also increases by less than 5 per cent, but by just enough to fully compensate for inflation. If inflation is more than 5 per cent, your pension increases by exactly 5 per cent, providing only partial protection against inflation. You must buy this type of annuity (or better – for example an RPI-linked annuity) with the fund built up through an occupational money purchase scheme or any of the contracted-out pension schemes which provide 'protected rights'. (The government has proposed that the maximum protection for pensions from an occupational scheme be reduced from 5 per cent to 2.5 per cent, but at the time of writing had not made clear whether this reduction would apply to other pensions covered by LPI rules.)

The big drawback with all increasing annuities is that your income at the start of retirement is a lot lower than the amount you would have had from a level annuity. In the past, unless inflation was running at very high levels, it would have taken many years before an escalating or RPI-linked annuity reached the amount of the equivalent level annuity. However, in recent years, the reduction in starting income has become much smaller. As the table in Example C shows, within the space of ten years, a 5-per-cent escalating annuity would be giving you a better income than a level annuity. And, at all but the lowest levels of inflation, an RPI-linked annuity would be giving the highest income within ten years. Moreover, an RPI-linked annuity offers full protection against inflation, however rapidly prices rise. Although, at the time of writing, inflation was running at 2.5 to 3 per cent a year, back in the 1970s it reached 27 per cent a year. Even if it seems unlikely that such high rates of inflation will return, the impact that would have on a level annuity is so devastating that you might feel taking out the insurance of an RPI-linked annuity would be worthwhile.

On the other hand, even when the escalating annuity or RPI-linked annuity has caught up with the level annuity, it will be several more years before you will have received the same amount of income in total. In Example C, only after 18 years would the 5-per-cent escalating annuity have paid Doug the same in total as the level annuity (18 × £2,663 = £47,934). If inflation averaged 2.5 per cent a year, Doug would wait 20 years before the total he got from the RPI-linked annuity matched the total paid out by the level annuity (20 × £2,663 = £53,260). If you are well disciplined, you might be better off choosing the level annuity but setting aside some of the income in the early years to help you cope with rising prices later on.

Example C

Doug has a pension fund of £33,000. Instead of buying a level annuity, Doug could use his £33,000 fund to buy an increasing annuity. The table below shows how much his pension would be worth after 10, 20 and 30 years, depending on the type of annuity he chooses and the level of inflation during his retirement (see Examples A and B).

Average yearly inflation	Years since start of retirement	Type of annuity					
		Level		Escalating at 5% a year		RPI-linked	
		Income you would get	Which would buy same as this much today	Income you would get	Which would buy same as this much today	Income you would get	Which would buy same as this much today
Starting income	0	£2,663	£2,663	£1,706	£1,706	£2,109	£2,109
2.5%	10	£2,663	£2,080	£2,779	£2,171	£2,700	£2,109
	20	£2,663	£1,625	£4,527	£2,763	£3,456	£2,109
	30	£2,663	£1,270	£7,373	£3,515	£4,424	£2,109
5%	10	£2,663	£1,635	£2,779	£1,706	£3,435	£2,109
	20	£2,663	£1,004	£4,527	£1,706	£5,596	£2,109
	30	£2,663	£616	£7,373	£1,706	£9,115	£2,109
10%	10	£2,663	£1,027	£2,779	£1,071	£5,470	£2,109
	20	£2,663	£396	£4,527	£673	£14,188	£2,109
	30	£2,663	£153	£7,373	£423	£36,801	£2,109

Investment-linked annuities

Investment-linked annuities give you the chance of a higher income than you can get from level or increasing annuities. But they are more risky because:

- increases in income, although likely, are not usually guaranteed
- the size of the increases is unpredictable .
- with many investment-linked annuities, your income can fall as well as rise.

There are two types of investment-linked annuity – 'with-profits' and 'unit-linked'. They are described below.

1: With-profits annuities

There may be two parts to your income:

- **guaranteed minimum income** This is the minimum pension you will get. Usually it is pretty low, but whatever happens you will never get less than this. Not all with-profits annuities provide a guaranteed minimum.
- **bonuses** These are used as the basis for increasing (or reducing) your income year by year.

Each year, the annuity provider announces its with-profits bonus rate. It depends on a variety of factors, but the most important is stock-market performance. However, the bonus is not simply added to your annuity. The system is a little more complex.

When you first buy the annuity, typically you must choose an 'assumed bonus rate' (ABR). You choose it from a range set by the insurance company, running from 0 per cent up to, say, 5 per cent. Once chosen, your ABR stays the same for the whole life of the annuity.

The ABR determines the amount of income you get at the start of the annuity and the likelihood of increases as your retirement progresses:

- **high ABR** If you choose a high ABR, your starting income is high. When the annual bonus rate is announced, if it exactly equals the ABR, your income stays broadly the same. (In practice, it might fall slightly due to the impact of charges.) If the bonus rate is higher than your ABR, your income increases. But, if the announced bonus rate is lower than your ABR, your income falls – see Example opposite.

- **low ABR** If you choose a low ABR, your starting income is low. But there is an increased chance that the announced bonus rate each year will be higher than your ABR, so it is likely that your income will increase each year. Only if the announced bonus rate is lower than your ABR will your income fall.
- **0 per cent ABR** If you choose the lowest possible ABR – in other words, 0 per cent – your starting income will be very low, usually just the guaranteed minimum amount. But, provided the company announces any bonus at all, your income increases. If, exceptionally, there is no bonus at all, your income stays the same – it can never fall.

Choosing a low or zero ABR can be useful if you want to retire gradually – see 'Gradual retirement' on page 281.

Because there is usually a risk of your income falling as well as rising, with-profits annuities are generally suitable only if you have a fairly large pension fund to invest – say, £100,000 or more – or you are using the with-profits annuity to provide only part of your retirement income.

Example

Malcolm, 60, is about to retire and has a pension fund of £150,000. If he used it to buy a level annuity, he could get an income of about £9,400 a year. But he decides to buy a with-profits annuity. His starting income depends on the assumed bonus rate (ABR) he chooses:

- **0 per cent ABR** This is the lowest ABR he can choose. His income would be only £5,450 a year, but is virtually certain to increase each year.
- **5 per cent ABR** This is the highest ABR the insurer is offering. The starting income would be much higher at £9,100 a year. But the income will increase only in years when the announced bonus rate is more than 5%. Every time the insurer announces a bonus of less than 5% Malcolm's income will fall.
- **ABR more than 0 per cent but less than 5 per cent** This will give Malcolm an income somewhere between £5,450 and £9,100 a year.

Malcolm chooses the maximum ABR of 5 per cent. The table shows how his income might vary over the first few years of his retirement.

Year of retirement	ABR (fixed for retirement)	Announced bonus rate	How income changes	Income for the year
Start of retirement	5%	n/a	n/a	£9,100
Year 1	5%	7%	× (1+7%)/(1+5%)	£9,273
Year 2	5%	6%	× (1+6%)/(1+5%)	£9,361
Year 3	5%	4%	× (1+4%)/(1+5%)	£9,272
Year 4	5%	5%	× (1+5%)/(1+5%)	£9,272
Year 5	5%	3%	× (1+3%)/(1+5%)	£9,095
Year 6	5%	6%	× (1+6%)/(1+5%)	£9,182

2: Unit-linked annuities

Unit-linked annuities work in a similar way to with-profits annuities, but they are more risky. This is because the amount of income you get is linked directly to the performance of a fund of underlying investments. Unlike the with-profits annuity, the worst investment performance is not limited to 0 per cent (no growth at all) – it can be less, because the underlying investments could actually fall in value. This means there is no guarantee that you will get at least a certain amount of income.

You should not consider a unit-linked annuity unless you can cope with the extra risk. In general, you will need a substantial pension fund to invest or other sources of retirement income to fall back on.

As with other types of unit-linked investments, you can choose which type of fund you will link your annuity to. For medium risk, you should normally choose a broadly based fund or a tracker fund. More specialist funds expose you to higher risks. See page 363 for a summary of the unit-linked funds available. The more risky the fund you choose, the more your income will tend to swing up and down.

Annuities if someone depends on you

All types of annuity can be arranged on a 'single-life' or 'joint-life last-survivor' basis. A single-life annuity pays out just for the duration of your own lifetime. A joint-life last-survivor annuity pays out as long as both or one of two people are alive. On the first death, some annuities carry on paying the same amount to the survivor. With others, the amount is reduced – for example, by a third or by half.

The person you have the annuity with does not have to be someone who is financially dependent on you. But certainly if anyone is dependent on you – for example, your wife, husband or other partner – you should normally choose a joint-life last-survivor annuity – see Example opposite.

With contracted-out pension schemes, you have no choice – you must buy an annuity which provides a pension for your widow or widower equal to half your pension.

Example

Philip is 65 and his wife Doris is 60. Philip retires with a pension fund of £50,000. If he used this to buy a single-life level annuity, he could get a pension of £807 for each £10,000 of pension fund. This would give him:

£807 / £10,000 × £50,000 = £4,035 a year.

Doris and Philip would cope well provided Philip was alive. But, if Philip dies before Doris, the £4,035 a year would stop and Doris would be left with nothing but her state pension to live on.

Therefore, Philip opts for a joint-life last-survivor level annuity reducing by one-third on the first death. This provides a pension while Philip is alive of £613 a year for each £10,000 of fund – in other words:

£613 / £10,000 × £50,000 = £3,065 a year.

If Philip dies, the pension is reduced by one-third to £2,043 a year and this reduced amount is paid to Doris for the rest of her life.

Guarantee period

If you died soon after taking out an annuity, it would not have paid out for long, so would not seem a very good deal. You can insure against this possibility by choosing an annuity with a guarantee period. All the annuities described above can be set up with this option.

Typically, the guarantee ensures that the income is paid for at least five (or sometimes ten) years, even if you die within the guarantee period.

If you do die during the guarantee period, the remaining income generally continues to be paid out as a regular income. In some circumstances, the income may be rolled up and paid as a lump sum to your estate.

Do not look on a guarantee period as a way of providing for survivors who were financially dependent on you:

- you might survive the guarantee period but still die before your dependant, in which case he or she will get nothing
- even if you die during the guarantee period, unless your survivor also dies within that period, there will come the day when his or her income abruptly stops.

Gradual retirement

Occupational schemes

Your pension usually starts on a single date. However, from 30 June 1999 onwards, you can take the proceeds of money purchase AVC and FSAVC schemes at any time, regardless of whether you have started taking a pension from your occupational scheme and regardless of whether you have stopped work. Therefore you could use the AVCs or FSAVCs to provide a small pension to supplement your earnings while you reduce the hours you work.

Stakeholder schemes and personal pensions

You do not have to convert all the pension you have built up under a stakeholder scheme or personal pension into one annuity taken out on a single date. Instead, you can take out lots of different annuities on as many different dates as you choose.

In the past, this was done by dividing your pension scheme into a cluster of segments. Each segment was technically a separate pension scheme, so could be used to buy an annuity quite independently of the other segments. If your own scheme was not set up on a segmented basis, you could transfer to another which was – but there would normally be charges for making the transfer.

Since April 2001, even where a scheme is not segmented, it can have multiple pension dates, so you can buy several annuities each at a different time.

Other ways to phase a gradual retirement include:

- having several pension schemes with different providers and taking an annuity from each at different times

- opting for a with-profits annuity with a low or zero ABR (see page 277); the pension will be low at the outset but virtually guaranteed to increase as the years go by
- pension fund withdrawal (see below).

Pension fund withdrawal

Pension fund withdrawal (also called 'income drawdown') is an option with personal pensions, stakeholder schemes and those occupational money purchase schemes which decide to allow it as an option.

To start taking a pension, you do not buy an annuity. Instead, you take an income direct from your pension fund while leaving the bulk of the fund invested. Under current rules, by age 75, you must convert your remaining fund to one or more annuities (which can be taken at different dates), though you should keep the situation under review and buy an annuity before then if appropriate.

If you want to take part of your pension fund as a tax-free lump sum (see page 267), you do this before starting to take your income direct from the fund. The income itself is taxable.

The Inland Revenue limits the amount of income you can take from the pension fund. The maximum is broadly the same as a level annuity for a single person (see page 273). You must take at least a minimum income which is set at 35 per cent of the maximum.

The insurance company you invest with must review your arrangement every three years. The minimum and maximum income limits will then be revised in line with changes in annuity rates and your increasing age. This means your pension may be reduced if you have been drawing the maximum or increased if you have been drawing the minimum. You must be able to cope with these changes in income.

There are two main advantages of pension fund withdrawal. First, at least until age 75, you are not forced to commit yourself to an income based solely on the annuity rates available at the point of retirement. This gives you scope to avoid buying an annuity when rates are low. However, if annuity rates generally continue to fall as your retirement progresses, you could eventually be worse off. Second, with pension fund withdrawal, your heirs can inherit whatever remains of your pension fund (after deduction of tax at 35 per cent in 2003–4). With an annuity, any of your pension fund not used up paying your annuity is usually kept by the annuity company

To make pension fund withdrawal worthwhile you will normally have to leave the bulk of your pension fund invested in shares and similar investments. This is more risky than buying an annuity, because your invested fund could fall in value or not grow fast enough to give you a better pension than an annuity would have done.

Because of the increased risks and the ongoing charges involved in leaving your pension fund invested, pension fund withdrawal is usually an option only if you have a substantial pension fund – say, £100,000 or more – or you are using pension fund withdrawal to provide only part of your retirement income. It is a complicated decision and you would normally be wise to get advice before going down this route.

Changes on the way

Drawdown is generally an option only for people with reasonably large pension savings. Otherwise, under current rules you are limited to annuities. Many people are unhappy with this 'Hobson's choice'. Annuity rates have virtually halved since 1990 and, once you have bought an annuity, you can't get your money back. So an annuity may seem a poor deal, especially if you die soon after taking one out.

Therefore the government is proposing to change the rules concerning your choices at retirement to give you more flexibility. However, flexibility invariably comes at a price – either in terms of your taking more risk with your pension savings or receiving a lower income. So, for many people, buying a traditional annuity may still remain the most suitable option.

The new rules are likely to come into effect from spring 2005. There will be a framework of general rules and broadly you will be free to make any choices within that framework. The general rules are very similar to the current regime and include:

- you must start to take a pension income from your savings no later than age 75
- the income must last for the rest of your life
- the pension must be paid out in regular instalments at least once a year
- the amount of pension must lie between minimum and maximum limits unless the amount is already determined by, say, an annuity or your employer's pension scheme
- the pension must be taxable.

What has gone under the new rules is any requirement to buy an annuity by age 75. You must still take a pension by that age, but it can be in a different, non-annuity form. But to prevent you using pension savings as a tax-efficient way of passing money on to your heirs, there are new rules if you opt for drawdown that prevent your survivors taking your remaining pension fund as a lump sum if you were aged 75 or over. Instead they would only be able to use the remaining fund to provide a taxable pension.

The new framework deliberately leaves open the method by which your pension might be provided in order to encourage the pensions industry to come up with new products that might overcome the perceived drawbacks of traditional annuities. In particular, the government sees a role for two new types of annuity:

- **limited period annuity** You use part of your pension fund to buy an annuity that will pay you an income for a set number of years – say, three or five. The rest of your pension fund is left invested to grow. At the end of the three/five years, you use a bit more of your pension fund to buy another annuity for a set period, and so on. At any stage, you can use all of the remaining fund to buy a traditional annuity that will pay you an income for life. The advantage of temporary annuities is that you are not locked into a single provider for life, but can shop around every few years for a better deal. The drawback is that to make this arrangement worthwhile, you must usually leave your pension fund invested in shares, so you run the risk of your pension fund falling in value if share prices slump. In other words, the price of flexibility is more risk.

- **value-protected annuity** This is like a traditional annuity but, in exchange for a lower income, the annuity will pay out a lump sum to your heirs if you die before age 75. Typically, the lump sum would equal the amount you paid for the annuity less the sum of the pension payments you had received up to the date of death. This innovation addresses the problem of not being able to get your capital back even if you die soon after the pension starts. But the price you pay for this type of flexibility is the lower income.

Action list at retirement

Before choosing an annuity you should take the following steps.

- Decide whether to take a lump sum.
- If you have any type of defined contribution (DC) scheme, ask the provider whether you have an 'open-market option'.
- If you do have an open-market option, check whether your current pension company offers a guaranteed annuity rate and/or makes hefty charges if you transfer to another annuity provider.
- In most cases, you can increase your pension by hundreds of pounds if you shop around for the best annuity.
- Work out what sort of annuity you want given your views about inflation and your duty towards any dependants.
- Check out annuity rates (see 'More information', below).
- If you have a large pension fund (six figures or more), check out income drawdown as an alternative to an annuity.

More information

You can find out about your occupational pension scheme options from your scheme booklet and your occupational pension scheme administrator. The scheme should be in touch with you a few months before retirement to check what you would like to do and how you want your pension to be paid.

Find out about your choices under other schemes from the scheme literature and the pension provider. Again, they should be in touch in the months before retirement.

If you have lost contact with any pension schemes you have belonged to or had in the past, you may be able to trace them through the Pension Schemes Registry.★

To shop around for the best annuity, check out annuity rates. These are published in a variety of places, including personal finance sections of newspapers, specialist magazines such as *Money Management*★ and *Pensions Management*★. If you have access to a fax machine, try the Fax services★ from *Moneyfacts*. The FSA★ publishes comparative tables for annuities.

If you want advice about choosing annuities, some IFAs★ specialise in this area and will select the best annuity for your circumstances, usually for a flat fee. The websites of these IFAs generally have useful background information as well as indications of the annuity rates currently available.

Pension fund preference

Ian is 59 and looking soon to retire or work part time. He has a personal pension and his fund is worth more than £150,000. Ian knows he can use his fund to buy an annuity from the provider with whom he built up his fund. However he's not sure whether this would be the best deal for him, especially as he doesn't need the maximum income from his fund because of other investments.

Because he needs only a small income, income drawdown could be suitable. Ian's pension fund could remain invested until he wants to use all or part to buy an annuity. The fund would be available to Ian's wife in the event of his death. He understands the risks and cost of this approach.

Which? February 1997

It pays to shop around

John boosted his pension by £219 a year by shopping around. This may not be a lottery-winning amount, but John receives the extra money – 12 per cent more than his pension company offered him – every year until he dies. John's pension company told him his £30,700 pension fund could buy an annual income of £1,817. But a specialist IFA found him an annuity paying £2,036 a year. The extra income meant the IFA's £59 fee was recouped in around three months.

Which? May 2000

Chapter 14

Basic investment planning

Chapter 4 should have given you a good idea of your financial objectives and the priority you attach to each one. Some of these objectives will concern your protection needs and have been dealt with in earlier chapters. Pension objectives have also been dealt with separately. What you should be left with now are your mainstream savings and investment objectives. Clearly, these will vary from person to person, but essentially they will fall into three broad types:

- providing a lump sum some time in the future either by investing a lump sum now or by saving regularly
- providing an income now by investing a lump sum
- providing an income some time in the future either by investing a lump sum now or by saving regularly.

The charts on the next few pages suggest how you might narrow down your choice of investments and methods of saving to find the most appropriate ways to meet your financial targets. A wide range of factors should be taken into account; these are discussed in the following pages. The charts concentrate largely on risk, because this is the factor above all others which most often seems to cause problems. Numerous financial scandals have revolved around investors being seduced into products which promised exceptional returns at seemingly little or no risk. Sometimes governments issue such investments, but in the commercial world risk and reward *always* go hand in hand. If you want the chance of high returns, you must be prepared to take on extra risk.

You should always treat a high-return, low-risk deal with suspicion. When interest rates are low and the stock market is in the doldrums, it can be especially tempting to believe the marketing hype for a deal offering above-average, safe returns, but there is bound to be a catch. An example from recent times has been some types of split-capital investment trusts (see page 372). These can offer some very sensible, moderate-risk ways to save. But during the stock-market slump of 2000 to 2003, some variants were offering unusually high returns. Closer inspection revealed that, unlike their less risky counterparts, these trusts were often heavily reliant on borrowed funds and/or investment in other split-capital trusts. This made the trusts much more risky and vulnerable to a collapse in share prices.

The charts that follow invite you to think of risk as a continuous scale from one to ten. If you place yourself at one, you are very averse to risk and should select savings and investments which carry the minimum of risk. Moving along the scale, you become more comfortable with risk and, at ten, you positively enjoy taking a gamble. How you assess your attitude towards risk was looked at in greater detail on page 83. As mentioned there, for a particular financial decision, your attitude towards risk may be influenced by the extent to which you are already on course to meet your most important financial targets. You should work through the charts for *each* financial target you have identified, bearing in mind the priority attached to each one. For example, if you are at the start of your financial plan, needing to build up an emergency fund and with little cash to spare, you should normally be very averse to risk. But as your main financial building-blocks fall into place, you may be comfortable taking greater risks with the lower-priority targets – see the diagram overleaf.

How to choose savings and investments

You need to consider a combination of factors when thinking about whether one type of savings or investments or another will best meet your needs. Here, the main factors are looked at in turn. They provide the framework for Chapters 15–17, which describe how the most common savings and investments work. Chapter 18 puts into practice matching specific savings and investments to your financial 'skeleton'.

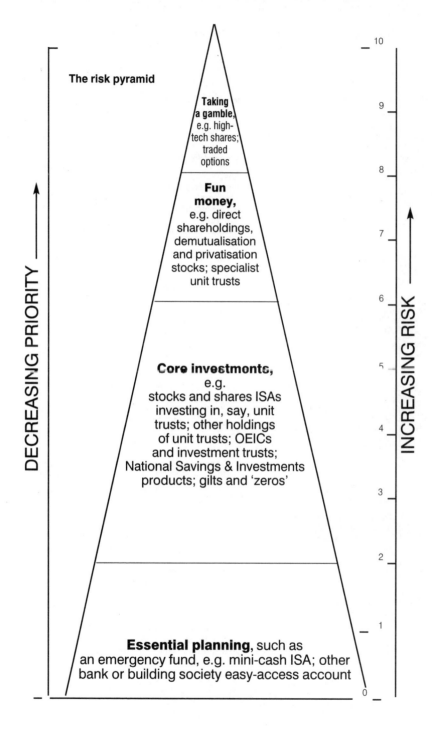

The risk pyramid

DECREASING PRIORITY ⟶

INCREASING RISK ⟶

10

9

8

7

6

5

4

3

2

1

0

Taking a gamble, e.g. high-tech shares; traded options

Fun money, e.g. direct shareholdings, demutualisation and privatisation stocks; specialist unit trusts

Core investments, e.g. stocks and shares ISAs investing in, say, unit trusts; other holdings of unit trusts; OEICs and investment trusts; National Savings & Investments products; gilts and 'zeros'

Essential planning, such as an emergency fund, e.g. mini-cash ISA; other bank or building society easy-access account

Building up a lump sum through regular saving

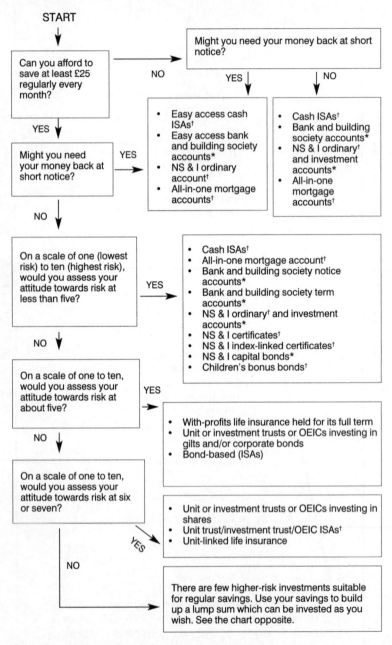

* May be particularly worth considering if you are a non-taxpayer.
† May be particularly worth considering if you pay tax at the higher rate.

Investing a lump sum to make it grow

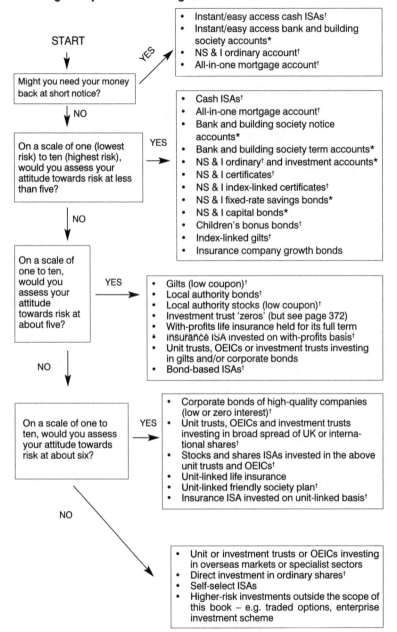

START

Might you need your money back at short notice?

YES
- Instant/easy access cash ISAs[†]
- Instant/easy access bank and building society accounts*
- NS & I ordinary account[†]
- All-in-one mortgage account[†]

↓ NO

On a scale of one (lowest risk) to ten (highest risk), would you assess your attitude towards risk at less than five?

YES →
- Cash ISAs[†]
- All-in-one mortgage account[†]
- Bank and building society notice accounts*
- Bank and building society term accounts*
- NS & I ordinary[†] and investment accounts*
- NS & I certificates[†]
- NS & I index-linked certificates[†]
- NS & I fixed-rate savings bonds*
- NS & I capital bonds*
- Children's bonus bonds[†]
- Index-linked gilts[†]
- Insurance company growth bonds

↓ NO

On a scale of one to ten, would you assess your attitude towards risk at about five?

YES →
- Gilts (low coupon)[†]
- Local authority bonds[†]
- Local authority stocks (low coupon)[†]
- Investment trust 'zeros' (but see page 372)
- With-profits life insurance held for its full term
- Insurance ISA invested on with-profits basis[†]
- Unit trusts, OEICs or investment trusts investing in gilts and/or corporate bonds
- Bond-based ISAs[†]

NO ↓

On a scale of one to ten, would you assess your attitude towards risk at about six?

YES →
- Corporate bonds of high-quality companies (low or zero interest)[†]
- Unit trusts, OEICs and investment trusts investing in broad spread of UK or international shares[†]
- Stocks and shares ISAs invested in the above unit trusts and OEICs[†]
- Unit-linked life insurance
- Unit-linked friendly society plan[†]
- Insurance ISA invested on unit-linked basis[†]

NO

- Unit or investment trusts or OEICs investing in overseas markets or specialist sectors
- Direct investment in ordinary shares[†]
- Self-select ISAs
- Higher-risk investments outside the scope of this book – e.g. traded options, enterprise investment scheme

*May be particularly worth considering if you are a non-taxpayer.
[†] May be particularly worth considering if you pay tax at the higher rate.

Using a lump sum to provide an income immediately

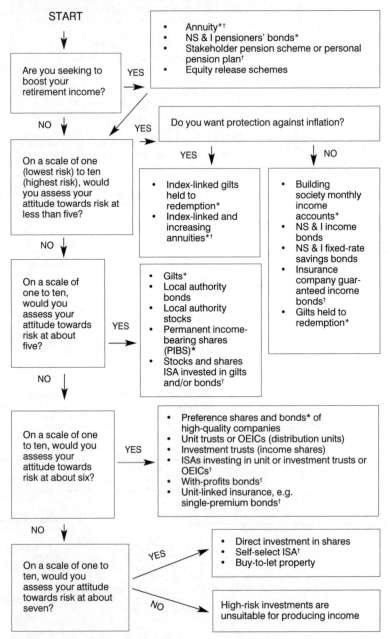

*May be particularly worth considering if you are a non-taxpayer.
† May be particularly worth considering if you pay tax at the higher rate.

Using a lump sum or regular savings to provide an income later on

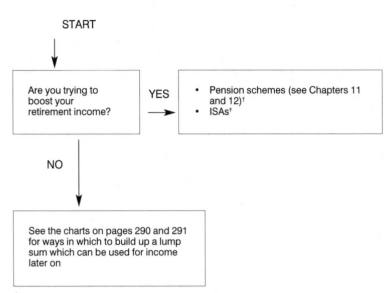

START

| Are you trying to boost your retirement income? | YES → | • Pension schemes (see Chapters 11 and 12)[†]
• ISAs[†] |

NO ↓

See the charts on pages 290 and 291 for ways in which to build up a lump sum which can be used for income later on

[†] May be particularly worth considering if you pay tax at the higher rate.

How much can you save or invest and how regularly?

With most savings and investments, there is a minimum amount you can invest. Sometimes, where there is no minimum, charges still make it uneconomic to pay in small sums. Where a type of saving or investment enjoys favourable tax treatment, there is usually a maximum you can invest. This can apply to other products too.

Some investment products are specifically designed to accept regular savings – monthly or annual sums, for instance – and there may be penalties if you fail to keep up the payments. There is quite a debate, especially in the insurance and pensions world, over whether regular saving is a 'good thing'. Regular saving has the advantage of creating a discipline which you might find helpful. It also takes away tricky decisions about when is the right time to buy investments whose price rises and falls. On the other hand, by committing yourself to regular saving, you lose flexibility over what, when and with whom you invest, because you are locked into the savings arrangement. This can be a problem if either your circumstances change or better products come on to the market.

It is also commonly argued that charges from regular-savings insurance and pensions products are higher than for equivalent single-premium products (where you pay in a single lump sum). On the face of it, this is true. However, you must consider how you would use single-premium products. If, for you, the alternative to taking out a regular-premium plan would be to take out a series of single-premium plans as and when you could afford to, you must compare charges for the *whole* series of lump-sum plans (and not just one of them) against the charges for the regular-savings plan.

For how long can you tie up your money?

Crucially important when choosing any investment is: can you get your money back, when, and are there penalties for doing so? Some products are designed to last for a specified period – five or ten years, for example. Obviously, you should not invest unless you can leave your money for the full period. Other investments do not have a specified term, but they may clearly be best suited to long-term investment, and may make an unwise choice if you know you want to save only for a year or two or might need funds in a hurry.

However sensibly you choose your investments at the outset, life can be unpredictable, so you should check what happens if you need your money back sooner: maybe you simply would not be able to have it back, perhaps you would lose interest, there might be surrender charges or, with an investment whose price rises and falls, you might run the risk of a loss.

What type of return do you need?

The need for either growth or income now, or income in the future, has already been considered. A further consideration is whether you want a fixed return or one which varies. Variable returns can be a problem if you are heavily reliant on them: for example as a major source of retirement income. Fixed returns, which go hand in hand with investing for a fixed period, are attractive if you expect returns on competing investments to fall. If, in fact, the competing returns rise over the period, you will lose out, so do not assume that choosing a fixed return is necessarily less risky than a return which can vary.

A fixed return loses value, in terms of what it can buy, if prices rise. A few products offering index-linked returns, which protect your investment against the impact of inflation, are available.

What return will you get?

Only a handful of investments offer a fixed or guaranteed return. Even then, you should check carefully so that you understand the nature of the guarantee – for example, will you get the promised return regardless or does the guarantee hold only as long as certain conditions are met?

With most savings and investments, you cannot know in advance what return you will get. As a rough guide, there is a trade-off between risk and return. For example, an investment that promises you will not lose any of your original capital is likely to offer a lower return than an investment where there is some capital risk. (See below for more about risk.)

Salespeople and advisers often make much of past performance data. They point out that an investment fund has grown strongly in the past, implicitly suggesting that it will do just as well in future. Take all this with a pinch of salt. Academic studies suggest only a weak link, if any, between past and future investment performance. What link there is suggests that investment funds that have performed poorly in the past are more likely than average to perform poorly in future. So there is some basis for avoiding the worst performing investments. But sadly there is no magic rule to help you pick the future winners.

How is the return taxed?

Chapter 4 examines the tax system to help you identify your own tax position. Now, you need to marry your personal tax treatment to the tax treatment of the investments you choose. Some investments and savings have particular tax advantages for certain types of investor; these are explained more fully in the chapters that follow. Some broad points to consider are as follows:

- Look at the after-tax (net) return you will get personally, given your income tax rate and capital gains tax position, not the before-tax (gross) return.
- Non-taxpayers gain nothing extra from tax-free investments.
- It is more convenient for non-taxpayers to receive returns from which no tax has been deducted than to have to claim back such tax.
- Tax-free returns are especially valuable to higher-rate taxpayers.

- Even if your income is taxed, you can often make capital gains without having to pay any tax on them because of the generous tax allowances.
- Income from most types of savings is taxed only at the savings rate. Basic-rate taxpayers have no further tax to pay. Higher-rate taxpayers have extra to pay. Non-taxpayers can, in most cases, reclaim any tax already deducted and starting-rate taxpayers can reclaim some of the tax. This treatment applies to interest from bank and building society accounts, income from annuities and interest from gilts and corporate bonds.
- Dividends from shares and distributions from most unit trusts and open-ended investment companies (OEICs) are taxed in a special way. Even non-taxpayers pay some tax (at 10 per cent) on this type of income (unless, until April 2004, they invest through an ISA or PEP).

What are the costs?

Just as you need to know the after-tax return for you personally, so you need to know the after-all-charges return to build a clear idea of what you stand to gain through a particular savings or investment medium. Some products are very straightforward. For example, when you save with a building society, you are quoted a particular rate of interest. The rate has been pitched at a level which (taking other factors into account) is expected to cover the society's costs. What you are quoted is what you get net of charges. Well, almost – you do have to watch out for interest penalties if you cash in term or notice accounts.

Most packaged products (life insurance, unit trusts, pension schemes) are more complex, with a variety of different charges – management fees, upfront charges, surrender penalties, switching fees, and so on. Trying to understand the impact of all these charges can be a nightmare. But life insurance and pension providers have to provide illustrations of the possible return from their products, netting out the impact of their own charges on the return you get (see Chapter 3 for details).

A third group of investments are those which run up dealing or transaction costs when you buy and sell them. These include most shares, gilts and corporate bonds. When assessing the return you might get, you should deduct what you will pay in stockbroker's commission, stamp duty, and so on.

What are the risks?

When people talk about investment risk, they usually mean the possibility of losing some or all of their original stake. But this is only part of the picture. There are four main types of risk:

- **capital risk** If you put your money into deposit-based savings, such as building society accounts, you know that you will always get back at least the amount of your original capital – that is, there is no capital risk. With investments like shares and unit trusts, which are bought and sold in a marketplace, you cannot be sure of this, because their price may have fallen during the time you have owned them. Another less obvious threat to capital is where charges are deducted from that capital rather than from the return. You also need to consider the standing of the organisation with whom you are investing. If you lend money to the British government, it is very unlikely that the government will default and be unable to pay you back as promised. But if you buy the bonds or shares of a small company struggling to break into new markets, there is a distinct possibility of your losing all your investment if the company goes out of business.
- **inflation risk** The big problem with deposit-type investments is that, over the long term, their returns tend to be lower than those from investments such as shares, and can be so low that they do not even compensate you for the impact of rising prices. This means that, although you can be sure of getting back your original outlay, it may be worth a lot less in terms of what you can buy with it. A few investments are specifically designed to protect you against inflation, but are not always the most appropriate choice. In the main, if you are investing for the long term, you should consider investments either in shares or linked to shares (such as unit trusts) as a way of hedging against inflation.
- **shortfall risk** If you have a set target – for example, saving enough to provide a certain level of retirement income, building up a lump sum to pay off a mortgage at the end of its term, or saving in advance to fund your child through university fees – there is often a risk that you will fail to meet your target. A way to reduce this risk would be to invest for a

guaranteed return, or to stick to safe investments like deposits, but the return on these is usually relatively low. So you would have to save more to reach your target, which could make the goal too expensive to be achievable at all. For example, the table below shows that for each £10,000 you needed in ten years' time, you would need to save £76 a month if you could get an after-tax return of only 2 per cent (as might be the case with, say, a building society savings account) but only £61 a month if you could invest at 6 per cent a year. Perversely, a more affordable way to reduce shortfall risk is to invest at least some of your money in equity-based investments which, although exposing you to capital risk, also give you the chance of a higher return over the long-term.

Amount you would need to save to build up a lump sum of £10,000 over ten years through regular saving

If the yearly rate of return was:	10.00%	8.00%	6.00%	4.00%	2.00%
You would need to save this much each month:	£50	£55	£61	£68	£76

- **the risk of being locked in (or out)** Accepting a fixed return over a set period or agreeing to a contract with onerous early-surrender penalties can prevent you from benefiting from improved returns elsewhere. Equally, though, keeping your options open can mean that you have to accept falling returns when others have protected their position by taking on fixed-rate deals.

You can see that there is no such thing as a completely 'safe' investment. Inevitably, you have to trade risk against return, and the different risks against each other.

In the charts on pages 290–3 and in Chapters 15–17 each type of investment is given a risk rating of one (lowest risk) to ten (highest risk). These ratings attempt to take into account all the various risks and give you a rule of thumb for comparing the riskiness of one type of investment with another. However, the ratings are not based on objective measures of probabilities and volatility, and the riskiness

Investing for income

Eileen, 48, earns around £350 a month, has no dependants and owns her home outright. Her only other asset is £120,000 from a divorce settlement, currently invested in a building society account. The combined income from her earnings and savings comes to about £674 a month putting her just in the basic rate tax bracket. Eileen needs all her income and wants to invest her capital to continue providing income but also sufficient growth to keep pace with inflation. She feels comfortable taking moderate risks with her money but, because her resources are limited, a cautious approach is suitable. At the time of investing (late 2002), investment conditions were exceptionally difficult. Interest rates were very low, gilts offered low returns to new investors, residential property prices had soared but looked to be near their peak. Commercial property prices were also starting to look high. Share prices were still volatile, but perhaps offered better value for longer-term investors than other assets, provided they could put up with some risk.

Financial plan: Eileen should continue to keep a sizeable chunk of her money (25 per cent) in deposit-based investments. She should use a spread of bonds (29 per cent of her money), property (8 per cent) and equities (38 per cent) to generate a bit more income (around £150 a month extra in late 2002) and give her a reasonable chance of enough capital growth to keep pace with inflation. Although some of the individual investments involve capital risk, it is important to look at all the investments as a whole. Collectively, they give a low to medium level of risk compatible with cautious investment.

Which? February 2003

sometimes varies depending on how you plan to use a particular type of investment: for example, holding it until repayment rather than selling in a volatile market, or combining it with other types of investment with a different degree of riskiness. Use the risk ratings as a rough guide which you can match to your assessment of the degree of risk which you are willing to take.

Stakeholder products

At the time of writing, the government was proposing to create a suite of 'stakeholder products'. These are to provide a range of simple, transparent, good value savings and investments that the government hopes will encourage greater levels of saving especially among lower-income households who traditionally have saved little and so have less scope to plan their finances and achieve financial goals. However, it is likely that stakeholder products will be available to everyone and could be especially useful for people who want to be their own financial adviser.

The stakeholder range is expected to comprise:

- **stakeholder cash ISA**. This will be suitable for short-term saving. It is expected that this will be the same as the present CAT-standard cash ISA (see page 310) simply rebranded as a stakeholder product.
- **stakeholder medium-term product.** This will be a range of products available both as unit trusts (or similar products) – see page 368 – and as insurance products. They must allow you to invest for as long as you like, not tie your money up for any set period and impose no penalties if you want to cash in early. There may also be a cap on the charges you have to pay each year, but the government is consulting further on that aspect. With-profits (see page 337) versions will be allowed but only in a transparent form that makes charges and the process of setting bonuses clear. These medium-term products will be available as ISAs (see page 376) and the present CAT standard for stocks-and-shares ISAs (see page 377) will be modified and re-branded as the stakeholder medium-term product.
- **stakeholder pension.** Current stakeholder pensions (see Chapter 12) will be taken into the new suite of stakeholder products with some modifications. In particular, the 'default' investment fund (see page 244) will have to be a lifestyle fund. This is a fund where the proportion of your money invested in lower-risk investments such as bonds and deposits automatically increases as you get closer to your chosen retirement age.

The new child trust fund (see page 313) is also to be a 'stakeholder product'. The suite of stakeholder products is due to be available from spring 2005 onwards.

Building a portfolio

In general, each investment target you have will require its own strategy for achieving it. But you are not simply limited to the particular risk and return offered by each product. By combining different investments, you can build a portfolio which has its own balance of risks and rewards. This gives you the scope to tailor your savings and investments closely to your own targets, circumstances and preferences.

You can see how this works by considering the example of shares. Buying shares in just one company would be a high-risk strategy; you would face three levels of risk:

- **market risk** The whole stock market could fall – because of economic recession, say.
- **industry or sector risk** The particular industry your company is part of could suffer some blow – a sudden increase in the price of raw materials, for example.
- **company risk** Your particular company could run into diffi-culties – for example, fierce competition from an aggressive new player – and could even go bankrupt, in which case you would most likely lose all your investment.

You can reduce your exposure to company risk by investing in the shares of a number of different companies. You can reduce your exposure to sector risk by making sure those companies come from a spread of different industries. And you can lessen the market risk by investing not just in the UK stock market but in, say, Europe, Japan and the United States, and by investing in a range of other investments, such as bonds and property, which respond in a different way to economic factors.

In the same way, you can combine different 'asset classes' to adjust the mix of risk and return. The four main asset classes are:

- **cash** Deposit-based investments like bank and building society accounts
- **bonds** In effect loans to governments and companies. But these can be bought and sold on the stockmarket
- **property** Either direct investment in property – usually commercial buildings like office blocks and shopping centres – or investment in the shares of companies that own and manage

such properties
- **equities** Shares in companies.

In this way you build an investment portfolio with the combination of risk and expected returns which suits you. You can buy into 'ready-made' portfolios by investing in 'pooled investments', such as unit trusts, investment trusts and investment-type life insurance.

More information

The chapters that follow outline the main investment and saving tools. For a more detailed look at them, see *Which? Way to Save and Invest*, published by Which? Books.★ Many books are devoted to developing your understanding of investment strategy and portfolio building: browse around a good bookshop. Regular journals to consider include *Which?*,★ *Money Management*,★ *Investors Chronicle*,★ *Moneywise*★ and *Money Observer*.★

When it comes to organising your investments, you might find it helpful to use a computer. A spreadsheet program, such as Microsoft Excel, is ideal if you are comfortable setting up your own system for logging your investments, calculating their values, working out any tax due, and so on. But you can also get tailor-made packages: for example, for managing a portfolio of stocks and shares, handling your tax, and so on. Many personal finance and stock-brokers' websites include portfolio managers. If you prefer to install your own software, have a browse around a computer warehouse or the advertisements in the various computer magazines stocked by most newsagents to see what is available. For a general outline of how computers can help, see *The Which? Guide to Computers*, published by Which? Books.★

Chapter 15

Lower-risk investments

This chapter gives you basic information about those investments that do not involve any risk of losing your original money. However, you should bear in mind that most of them are vulnerable to the impact of inflation. This is particularly so if you are using these investments to provide an income, because the amount of your capital stays the same in money terms but gets progressively smaller in terms of what you can buy with it. If you reinvest the interest earned, not only is your capital growing by the reinvested amount, but you earn interest on the reinvested interest (a process called 'compounding'), which further boosts the value of your investment. But even if you do let the interest accumulate, the return on these investments might still fall short of inflation, and, over the long term, generally lags behind returns available elsewhere. This makes them unsuitable as the only home for long-term saving, although they might form part of a more widely invested portfolio. Balancing the risks, each product has been given a risk rating on a one (lowest risk) to ten (highest risk) scale, which should help you to match the various forms of saving and investment to your assessment of your own attitude towards risk (see also Chapters 4 and 14).

Bank and building society savings and investments

Current accounts

What they are Current accounts are the prime tool for basic money management. You deposit money – often your main source of income – and have various ways of instructing the bank or building society to make payments from the account: cheque, debit card, standing order, direct debit, for example. Access to cash is usually through visits to a branch or an automated teller machine, so convenience of these to your home/work may be a key factor in your choice of account. Small sums can also be obtained through 'cashback' arrangements at supermarkets. In some areas or for some banks, there are arrangements to bank through post offices. Most bank current accounts and a few building society accounts allow you to borrow through your current account in the form of an overdraft.

Minimum investment Often none, although the minimum investment in high-interest current accounts may be thousands of pounds.

Maximum investment None.

Type of return Many personal current accounts pay a very small rate of interest on balances which are in credit. The amount is so small that it should not be a major factor in your choice of account. High-interest accounts pay better rates but usually require you to keep a substantial minimum balance; you might do better to invest surplus funds in a proper savings product. The best returns are often to be had with Internet-based accounts.

Tax treatment Interest is taxable and usually paid with tax at the savings rate (20 per cent in 2003–4) already deducted. Non-taxpayers can reclaim tax overpaid, or, better still, arrange for interest to be paid gross by completing Form R85 from the bank, building society or your local tax office. Starting-rate taxpayers can reclaim part of the tax. There is no further tax for basic-rate taxpayers to pay. Higher-rate taxpayers must pay extra.

How long you invest for No set time. You can withdraw your money whenever you like, though there may be an upper limit on cash and/or withdrawals in any one day.

Charges With most personal current accounts, there are no charges if the account is in credit. If the account is overdrawn, there may be charges for each transaction credited to and debited from the account. Usually, there are charges for overdrafts, which are much higher if you do not arrange the overdraft in advance. A few accounts let you overdraw by a small, set limit without charge.

Risk No capital risk. Vulnerable to inflation, so do not keep surplus funds idle in a current account. Risk rating: one.

More information Regular surveys in *Which?*,★ personal finance magazines and the personal finance pages of newspapers, summaries in *Moneyfacts*,★ fax services,★ Ceefax★ and Teletext★ (for high-interest accounts).

How to open an account For a branch-based account, visit the local branch. Most banks and building societies offer telephone banking accounts which you can open by phoning the number given in advertisements or *Yellow Pages*. There are now many computer-based accounts. These fall into two types: home computer-based accounts, which you usually open through a branch or by post; and Internet-based accounts, which you open or transfer through the Internet.

All-in-one mortgage accounts

What they are A mortgage, current account and savings facility combined. This is a holistic approach to handling your finances. You overpay your mortgage either by paying off larger amounts than the contractual minimum or by arranging to have your whole salary or other earnings paid into your mortgage account. Using normal current account tools – cash card, debit card and chequebook, for instance – you draw against the overpayment whatever money you need to cover your normal living expenses and other spending. Any surplus remains in the mortgage account, so reducing the mortgage debt. This in effect, means that the difference between your over-payment and your spending – that is, your savings – earns whatever is the current mortgage rate (since it reduces the mortgage debt on which you pay the rate).

Minimum investment Not relevant. You must take out a mortgage and there may be a minimum for this – for example, £50,000 – and you must agree to have your earnings paid into the account. As is normal practice, the lender will usually restrict the maximum mortgage to a given multiple of your earnings.

Maximum investment In effect, the size of your mortgage.

Type of return Saving in interest on the mortgage loan if you pay off more than the minimum required. In effect, your savings are earning the mortgage rate, which is usually significantly higher than the rate on a comparable deposit account.

Tax treatment You do not receive interest as such; instead you save the interest which would otherwise be paid on the mortgage loan.

Therefore, there is no tax – in effect, the return on your savings is tax-free.

How long you invest for The mortgage term, or a shorter period if you pay off your mortgage at a faster rate.

Charges Normal charges associated with taking out a mortgage (see Chapter 9).

Risk No capital risk. Inflation has both positive and negative effects, since it erodes the value of your mortgage loan as well as the value of your income/savings. If you have a variable-rate mortgage, the account is vulnerable to rising interest rates and although this in effect increases the return on your 'savings', rising rates increase the cost of the mortgage and leave a smaller surplus from your income to be 'saved'. Risk rating: one.

More information Summaries in *Moneyfacts*.★ Occasional articles in personal finance magazines and personal finance sections of newspapers.

How to open an account Contact providers direct or through a financial adviser. Some of these accounts are available by Internet.

Instant access/easy access accounts

What they are Instant access accounts let you withdraw your money at any time without notice or penalty. However, there may be limits on the amount of cash or cheque withdrawals you can make in any one day. Easy access accounts give you rapid, though not necessarily instant, access to your money – for example, they include postal accounts where you have to wait for a cheque to be sent and telephone accounts where transfers to your current account may take, say, a few days. Both instant access and easy access accounts make a suitable home for an emergency fund.

Minimum investment Often none.

Maximum investment None.

Type of return Interest, which is variable. Usually tiered accounts, meaning that small balances earn little or no interest, and higher rates are paid as your balance reaches set thresholds.

Tax treatment Interest is taxable and usually paid with tax at the savings rate (20 per cent in 2003–4) already deducted. Non-taxpayers can reclaim tax overpaid, or, better still, arrange for interest to be paid gross by completing Form R85 from the bank, building society or your local tax office. Starting-rate taxpayers can reclaim part of the tax. Basic-rate taxpayers have no further tax to pay. Higher-rate taxpayers have extra to pay.

How long you invest for No set period.

Charges No explicit charges. The bank's or building society's costs are one factor influencing the interest rates offered.

Risk No capital risk. Vulnerable to inflation. Vulnerable to falling interest rates. Risk rating: one.

More information Regular surveys in *Which?*,★ personal finance magazines and the personal finance pages of newspapers, summaries in *Moneyfacts*,★ fax services,★ Ceefax★ and Teletext.★

How to invest For branch-based accounts, contact your local branch. For postal or telephone accounts, contact the telephone number (or address) in advertisements or *Yellow Pages*. Register for Internet-based accounts through the Internet.

Notice accounts

What they are Savings accounts which let you withdraw your money without penalty only if you give a specified period of notice, such as a month or 90 days, depending on the account. Earlier withdrawal is usually (but not always) possible on payment of an interest penalty.

Minimum investment Varies from, say, £500 to £10,000.

Maximum investment None.

Type of return Interest, which is variable. Often tiered accounts, paying higher rates if the amount you have invested exceeds specified thresholds.

Tax treatment Interest is taxable and usually paid with tax at the savings rate (20 per cent in 2003–4) already deducted. Non-taxpayers can reclaim tax overpaid, or, better still, arrange for interest to be paid gross by completing Form R85 from the bank, building society or your local tax office. Starting-rate taxpayers can reclaim part of the tax. No further tax for basic-rate taxpayers, but higher-rate taxpayers pay extra.

How long you invest for No set term, but you should aim to give the full notice period when you want to make withdrawals.

Charges No explicit charges, apart from penalties or notice periods on withdrawal. The bank's or building society's costs are one factor influencing the interest rates offered.

Risk No capital risk. Vulnerable to inflation. Vulnerable to falling interest rates, especially since you cannot readily switch to another investment. Risk rating: two to three, depending on length of notice period.

More information Regular surveys in *Which?*,★ personal finance magazines and the personal finance pages of newspapers, summaries in *Moneyfacts*,★ fax services,★ Ceefax★ and Teletext.★

How to invest At local branch. By post or phone, if postal or phone-based account.

Term accounts and bonds

What they are You invest for a set period – one or two years, say – and either cannot get your money back earlier or withdrawals are subject to strict rules: for example, you must leave a certain sum invested, or make only one withdrawal of up to ten per cent of the value of the account, and so on. There are many variations: with some, the return is paid at the end of the term when the account or bond matures; with others, you can take a monthly income.

Minimum investment Varies: £2,500 or £10,000, for example.

Maximum investment None.

Type of return Interest, which may be fixed or variable, depending on the particular account or bond.

Tax treatment Interest is taxable and usually paid with tax at the savings rate (20 per cent in 2003–4) already deducted. Non-taxpayers can reclaim tax overpaid, or, better still, arrange for interest to be paid gross by completing Form R85 from the bank, building society or your local tax office. Starting-rate taxpayers can reclaim part of the tax. No further tax for basic-rate taxpayers, but higher-rate taxpayers have extra to pay.

How long you invest for The specified term.

Charges No explicit charges. The bank's or building society's costs are one factor influencing the interest rates offered.

Risk No capital risk. Vulnerable to inflation. Variable rates are vulnerable to falling interest rates, but you would lose out if locked into fixed rates when other interest rates were rising. Risk rating: three.

More information Regular surveys in *Which?*,★ personal finance magazines and the personal finance pages of newspapers, summaries in *Moneyfacts*,★ fax services,★ Ceefax★ and Teletext.★

How to invest At local branch. By post or phone, if postal or phone-based account.

Monthly income accounts

What they are These can be based on several types of deposit: for example, instant access or notice account, term account or bond. Most commonly they are notice accounts. Instead of accumulating interest within the account or bond, the interest is paid out monthly as income. This form of investment is popular with pensioners seeking to boost their income.

Minimum investment Varies: can be as low as £500, but is more often £5,000 to £10,000.

Maximum investment None.

Type of return Interest, which may be fixed or variable, depending on the particular account or bond.

Tax treatment Interest is taxable and usually paid with tax at the savings rate (20 per cent in 2003–4) already deducted. Non-taxpayers can reclaim tax overpaid, or, better still, arrange for interest to be paid gross by completing Form R85 from the bank, building society or your local tax office. Starting-rate taxpayers can reclaim part of the tax. No further tax for basic-rate taxpayers, but higher-rate taxpayers have extra to pay.

How long you invest for Depends on the type of account or bond. Most commonly, these are notice accounts where you can have your money back at any time provided you give the required notice – for example, 60 or 90 days – or alternatively pay an interest penalty.

Charges No explicit charges. The bank's or building society's costs are one factor influencing the interest rates offered.

Risk No capital risk. Vulnerable to inflation. Variable rates are vulnerable to falling interest rates, but you would lose out if locked into fixed rates when other interest rates were rising. Risk rating: one to three, depending on type of account or bond.

More information Regular surveys in *Which?*,* personal finance magazines and the personal finance pages of newspapers, summaries in *Moneyfacts*,* fax services,* Ceefax* and Teletext.*

How to invest At local branch. By post or phone, if postal or phone-based account.

Cash individual savings accounts (ISAs)

What they are A bank, building society or National Savings & Investments (NS&I) account which gets favourable tax treatment. You have to be aged at least 16 to take out a cash ISA. Some ISAs are 'CAT-marked' which means they meet government standards regarding Charges, Access and Terms. The CAT mark tells you that the account offers a fair deal – the table below sets out the main requirements for a CAT-marked cash ISA. ISAs which do not meet the CAT standards are not necessarily bad products, they are just different – for example, they might require a longer notice period for withdrawals but offer a higher return to compensate for this. CAT-standard cash ISAs are due to be rebranded as 'stakeholder cash-ISAs' probably from April 2005. For more about stakeholder products, see Chapter 14.

Tip

If you are a non-taxpayer, you can arrange to receive interest from your bank or building society account without any tax having been deducted by completing Form R85, which the branch or your tax office can supply. This saves you the trouble of having to reclaim tax later on. For more information, see Inland Revenue* leaflet IR110 *A guide for people with savings.*

CAT standards for cash ISAs

Standard	Main requirements
Charges	No one-off or regular charges
Access	• Minimum transaction size no more than £10
	• Withdrawals within 7 working days or less
Terms	• Interest not to be less than 2% below base rate
	• Interest must increase within one month of a base rate increase
	• No other special terms allowed (e.g. restricting number of withdrawals)

Minimum investment None for tax purposes, but provider might set its own minimum (e.g. from £10 up to £250). To qualify for CAT status, the minimum must be no more than £10.

Maximum investment £3,000 each tax year up to 2005–6; £1,000 a year in subsequent years.

Type of return Interest, which is usually variable, occasionally fixed. To meet the CAT standards, interest must be variable.

Tax treatment Interest is tax-free.

Charges No explicit charges. The provider's costs are a factor in deciding what interest rate to offer. There may be penalties or loss of bonuses if you withdraw your money – these are not permitted with CAT-standard ISAs.

Risk No capital risk. Vulnerable to inflation. Variable rates are vulnerable to falling interest rates. Risk rating: one to three depending on account features.

More information Regular surveys in *Which?*,* personal finance magazines and personal finance pages of newspapers, summaries in *Moneyfacts.** See Inland Revenue* leaflet IR 2008 *ISAs, PEPs and TESSAs.*

How to invest At local branch. By post or phone, if postal or phone-based account.

TESSA-only ISAs

What they are A special type of cash-ISA which receives the capital from a maturing Tax-Exempt Special Savings Account (TESSA) – these were tax-efficient bank or building society accounts designed to last for a maximum of five years. The last TESSAs are due to mature by 5 April 2004. Like ordinary cash ISAs, TESSA-only ISAs can be instant access or term accounts and, if they meet the rules set out in the table opposite, they can be CAT-standard ISAs.

Minimum investment None for tax purposes, but provider might set its own limit (e.g. from £10 up to £250). To qualify for CAT status, the minimum must be no more than £10.

Maximum investment The amount of capital (but not any return on it) which you get back from your maturing TESSA. (The maximum capital you could get back is £9,000.) This is in addition to anything you invest in an ordinary cash ISA.

Type of return Interest, which is usually variable.

Tax treatment Interest is tax-free.

Charges No explicit charges. The provider's costs are a factor in deciding what interest rate to offer. There may be penalties or loss of bonuses if you withdraw your money – these are not permitted with CAT-standard ISAs.

Risk No capital risk. Vulnerable to inflation. Variable-rate ISAs are vulnerable to falling interest rates. Risk rating: one to three, depending on account features.

More information Summaries in *Moneyfacts*.★ Occasional surveys in *Which?*,★ personal finance magazines and personal finance pages of newspapers. See Inland Revenue★ IR 2008 *ISAs, PEPs and TESSAs*.

Tip

It makes sense to use your ISA allowance every year. ISAs can be used to invest in a wide range of savings and investments which are suitable for an equally wide range of financial targets. In particular, cash ISAs can be a good home for an emergency fund or short-term savings. See page 376 for more about the different types of ISA you can choose.

Warnings

- If you take out a cash ISA, you reduce the maximum you can invest in a stocks and shares ISA – see page 379.
- There are strict rules about the types of ISA you can have and the amounts you can invest each year. If you break the rules, the last ISA(s) you took out will usually be declared void and you'll have to pay tax on the proceeds after all. For example, if you take out two ISAs taking you over the annual limit, the second ISA will be made void.

How to invest At a local branch. By post or phone, if postal or phone-based account.

Children's accounts

What they are Accounts especially for children (variously defined: for example, up to age 16, 18 or 21), usually offering introductory gifts, magazines, money-boxes, etc. Some accounts include cash cards for older children (aged 11 or more, say). Children's accounts are useful as a way of getting children into the savings habit or introducing them to the rudiments of budgeting.

Minimum investment Often as low as £1.

Maximum investment Usually none.

Type of return Interest, which is variable.

Child trust fund

In Budget 2003, the government announced that every child born from September 2002 onwards would be entitled to a child trust fund (CTF). At the time of writing, only the broad outline of the scheme was available. It was envisaged the scheme would work as follows.

Each child will qualify at birth for a cash sum from the government of £250 or £500 if the child's family has a low income (measured as qualifying for the full child tax credit). The cash will be invested in the child's CTF where it will grow until the child reaches the age of 18. At that time, the young person can withdraw the money in the fund to use for any purpose or roll the money into some other form of savings vehicle. There will be no access to the fund before age 18. The government might add further sums to each CTF, for example, on starting primary school and again on starting secondary education.

Parents, other relatives and friends will also be able to add to the child's fund. Additions from all non-government sources will be capped at £1,200 a year.

The child trust fund will have to be invested in a special account. Private businesses – for example, banks and building societies – will be invited to set up these accounts. The government expects them to be up and running by 2005 and the accounts will then be backdated to eligible children's birth. It is expected that the account will grow tax-free.

Tax treatment Interest is taxable and, if you do nothing, it will be paid with tax at the savings rate (20 per cent in 2003–4) already deducted. However, non-taxpayers (which includes most children) can have interest paid gross if Form R85 from the bank, building society or your local tax office is completed. Watch out for interest being treated as income of the parent (see Chapter 18).

How long you invest for Usually, these are instant access accounts, but some do not allow withdrawals before a given age.

Charges No explicit charges. The bank's or building society's costs are one factor influencing the interest rates offered.

Risk No capital risk. Vulnerable to inflation. Variable rates are vulnerable to falling interest rates. Risk rating: one.

More information Regular surveys in *Which?*,★ personal finance magazines and the personal finance pages of newspapers, summaries in *Moneyfacts*.★

How to invest At local branch.

National Savings & Investments products

These are investments offered by the government and run by National Savings & Investments (NS&I).★

NS&I ordinary account

What it is A savings account which gives you limited immediate access to your money. A small amount of interest each year is tax-free, which could be useful for higher-rate taxpayers, but overall the ordinary account is of limited use because the rate of interest paid is very low.

Minimum investment £10.

Maximum investment £10,000 (including reinvested interest).

Type of return Interest, which is variable. A higher rate is paid if the balance is £500 or more and you've had the account for at least a year. Interest is credited to your account annually.

Tax treatment The first £70 (£140 from a joint account) a year of interest is tax-free. Above that limit, interest is taxable but paid out gross, that is, without the tax already deducted.

How long you invest for No time limit. You can withdraw up to £100 instantly through post offices, or £250 if you regularly use one branch; otherwise withdrawals are made by post and take a few days.

Charges No explicit charges. NS&I's underlying costs are one factor influencing the interest rates offered.

Risk No capital risk. Vulnerable to inflation. Vulnerable to falling interest rates. Risk rating: one.

More information Post offices, direct from NS&I,★ occasional reviews of these products in *Which?*,★ personal finance magazines and the personal finance pages of newspapers, summaries in *Moneyfacts*.★

How to invest Via post offices or deal direct with NS&I.★

NS&I investment account

What it is A one-month notice account.

Minimum investment £20.

Maximum investment £100,000 (including reinvested interest). The same limit applies regardless of whether this is an account in a single name or a joint account.

Type of return Interest, which is variable. This is a tiered account with higher rates of interest payable as your balance reaches £500, £5,000, £10,000, £25,000 and £50,000. Interest is credited once a year.

Tax treatment Interest is taxable but paid out gross, that is, without the tax already deducted, making this a useful investment for non-taxpayers.

How long you invest for No time limit, but you have to give one month's notice to withdraw any money from the account or give no notice but lose 30 days' interest.

Charges No explicit charges. NS&I's underlying costs are one factor influencing the interest rates offered.

Risk No capital risk. Vulnerable to inflation. Vulnerable to falling interest rates. Risk rating: two.

More information Post offices, direct from NS&I,★ occasional reviews of these products in *Which?*,★ personal finance magazines and the personal finance pages of newspapers, summaries in *Moneyfacts*.★

How to invest Via post offices or deal direct with NS&I.★

NS & I certificates

What they are Two-year- or five-year-term investment producing a guaranteed tax-free return, which makes them attractive for taxpayers, especially those paying at the higher rate.

Minimum investment £100.

Maximum investment £10,000 in the current issue, plus a further unlimited amount if you are reinvesting the maturity proceeds of an earlier issue. This is in addition to holdings of previous issues.

Type of return Interest, which is fixed and paid out at the end of the two-year or five-year term or on earlier encashment. The rate of interest increases each year you hold the certificates.

Tax treatment Tax-free.

How long you invest for You choose either a two-year or a five-year term. You can get your money back earlier, but you'll get interest only at the reduced rates which apply to the earlier years. If you cash in during the first year, you get no interest at all (except on reinvested certificates). At the end of two or five years, make sure you cash in the certificates or reinvest in a new issue, otherwise they usually revert to a standard rate of interest called the 'General Extension Rate', which is very low.

Charges No explicit charges. NS&I's underlying costs are one factor influencing the interest rates offered.

Risk No capital risk. Vulnerable to inflation. Because you are locked in at a fixed rate, you'll lose out if other interest rates rise. Risk rating: three.

More information Post offices, direct from NS&I,★ occasional reviews of these products in *Which?*,★ personal finance magazines and the personal finance pages of newspapers, summaries in *Moneyfacts*.★

How to invest Via post offices or deal direct with NS&I.★

Index-linked NS&I certificates

What they are Investments producing a guaranteed tax-free return which is inflation-proofed. At the time of writing, available with either a three- or five-year term. (Earlier certificates available with two-year term.) Useful if you are concerned to protect your savings against rising prices (or if you want to take a gamble on inflation rising to high levels). The tax-free status makes them attractive for taxpayers, especially those paying at the higher rate.

Minimum investment £100.

Maximum investment £10,000 in the current issue, plus a further unlimited amount if you are reinvesting the maturity proceeds of an earlier issue. This is in addition to holdings of previous issues.

Type of return Interest made up of two elements: first, you get interest at set rates which increase for each year you hold the certificates; second, you get the amount needed to protect your capital and the interest already earned against inflation as measured by changes in the Retail Prices Index. The return is paid out at the end of the two-year or five-year term or on earlier encashment.

Tax treatment Tax-free.

How long you invest for You choose either a three-year or five-year term. You can get your money back earlier, but you'll get only the extra interest at the reduced rates which apply to the earlier years. If you cash in during the first year, you get no interest at all (except on reinvested certificates). At the end of three or five years, make sure you cash in the certificates or reinvest in a new issue, otherwise they usually revert to a lower rate of interest (still index-linked) or just index-linking.

Charges No explicit charges. NS&I's underlying costs are one factor influencing the interest rates offered.

Risk No capital risk. Because you are locked in at a fixed rate, you'll lose out if other interest rates rise, though what is relevant here is 'real' interest rates, that is, interest less the inflation rate. Risk rating: two.

More information Post offices, direct from NS&I,★ occasional reviews of these products in *Which?*,★ personal finance magazines and the personal finance pages of newspapers, summaries in *Moneyfacts*.★

How to invest Via post offices or deal direct with NS&I.★

NS&I fixed-rate savings bonds

What they are Fixed-term investments. The terms available vary. At the time of writing you could choose bonds lasting one, three or five years. They produce a guaranteed return which can either be paid out as a lump sum at the end of the term or as a regular monthly or yearly income. The only NS&I products paying a net-of-tax return, making them convenient for basic-rate taxpayers.

Minimum investment £500.

Maximum investment £1 million.

Type of return Interest, which is fixed. You get a higher rate of interest if you invest £20,000 or more and higher again if you invest £50,000 or more. You choose whether to have interest added automatically to your bond or paid out to a bank or building society account.

Tax treatment Interest is paid with tax at the savings rate (20 per cent in 2003–4) already deducted. Non-taxpayers and starting-rate taxpayers can reclaim all or part of the tax, respectively (but would generally do better to consider alternative investments). Basic-rate taxpayers have no further tax to pay. Higher-rate taxpayers must pay extra.

How long you invest for You choose from the terms available, currently one, three or five years. You can get your money back earlier but you will then lose 90 days' interest.

Charges No explicit charges. NS&I's underlying costs are one factor influencing the interest rates offered.

Risk No capital risk. Vulnerable to inflation. Because you are locked in at a fixed rate, you will lose out if other interest rates rise. Risk rating: two to three, depending on the term you choose.

More information Post offices, direct from NS&I,* occasional reviews of these products in *Which?*,* personal finance magazines and personal finance pages of newspapers, summaries in *Moneyfacts*.* **How to invest** Via post offices or deal direct with NS&I.*

NS&I income bonds

What they are Bonds which produce a monthly income. At present, you can hold the bonds indefinitely (they have a guaranteed lifetime of at least ten years from the time you buy them, but the government could redeem them after that if it decided to and gave six months' notice).

Minimum investment £500.

Maximum investment £1 million. The same limit applies regardless of whether this is an account in a single name or a joint account.

Type of return Interest, which is variable. A higher rate of interest is paid if you invest £25,000 or more. The interest is paid out each month and can be paid automatically into either your bank or building society account or an NS&I investment account.

Tax treatment Taxable, but paid gross, that is, without any tax deducted. This makes the bonds very convenient for non-taxpayers.

How long you invest for No set period. Either give three months' notice of withdrawal or no notice but lose 90 days' interest.

Charges No explicit charges. NS&I's underlying costs are one factor influencing the interest rates offered.

Risk No capital risk. Vulnerable to inflation. Vulnerable to falling interest rates. Risk rating: three.

More information Post offices, direct from NS&I,★ occasional reviews of these products in *Which?*,★ personal finance magazines and the personal finance pages of newspapers, summaries in *Moneyfacts*.★

How to invest Deal direct with NS&I;★ application forms are available at post offices.

NS&I pensioners' bonds

What they are One-, two- or five-year bonds which produce a fixed monthly income and are available only to people aged 60 or more.

Minimum investment £500.

Maximum investment £1 million (all bonds held, whether in single or joint names).

Type of return Interest, which is at a fixed rate guaranteed for the one-, two- or five-year term. Interest is paid each month into either your bank or building society account or an NS&I investment account.

Tax treatment Taxable, but paid gross, that is, without any tax deducted. This makes the bonds very convenient for non-taxpayers.

How long you invest for The interest rate is fixed for one, two or five years at a time, though you can invest for longer. If you cash in a bond at maturity, you do not have to give any notice and you get your money back within a few days. If you cash in at any other time, you must either give 60 days' notice, during which time no interest is paid on the amount you are withdrawing, or lose 90 days' interest if you withdraw without notice.

Charges No explicit charges. NS&I's underlying costs are one factor influencing the interest rates offered.

Risk No capital risk. Vulnerable to inflation. Being locked into fixed rates means you could lose out if other interest rates rise. Risk rating: three.

More information Post offices, direct from NS&I,★ occasional reviews of these products in *Which?*,★ personal finance magazines and the personal finance pages of newspapers, summaries in *Moneyfacts*.★

How to invest Deal direct with NS&I;★ application forms are available at post offices.

NS&I capital bonds

What they are Bonds which produce a guaranteed return payable at the end of five years.
Minimum investment £100.
Maximum investment £1 million. This includes holdings of previous issues (except Issue A) as well as the current issue and the same limit applies whether the bonds are in sole or joint names.
Type of return Interest, at fixed rates which rise each year and are guaranteed for five years from the time you invest. Interest is credited to the bond each year.
Tax treatment Taxable, but paid gross, that is, without any tax deducted, which is convenient for non-taxpayers. However, although interest is not paid until the end of five years, taxpayers are taxed on the interest each year as it is credited to the bond, so you need to make sure you have money available from elsewhere to meet the tax bill.
How long you invest for You should aim to invest for the full five years. If you cash in earlier, you receive the lower rates of interest which apply to the earlier years. And if you cash in during the first year, you get no interest at all.
Charges No explicit charges. NS&I's underlying costs are one factor influencing the interest rates offered.
Risk No capital risk. Vulnerable to inflation. Being locked into fixed rates means you could lose out if other interest rates rise. Risk rating: three.
More information Post offices, direct from NS&I,★ occasional reviews of these products in *Which?*,★ personal finance magazines and the personal finance pages of newspapers, summaries in *Moneyfacts*.★
How to invest Deal direct with NS&I;★ application forms are available at post offices.

NS&I children's bonus bonds

What they are Bonds bought by adults (defined as anyone over 16) on behalf of children up to the age of 16. The bonds can run until the child reaches age 21, building up a tax-free lump sum. The return is fixed for five years at a time and reviewed on each five-year anniversary.

Minimum investment £25.

Maximum investment £1,000 per child in the current issue. This is in addition to holdings of previous issues.

Type of return Interest, at fixed rates guaranteed for five years at a time, including a bonus payable on each five-year anniversary.

Tax treatment Tax-free. Bearing in mind that children's income may be treated as income of the parents (see Chapter 18), the tax-free status means that these bonds can be particularly useful as gifts from parents to their child.

How long you invest for Money can remain invested in the bonds until the child reaches age 21, when the bonds stop earning interest. They can be cashed in before then. If you cash in a bond within one week after a five-year anniversary, you do not have to give any notice, and the money is paid over to the child's parent or guardian within a few days. If you cash in at any other time, you must give one month's notice, and you will forfeit the five-year bonus. If you cash in during the first year, you get no interest at all.

Charges No explicit charges. NS&I's underlying costs are one factor influencing the interest rates offered.

Risk No capital risk. Vulnerable to inflation. Being locked into fixed rates means the child could lose out if other interest rates rise. Risk rating: three.

More information Post offices, direct from NS&I,★ occasional reviews of these products in *Which?*,★ personal finance magazines and the personal finance pages of newspapers, summaries in *Moneyfacts*.★

How to invest Via post offices or deal direct with NS&I.★

Tip

Because they offer a tax-free return, children's bonus bonds make a good gift for parents if they are worried that income from the child's investments would otherwise be taxed as the parents' income – see page 388.

Premium bonds

What they are Strictly, these are a gamble rather than an investment. You buy the bonds, and they are entered into a monthly prize draw where each bond stands a 1-in-30,000 chance of winning a prize ranging from £50 to £1 million (figures for November 2003). Unlike most other forms of gambling, though, you never lose your stake money.

Minimum investment £100.

Maximum investment £30,000 (plus automatically reinvested prizes).

Type of return The money invested in premium bonds is placed in a prize fund from which over 700,000 prizes are paid out each month. Prizes range from £50 to £1 million. Small prizes (£50 to £1,000) can be automatically reinvested to buy new bonds. From November 2003, the prize fund represented 2.15 per cent of the total invested in the bonds.

Tax treatment Prizes are tax-free.

How long you invest for Up to you. Bonds must be held for one complete calendar month before they are eligible for the prize draws. You can withdraw your money at any time, though this is done by post and takes a few days.

Charges No explicit charges. NS&I's costs are one factor influencing the return on the prize fund (and hence the overall payout in prizes).

Risk No risk to capital. Vulnerable to inflation. Return can range from nil to £1 million. Risk rating: three.

More information Post offices, direct from NS&I,★ occasional reviews of these products in *Which?*,★ personal finance magazines and personal finance pages of newspapers.

How to invest Via post offices or deal direct with NS&I.★

Tip
Premium bonds are an interest lottery. You do not gamble with your capital, only the interest from it. You could set up your own interest lottery by investing a lump sum in a bank or building society account and using the interest to buy National Lottery tickets, back horses, and so on.

Summary of lower-risk investments

Investment	Minimum period for which you should aim to invest	Type of return	Risk rating
Bank and building society savings and investments			
Current accounts	No set period	Variable, taxed,* if interest paid at all	1
All-in-one mortgage accounts	Mortgage term or shorter	Tax-free interest	1
Instant access/easy access accounts	No set period	Variable, taxed*	1
Notice accounts	No set period	Variable, taxed*	2–3
Term accounts and bonds	The specified period, e.g. 1 or 2 years	Fixed or variable, taxed*	3
Monthly income accounts	Varies	Fixed or variable, taxed*	1–3
Cash ISAs	No set period	Variable (or occasionally fixed), tax-free	1–3
TESSA-only ISAs	No set period	Usually variable, tax-free	1–3
Children's accounts	Usually, no set period	Variable, taxed*	1
National Savings & Investments (NS&I) products			
Ordinary account	No set period	Variable, taxable*	1
Investment account	No set period	Variable, taxable*	2
NS&I certificates	2 or 5 years	Fixed, tax-free	3

Summary of lower-risk investments (*continued*)

Investment	Minimum period for which you should aim to invest	Type of return	Risk rating
National Savings investments (continued)			
Index-linked NS&I certificates	3 or 5 years	Fixed, inflation-proofed, tax-free	2
Fixed-rate savings bonds	1, 3 or 5 years	Fixed, taxed	2–3
NS&I income bonds	At least a year	Variable, taxable*	3
NS&I pensioners' bonds	1, 2 or 5 years	Fixed, taxable*	3
Capital bonds	5 years	Fixed, taxable*	3
Children's bonus bonds	5 years	Fixed, tax-free	3
Premium bonds	No set period	Tax-free prizes	3

* Income is paid out before deduction of tax, or non-taxpayers can arrange to receive income gross, that is, before deduction of tax.

Chapter 16

Medium-risk investments

People who would like to achieve their investment or savings targets over a period of, say, five years or more would be unwise to rely too heavily on the lower-risk products described in Chapter 15: the returns tend to lag behind those of other investments and might not even keep pace with inflation. But going after higher returns inevitably means accepting some extra degree of risk. Chapter 17 outlines those investments where the value of your capital is fairly exposed. This chapter concentrates on the middle ground – a mixture of investments where either your capital is not at risk, though it may be tied up for some time, and/or you may have to accept that the return on it is unpredictable; or where the risk to your capital is generally fairly low.

Investments from the government

Gilts (British government stocks)

What they are Loans you make to the government in the form of bonds which usually have a fixed lifetime. You do not have to hold them for that set period because you can buy and sell them on the stock market. At the time of writing, there are 43 different conventional British government stocks (as well as index-linked stocks – see page 329). Stocks are often described in terms of their 'nominal' or 'par' value of £100. This is a convenient way of dividing the stocks into units, but if you bought a nominal £100 stock, for example, what you pay could be more or less than that amount. British government stocks are called 'gilts' (or 'gilt-edged'), reflecting the very sound nature of these stocks because of the unlikelihood that the government would ever default on them.

Minimum investment There are two ways to buy. If you buy stock when it is newly issued, you can do so direct from the Debt Management Office* (which issues stock on behalf of the government). New stock is auctioned and you must bid for at least £1,000 of stock. There are no dealing charges on stock you buy this way.

Alternatively, you can buy stock which has already been issued and is traded on the stock market. You can buy this way through a stockbroker or through the Bank of England Brokerage Service.* There is no set minimum investment, but dealing charges make buying small amounts (less than, say, £1,000) uneconomic. However, the Bank of England Brokerage Service charges (see page 329) tend to be lower than a stockbroker's for smallish transactions.

Maximum investment None.

Type of return The return is made up of two parts: while you hold the stock, you are paid a fixed amount of interest every six months; when the stock is sold or comes to the end of its life, you make a capital gain or loss. Some stocks pay a very low amount of interest and are useful only for people who are mainly after capital gains. Other stocks pay a high level of interest and are particularly useful for people who need income immediately; it may even be worth reckoning on some capital loss (by buying the stock at more than its nominal value) if a high income is a major priority.

If you hold the stock until the end of its life (until it is 'redeemed'), you will get back a known amount of £100 for each nominal £100 of stock you hold. This means that you know from the time you buy exactly what return you will get overall if you hold the stock to redemption: that is, the return is fixed and guaranteed. Alternatively, you can sell the stock before redemption, in which case you cannot be certain in advance what capital gain or loss you stand to make. So the nature of the return depends on how you choose to use these stocks.

Since 1997, you have also been able to buy 'gilt strips'. A single gilt-edged stock provides a stream of income payments plus the capital payment at redemption. Some stock can now be split up ('stripped') into components, each producing one payment. For example, a gilt with two years until redemption would produce four interest payments and a redemption payment. This could be split into five strips, one for each payment. Each strip (which is in effect a 'zero coupon bond') is traded separately. Gilt strips provide a very flexible form of investment and can be used, for example, to design an income flow tailored to your needs.

Tax treatment The income from all gilts is normally paid gross – that is, without any deduction of tax – which is especially convenient for non-taxpayers. But the income is taxable, unless you are a non-taxpayer. You can request to receive the income from gilts net of tax, in which case you will receive interest after deduction of tax at the savings rate of 20 per cent. There is no further tax to pay if you are a basic-rate taxpayer. Higher-rate taxpayers have extra to pay. If you are a starting-rate taxpayer, you can reclaim part of the tax deducted but it would be more sensible for you to opt to receive gross interest. Before 6 April 1998, income from gilts was normally paid net of tax if you bought through a stockbroker. Under transitional rules, if you already held gilts on that date, you will continue to receive the income net unless you request to switch to gross payments.

Capital gains on gilts are tax-free. This means that stocks paying low interest, whose return is likely to be largely in the form of capital gain, can be particularly attractive for higher-rate taxpayers and people who would normally pay tax on their gains.

How long you invest for If you want to hold stocks until redemption, there is a large range of redemption dates, from stocks just about to mature up to lifetimes of 30 years or more. But, of course, you can sell at any time before then on the stock market, and some stocks, called 'irredeemables', have no redemption date at all, so you *have* to sell to cash in your investment.

Traditionally, gilts are divided into three groups:

- shorts (five years or less to redemption),
- mediums (five to fifteen years), and
- longs (over fifteen years).

The groups tend to behave in different ways. As short-dated stocks get closer to their redemption date, their prices tend towards the nominal value at which they will be redeemed; other short-dated stocks tend to react to changes in general interest rates. Longer-dated stocks are influenced more by the inflation outlook and wider-ranging economic factors.

Charges If you deal through a stockbroker. Typically, you might pay, say, 1 per cent on deals up to £7,000 with a minimum charge of

£17.50. The Bank of England Brokerage Service★ is cheaper (see overleaf). There is also a 'spread' between the price paid by buyers and sellers, with buyers paying a little more than the quoted mid-market price and sellers getting a little less.

Risk This varies, depending on how you use the stocks. If you intend to hold them until redemption (or you invest in 'gilt strips'), you know exactly what will happen to your capital, and your total return is fixed – though you are not locked into this because you could change your mind and sell before redemption. If you are holding conventional gilts for their income, bear in mind that the income is vulnerable to inflation (though see the section below on index-linked gilts). You can also buy and sell gilts on a more speculative basis, though their price movements tend to be more modest than those of shares. Buying through the Bank of England Brokerage Service, you deal by post and so cannot be certain of the price at which your deal will be struck, which makes buying and selling in this way more risky than buying through a stockbroker. Risk rating: around four when held as medium- to long-term investments.

More information For a fuller discussion of gilts and how you can use them, see *Which? Way to Save and Invest*, published by Which? Books.★ The Debt Management Office★ publishes an excellent booklet explaining how gilts work and how to invest, *Investing in gilts – the private investor's guide to British Government stock*. For stockbrokers (including many high-street banks and some building societies which run their own stockbroking arms), contact the Association of Private Client Investment Managers and Stockbrokers (APCIMS)★ for a free directory of its members or the London Stock Exchange★ for a list of brokers. Quality daily newspapers carry full lists of gilts, including their prices and returns. Articles in *Which?*,★ personal finance magazines and the personal finance pages of newspapers are other good sources of information.

How to invest To use the Bank of England Brokerage Service,★ get a form from a post office or from the Bank of England. Otherwise, deal through a stockbroker. If you are buying gilts within an ISA (see page 361), you will have to buy through your ISA manager – who will usually be a stockbroker or the broking arm of a bank or building society. If you invest in new issues, do so via a stockbroker or by contacting the Debt Management Office★ for a prospectus or look for a prospectus printed in the press.

Bank of England Brokerage Service charges for buying and selling gilts

Type of deal	Commission rate	Minimum charge	Example
Buy up to £5,000	0.7%	£12.50	• If you buy £1,000 of stock, commission costs £12.50 • If you buy £3,000 of stock, commission costs £21
Sell up to £5,000	0.7%	None	• If you sell £1,000 of stock, commission costs £7 • If you sell £3,000 of stock, commission costs £21
Buy or sell over £5,000	£35 plus 0.375% of the excess over £5,000	£35	• If you buy or sell £7,000 of stock, commission costs £42.50 • If you buy or sell £10,000 of stock, commission costs £53.75

Index-linked gilts

What they are Basically, these are much the same as conventional gilts (see above), but both the income and the amount you get back at redemption are increased in line with inflation (measured as changes in the Retail Prices Index, subject to an eight-month lag). Their stock-market prices will *tend* to increase along with the rising redemption value, but are, of course, subject to other forces as well, such as returns available on other investments, confidence in the economy, and so on.

Minimum investment As for conventional gilts.

Maximum investment As for conventional gilts.

Type of return Income is inflation-proofed, which is useful for, say, retired people wanting an income to supplement their pensions. Your capital would be inflation-proofed too if you bought a stock when it was first issued and held it until redemption, but this link to inflation is weakened when you buy and sell on the stock market at prices which may be out of line with the indexation.

Tax treatment As for conventional gilts.

How long you invest for At the time of writing there were 10 index-linked gilts with redemption dates ranging from 2004 to 2035.

Charges As for conventional gilts.

Risk In the main, as for conventional gilts, with one important exception: income and to some extent capital are protected against inflation. Risk rating: around three to four when held as a medium- to long-term investment.

More information As for conventional gilts.

How to invest As for conventional gilts.

Local authority bonds and stocks

What they are Loans to local government. Some loans are in the form of fixed-term bonds which must be held to redemption. Others are stocks, similar to gilts, which can be bought and sold on the stock market.

Minimum investment For bonds, this varies from, say, £200 upwards. With stocks, there is no set minimum, but dealing costs would make less than, say, £1,000 uneconomic.

Maximum investment None.

Type of return Fixed-term bonds give you fixed interest, which is usually paid every six months. Stocks are similar to gilts, paying you a fixed income plus a capital gain or loss, depending on the prices at which the stocks are bought and sold (or redeemed). The interest rate on local authority stocks tends to be higher than on gilts, reflecting the higher risk (see below).

Tax treatment Interest from both bonds and stocks is taxable and paid with income tax at the savings rate (20 per cent in 2003–4) already deducted. Non-taxpayers and starting-rate taxpayers can reclaim all or part of the tax respectively. Basic-rate taxpayers have no further tax to pay. Higher-rate taxpayers have extra to pay. Capital gains on stocks are tax-free.

How long you invest for Terms vary. Like gilts, stocks can be sold before redemption on the stock market. Bonds are typically for two to eight years, and you are locked in for the whole period as these cannot be traded and there is generally no way to get your money back early.

Charges None for bonds. Stockbroker's commission and a spread between buying and selling prices for stocks.

Risk Bonds: the only risk to your capital is that the local authority might default on the loan and be unable to repay it, but this risk is slight; vulnerable to inflation; the fixed term and return mean you could lose out if other interest rates rose. Stocks: similar to conventional gilts, except for possible problems buying and selling, since the market for these stocks is sometimes not very active; slight risk that the local authority might default. Risk rating for both: around five.

More information Bonds: direct from local authorities, summaries in *Moneyfacts*.* Stocks are listed in quality newspapers with details of their prices and returns.

How to invest Bonds: contact the relevant local authority. Stocks: deal via a stockbroker.

Investments from commercial organisations

Annuities

What they are Investments offered by insurance companies whereby you swap a lump sum for a regular income. You cannot get your original investment back as a lump sum, though you are treated as if part of each income payment is in fact a bit of your original capital coming back (see Tax treatment, below). Annuities can be for life ('lifetime annuity') or for a set period of years ('temporary annuity'). Pensions from money purchase pension schemes and plans (see Chapter 13) are usually a type of lifetime annuity and are called 'compulsory purchase annuities'. Non-pension annuities are called 'purchased annuities'.

Minimum investment Varies, but you would usually pay thousands of pounds for a lifetime annuity.

Maximum investment None.

Type of return Income, which can be fixed or can increase each year either by a fixed percentage or in line with prices – you decide on the type of return at the time you invest. You can also choose annuities which guarantee to pay out for a fixed period – for example, five or ten years – even if you die during that period. The return from lifetime annuities depends heavily on the average life expectancy for someone of your age, so rates are generally higher the older you are and are higher for men than for women. Some providers offer annuities for people in poor health ('impaired life annuities') and these pay higher than normal rates.

Tax treatment With the exception of annuities used to provide a pension, part of each regular payment is deemed to be the return of part of your capital and is tax-free. The remaining part is income, which is usually paid with tax at the savings rate already deducted, but you may be able to arrange to have it paid gross if you are a non-taxpayer (if not, you can reclaim the tax). Starting-rate taxpayers can reclaim part of the tax. Basic-rate taxpayers have no further tax to pay. Higher-rate taxpayers must pay extra. The whole of the income from a pension annuity is taxable at your top rate of income tax and is generally paid with the correct amount of tax deducted using the PAYE system.

How long you invest for A lifetime annuity is literally for life: having made your decision to invest, you have no chance to reverse it. Temporary annuities are for set periods: for example, five years. You are committed to investing for the full period and cannot get your capital back as a lump sum.

Charges No explicit charges. The insurance company's costs are one factor determining the annuity rates on offer.

Risk No access to your capital as a lump sum once you have invested. Annuities with no built-in increases are vulnerable to inflation: you are locked in at whatever annuity rates apply at the time you invest, and you will lose out if annuity rates subsequently rise. (However, the trend in recent years has been for annuity rates to fall.) Risk rating: around four for annuities paying a fixed income; around three for annuities which provide some protection against inflation.

More information Example annuity rates are listed in a wide range of personal finance magazines, some newspapers and in *Moneyfacts Life & Pensions*.* A number of fax services* also give up-to-date rates. A few IFAs specialising in annuities,* such as the Annuity Bureau and Annuity Direct, focus on finding the best annuities for

---

Warning
The annuity rate at the time you invest determines the income you will get for the rest of your life in the case of a lifetime annuity or for the whole term in the case of a temporary annuity. Therefore, it is important to avoid investing at times when annuity rates are low. If you're not sure whether the timing is right, get advice.

clients. If you have access to the Internet, you can find annuity rate comparisons on some personal finance and IFA websites, for example www.moneyfacts.co.uk, www.annuity-bureau.co.uk and www.annuitydirect.co.uk.

How to invest Either contact the insurer offering your chosen annuity or use one of the IFAs which specialise in annuities.

Insurance company guaranteed income and growth bonds

What they are Investments based on either single-premium insurance policies and/or annuities which give you a fixed income or fixed rate of growth over a set period and then return your original investment at the end of the period.

Minimum investment Varies from £1,000 upwards.

Maximum investment None.

Type of return You get either fixed income from income bonds or a fixed rate of growth from growth bonds (paid when the bond matures).

Tax treatment Depends on the underlying investments which make up the bond, but usually there is no basic-rate tax for you to pay. The insurance company has often already paid tax on the underlying investment, but this is the company's own tax bill, so non-taxpayers and lower-rate taxpayers cannot reclaim any tax. Higher-rate taxpayers may have to pay extra, though, with some types of bond, tax is deferred until the end of the term and based on the taxpayer's tax position in that year.

How long you invest for Depends on the fixed term of the bond, which is generally from one year to ten years. You cannot usually get your money back early.

Charges No explicit charges, although the insurance company's costs are one factor taken into account when setting the rate of return.

Risk No risk to capital. Vulnerable to inflation. Being locked into a fixed return, you will lose out if returns on other investments rise. Risk rating: around four. Do not confuse with other types of insurance company bond where return of capital is not guaranteed – see, for example, pages 341 and 367.

More information Details of bonds available are included in many finance magazines, including *Money Management*★ and *Moneyfacts Life & Pensions*.★ Regular summaries are also given in the personal finance sections of quality newspapers. For information about specific bonds, contact the insurer direct or use an independent financial adviser (IFA).★

How to invest Either contact the insurer direct or invest through an independent financial adviser.

Permanent income-bearing shares (PIBSs)

What they are Loans to building societies in the form of stocks which have no redemption date at all and which are bought and sold on the stock market. (Holding PIBSs often makes you a member of the building society. If the society converted to a bank or was taken over, you could be eligible for a cash or share windfall.)

Minimum investment Varies from £1,000 upwards.

Maximum investment None.

Type of return Fixed interest paid out twice a year, which makes PIBSs popular investments with people seeking an immediate income. The rate of interest is usually higher than it is on gilts, reflecting the higher risk you take with PIBSs (see below). Depending on the prices at which you buy and sell, you may make a capital gain or a capital loss.

Tax treatment Interest is taxable and, since 1 April 2001, paid before deduction of tax. Income tax is due at your highest rate, unless you are a basic rate tax payer, in which case tax is due at the savings rate (20 per cent in 2003–4). Capital gains are tax-free.

How long you invest for No set period, but this is not a suitable home for money you might need back at a particular time or at short notice because prices may be low at that time.

Charges Stockbroker's commission and spread between the prices at which you buy and sell.

Risk Capital risk on three counts: prices can fall, the market in these stocks is not very active (so you might have problems selling – and buying), and there is a small risk that the building society might go out of business (though in the past the few societies that have run into difficulties have been absorbed into other societies rather than allowed to go bust). There is also a slight risk to income, because the building society is allowed to waive the interest if it is facing financial difficulty. The fixed income is vulnerable to inflation. Risk rating: around five.

More information Stockbrokers, the personal finance sections of some newspapers, occasional articles in personal finance magazines.
How to invest Via a stockbroker.

Corporate bonds

What they are These work in a similar way to gilts, except they are loans to companies in the form of stocks which are bought and sold on the stock market. There are various types of corporate bond: for example, those which are 'secured' either against the general assets of the company or against specific assets which can be seized and sold if the company defaults on the loan (in contrast to 'unsecured' loans, which are not backed by specific assets). There are also 'convertibles', which can be swapped for shares in the company at a set price at or before some specified date.

Minimum investment No set minimum, but dealing charges would make less than, say, £1,000 uneconomic.

Maximum investment None.

Type of return Usually, corporate bonds offer a fixed rate of interest, paid half-yearly. You also stand to make a capital gain or loss, depending on the prices at which the bonds are bought and sold, redeemed or converted.

Tax treatment Interest is taxable and, since 1 April 2001, paid before deduction of tax. Income tax is due at your highest rate; unless you are a basic rate taxpayer, in which case tax is due at the savings rate (20 per cent in 2003–4). Capital gains are generally tax-free.

How long you invest for Most bonds have a fixed lifetime, after which they are redeemed by the company. But of course you can sell on the stock market before then. This is not the home for money you might need back at short notice because prices could be low when you want to sell.

Charges Stockbroker's commission: for example, 1 per cent on deals up to £5,000 or so, with a flat-rate minimum commission of £15–£20. There is also a spread between the prices paid by buyers and sellers.

Risk There is a risk to your capital because bond prices can fall. You also have the risk that the company might go out of business and be unable to repay the loan, in which case you would lose all your capital. This latter risk should be reasonably small if you invest in the bonds of a large, well-established company (though, as the collapse of Barings Bank showed, bondholders in even the most seemingly sound company can lose). The risk of default can be substantial if you pick new and/or struggling companies. Fixed incomes are vulnerable to inflation. Risk rating: from around five for the most sound ('blue chip') companies to ten for companies which are unproven or in difficulty.

More information Stockbrokers.

How to invest Via a stockbroker. If you invest in new issues, via a prospectus from the company's agents or printed in the press.

Preference shares

What they are Unlike loans to a company, buying shares gives you a stake in the ownership of a company. Ordinary shares are described in Chapter 17, but preference shares are included here because they have various characteristics which are more akin to corporate bonds. Preference shares usually offer a fixed income, which is paid before any dividends to ordinary shareholders. Some preference shares have a redemption date, at which time they are bought back by the company, while others are irredeemable. In either case you can buy and sell them on the stock market. Convertible preference shares give you the right to switch to ordinary shares in the company at a set price at or before some specified date, which gives you the option to switch from a fixed to a variable income and participate in the generally more volatile movement of ordinary share prices.

Minimum investment No set minimum, but dealing charges would make investing less than, say, £1,000 uneconomic.

Maximum investment None.

Type of return Income is in the form of dividends, usually at a fixed rate and paid half-yearly. You also stand to make a capital gain or loss, depending on the prices at which the shares are bought and sold.

Tax treatment Income is taxable. The dividends are paid net of income tax at a special 10 per cent rate. Non-taxpayers cannot reclaim the tax deducted. Both starting-rate and basic-rate taxpayers have no further tax to pay. Higher-rate taxpayers have further tax to pay. Capital gains are taxable, though you may have allowances to set against them (see page 83).

How long you invest for No set period, because you can sell at any time on the stock market. But this is not the home for money you might need back at short notice or at a set time, since share prices might then be low.

Charges Stockbroker's commission and spread between the prices which buyers pay and sellers receive.

Risk Capital risk because of fluctuating share prices. You also have the risk that the company might go out of business. If it does, preference shareholders are in line for a payout ahead of ordinary shareholders, but the company might not have enough assets to stretch even to the preference shareholders, in which case you would lose all your capital. This should be a small risk with large, well-established companies, but a major consideration with companies struggling to get established or going through a bad patch. Fixed incomes are vulnerable to inflation. Risk rating: around five for 'blue chip' companies to ten for riskier ventures.

More information Stockbrokers, specialist magazines such as *Investors Chronicle*.★ Prices and so on are included in share listings in daily newspapers.

How to invest Via a stockbroker. If you invest in new issues of shares, via a prospectus from the company's agents or published in the press or, more commonly, through a stockbroker which offers a new issues service.

Pooled investments

Pooled investments are ready-made portfolios of particular types of assets, such as shares of a particular country, or a range of different assets, such as shares, gilts and property. They give you a way of spreading risks, investing relatively small sums and keeping down dealing costs. Against these advantages you must weigh the charges levied by the managers who run these investments and whether you are happy that the investment policy of the managers fits sufficiently well with your own investment aims.

With-profits life insurance

What it is This is one form of investment-type life insurance offered by insurers and by friendly societies – organisations which started life as mutual self-help organisations to help people cope financially with crises such as illness and death. (Pension schemes – see Chapters 11–13 – can also be invested on a with-profits basis, in which case they work in basically the same way as outlined here.) Your premiums are invested by the insurer in gilts, shares, property, and so on to form a fund out of which it meets claims and the costs of running its business. But insurers tend to be prudent people and so, normally, the investments produce more than the amount needed to meet claims, costs, dividends to shareholders (if the insurer is set up as a company) and reserves. The excess is distributed to the with-profits policyholders as bonuses. The insurer's actuary advises on how much can be paid out in bonuses each year. Usually, some kind of smoothing is applied to avoid sharp variations in bonuses from year to year. This means that some of the profits from a good year are held back in reserve instead of being paid out as bonuses. The reserves are then used to maintain bonus levels in years when the with-profits fund does not perform well. In this way, a with-profits policy should normally give you reasonably steady growth from year to year. You should not expect to do as well in the boom years as you would investing directly in the stock market, but equally, you should be insulated to some extent from falls in the market. But watch out for market value reductions (MVRs) if you cash in or transfer early – see 'Charges' later in this section.

Minimum investment Varies, depending in part on the type of policy or plan you are looking at. But some regular-premium policies accept sums of less than £10 a month. Single-lump-sum premiums tend to start in hundreds of pounds.

Tip

The return from most investment-type life insurance is not tax-free because the insurer has had to account for tax (which you can't reclaim) on the underlying investments. But friendly society tax-exempt plans (of which 'baby bonds' are an example) and insurance ISAs are completely tax-free until 5 April 2004 (when dividend income is due to become taxable at 10 per cent).

Maximum investment Insurers may set their own maxima, in particular limiting the amount of life cover they are willing to give. Tax rules may also play a part: for example, friendly societies cannot accept more than £25 a month (£270 a year) into their tax-exempt plans (see page 340).

> **Warning**
> With-profits life insurance policies are generally contracts designed to run for the long term. Their investment value builds up gradually. If you cash in the policy or stop paying premiums in the early years, your policy may be worth less than you have paid in premiums, or even worth nothing at all.

Type of return There are two types of bonuses: reversionary bonuses are added regularly, usually every year. Once added to the value of your policy, they cannot be taken away provided you keep the policy going for its original term. But if you cash in or transfer your policy early, even reversionary bonuses can be reduced by MVRs (see page 342). A terminal bonus is paid when the policy matures or on death – but not if it is cashed in or transferred early. The terminal bonus can account for a large proportion – for example a half – of the total return.

Tax treatment The return you get counts as income. With a few exceptions, the insurer has to pay or allow for tax on the underlying investment fund. This is deemed to be equivalent to having had basic-rate income tax already paid when you get the bonuses, so basic-rate taxpayers do not have any tax to pay themselves. However, non-taxpayers cannot reclaim any of the tax deemed to have been paid. Higher-rate taxpayers do not have to pay any extra tax, provided the policy counts as a 'qualifying' one (this means that the policy meets certain rules and so qualifies for advantageous tax treatment; most regular-premium policies designed to last for at least ten years meet these rules). If the policy is not a qualifying one, there could be some higher-rate tax. 'With-profits bonds' often allow you to take up to a given level of income each year, but put off paying tax on the income until the policy eventually matures. The limit on the yearly income is one-twentieth of the premiums paid. Any amount not used up in one year can be carried forward to future years. The proceeds of the bond, including the earlier income withdrawals, are then taxed when you finally cash in the bond. Although only higher-rate taxpayers would then have tax to pay on the bond itself, the payout can also affect other taxpayers if they are claiming income-related allowances or benefits, such as age

Investment-type life insurance

Investment-type life insurance is usually invested on either a with-profits basis (see page 337) or a unit-linked basis (see page 363). Here, the variations common to both the with-profits and unit-linked routes are described. See also page 367.

Endowment policies These are designed to run for a specified length of time (the 'endowment period'), during which you pay regular premiums (usually monthly) and at the end of which the policy pays out a cash sum. The policy also pays out if you die during the policy term but, if it's life cover you need, term insurance is a cheaper option. In the past, endowment policies have been used widely as an all-purpose way of building up your savings: for example, as part of an endowment mortgage, to pay school fees, or to accumulate a nest egg for non-specific purposes. This made some sense, because premiums to most policies qualified for some tax relief, but that premium relief was abolished in 1984. Nowadays, individual savings accounts (ISAs) are a more tax-efficient route for tackling medium- to long-term savings objectives.

Friendly society tax-exempt plans and 'baby bonds' These are usually endowment policies, but, unlike most life insurance plans, the return on the invested premiums is completely tax-free. This makes such plans useful for all taxpayers, especially those who pay at the higher rate. However, dividend and similar income building up in these plans is due to become taxable at 10 per cent from 6 April 2004 onwards

'Baby bonds' are simply versions of the tax-exempt plans aimed at children, and they are useful as gifts from parents who would otherwise be taxed on their child's income (see page 388). There is a snag: the government restricts the amount you can invest in these plans (in 2003–4 to just £25 a month or £270 a year). The low amount invested means that any flat-rate charges can eat heavily into the value of the plan. Some friendly societies offer lump-sum versions of the plans whereby your money is invested in, say, an annuity to meet the regular premiums for the tax-exempt plan.

Whole-of-life policies As the name suggests, these are designed to run for the whole of your life. Because the life cover element will inevitably have to pay out one day, such policies build up a cash value, which can be cashed in to provide an investment return. Whole-of-life plans, invested on a unit-linked rather than a with-profits basis, are used as **maximum protection plans** and **universal plans,** which package together life insurance, investment and often other types of insurance.

Single-premium bonds (including with-profits bonds) These are single-premium whole-of-life policies, though that doesn't mean you have to keep them for the rest of your life. With most bonds, you can invest for as long or as short a period as you like, but they are designed to run for the medium to long term (say, at least five to ten years) and you could face hefty surrender charges if you cash in during the first few years. They can be used to provide growth or income.

With-profits bonds (i.e. single-premium bonds that are invested on a with-profits basis) are especially popular with income-seekers. This is in part because the tax rules for single-premium bonds let higher-rate taxpayers take a limited income each year while putting off any tax bill until the year the bond is cashed in (see page 339). Investors who are not higher-rate taxpayers do not in any case have any tax to pay, though the equivalent of basic-rate tax has already been deducted and can't be reclaimed (see page 339).

With-profits bonds' popularity with income-seekers stems also from the fact that the bonds generally offer a higher return than bank and building society accounts but are less risky than fully fledged stock-market investments (such as unit trusts). But the returns are not guaranteed and depend on the insurer's ability to maintain bonus levels (see 'Risk' on page 343). Although you may receive the advertised income, the full return of your capital usually depends on bonus rates throughout the life of the bond. If bonuses fall short of target, you will not get all of your capital back – which, is of course, a very different situation from investing in a bank or building society account.

allowance or child tax credit. Friendly societies can offer plans which are invested in a tax-free fund (except that dividend and similar income is due to become taxable at 10 per cent from 6 April 2004 onwards) and whose proceeds are completely tax-free whatever your normal rate of tax.

How long you invest for This depends on the type of policy or plan you have, because many different sorts of policy can be invested on a with-profits basis. The main ones are shown in the box on pages 340–1. In general, though, with-profits life policies are long-term investments, often designed to last at least ten years, which will give you a very poor investment if you pull out early. Stopping a policy early crystallises charges (largely commission paid to advisers and salesmen) which would otherwise have been spread out over the lifetime of the policy. People are often taken by surprise by the fact that, once those charges have been taken into account in arriving at the surrender value, their policy may have a very low value indeed.

Charges An administration fee is usually deducted from each premium. If you give up the policy early, there will usually be surrender penalties. In addition, there may be a market value reduction (MVR) – sometimes also called a market value adjustment (MVA). These days, most with-profits insurers retain the right to impose an MVR if you cash in or transfer your policy before the end of its original term. Until recent years, not much attention was paid to MVRs. Insurers gave the impression that they would be imposed only in very exceptional market conditions. However, with a three-year slide in the stock market between 2000 and 2003, the exceptional conditions arrived and MVRs have become commonplace. The aim of an MVR is to ensure that poli-cyholders who quit do not take away more than their fair share of the with-profits fund to the detriment of policyholders who stay behind. The MVR reduces the cash-in value or transfer value of your policy (which is likely already to have been reduced by surrender charges), commonly by 5, 10 or even 20 per cent. MVRs are not levied if you hold your policy to the end of its term.

With a traditional with-profits policy, other charges are not explicit – they are simply one of the factors determining the bonus rates. However, many policies these days are 'unitised' with-profits plans – with these charges made explicit and usually expressed as an upfront charge deducted from the amount you invest plus an annual management fee ranging from, say, 1 to 3 per cent of the value of the money invested.

Risk Provided you do not have to cash in your investment early, there is no capital risk. Because bonuses are linked to a broadly based investment fund, you stand a good chance of beating inflation. But bonuses are unpredictable, especially the terminal bonus. You should be wary of simply assuming that past bonus levels will be maintained, or improved on, for the future: in recent times, many companies have cut their reversionary bonuses. A useful indicator of an insurer's ability to keep up future bonus levels is some measure of their 'financial strength', which looks at factors such as the level of reserves, the nature of the assets held by the insurer, and so on – this is covered in the with-profits guide (see page 55), which, however, is seldom read and poorly understood by most investors. The FSA is currently looking at ways of improving the information given to consumers about with-profits policies. Risk rating: about five provided you keep the policy going until the end of its term. If you are not sure you will be able to do this, your returns become much more uncertain and risk rises to around six to seven.

More information If you are interested in a particular insurer's or friendly society's products, the company must provide you with product details set out in a Key Features or Key Facts document; a with-profits guide, available on request, explaining how the company sets bonus levels; and an illustration or personal example if you request one. (See Chapter 3 for more about these documents.) *Money Management*★ publishes regular surveys of with-profits performance and financial strength. *Moneyfacts Life & Pensions*★ gives performance details and premiums for with-profits policies and a summary of insurers' bonus declarations. For more information about the different forms of investment-type life insurance which can be invested on a with-profits basis, see *Which? Way to Save and Invest*, published by Which? Books.★

How to invest If, from your research, you have picked out a particular insurer's products, deal with the insurer direct if it allows this. Otherwise, use an independent financial adviser (IFA).★

Insurance ISAs

Insurance ISAs can be used to invest in investment-type life insurance plans. They can be either with-profits plans or unit-linked. The difference between an insurance ISA and a non-ISA insurance plan is that the proceeds from the insurance ISA are completely tax-free (except dividends are due to be taxed at 10 per cent from 6 April 2004). For more about ISAs, see Chapter 17.

Gilt and fixed-income unit trusts

What they are Unit trusts are discussed more fully in Chapter 17. The gilt and fixed-income versions are professionally managed funds investing at least 80 per cent of the fund in gilts and other investments offering a fixed income, such as corporate bonds and/or preference shares. You invest by buying units in the trust.

Minimum investment Varies from, say, £500 upwards as a lump sum and from £25 a month through a regular savings scheme run by the trust management company.

Maximum investment None.

Type of return Units earn income (called 'distributions'), which can either be paid out regularly or, if you hold what are called 'accumulation units', automatically reinvested in the fund. Gilt and fixed-income trusts are particularly useful for investors seeking a regular income immediately. It is important to note that, although the underlying investments produce fixed income, the income from the trust itself is variable, because of the changing mix of underlying investments. You also stand to make a capital gain or loss, depending on the prices at which you buy and sell your units.

Tax treatment Distributions are paid or credited with income tax at the savings rate (20 per cent in 2003–4) already deducted. You get a tax credit showing the amount of tax paid, which you use to reclaim tax if you are a non-taxpayer. If you are a starting-rate taxpayer, you can reclaim part of the tax. Basic-rate taxpayers have no further tax to pay. Higher-rate taxpayers have extra to pay. Capital gains count as taxable, but you may have allowances you can set against them (see page 83). Since April 1999, provided the bulk of the trust (taken to be 60 per cent or more of the marketable value of its investments) is invested in interest-bearing investments, such as corporate bonds or gilts, this tax treatment continues unchanged. However, if the trust does not meet this condition – for example, if it has sizeable investments in preference shares – the distributions will be treated as if they are made from a share-based unit trust – see page 369. Note, in particular, that non-taxpayers would not then be allowed to reclaim the tax already paid.

How long you invest for No set period, but this is not the home for money you might need back at a set time or at short notice when unit prices could be low. Treat as a medium- to long-term investment.

Charges There is an annual management charge (often around 1–1.5 per cent of the underlying fund) and usually a spread between the prices at which you buy ('offer price') and sell ('bid price') units. This spread incorporates what is called the 'initial charge' – often around 3–5 per cent of the amount invested – but the total you pay upfront is effectively the spread, which tends to be 1 or 2 per cent more.

Risk These trusts give you a stake in a spread of different fixed-interest investments, which is generally a lower-risk strategy than investing direct in just one or two such stocks. They are a particularly useful way of spreading risk if you want to invest in corporate bonds. Bear in mind that income is variable. Risk rating: about five.

More information For general information, contact the Investment Management Association (IMA).★ Performance of trusts is published daily in quality newspapers and in specialist magazines, such as *Money Management*.★ *Which?*,★ personal finance magazines and the personal finance pages of newspapers all run regular articles about unit trusts. Personal finance websites, such as MoneyeXtra and FT Your Money, have search tools to help you choose unit trusts. There are now numerous fund supermarkets which both help you choose and buy unit trusts. (For these websites, see Appendix III.) Having selected several trusts which interest you, contact the management companies for product details and illustrations (see Chapter 3 for more about these).

How to invest If, having done your initial research, you know which trust(s) you want to invest in, you could contact the management companies direct. But you may get a better deal through a discount broker★, fund supermarket (see Appendix III), or an IFA★.

Stocks and shares ISAs

Stocks and shares ISAs can be used to invest in a wide range of underlying assets. These include gilts, corporate bonds and preference shares which would give you a medium-risk investment in a similar way to bond-based PEPs (see below). See Chapter 17 for full details about investments within ISAs. Note that many fund super-markets (see Appendix III) let you mix and match unit trusts (and sometimes investment trusts) from different providers within the shelter of a single ISA.

Bond-based personal equity plans (bond-based PEPs)

What they are (PEPs themselves are discussed more fully in Chapter 17.) From mid-1995 to April 1999, people were able to use

---

Open-ended investment companies ('OEICs')

Open-ended investment companies ('OEICs') are, from the investor's point of view, basically the same as unit trusts, though technically they are different. They are a cross between investment trusts (see page 372) and unit trusts. Like investment trusts, OEICs are companies which invest in funds – you invest by buying the OEIC's shares. Like unit trusts, though, the size of the fund varies with the number of investors involved, because shares are created and cancelled as investors come and go. This means that the price of OEIC shares behaves more like the price of units in a unit trust than shares in an investment trust, being directly related to the value of the underlying fund.

OEICs were developed largely as a way of widening the appeal of UK pooled investments. Foreign investors are unfamiliar with the trust status of unit trusts and feel more comfortable with corporate status. There is just one price at which shares in an OEIC are both bought and sold; this is in line with the way in which most Continental and US funds are priced. The price is based directly on the value of the investments in the fund, with charges shown sepa-rately. OEICs are taxed in the same way as unit trusts.

At the time of writing, OEICs are still fairly novel, but newly created collective investment schemes are tending to adopt the OEIC model and some unit trust managers are converting existing trusts to the new OEIC structure. The views of existing unit trust investors have to be taken into account before this can happen, but in general your investment should be broadly unchanged.

---

general PEPs to invest in corporate bonds and preference shares (but not gilts). Since 6 April 2001, PEPs can invest in the same range of investments as ISAs, which includes gilts. Two types of bond-based PEP originally emerged:

- those using the PEP to invest in fixed-interest unit trusts. Some trusts invest in a whole range of corporate bonds and shares; others specialise in, say, preference shares. Basically, from your point of view, this is simply investing in a unit trust (as described above) except that you gain certain tax advantages
- those investing in a single, newly issued corporate bond. The few which were launched offered a fixed return over a fixed period. The return is either payable as income or rolled up and paid out when the bond matures.

Minimum investment You can no longer newly invest in PEPs.

Maximum investment You can no longer newly invest in PEPs.

Type of return If it is a unit trust PEP, the same as for direct investment in the trust – see page 344. Most unit trust bond PEPs aim to provide a high income which is variable. For single-bond PEP, could be either fixed income or fixed growth.

Tax treatment The return on investments held in a PEP is completely tax-free. This will continue to be the case, provided the majority of the trust (taken to be 60 per cent or more of the marketable value of the investments) is invested in interest-bearing investments, such as corporate bonds. But if the trust does not meet this condition – for example if it has a sizeable investment in preference shares – the distributions will be treated as if made from a share-based PEP (see Chapter 17). This means that from April 2004 onwards the PEP manager would no longer be able to reclaim the tax credit on distributions from the trust.

How long you invest for For a unit trust PEP, no set period, but this is not the home for money you might need back at a particular time or at short notice, when unit prices might be low. For single-bond PEPs, there may be a fixed period, such as five years, during which you cannot get your money back at all.

Charges PEP managers may make extra charges (on top of those applying to the underlying investment), although in practice most unit trust managers do not. With single-bond PEPs, there are usually no charges.

> **Warning**
> Although most bonds offer a fixed income, the income from bond-based unit trusts, bond-based ISAs and most bond-based PEPs is variable.

Risk For unit trust PEPs, the same as for the underlying trust. Risk rating: about five.

For single-bond PEPs, you run the risk that the company issuing the bond might default, in which case you would lose all your capital, but this risk should be slight with a blue chip company. You are also locked into a fixed-interest, fixed-term investment and could lose out if other interest rates rose. Risk rating: from around five for the most sound companies to ten for those with no track record or experiencing difficulties.

More information For unit trust PEPs, as for unit trusts (see page 345). For single-bond PEPs, contact the issuers direct or through an independent financial adviser.

How to invest You can no longer newly invest in PEPs. However, you can still switch your investment from one fund to another within the same PEP and from one PEP manager to another. From 6 April 2001 onwards, the tax rules let you transfer just part of a PEP as well as whole plans and PEPs can be merged.

> **Warning**
> Trust managers usually set their charges against income earned by the investments in the trust. With bond trusts, charges may instead be deducted from capital. This makes the income you get look higher, but be aware that your capital may be eroded – i.e. in effect you will be swapping part of your capital for an income now.

Guaranteed equity investments

What are they A group of investments aimed at people who want better returns than the bank or building society can provide but do not want any risk of losing their capital. Guaranteed equity bonds can be based on deposit bonds (offered by banks, building societies and National Savings & Investments), insurance bonds or unit trusts, which all work in different ways (see the box on page 351). What they all have in common is that they offer a return linked to the stock market – typically, linked to the rise in the FTSE 100 Index or some other measure of stock-market performance – but aim to return your capital in full at the end of a set period. In the case of bank, building society and NS&I bonds, this aim usually takes the form of a guarantee to return your full capital. But, with the insurance- and unit-trust-based versions, the 'guarantee' generally holds only provided certain conditions are met, so it is important to read the terms and conditions thoroughly. For example, the guarantee may cease if the relevant stock-market indices fall more than a given amount and this can trigger large capital losses.

Minimum investment Varies from as little as £500 with some providers up to, say, £10,000.

Maximum investment Often none per investor. But many of these investments are offered for only a short period of time with a fixed limit on the amount that can be invested by all the investors in total.

Type of return Lump sum paid at the end of the guarantee period. If this is a deposit-based bond, the return counts as interest. The return from an insurance bond counts as income. The return from a unit trust will usually count as a capital gain.

Tax treatment Deposit bonds: the same as for bank and building society accounts (see Chapter 15) but some can be set up as cash ISAs in which case the return is tax-free (see page 310). Insurance bonds: as for non-qualifying policies (see page 339) and mainly suitable for people who are higher-rate taxpayers or who usually use up their full capital gains tax allowance each year (see page 83). Unit trusts: as for unit trusts (see page 369).

How long you invest for Deposit bonds have a set term, which is usually from one year up to five years and you can't normally get your money back early. You must normally hold an insurance bond for at least a minimum period – say, five or six years – for the return of your capital to be guaranteed. You can generally cash in earlier but in that case you probably will not get back all your capital. Usually you can leave your money invested beyond the initial guarantee period. With the unit trust versions, the guarantee generally runs for three months at a time and you can continue investing for further three-month periods for as long as you like.

Charges Deposit bonds: as for bank and building society accounts, though a few of these bonds have an upfront arrangement fee. Insurance bonds: as for unit-linked insurance policies. Unit trusts: as for unit trusts.

Risk Deposit bonds: in general, no capital risk provided you invest for the full guarantee period or term. Unit trust versions aim to return your full capital but generally do not give an absolute guarantee. Check the small print of insurance bonds carefully – with some, you are guaranteed a full return of your capital only if the stock market does not fall by more than a set amount (say, 27 per cent). If it does fall by more, you could lose a substantial sum. All these guarantees come at a price. Although you share in stock-market growth, you usually get only a proportion of the growth and you do not get any of the income that shares and share-based investments generally produce. If the stock market falls you get no return at all beyond return of your capital. Risk rating for bank and building society guaranteed investments: around five. Risk rating for unit trust versions: five to six. Risk rating for insurance bonds: five to seven depending on the small print. Do not confuse the guaranteed version of unit trusts with protected unit trusts (which are much higher-risk) – see the box opposite.

More information From banks, building societies, National Savings & Investments*, insurance companies and unit trust management companies that offer these investments and from IFAs. *Moneyfacts Life & Pensions** lists many of the bonds available. The IMA's* information service includes details of guaranteed and

---

Warning

The whole proceeds of both bank or building society guaranteed equity bonds and insurance guaranteed equity investments count as income for the year the bond comes to an end or is cashed in. If you are then aged 65 or over, the return from the bond could take you over the income limit for age allowance (see page 80). In that case, you would lose some or all of the allowance and have to pay extra tax as a result. Ways to avoid this problem include opting for an ISA version of a bank or building society bond or choosing a unit trust guaranteed investment instead.

How guaranteed equity investments work

Bank and building society guaranteed and National Savings & Investments equity bonds These are fixed-term deposit accounts. The bond earns interest which is paid out when the bond comes to an end, together with the full return of your capital. The amount of interest you get depends on the performance of a stock-market index, such as the FTSE 100, a group of several stock-market indices or a basket of shares. For example, you might get 50 per cent of the growth in the FTSE 100 Index, or a return of 6.5 per cent a year provided the FTSE 100 Index rises or stays at the same level, or growth in a basket of five specific shares up to a maximum return of 30 per cent.

Insurance guaranteed equity investments You take out a single-premium life insurance policy and your money (less any upfront charges) is put in an investment fund. Provided you invest for the full guarantee period, you get back your capital plus the growth of the fund or alternatively growth linked to one or more stock-market indices – for example 100 per cent of the average growth of the FTSE 100, S&P 500, Nikkei 25 and Eurostox 50, or growth in the FTSE 100 up to a maximum return of 30 per cent. A few of these insurance bonds invest in a fund which works in the same way as the unit trust versions described below.

Guaranteed unit trusts When you pick the trust, you choose the level of protection you want. Only a '100-per-cent fund' tries to return your capital in full. Typically, the investment is divided into three-month periods. At the end of each three-month period, the trust aims to return at least the amount you invested at the start of the period, by investing the bulk of your money to earn interest. It also aims to give you a proportion of any increase in a stock-market index by investing in financial futures.

Not all protected unit trusts are 100-per-cent funds. For example, a '95-per-cent fund' aims only to ensure you get back at least 95 per cent of your original investment at the end of the three-month period. But this allows more of your money to be put into futures, so increasing the amount you stand to gain if the market rises. These types of protected funds are not guaranteed investments and expose you to higher risks.

protected funds. See occasional articles in *Which?*★ and *Money Management*★.

How to invest If you've identified specific guaranteed investments you want to invest in, contact the providers directly. Otherwise, consult an IFA.★ Note that the deposit bonds and insurance bonds are often on sale only for a short period of time. The unit trust versions are continuously available.

Summary of medium-risk investments

Investment	Minimum period for which you should aim to invest	Type of return	Risk rating
Investments from the government			
Gilts	a) Until redemption	a) Fixed income, taxed or taxable; fixed capital gain or loss, tax-free	4
	b) No set period	b) Fixed income, taxed or taxable; capital gain or loss, tax-free	4–5
Index-linked gilts	a) Until redemption	a) Fixed income, inflation-proofed, taxed or taxable; capital gain or loss, ignoring the increases in line with inflation, is fixed at the time you invest, tax-free	3–4
	b) No set period	b) Fixed income, inflation-proofed, taxed or taxable; capital gain or loss, tax-free	4
Local authority bonds	Set period – usually 1–8 years	Fixed, taxed	5
Local authority stocks	As for gilts	As for gilts	5

Investments from commercial organisations

Annuities	For life or for a set period	Fixed or with built-in increases, taxed	3 or 4
Insurance company income and growth bonds	Set period – usually 1–10 years	Fixed, taxed	4
Permanent income-bearing shares (PIBS)	No set period	Fixed, taxable	5
Corporate bonds	As for gilts	Fixed income, taxable; capital gain or loss, tax-free*	5–10, depending on quality of issuing company

Investment	Minimum period for which you should aim to invest	Type of return	Risk rating
Preference shares	No set period	Fixed income, taxed; capital gain or loss, taxable*	5–10, depending on quality of issuing company

Pooled investments

Bank and building society guaranteed investments	Set period, usually 1–5 years	Growth, taxed as interest*	About 5
With-profits life insurance	Set period, often 10 years or more	Bonuses, effectively taxed*	About 5
With-profits friendly society tax-exempt plans	Set period, often 10 years or more	Bonuses, tax-free†	About 5
Gilt and fixed-income unit trusts and OEICS	No set period	Income, variable, taxed; capital gain or loss, taxable*	About 5
Unit trust bond-based PEPs	No set period	Income, variable, tax-free; capital gain or loss, tax-free	About 5

Guaranteed unit trusts	No set period (but multiple of 3 months)	Capital Gain, taxable	5–6
Insurance guaranteed equity investment	Set period – after 5 or 6 years	Income, variable taxed	5–7
Single-bond-based PEPs	Fixed period, e.g. 5 years	Income or growth, fixed, tax-free	5–10, depending on quality of issuing company

* You can invest in these investments through an ISA (see Chapter 17), in which case the return will be tax-free.

† But dividend and similar income building up within a plan is due to become taxable at 10 per cent from 6 April 2004 onwards.

Chapter 17

Higher-risk investments

When it comes to any serious longer-term savings targets, you should consider investments whose returns are linked in some way to shares. This does not mean you have to buy shares in individual companies yourself (although this is one option, of course): a number of pooled investments gives you cheaper and possibly more convenient access to a well-balanced portfolio. This chapter looks at the mainstream ways of investing in shares in the context of basic financial planning; it does not look at more esoteric investments, such as traded options, the Enterprise Investment Scheme, venture capital trusts, and so on. These may well have a place in your personal finances but, given their inherently higher risks, they should perhaps be viewed as fun investments rather than ways of achieving particular financial objectives. On that basis, they fall outside the scope of this book.

Direct investment in shares
Ordinary shares

What they are The shareholders of a company are its owners and share in the profits of the company. Your shares also give you the right to have a say in how the company is run (by exercising your voting rights at shareholder meetings) – but see page 357.

Minimum investment No set minimum, but dealing charges mean that buying less than, say, £1,000–£1,500-worth of a company's shares at a time is usually uneconomic.

Maximum investment None.

Type of return This can come in two forms. An established company usually pays dividends every six months (with some companies, every three months) to its shareholders. The amount paid is variable, although most companies are reluctant to reduce or miss a dividend payment. Companies still establishing themselves or those facing difficulties might not pay any dividends at all. Shareholders might be quite happy to accept this, if they can see profits being ploughed back into the growth of the company, giving the promise of future rewards.

Because shares are traded on the stock market, you also stand to make a capital gain or loss if you sell your shares, depending on the prices at which you bought and sold them.

Tax treatment Dividends count as income for tax purposes. They are paid after deduction of tax at a special rate of 10 per cent, and you receive a tax voucher along with the dividend cheque showing how much tax has been deducted. Both starting-rate and basic-rate taxpayers have no further tax to pay. Non-taxpayers cannot reclaim the tax. Higher-rate taxpayers have a further tax to pay, bringing their total tax rate on dividends to 32.5 per cent – see Example below. Capital gains on shares are taxable, though you can set your capital gains tax allowances against them (see page 83). Gains on employee shares and unquoted shares in trading companies – including those listed on the Alternative Investment Market (AIM) qualify for the higher rates of taper relief that apply to business assets, so reducing the tax you pay.

How long you invest for No set period, but this is not the home for money you might need back at a set time or at short notice, when share prices might be low.

Charges For the purchase of newly issued shares, no charges. For other shares, stockbroker's commission; the table on page 360 gives

---

Example

In 2003–4, Jules receives £540 in share dividends. These have already had tax at 10 per cent deducted. The before-tax value of the dividends is £600 (which equals £540 plus a £60 tax credit).

Since Jules is a higher-rate taxpayer, he is liable for tax at 32.5 per cent on the £600 dividends. This comes to 32.5% × £600 = £195. But £60 tax has already been deducted from the dividend payout, so Jules just has the excess to pay, in other words £195 – £60 = £135.

---

an indication of the amount you might pay. Stamp duty of 0.5 per cent on purchases but not sales. The spread between the prices at which you buy and sell: say, 1.5 per cent for large, well-established companies, but a much higher percentage for small companies whose shares are not often traded. In addition, on a purchase or sale of £10,000 or more, you have to pay a small PTM levy, which helps fund the City's Panel on Takeovers and Mergers. Some brokers also make a separate 'compliance charge', which goes towards the cost of meeting the regulatory rules for the industry.

You may be encouraged to hold your shares in electronic form through your broker's 'nominee account' (see page 359). Using a nominee account might be free or there could be charges: for example, on a regular basis or each time the broker hands over dividends. With nominee accounts, watch out too for extra charges if you want to receive company reports and accounts or to attend a company's AGM. (You could avoid a charge for company accounts by getting them direct from the company registrar or through a free service such as that run by the *Financial Times* – see 'More information' below.) As an alternative to using a nominee account, you could become a 'sponsored member' of Crest, in which case you directly hold your electronic shares. You must be sponsored usually by a broker who will make a charge. You do not have to hold shares electronically but, if you choose to hang on to paper share certificates, you will probably face higher charges when you sell or buy. Also, you will probably need to deal under a slower system than

---

Warning

Beware of stock-market 'bubbles'. Throughout the centuries, there have been periods when investors get overly enthusiastic about a particular company or sector. One of the most notorious incidents was the South Sea Bubble in the 1700s; one of the most recent has been the passion for 'dotcom shares'. If you get in on a bubble early and sell your shares before the bubble bursts, you can make a real killing. But don't be the last one left holding the shares when their price suddenly plunges back to reality. Chasing stock-market bubbles must be viewed as a high-risk 'fun investment' – not a tool of financial planning.

Tip

Gains from shares will be tax-free if you invest through an individual savings account (ISA) – see page 361.

---

normal or else face fines if your money or certificates do not reach your broker in time. For more details see opposite.

Risk Capital risk, because the value of your shares can fall as well as rise. In addition, there is the risk that a company you invest in goes out of business, in which case you would lose all your capital. On the inflation front, shares offer a good chance of keeping abreast of, or bettering, inflation over the long term – but no guarantee of doing so. Income can vary. You can reduce risk by investing in shares of different companies from different sectors. Risk rating: from around seven for shares in a single, sound, well-established company to ten for a high-risk venture.

More information One of the best ways to keep abreast of company information and share prices is via the Internet. Numerous websites and many online dealing services now exist which can help you do this. A selection of the most useful websites is given in Appendix III. Share prices are listed in many daily newspapers, on Ceefax★ and Teletext★ and on the Internet. ProShare★ is an independent organisation set up to promote direct investment in shares; it produces information packs, runs conferences, and so on. Among other perks, membership of ProShare gives you access to a telephone share information service. The *Financial Times*★, *Investors Chronicle,*★ other specialist magazines such as *Shares*★ and

---

Warning

Many small investors buy shares as new issues, attracted by the simplicity of the transaction and the fact that there are no charges. Privatisation issues, which were attractively priced at issue and have on the whole produced good profits, have fuelled this interest. However, companies try to launch their new issues when stock-market conditions look set to raise the maximum possible money for the company. That is the worst time at which investors should buy. Waiting and buying 'second-hand' might be a better deal.

Growth Company Investor★ and, to a lesser extent, the City pages of newspapers give reports and analysis of a wide range of individual companies. A number of fairly costly, but comprehensive, company guides is available, for example *The Pinsent Communications Company Guide*★; these give you essential statistics about companies and summaries of stockbrokers' recommendations. Company reports and accounts can be obtained direct from companies, and the *Financial Times*★ and *Investors Chronicle*★ run a report and accounts service for readers. For a general introduction to investing in shares, see *The Which? Guide to Shares*, published by Which? Books.★ Numerous books have been written about how to analyse shares and how to make a million – try your local bookshop. Consult a traditional stockbroker★ for advice on which shares to buy and sell or the timing of deals.

How to invest To buy new issues, register with a broker offering a new-issue service or, in the case of privatisations, see details in the press. For other shares, buy and sell through a stockbroker. If you need advice, choose a traditional stockbroking 'execution-and-advice' service. If you are confident about dealing without advice, opt for an 'execution-only' (also called 'dealing-only') service. The latter should be cheaper than a service which includes advice.

There are now numerous websites through which you can buy and sell shares. Most are execution-only. They work in two ways:

- **via a direct link to the dealing facility** The trading computer supplies you with a real-time share price at which you can trade. You generally have 15 to 20 seconds to accept or reject it. If accepted, your trade is executed instantaneously.
- **via a link to the broker's dealing desk** Your order is delivered by email. A human dealer picks it up and carries out the trade in the normal way. This is essentially the same as placing an order by phone. Price information may be supplied on the website but it will not necessarily be real-time.

Three-day trading, nominee accounts and all that

In order to compete with stock markets around the world, the London Stock Exchange has been speeding up the pace at which deals are completed. On 5 February 2001, 'three-day trading' was introduced, meaning that payment takes place just three working

Stockbrokers' commissions when you invest in shares

	Typical traditional stockbroker's service including advice	Example of a dealing-only service
Commission levels	• 1.5% on first £7,000 • 0.55% on next £8,000 • 0.5% on anything above £15,000. Minimum £20	1% Minimum £14
For example, commission on:		
Small deal (£500)	£20	£14
Medium deal (£2,500)	£37.50	£25
Large deal (£10,000)	£121.50	£100

days after shares are bought or sold. (This replaced five-day trading, and, previously, ten-day trading, which itself replaced an earlier, rather more leisurely system of settling deals in bulk at the end of fortnightly account periods.)

Three-day trading is no problem for professional investors, but it is near impossible for those small investors who are generally reliant on the postal system to receive transfer documents and deliver share certificates or cheques within just three days. Therefore, many brokers encourage their smaller clients to hold their shares through 'nominee accounts' and to open deposit accounts with the broker from which payments for deals can be made. With a nominee account, you cease to be the direct owner of your shares; instead, the broker owns the shares on your behalf. There are a number of potential drawbacks with this arrangement:

- As you are no longer the direct owner, you lose your automatic right to receive reports and accounts, to attend company meetings, to vote, and also the right to any share perks. Whether or not you can still exercise these rights depends on the services the broker offers as part of the nominee account.
- You may have to pay an annual fee for the nominee account, and there may be extra charges for collecting dividends, passing on

information about company meetings, and so on.

• Deposit accounts with brokers typically pay less interest than a comparable building society account.

You do not have to hold your shares through a nominee account. You can carry on dealing outside the three-day trading system, allowing longer for settling your deals – usually, this means using the old ten-day system instead. However, you may have to pay higher charges and/or accept a worse deal on share prices if you use the slower ten-day system. If you deal only occasionally, the slower system is likely to be best for you.

If you are a very active trader, consider the nominee route, but shop around for a service which suits you. Alternatively, consider becoming a 'sponsored member' of Crest (an electronic share settlement system). With this route, you have your own Crest account (in the same way that stockbrokers do), in which you hold your own shares electronically, which means they can be rapidly delivered when you sell them. For more details, see *The Which? Guide to Shares*, published by Which? Books.*

Self-select individual savings accounts (ISAs)

An ISA is not itself an investment. It is a wrapper you can put around all sorts of savings and investment products, making the returns from those products tax-free (or largely so). Many products – such as unit trusts – come ready-made in standard ISA and standard non-ISA forms. You can also opt for a self-select ISA. This lets you pick and mix, putting the investments of your choice within the ISA wrapper. It can be ideal, if you like to hold shares directly.

In general, only quoted shares can be included within an ISA. In the UK, this includes Techmark shares along with other shares listed on the main London Stock Exchange. However, you can include employee shares which you have received through a savings-related share option scheme or an approved profit-sharing scheme at work, even if they are unquoted. You must make the transfer within 90 days of acquiring the shares. An ISA cannot include shares traded on the Alternative Investment Market (AIM), Ofex or Tradepoint. Shares traded on foreign stock markets are eligible provided they are listed on a recognised stock exchange.

Self-select ISAs are offered by many stockbrokers and broking subsidiaries of some banks and building societies. Make sure that the charges for running the ISA do not outweigh the tax gains from putting your shares within the ISA wrapper.

Single-company personal equity plans (PEPs)

What they are A PEP is not in itself an investment. It is a tax-efficient wrapper which you can use to invest in shares and certain other investments. PEPs were originally introduced by the government to encourage direct investment in shares, but their scope was expanded over the years to encompass a much wider range of investments. You can no longer newly invest in a PEP. However, PEPs you already held on 5 April 1999 can continue. Originally you could have either general PEPs (investing in a range of investments) or single-company PEPs which, as the name suggests, hold the shares of just one company at a time, although you can switch from one company to another. However, from 6 April 2001, you can merge your general and single-company PEPs if you want to. From the same date, the range of investments you can hold in a PEP was expanded and brought into line with the range of investments eligible for stocks and shares ISAs (see page 361).

Minimum investment You can no longer newly invest in PEPs. However, you can switch from one PEP manager to another.

Maximum investment You can no longer newly invest in PEPs.

Type of return As for direct investment in shares – see page 355. PEPs are not themselves investments; they are a tax-efficient 'wrapper' under which you invest.

Tax treatment In general, income from investments held in a PEP is tax-free. However, from 6 April 2004, income from shares held in a PEP is due to become taxable to the extent that your PEP manager will no longer be able to reclaim the tax already deducted from dividends (see page 356). Capital gains are tax-free.

How long you invest for As for direct investment in shares. The PEP rules do not require you to invest for any specified length of time.

Charges In addition to the charges associated with buying and selling shares, extra charges may be made to cover the costs of running the PEP. They vary, so you should shop around.

Risk As for direct investment in shares. Your PEPs should be viewed in the context of the full range of investments that you hold.
More information The Association of Private Client Investment Managers and Stockbrokers (APCIMS)★ produces a free directory of members which includes details of those who offer a PEP service. *Which?*,★ personal finance magazines and the personal finance sections of newspapers run occasional articles about PEPs. See Inland Revenue★ leaflet IR2008 *ISAs, PEPs and TESSAs*.
How to invest As for direct investment in shares.

Warning

If investing directly in shares, you should ideally invest a minimum of around £15,000 to £20,000 in a dozen or more different companies to protect yourself adequately from risk and to avoid dealing charges eating too heavily into your profits. For many investors, pooled investments, such as unit trusts, OEICs, investment trusts and exchange-traded funds, will be the better option.

Pooled investments

Unit-linked life insurance

What it is This is a form of investment-type life insurance. (Pensions can also be invested on a unit-linked basis – see Chapters 11 to 13.) The bulk of your premiums buys units in one or more funds investing in shares and/or other investments. The value of your policy depends directly on the value of these underlying fund(s), so if the prices of the shares in a share-based fund fall, so too will the value of your units. There is usually a very wide range of different investment funds to choose from, including:

- **deposit-based fund** (often called 'money fund', 'cash fund' or 'deposit administration') This invests in high-interest bank and building society accounts and/or money market funds. Like the underlying deposits, the value of these funds cannot fall, so a deposit-based fund is useful to switch into if you want to consolidate gains on a policy or you want to switch out of a falling stock market.

- **unitised with-profits fund** This works in a similar way to traditional with-profits insurance, with bonus units being added to the plan, but the charges are explicit and the insurer usually reserves the right to adjust unit values downwards in exceptional investment conditions (although there may be a value below which the fund is guaranteed not to go).
- **fixed-interest fund** This invests in gilts, corporate bonds, and so on.
- **property fund**, investing in, say, shopping centres and office blocks which provide rental income.
- **managed fund**, investing in a wide range of assets which might include gilts, shares and property.
- **share fund** – for example, those in the UK, Europe, the United States, Japan, or Australia, or shares in companies which are in the doldrums but expected to grow strongly in future.
- **tracker fund**, whose value rises and falls in line with a selected stockmarket index – most commonly the FTSE 100 or FTSE All Share Index. Tracker funds (also called 'passively managed funds) tend to buy and sell shares in the fund less frequently than other ('actively managed') funds, so should benefit from lower costs.
- **commodities and metals**.

Minimum investment Varies, depending on the type of policy. But for regular-premium policies, payments start at under £10 a month. For single-premium policies, you might need a lump sum of at least £500, say.

Maximum investment As for with-profits policies – see page 338.

Type of return Your policy builds up a value according to the value of the underlying investment funds. How this value is used depends on the type of policy: for example, a maximum investment plan is designed to pay out a lump sum at the end of ten years, but a single-premium bond can be used to provide an income. See 'Tax treatment' below for more detail.

Tax treatment As for with-profits policies. Special rules apply to single-premium bonds used to provide income. Each time you take any 'income' you are treated as cashing in part of the policy. Provided you cash in no more than a given limit, you can put off paying any tax due (which would be only higher-rate tax anyway) until the policy eventually comes to an end, and tax would be charged according to your tax status at that time. The limit on the amount you can cash in each year is one-twentieth of the premiums paid so far; any amount not used up in one year can be carried forward to future years. The proceeds of the bond, including the earlier income withdrawals, are taxed when you finally cash in the bond. Although only higher-rate taxpayers would then have tax to pay on the bond itself, the payout can also affect other taxpayers if they are claiming income-related allowances or benefits, such as age allowance or child tax credit.

How long you invest for This depends on the type of policy or plan – see the boxes on pages 340 and 367. Many unit-linked life insurance products are designed to be long-term investments and will give you a very poor return if you pull out early. Stopping a policy early crystallises charges (largely commission paid to advisers and salespeople) which would otherwise have been spread out over the lifetime of the policy. As a result, the surrender value of your policy could be less than you have paid in premiums, or even nothing at all.

Charges There are several charges to consider. First, there will be some form of policy or administration fee deducted from each premium; this will often be a flat-rate fee, so it can eat heavily into small payments. Next, you need to consider the 'unit allocation', which tells you what proportion of the remaining premiums will be

---

Tip and warning

If you are currently a higher-rate taxpayer, but expect to pay tax at a lower rate later on, a single-premium insurance bond can be a tax-efficient way of providing income because no tax is charged at the time you take out any income (provided this is below a certain limit). When the policy matures, only higher-rate tax is levied, so if you are a basic-rate or starting-rate taxpayer by then, there will be no tax at all to pay on the proceeds. But beware: if you are aged 65 or more when your single-premium insurance bond comes to an end and you qualify for age-related tax allowances (see page 80), you could lose some or all of the extra allowance and have extra tax to pay as a result.

> **Warning**
> Make sure you understand the nature of the unit-linked life insurance policy or plan you are investing in. If it is designed for the long term, you could get a very poor return if you pull out early.

used to buy units; this proportion might be low in the first year or two when the bulk of the costs (commissions, for example) are being paid by the insurer. Don't be too impressed by unit allocations of more than 100 per cent: this does not mean that more than you have paid in is being invested; the policy fee has already been deducted, so you are in effect getting a refund of part of the fee. Watch out for what are called 'capital units'; the distinctive feature of these is that they have a higher-than-usual annual management fee which persists for the lifetime of the policy. There is a spread between the offer price at which you are allocated units and the bid price at which you cash them in; typically, this is around 5 to 6 per cent. Finally, there is the annual management fee of around 1 per cent.

Assessing the impact of this hotchpotch of charges would be a difficult task. Fortunately, nowadays the work is done for you, as insurers are required by law to tell you about the impact of charges on your investment (see Chapter 3). They must also tell you what happens if you cash in or stop your policy early, when surrender charges can heavily dent the value of your policy. If you switch between investment funds, the first switch or two might be free; you will be charged for subsequent switches (though the charge is usually fairly low).

Risk There is a risk to your capital because the value of the underlying investments can fall as well as rise. On the other hand, by investing in a fund you are spreading your risks and reducing the impact that any one company's share collapse could have on your overall investment. Your choice of fund affects risk: a UK managed fund (see page 364), for example, is far less likely to see sharp swings in value than a small companies or commodities fund. By investing in shares and similar investments, you stand a good chance of keeping pace with or beating inflation (but if you choose a deposit-based fund, this would not be the case). Risk rating: deposit-based funds, around three; other funds, from six upwards.

Unit-linked life insurance plans

The box on pages 340–1 looks at the broad types of insurance policy which can be invested on either a with-profits or unit-linked basis. Here, two further plans, which are usually set up as unit-linked insurance, are considered briefly.

Single-premium bonds These are usually a form of whole-of-life insurance policy (see page 341) which provide minimal life cover and are intended to be used for investment purposes. There may be as many as 20 or so different funds to which you can link. You can invest in more than one fund simultaneously and switch between them at any time. The insurance company has to account for tax on both income and gains from the underlying investment funds, and you cannot reclaim any of that tax. This makes the bonds unattractive for basic-rate, starting-rate and non-taxpayers and anyone with unused capital gains tax allowances, who would do better generally to invest in unit and investment trusts. These bonds are therefore most suitable for higher-rate taxpayers and those who particularly want to switch funds regularly.

Maximum investment plans These are ten-year endowment policies designed to build regular savings into a lump sum. Life cover is kept to a minimum, and you can choose from a wide range of investment funds. As with single-premium bonds, the tax treatment means that these plans are generally not suitable unless you are a higher-rate taxpayer or particularly need a cheap route for switching between different investment sectors.

More information Price and performance details of insurance funds are included in quality daily newspapers and various personal finance magazines, such as *Money Management*,★ and *Moneyfacts Life & Pensions*,★ which publishes annual surveys of fund managers' performance. Articles in *Which?*★ and the personal finance pages of newspapers are also useful sources of information. For individual policies and plans, the insurer or friendly society will provide product details and illustrations (see Chapter 3).

How to invest If you are interested in a particular product, deal directly with the insurer or friendly society if they allow this. Otherwise, buy through an independent financial adviser (IFA).★

Unit trusts

What they are These are professionally managed funds investing in shares and/or other stock-market investments. They can also (though only a few do this) invest in other assets, such as property and futures and options (the last two let you speculate on which way the future prices of shares and other assets will move without your actually holding the shares or assets themselves). The fund is divided up into units, and you invest by buying these units. The value of your holding depends on how the price of those units moves. Often, the unit trust management company operates a range of different trusts, for example:

- **UK all companies**, investing in shares of UK companies and aiming to produce a mixture of income and growth
- **UK growth**, again investing in UK companies, but specialising in shares expected to produce capital gains
- **UK equity income**, concentrating on shares with high dividend yields; the income can be reinvested rather than paid out
- **'index' or 'tracker' funds**, which mimic the movement of a particular stock-market index, such as the FTSE 100, and which often have lower annual management fees because the underlying investments are less actively traded
- **gilt and fixed-interest**, investing in gilts (see page 325), corporate bonds (see page 335), preference shares (see page 336) and similar investments
- **convertibles**, investing in convertible corporate bonds (see page 335)
- **balanced**, investing in a mixture of shares and fixed-interest
- **international funds**, investing in shares etc. from a wide range of stock markets around the world
- **smaller companies**
- **particular countries**, for example European countries or Japan
- **fund of funds**, investing in other unit trusts.

Minimum investment Varies, but could be as low as £25 a month if the management company runs a regular-savings scheme, and from, say, £250 as a lump sum.

Maximum investment None.

Type of return You can use most unit trusts to provide either growth or income, though some are better for one purpose than the other, and a few trusts can be used only for growth. Income is in the form of distributions, which are similar to dividends from shares. If you want to receive an income, choose 'distribution units'; if you do not, choose 'accumulation units', whose income is automatically used to buy you further units.

Tax treatment Distributions count as income for tax purposes. Distributions from unit trusts investing wholly or mainly in shares are taxed in the same way as dividends from shares. In other words, you receive the distributions with tax at a special rate of 10 per cent already deducted. If you are a non-taxpayer, you cannot reclaim the tax. Starting-rate and basic-rate taxpayers have no more tax to pay. Higher-rate taxpayers must pay extra tax, bringing the total rate they pay on the distribution to 32.5 per cent. Capital gains on units are taxable, though you may have allowances to set against them (see page 83).

How long you invest for No set period, but this is not the home for money you might need back at a set time or in a hurry, as unit prices might be low when you come to sell.

Charges There is an annual management charge (usually around 0.75–1.5 per cent of the underlying fund) and a spread between the prices at which you buy ('offer price') and sell ('bid price') units. This spread incorporates what is called the 'initial charge' – commonly 5 per cent of the amount invested – but the total you pay upfront is effectively the spread, which tends to be 1 or 2 per cent more. Some trusts have reduced or scrapped their initial charge and make an 'exit charge' instead if you sell within, say, five years. The initial charge is reduced or waived altogether if you buy through a discount broker★ or fund supermarket (see Appendix III).

Risk There is a risk to your capital because the price of units can fall as well as rise. Your choice of trust affects this risk: a UK all-company trust, for example, is far less likely to see sharp swings in value than a smaller-companies or trust. By investing in shares and similar investments, you stand a good chance of keeping pace with or beating inflation. Risk rating: from six upwards.

More information The Investment Management Association (IMA)★ produces leaflets and has a useful website explaining how unit trusts work, the types of trust available and how you can use them. The information service also publishes a directory of its members. Price and performance details of unit trusts are included in quality daily newspapers and various personal finance magazines, such as *Money Management*★ and *Moneyfacts Life & Pensions*★ (which also covers unit trusts). Articles in *Which?*★ and the personal finance pages of newspapers are also useful sources of information. For individual trusts, the management company will provide product details and illustrations (see Chapter 3). If you are an Internet user, you can find many sites producing performance statistics and risk ratings, including for example Trust Net and Standard & Poors (see Appendix III).

Exchange traded funds (ETFs)

Exchange traded funds have been available in the USA for some years. In April 2000, the first ETF went on sale in the UK. An ETF is an investment fund set up as a company. You invest by buying its shares, which are traded on a stock exchange. You buy ETF shares in the same way as any other stocks and shares – see page 359.

Investment trusts (see overleaf) are also traded on the stock exchange, but ETFs are different because, like unit trusts and OEICs, they are 'open-ended funds'. This means that extra ETF shares are created when there are more buyers than sellers, and shares are cancelled when sellers outnumber buyers. Because the size of the ETF adjusts with supply and demand, its price is not affected by demand for and supply of the shares (unlike an investment trust). So the ETF's price reflects just the value of the investments in the fund.

In the USA, ETFs are very popular and as a result the spread between the buying and selling price of the shares has been driven as low as 0.1 per cent. So far, all ETFs have been tracker funds (though ETFs in managed funds are also under consideration). As tracker funds, they have low management costs too – for example, 0.35 per cent of the fund per year for the UK's first ETF. But, as with other shares, you'll have to pay dealing charges when you buy and sell (though there is no stamp duty on purchases). This makes ETFs suitable only if you have a lump sum of, say £1,000 or more to invest. To find out about ETFs, visit the website www.ishares.net.

Open-ended investment companies (OEICs)
You may come across funds which are set up as OEICs rather than unit trusts. From the investor's point of view, there is little difference between the two investments. See page 346 for details.

How to invest If you have already selected the trusts you want to invest in, you might be tempted to go directly to the trust management company. But often this will not be the cheapest way to buy. Typically, you'll pay less if you buy through a discount broker* or a fund supermarket (see Appendix III) because, with both, the initial charge is reduced or cut completely so that more of your money is invested. If you need advice choosing a fund, contact an independent financial adviser (IFA).*

Pound-cost averaging
Some advisers suggest, when buying unit trusts and similar funds, there is an advantage in choosing regular saving over investing a lump sum because of 'pound-cost averaging'. The essence of the argument is that, when unit prices are low, your set regular sum buys more units than when unit prices are high. Therefore, the average price you pay for your units is less than the average unit price.

For example, suppose you invest £100 a month. If the unit price is 100p, you get £100 / 1.00 = 100 units. If next month the unit price is 50p, you would get £100 / 0.50 = 200 units. In total you would have 300 units at a price of £200, i.e. an average price to you of £200 / 300 = 66.7p per unit. This compares with an average price over the two months of (100 + 50) / 2 = 75p. Sounds like a bargain.

But there is nothing magic about the sums. They merely show how regular saving takes the 'timing risk' out of your investment: you avoid the problem of investing all your money when unit prices are high, but equally you lose the opportunity of investing all your money when unit prices are low. So pound-cost averaging may reduce your potential losses but it also reduces your potential gains. Whether that appeals to you depends on your attitude towards risk. Bear in mind that you still have to worry about the timing when you come to sell your units.

Investment trusts

What they are Investment trusts are companies that are quoted on the stock market. Their business is managing funds invested in shares and other assets. You invest by buying the shares of the investment trust. There are different types of investment trust, specialising in different areas of investment, in much the same way as unit trusts. But there are some important differences between unit trusts and investment trusts:

* Unit trusts are open-ended, meaning that when there are more people wanting to invest than to cash in, new units are created, expanding the size of the trust, and this new money is used to buy further investments in the fund. By contrast, investment trusts are closed-ended funds, because there is a finite pool of shares in the company. If more people want to buy than to sell, this drives up the share price. The unit price of a unit trust will, then, largely

---

Investment trust zero-dividend preference shares ('zeros')

Zeros can be a useful way of investing for growth over periods of, say, five to ten years.

Zeros are capital shares in a split-capital investment trust. They do not receive any income but, when the trust is wound up on a pre-set maturity date, they receive part of the capital growth of the assets held by the trust. The longest available periods to maturity are usually ten years.

Because zeros are preference shares (see page 336), they are among the lower-risk types of shares which you can hold. When the investment trust is wound up, the zeros receive a set share of the capital growth before any ordinary shareholders get a look-in.

In a complex investment trust, there may be many different classes of shares, including several types of preference share. Before investing, check that the zeros you have chosen are high up in the pecking order – 'first order preference shares' would get the first cut.

Bear in mind that, if you need to sell before maturity, you cannot be sure of the share price at which you can sell.

On a one-to-ten risk scale, zeros would generally score about five or so.

---

reflect the value of the underlying assets in the trust. But the underlying assets are only one factor influencing the share price of an investment trust.

- Investment trusts, but not unit trusts, can borrow money to invest. This has what is called a 'gearing effect', which magnifies gains on a successful investment but also magnifies losses on a poor one.

Minimum investment Varies from, say, £25 a month through a savings scheme run by the investment trust management company; savings schemes also accept *ad hoc* lump sums as small as, say, £250. Otherwise you buy through a stockbroker, and dealing charges would tend to make deals under £1,000 uneconomic.

Maximum investment None.

Type of return With some investment trusts, just one class of shares will automatically give you income (in the form of dividends) and growth (if the share price rises). But 'split capital trusts' give you

However, risk can vary enormously. In particular, investment trusts that are highly geared (i.e. are borrowing a high proportion of the money they invest) and/or have large amounts invested in the shares of other split-capital investment trusts have proved very high risk and vulnerable to the slide in the stockmarket during 2000 to 2003. Many small investors lost money and appear to have been mis-sold these trusts since neither the marketing literature nor their adviser (where they used one) had made the risks clear. At the time of writing, both the Financial Services Authority (the financial regulator) and the Financial Ombudsman Service are investigating claims for compensation and the Association of Investment Trust Companies has made arrangements to pay compensation to investors suffering the greatest financial hardship (defined as investors with less than £16,000 in savings and investments) because of losses on split capital trusts.

Understandably, the recent history of these split-capital investment trusts has given all such investments, including zeros, a bad name, but it would be wrong to tar them all with the same brush. The zeros of those split-capital trusts that are not highly geared and do not invest in other trusts' shares are still worth considering as a useful growth investment.

a choice of shares. A split capital trust is set up for a fixed period. During that time, some of its shares (the 'income shares') receive all or most of the income from the trust; when the trust is wound up, the 'capital shares' receive all or most of the growth. There are some exotic variations on this theme: for example, zero dividend preference shares (see page 372) and capital indexed shares, both of which require some homework before you use them. Income shares can be useful for investors seeking a high income immediately, provided they are prepared to sacrifice capital growth.

Tax treatment The same as for direct investment in shares. Capital shares in split capital trusts can be particularly useful for higher-rate taxpayers.

Charges The same as for direct investment in shares – see page 355 – if you buy through a stockbroker. The cost of investing is generally lower if you use a savings scheme run by many of the investment trust management companies (because they can then buy and sell

---

Unit trust or investment trust?

Having decided to invest in a fund, should you go for a unit trust (or OEIC) or an investment trust? You will have to weigh up a variety of factors:

- Investment trusts that borrow money to invest in the fund are more risky (i.e. there is more risk of losing money but also a greater opportunity for gain) than the equivalent unit trust (which is not allowed to use borrowed money).
- Investment trusts tend to be more risky/offer the opportunity for greater return than unit trusts because the value of your investment does not just reflect the value of the underlying fund but also the relative demand for the investment trust shares.
- The different charges: for example, with investment trusts, you usually have dealing costs when you buy and sell the shares. On the other hand, the annual management charge is sometimes lower than for an equivalent unit trust.
- How well the return is tailored to your goals: in particular, split-capital investment trusts offer different shares particularly suited to either capital growth or regular income.

---

in bulk and pass on cost savings to investors). There is a spread between the price at which you can buy shares and the price at which you can sell them. The management company's annual charge for its services is usually fairly low: for example around 0.5 per cent.

Risk There is a risk to your capital because share prices can fall as well as rise. A trust which has a high level of borrowing – that is, it is highly geared – will tend to have a more volatile share price than a less highly geared trust. Similarly, if the trust invests in inherently more risky companies – smaller companies or emerging markets, for instance – the share price can be expected to vary more widely and your risk will be greater. In recent times, some high-risk versions of split-capital trusts have appeared, which rely on complicated arrangements for borrowing and/or investing in the shares of other split-capital trusts. If you are not happy taking high risks, you should avoid these types of trust. To help you assess the risks, the Association of Investment Trust Companies (AITC)★ has started to publish information about trusts' investment in other trusts. As with all share-based investments, you stand a good chance of keeping pace with or beating inflation over the long term. Risk rating: from six or seven upwards.

More information The AITC★ produces a number of useful explanatory booklets and a directory of investment trust companies. Price and performance details of investment trusts are included in quality daily newspapers and various personal finance magazines, such as *Money Management*.★ Articles in *Which?*★ and the personal finance pages of newspapers are also useful sources of information. Like all quoted companies, investment trusts must produce an annual report and accounts; you can get these direct from the trust management company or, for example, through the *Financial Times*★ service to readers. You can also get advice from stockbrokers offering a traditional dealing and advice service. Useful websites include Trust Net and, for split-capital investment trusts, Splits Online (see Appendix III).

How to invest Through a stockbroker (see page 359) or, if there is one, through a savings scheme run by the investment trust management company: contact the company directly (details from the AITC★ directory). Some fund supermarkets (see Appendix III) offer investment trusts as well as unit trusts and OEICs.

Individual savings accounts (ISAs)

What they are ISAs are not themselves investments. They are a tax-free wrapper which you can use to invest in a very wide range of underlying investments. The ISA must be run by an account manager which can be the provider offering the underlying investment or a third party, such as a stockbroker.

There are two types of ISA ('mini-ISAs' and 'maxi-ISAs') and three different 'components' corresponding to different types of investment:

- **cash component** This is invested in deposits, such as bank, building society and National Savings accounts.
- **insurance component** This covers investment-type insurance plans.
- **stocks and shares component** This includes shares, unit trusts, open-ended investment companies, investment trusts, corporate bonds, futures and options, gilts, and so on. The investments must have at least five years of life left when they are first included in the ISA.

A mini-ISA invests in just one of the above components. A maxi-ISA must have a stocks and shares component and can also include either one or both of the other two components. In any one tax year, you choose whether to invest in up to three mini-ISAs (one of each type) or in a single maxi-ISA.

In addition, you can have a TESSA-only ISA which accepts reinvested capital from a maturing tax-efficient special savings account (TESSA) – see page 311. You must be aged at least 18 to take out most ISAs, but you can start cash ISAs from 16 onwards.

At any time in the tax year, you can have just one manager for your maxi-ISA or just one manager each for your mini-ISAs. But you can switch from your current manager to a different one. And you can choose different managers for the ISAs you take out in subsequent tax years.

Some ISAs are 'CAT-marked' which means they meet government standards regarding Charges, Access and Terms. The CAT mark tells you that the account offers a fair deal – the following table sets out the main requirements for a CAT-marked insurance or stocks and shares ISA. (See Chapter 15 for cash ISA CAT standards.) ISAs which do not meet the CAT standards are not necessarily bad products, they are just different – for example, they might have higher charges but offer a wider range of investment choices in return.

Probably from April 2005, the CAT-standard for insurance ISAs is due to be withdrawn and the CAT-standard for stocks-and-shares will be altered and apply only to a new 'stakeholder medium-term product'. For more about stakeholder products, see Chapter 14. These changes affect only the CAT standards. Non-CAT standard stocks-and-shares ISAs and insurance ISAs will still be available as now.

CAT standards for ISAs*

Standard	Main requirements
Insurance ISA	
Cost	Annual charge up to 3%; no other charges
Access	Minimum investment no more than £250 a year or £25 a month
Terms	Surrender value to reflect value of underlying investments; by the third year, surrender value must at least match premiums paid in
Stocks & shares ISA	
Cost	Annual charge up to 1% of fund; no other charges
Access	Minimum investment no more than £500 a year as a lump sum or £50 a month
Terms	Unit trusts, etc: at least 50% of underlying investment in UK and/or other EU stocks and shares; units and shares must have single price (i.e. no bid–offer spread); level of risk must be made clear in account literature

* See page 310 for CAT standards for cash ISAs.

Minimum investment None for tax purposes, but providers might set their own minimum. To qualify for CAT status, the minimum must be no more than the limits shown in the table overleaf.

Maximum investment Up to 2005–6, you can invest a maximum of £7,000 a year in ISAs. In subsequent tax years, you can invest up to £5,000. Any unused allowance in one year cannot be carried forward.

If you opt for one or more mini-ISAs, the maximum you can invest in each component is: cash, £3,000 in each tax year up to 2005–6, and £1,000 in subsequent years; insurance, £1,000 a year; stocks and shares, £3,000 a year.

If, instead, you choose a maxi-ISA, you can invest up to the full £7,000 in the tax years up to 2005–6 (£5,000 in later years) in stocks and shares. Anything you invest in the other two components reduces the amount left to invest in stocks and shares. The maximum you can invest in cash is £3,000 up to 2005–6, and £1,000 in subsequent years. The maximum for the insurance component is £1,000 a year.

If you want to invest the maximum possible in stocks and shares, you should choose a maxi-ISA.

The limits apply to the amount you pay into your ISAs regardless of any withdrawals made during the same tax year. For example, if you invest the full £7,000 in a stocks and shares ISA in 2003–4 but withdraw £1,000 of this before the end of the tax year, you are left with only £6,000 in the ISA. But this does not mean you can invest a further £1,000 in the ISA – you continue to be treated as having used up your full annual allowance.

Type of return As for the underlying investments.

Tax treatment Until 5 April 2004, the whole return is tax-free. After that date, the account manager will no longer be able to reclaim the tax credit on share dividends and distributions from unit trusts and OEICs. Other income and capital gains will continue to be tax-free.

Charges Expect to pay the normal charges for the underlying investments. Check whether your ISA manager adds on any extra costs. To meet the CAT standards, costs must be no more than the limits given in the table on page 377.

Risk In general, as for the underlying investments. However, within your ISA you could build a mixed portfolio of trusts and shares, say, giving you a more tailored exposure to risk.

Warning

If you want to invest more than £3,000 in stocks and shares in any tax year through an ISA, you must choose a maxi-ISA. Bear in mind that if you have already taken out a mini-cash ISA for the year, you will not be eligible to take out a maxi-ISA.

How much you can invest within ISAs each year

ISA component	If you invest in one, two or three mini-ISAs		If you invest in a single maxi-ISA	
	Up to 2005–6	2006–7 onwards	Up to 2005–6	2006–7 onwards
Cash	£3,000	£1,000	£3,000	£1,000
Insurance	£1,000	£1,000	£1,000	£1,000
Stocks and shares	£3,000	£3,000	£7,000*	£5,000*
Overall maximum for all components	£7,000	£5,000	£7,000	£5,000

*Reduced by any amount invested in the cash and/or insurance components.

Tip

If you are interested in investing in unit and/or investment trusts, it usually makes sense to use your annual ISA allowance. If you are interested in investing in shares, you need to weigh ISA charges and any restrictions on the shares you can choose against the tax advantages.

More information The Investment Management Association (IMA)★ and the Association of Investment Trust Companies (AITC)★ can tell you which members offer ISAs. The Association of Private Client Investment Managers and Stockbrokers (APCIMS)★ can do the same. Many personal finance websites, such as MoneyeXtra and fund supermarkets (see Appendix III) give details of the ISAs available. Personal finance magazines and the personal finance sections of newspapers run regular articles about ISAs. See Inland Revenue★ leaflet IR2008 *ISAs, PEPs and TESSAs*.
How to invest As for the underlying investments. Note that many fund supermarkets (see Appendix III) let you mix and match investment funds from a variety of providers within a single ISA.

Personal equity plans (PEPs)

What they are A PEP is not itself an investment, but it is a tax-efficient method of investing in a range of qualifying assets. From

April 1999, PEPs were replaced by individual savings accounts (ISAs). From that date, you can no longer newly invest in PEPs. However, existing PEPs can continue and you can switch your investment from one PEP manager to another.

There were originally two types of PEP: general PEPs and single-company PEPs. However, from 6 April 2001 onwards, the distinction was dropped. You can now merge your single-company and general PEPs if you want to and the investments eligible for the PEP wrapper have been brought into line with those eligible for ISAs (see page 376).

Minimum investment You can no longer newly invest in PEPs.

Maximum investment You can no longer newly invest in PEPs.

Type of return As for the underlying investments.

Tax treatment Income and gains from investments held in a PEP are both completely tax-free. However, from 6 April 2004, income from shares held in a PEP will become taxable and your PEP manager will no longer be able to reclaim the tax already deducted from dividends (see page 356).

Charges Expect to incur the normal charges for the underlying investment. Charges for the PEP itself vary considerably, depending on the investments you choose and the PEP manager, which could be a unit or investment trust management company, a bank, a building society, a stockbroker, an independent financial adviser, a specialist PEP manager, and so on. Unit trust managers often make no extra charges at all (over and above the normal charges for the unit trust) if you use a PEP. By contrast, a PEP invested in your own selection of shares and managed by a stockbroker could be fairly costly.

Risk In general, as for the underlying investments. However, within your PEP you could build a mixed portfolio of trusts and shares, say, giving you a more tailored exposure to risk.

More information The directory of unit trust management companies published by the Investment Management Association (IMA)★ indicates those that offer PEPs. The directory of the Association of Investment Trust Companies (AITC)★ does the same for its members. Similarly, the directory of members of the Association of Private Client Investment Managers and Stockbrokers (APCIMS)★ includes details of those who offer a PEP service. *Which?*,★ personal finance magazines and the personal finance sections of newspapers run occasional articles about PEPs –

see, for example, *Money Management.★* For a listing of PEP details and performance, see *Moneyfacts Life & Pensions★* (which also covers unit and investment trust PEPs). See Inland Revenue★ leaflet IR2008 *ISAs, PEPs and TESSAs.*

How to invest As for the underlying investments.

Other investments

Buy-to-let property

What it is Buying residential property, not to live in yourself, but to let out in order to earn rental income. Most people do not have enough spare capital to buy a second or subsequent property outright, but in recent years it has become fashionable to take out a mortgage to buy such property. It is important to choose properties that are likely to attract a strong supply of tenants – for example, in a university town or large urban area with good employment opportunities.

Minimum investment No specific minimum, but usually the maximum mortgage is 60 to 85 per cent of the property's value, so you will need to find a sizeable chunk of the purchase price yourself.

Maximum investment None

Type of return Provided the rental income exceeds any mortgage payments and other charges, this can be a source of income. In addition you may make a capital gain from any rise in property prices.

Tax treatment Income is taxable – broadly, you are treated as if you are running a business and you can deduct all business-related expenses when working out your profits. A gain when you sell the property could be subject to capital gains tax but you can claim various allowances (see page 83).

Charges Cost of the mortgage (see Chapter 9): the interest rate for buy-to-let mortgages is generally slightly higher than on a mortgage to buy your own home. Costs associated with being a landlord: for example, maintenance and repairs. Cost of an agent if you pay one to look after the property and to find tenants.

Risk A portfolio of many properties would generally be a medium-risk investment – historically, residential properties have produced higher returns than gilts or equities with less variation in the returns (in other words, less risk). However, ready-made portfolios of residential property are not generally available to private investors (although they can invest in property unit trusts and investment trusts which are invested in commercial properties such as offices and shops). Investing in a single property carries a much higher risk. You might pick a property that you find is hard to rent out – perhaps because of its condition or the area it is in. The economic or social climate of the area might change, damaging your rental prospects. You might get a difficult tenant and incur substantial legal costs enforcing the terms of the lease or removing them. And house prices might have fallen at the time you want to sell. Worse still, you might not be able to find a buyer and so be unable to cash in your investment when you want to. Taking out a mortgage to buy a rental property is a form of gearing. It has the effect of magnifying both any profits you make and also any losses. In other words, borrowing increases the risks you are taking. Risk rating: varies from, say, seven upwards.

More information To find out about suitable properties, consult estate agents. For information about buy-to-let mortgages, contact lenders direct or check the summary tables in *Moneyfacts.*★ Occasional articles are published in magazines such as *Which?*★ and *Money Management.*★ For guidance on the tax position, see Inland Revenue★ leaflets IR150 *Taxation of rents – a guide to property income* and CGT1 *Capital gains tax – an introduction.*

How to invest Purchase properties through estate agents. Many lenders currently offer buy-to-let mortgages – contact them direct or use a mortgage broker.

Summary of higher-risk investments

Investment	Minimum period for which you should aim to invest	Type of return	Risk rating
Direct investment in shares			
Ordinary shares – direct investment	No set period, but generally at least 5 years	Variable income and/or growth, taxable	7 and above
ISAs investing direct in shares and single-company PEPs	No set period, but generally at least 5 years	Variable income and/or growth, tax-free★	7 and above

Summary of higher-risk investments *(contd)*

Investment	Minimum period for which you should aim to invest	Type of return	Risk rating
Pooled investments			
Unit-linked life insurance – regular-premium plans	Usually at least 10 years	Growth, effectively taxed at equivalent of basic-rate income tax	6 and above (but 3 for deposit-based funds)
Unit-linked life insurance – single-premium plans	Varies	Growth, but you can use partial withdrawals for income, effectively taxed at equivalent of basic-rate income tax	6 and above (but 3 for deposit-based funds)
Unit-linked friendly society tax-exempt plans	Set period, often 10 years or more	Growth, tax-free*	6 and above (but 3 for deposit-based funds)
Unit trusts, OEICs and exchange traded funds (ETFs)	No set period, but generally at least 5 years	Income, taxed; growth, taxable; or just growth	6 and above
Investment trusts	No set period, but generally at least 5 years	Income, taxed; growth, taxable; or just growth; or just income	6/7 and above
Investment trust 'zeros'	Up to ten years	Growth, taxable	About 5 (but some may be higher)
Share-based ISAs and PEPs	No set period, but generally at least 5 years	As for underlying investment; tax free*	6 and above
Buy-to-let property	No set period	Income, taxable; growth, taxable	7 and above

* Except dividends and similar income due to become taxable at 10 per cent from 6 April 2004 onwards

Chapter 18

Meeting your investment targets

The preceding chapters have described the array of savings and investment tools available, but which should you match to your own particular needs? Since targets are as varied and individual as people themselves, there is no simple answer. Chapter 14 looked at which investments you might use to meet broad investment and savings targets, such as growth or income either immediately or in the future. This chapter gives some guidance towards meeting a few of the most common specific financial targets.

An emergency fund

The most fundamental step in financial planning is ensuring that you have some cushion to fall back on in an emergency. This is not simply crisis management – mending a leaking roof, sudden car repairs, bailing out children stuck abroad penniless. It can also be an 'opportunist fund', letting you take advantage of special offers and events that arise unexpectedly.

Two decisions should be made about your emergency fund:

- How much do you need?
- Where should you keep it?

How much?

This depends crucially on your own circumstances, lifestyle, the type of emergencies you might have to cope with, and so on. If you are self-employed, for example, you might need quite a large buffer to cover short-term falls in receipts or a brief period of illness not covered by your income protection insurance (see Chapter 6).

Worse still, if your income would not be protected at all in the event of illness, you may be concerned to build up a sizeable emergency fund, though you should weigh up whether it would be better to divert some of those funds into appropriate insurance. If you have a large family, the probability of a crisis arising may be higher simply because, with more people involved, there's more risk of something going wrong. If you live in an older property, there may be a higher risk of unforeseen repairs being needed. You will have to examine your own situation and decide what size of emergency cushion feels right for you. Whatever you decide now should be reviewed periodically as your circumstances change: for example, if unemployment threatens, you may want to build up extra reserves, or as your children become independent, a smaller buffer may be enough. As a very rough guide, for most people an emergency fund of £1,000–£5,000 would probably be adequate.

Where to keep your fund

Conventional wisdom is that an emergency fund should be kept where you have instant access to it in times of need. Of course, you could meet that requirement by simply stuffing fivers under the mattress, but an emergency fund has other features too:

- It should be kept in a secure place. There should be no risk at all of losing the money put into your fund. At one level, this means that you shouldn't store it at home where it would be vulnerable to theft. At another, it means that you shouldn't invest it in assets whose value can rise and fall.
- Ideally, the money should not be idle. It should be earning you some return.

The best place for an emergency fund is in some form of deposit account run either by a building society, bank or National Savings & Investments (NS&I) (see Chapter 15). An instant access account is an obvious choice, and you might consider accounts which let you make withdrawals through cash machines so that you can cope with emergencies outside banking hours. Postal, phone-based and Internet accounts often offer the best rates of interest.

If you have instant access to credit – for example, you have a high spending limit on your credit card which you usually do not fully use – you could consider putting at least part of your emergency fund in an account which requires some short period of notice (up to a month, say) if, in exchange, you will get a better rate of interest.

> **Tip**
> You do not need *instant* access to an emergency fund if you can rely on credit in an emergency. This may allow you to invest for a better return.

Similarly, although £1,000–£5,000 might be enough as an emergency fund, you might consider adding it to other lower-risk savings if this would give you a large enough lump sum to cross an interest-rate threshold on a tiered account and so earn a better return.

If you do not need your whole ISA allowance for investing in share-based investments, it makes sense to put your emergency fund within a mini-cash ISA wrapper – that way, the interest it earns will be tax-free. You may need to do this gradually over two or three years, if your fund is larger than the annual ISA allowance. See pages 310 and 376 for information about ISAs.

If you have a mortgage, you might instead consider an all-in-one mortgage account as a possible home for your emergency fund – see page 305. The 'return' will generally be considerably higher than you could get on an instant access account and should also beat notice accounts.

The chart opposite summarises your choices for an emergency fund.

Investing for children

There are two main reasons for considering children's investments. The first is to help the child to understand how to value and use money; the second is to build up a nest egg for the child to use in later life. The chart on page 390 summarises the most useful options.

Learning about money

It's hard to beat a building society or bank account for teaching children to handle money sensibly. Essential features are an accessible

Choosing a home for your emergency fund

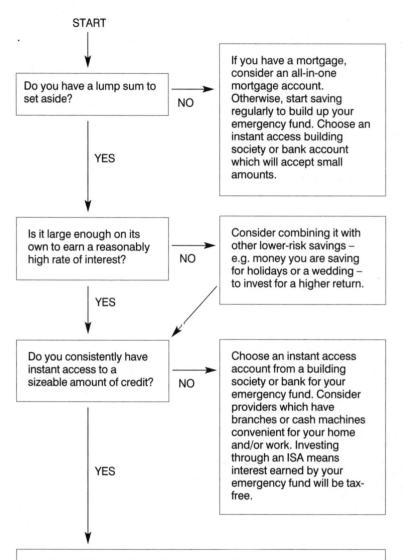

START

Do you have a lump sum to set aside?

NO → If you have a mortgage, consider an all-in-one mortgage account. Otherwise, start saving regularly to build up your emergency fund. Choose an instant access building society or bank account which will accept small amounts.

YES

Is it large enough on its own to earn a reasonably high rate of interest?

NO → Consider combining it with other lower-risk savings – e.g. money you are saving for holidays or a wedding – to invest for a higher return.

YES

Do you consistently have instant access to a sizeable amount of credit?

NO → Choose an instant access account from a building society or bank for your emergency fund. Consider providers which have branches or cash machines convenient for your home and/or work. Investing through an ISA means interest earned by your emergency fund will be tax-free.

YES

Consider relying on the credit for an immediate response to an emergency. Pay off the credit by drawing on an emergency fund invested for higher interest, for example in a notice account (with a notice period of up to one month) at a building society or bank or the National Savings investment account. Investing through an ISA means interest earned by your emergency fund will be tax-free.

branch, a low minimum balance, instant access and tolerant counter staff who don't mind counting a box full of change. Many banks and building societies have accounts especially aimed at children, often including free gifts, such as piggy-banks, magazines and birthday cards, but the interest offered is often pitifully low (though, if you are lucky, a small local society may offer better returns). Once your child reaches 11 or so, consider an account with a cash card (particularly useful as school-bound children may find it hard to visit a branch). From age 14 or so, a few accounts include a debit card which can be a good introduction to using plastic in shops or online. For the child's own larger sums, such as birthday money, consider too the NS&I investment account (see page 315).

Providing a nest egg

Parents giving, or building up, relatively large sums for their offspring (more than £2,000–£3,000, say) need to watch the tax rules. Even a child has a personal allowance to set against income tax – £4,615 in 2003–4. This means that most children are non-taxpayers (so make sure they receive income *gross*, that is, without tax deducted). A child can also make capital gains (over and above reliefs) of up to £7,900 in 2003–4 tax-free. However, to prevent tax avoidance, if you give money or an asset to your own child, any income it produces during a tax year counts as *your* income, not the child's, and is taxed at your top rate. This rule is waived if the total before-tax income from all sources produced by all gifts from a parent comes to no more than £100 during the tax year. This means that a child could receive up to £200 without problem if both parents made gifts. If the income exceeds that limit, then all of it (not just the excess) is taxed as your own. To avoid falling foul of these rules, choose investments for your child which produce a tax-free return or capital gains rather than income. Income produced by gifts from people other than parents counts as the child's own.

Tip
You may need to give the Inland Revenue proof that a gift to your child was not from you, so ask grandparents, godparents etc. to send a letter with money or investments they give your child.

Note that, even though the return from ISAs is tax-free, the gross income from a cash ISA taken out by someone under age 18 still counts as income of the parent if the ISA investment was the result of a gift from the parent and the £100 limit is breached.

To build up a nest egg to help a child in later years, longer-term investments offer the best prospect. As always, the particular choice of investment depends partly on the degree of risk you're willing to take. At the lowest end of the risk spectrum is the NS&I children's bonus bond (see page 320). As this offers a tax-free return, it is suitable as a gift from a parent.

A medium- to higher-risk product aimed specifically at children is the the so-called 'baby bond' (see page 340). These are variants of the tax-free insurance policies offered by friendly societies. They are useful for parents investing for children because there's no tax on the eventual payout. But what makes them special is that, unlike other insurance policies, there's also no tax on the fund in which the premiums are invested (except dividend and similar income is due to become taxable at 10 per cent from 6 April 2004 onwards). Premiums are invested on either a with-profits or a unit-linked basis. Unit-linking is more risky than with-profits because investment values may have taken a tumble at the time your child wants to cash in. Over the long term, a unit-linked bond should tend to outperform a with-profits one.

In theory, the baby bonds' tax-free status should ensure very competitive returns, but charges have a big impact on the value of the bonds, because the government limits each person's investment in them to a very low maximum (see page 338). If you are comfortable with the risk of a share-based investment for your child, you could do better by looking at unit trusts and investment trusts (see Chapter 17). Ideal for children's investments are the savings schemes run by many unit and investment trust managers. Some accept investments as low as £20 a month on a regular basis, and *ad hoc* lump sums from £200.

A popular gift for children is NS&I premium bonds (see page 322). Strictly speaking, these are not investments, although if the holding is big enough and the child has average luck, the 'return' can compare reasonably with middle-of-the-road bank and building society rates and, of course, there's always that outside chance of making a million. Children aged 16 or over can buy premium bonds

Investing for children

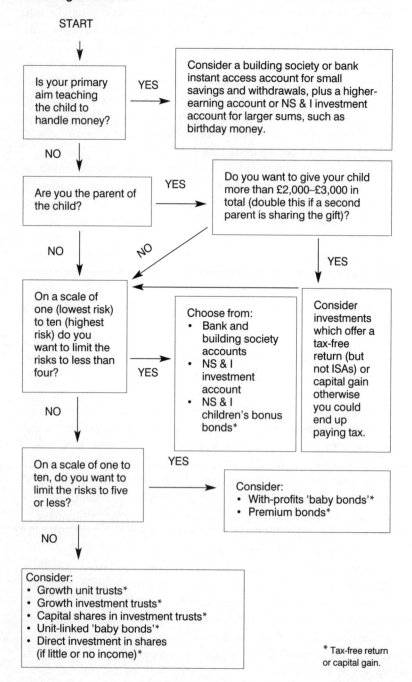

START

Is your primary aim teaching the child to handle money? → **YES** → Consider a building society or bank instant access account for small savings and withdrawals, plus a higher-earning account or NS & I investment account for larger sums, such as birthday money.

NO ↓

Are you the parent of the child? → **YES** → Do you want to give your child more than £2,000–£3,000 in total (double this if a second parent is sharing the gift)?

NO ↓   **NO** ↙   **YES** ↓ → Consider investments which offer a tax-free return (but not ISAs) or capital gain otherwise you could end up paying tax.

On a scale of one (lowest risk) to ten (highest risk) do you want to limit the risks to less than four? → **YES** → Choose from:
- Bank and building society accounts
- NS & I investment account
- NS & I children's bonus bonds*

NO ↓

On a scale of one to ten, do you want to limit the risks to five or less? → **YES** → Consider:
- With-profits 'baby bonds'*
- Premium bonds*

NO ↓

Consider:
- Growth unit trusts*
- Growth investment trusts*
- Capital shares in investment trusts*
- Unit-linked 'baby bonds'*
- Direct investment in shares (if little or no income)*

* Tax-free return or capital gain.

themselves. Otherwise, only parents, grandparents, great grand-parents and guardians can buy bonds for a child. Anyone else would need to give cash to, say, the parent who could then make the purchase in the name of the child.

Paying for school education

Figures from the Independent Schools Council Information Service (ISCis) show the number of both boarding and day pupils at private schools is on the increase. This is despite the high cost of private schooling. 'First-timers' – parents who didn't themselves go to private school – account for four out of ten parents choosing private schooling for their children. A survey of parents for ISCis found that many of the top reasons for choosing private education were non-academic and were to do with encouraging respect for other pupils and adults, fostering independence, pastoral care and firm discipline. But teaching in small classes and making full use of information technology were also important.

Sending your son or daughter to a private school is not an easy decision, with even the cheapest charging around £1,000 a term for day pupils. Sending a child to the most prestigious boarding-schools can cost over £20,000 a year for each child. There are basically three ways in which you can cope with school fees:

- Borrow now, for example by extending your mortgage, and pay off the loan over a number of years. Bear in mind that you could lose your home if you were unable to keep up the mortgage payments.
- Pay-as-you-go out of your current income or savings (maybe an inheritance). This could mean cutting other spending and/or taking on extra work. However, according to ISCis, nearly one-third of pupils receive some financial help from their school through scholarships, bursaries and so on. (Help for new pupils from the state, through the assisted places scheme, was abolished in 1998.) Some local authorities and charities can also help. Check with individual schools to find out what may be available.
- Plan ahead and start saving before your child gets to the entry age for the level of schooling you're interested in. The ISCis survey found that fewer than one-third of parents choosing private schooling plan ahead.

The last course offers several options for saving. If you have already chosen a particular school, contact the bursar to find out whether the school runs its own prepayment scheme, which is often called a 'composition fee scheme'. Such a scheme has an advantage, because your savings are paid into a charitable trust where they build up tax-free until needed. But check what happens if you want to change your choice of school.

A few insurance companies used to operate educational trusts which also had tax-free status and didn't commit you to a particular school. But the tax perks were removed from these schemes from April 1997 onwards, so your choice is now limited to the standard range of investments for providing an income in the future. The methods described below are suitable not only for school fees but also if you want to build up a sum to help your child through university – an increasingly important task for parents as student grants have now been abolished and tuition is no longer free.

Given the increase in school fees over the years, you are unlikely to build up an adequate sum using the lower-risk investments described in Chapter 15. But if you have only a few years until your child starts school, you would be unwise to choose higher-risk investments, so try to build up what you can using deposit-based investments. If there are fewer than five years to go until your child starts school, you might consider using a cash ISA, which at least gives you the advantage of tax-free growth. You can withdraw your money at any time without losing the tax advantage, but check whether the ISA provider makes any penalties.

Assuming you have a reasonable time to plan ahead (at least five years, say), you really should consider medium- and higher-risk investments. In the past, if you could save for at least ten years, advisers often promoted special school fee savings plans based on endowment insurance (see page 340). Three particular advantages are often cited:

- you pay in regular premiums – a useful discipline if you find it hard to save
- built-in life cover ensures that your child's schooling plans need not be upset if you were to die
- with-profits plans provide a middle course between deposit-based investments and higher-risk share-based investments, which is useful for people who want to limit their risks.

Providing for your child's school education

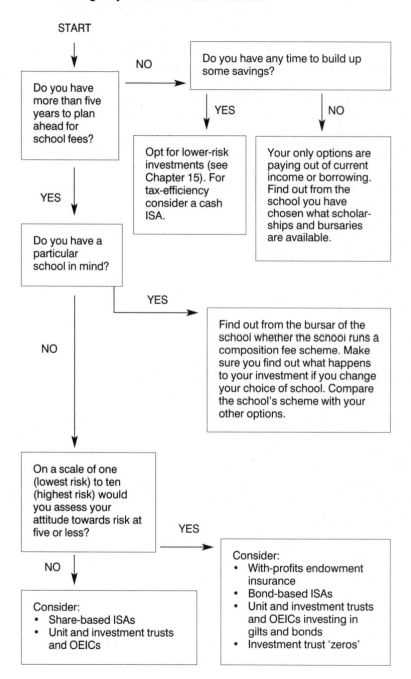

START

Do you have more than five years to plan ahead for school fees?

NO → Do you have any time to build up some savings?

YES → Opt for lower-risk investments (see Chapter 15). For tax-efficiency consider a cash ISA.

NO → Your only options are paying out of current income or borrowing. Find out from the school you have chosen what scholar-ships and bursaries are available.

YES

Do you have a particular school in mind?

YES → Find out from the bursar of the school whether the school runs a composition fee scheme. Make sure you find out what happens to your investment if you change your choice of school. Compare the school's scheme with your other options.

NO

On a scale of one (lowest risk) to ten (highest risk) would you assess your attitude towards risk at five or less?

YES → Consider:
• With-profits endowment insurance
• Bond-based ISAs
• Unit and investment trusts and OEICs investing in gilts and bonds
• Investment trust 'zeros'

NO

Consider:
• Share-based ISAs
• Unit and investment trusts and OEICs

But unit and investment trusts provide a more flexible and cost-efficient alternative and, if you invest via an ISA (see page 376), you get a largely tax-free return (previously completely tax-free but, from April 2004 onwards, dividends within an ISA are due to become taxable at 10 per cent). Admittedly, you do need more discipline to keep up a pattern of regular savings. And there is no built-in life cover, so you should take into account your commitment to paying school fees when assessing your overall life cover needs (see Chapter 5). If you prefer to avoid the risks of share-linked investments, bond-based trusts are possible alternatives to with-profits policies. But there is no reason why you should use a single investment tool to build up the fund you need. Choosing a combination of, say, unit trust ISAs and with-profits insurance might give you a good mixture of savings discipline, risk and tax-efficiency. For more information about bursaries and scholarships, see *The Which? Guide to Choosing a School*, available from Which? Books.*

If you have PEPs and TESSAs started before April 1999, you may be able to earmark these to cover education costs, if they are not already needed for another financial target.

The chart on page 393 summarises the main ways of providing for your child's school education.

Paying for your child's university education

The National Union of Students (NUS) estimates that, in 2002–3, it cost £8,400 a year to be a student in London and £7,317 a year outside London (living away from home). And these figures are set to rise if increased tuition fees come into effect from 2006. Parents are not expected to pay all of this and, from 2006, might not be required to pay anything towards these costs. However many parents would like to help their children through this stage so that they can start their working life without large student debts hanging over them.

Your options are very much the same as those described above for financing your child's school education. Namely, you could borrow, pay-as-you-go out of your income, plan ahead by building up some savings, or a combination of these options. If you decide to save, the types of investment that are suitable are the same as those suggested in the chart on page 393.

However, there is one other point worth bearing in mind. Although you may not want your child to run up large debts, student loans are in fact a very cheap way of borrowing. The amount that must be repaid increases in line with price inflation (running at around 2.5 to 3 per cent at the time of writing) but there is no other interest added. So it may be worth encouraging your child to take out the maximum available student loans. This allows you to keep some of your savings invested while your child is at university. Provided the savings grow faster than inflation (i.e. the effective cost of the student loans), this will be a better use of your finances. You can then use the sum built up to pay off the student loans when your son or daughter graduates.

An even more efficient strategy might be to leave your graduate son or daughter to pay off the student loan over a longer period and instead use the savings you've built up to help them, say, buy a home. This would reduce the amount of mortgage required. Since a mortgage is likely to be more expensive than a student loan, this strategy minimises the overall cost of your son's or daughter's borrowing.

For more details about student loans, tuition fees and what parents may be required to contribution towards university costs, see *The Which? guide to financing your child's future* available from Which? Books★. For an outline of how the system may change from 2006, see the Department for Education and Skills (DFES)★ booklet *The future of higher education. What it means to students and parents.*

Saving for further education

Duncan and Sheena are both teachers in their mid-thirties. Since the birth of their daughter, Poppy, last year, Duncan has gone part time but Sheena still works full-time. Poppy's arrival has changed their circumstances dramatically and they need to review their finances. One of their longer term goals is to build up a fund for Poppy's further education.

They have enough savings to cover their short- and medium-term goals. In particular, their emergency funds (in mini cash ISAs) are pretty high. They should start a stocks and shares ISA via a unit trust, for example. This would allow them to invest tax-free, which is important as Sheena is nearly a higher-rate taxpayer. It would be a good way to save for Poppy's further education. As they have a fairly cautious attitude towards risk, Sheena and Duncan should choose a low-risk investment fund.

Which? August 2001

> **Warning**
> Higher returns always go hand in hand with higher risks. If a deal looks too good to be true, it almost certainly is.

Boosting your retirement income

This is the holy grail of many pensioners and the target which seems most consistently to trigger cases of fraud and abuse among financial organisations. There is one basic lesson which you should never ignore: you cannot have an exceptionally high income without some risk to your capital. If you are offered a deal which promises high income from safe investments, be on your guard, take nothing at face value, ask questions, check documents and, ten to one, you'll find the deal is flawed. Don't touch it with a barge-pole, and report the providers to the main financial regulator, the Financial Services Authority (FSA),* or to the police if you suspect a fraud.

Chapter 14 examined the main ways in which you can produce an income by using a lump sum, and the chart on page 292 gives some guidance on choosing investments according to how much risk you are comfortable about taking. Understandably, many pensioners are very cautious about risk – after all, money lost at this stage of life generally cannot be replaced. However, if you stick exclusively with deposit-type investments, the value of your savings can be badly eroded by inflation as retirement progresses; ultimately, this means that the value of the income they produce will be a lot less too. You need to strike a balance between income, security and capital growth. No one single investment will meet all these aims. Instead, you need to consider a portfolio of investments which will sustain your income over a long period, while giving you partial protection against the full array of risks.

The investments in your portfolio, and their mixture, is a matter of personal choice, but will probably include some from each of the lower-risk, medium-risk and higher-risk investments described in Chapters 15–17. So, for example, you might have a third of your money invested in monthly income building society accounts, cash ISAs and NS&I pensioners' bonds; a third in gilts, bond-based ISAs and insurance company guaranteed growth bonds; and a third in a range of unit trusts and share-based ISAs. The balance of the portfolio should shift as investment conditions alter: for example, with less in unit trusts if the stock market seems likely to fall, more in deposits if interest rates are high. If inflation is a particular concern, index-linked NS&I certificates and index-linked gilts would play a part in the portfolio too.

In addition to this general portfolio building, you could consider using an equity release scheme.

Equity release schemes

How can you increase your income if you do not have a lump sum to spare? Many elderly people are 'cash poor, asset rich', having capital tied up, particularly in the home in which they live. Equity release schemes (also known as home income plans or HIPs) let you release some of that capital and convert it into income. There are two basic types of scheme:

- **mortgage-based plans** (sometimes called 'lifetime mortgages') You take out an interest-only mortgage on your home (generally on up to 75 per cent of its value) and use the proceeds to buy an annuity which pays you a set income after the mortgage interest payments have been automatically deducted. The loan is eventually repaid out of your estate after your death (or the death of both you and your husband, wife or partner), or out of the proceeds of selling the home if you move before then. Essential features making these plans safe are that the mortgage rate is *fixed*, the interest is paid as you go along (and *not* added to the outstanding loan), and the income is set and payable for life (so you're *not* relying on stock-market performance).
- **reversion schemes** Instead of taking out a mortgage, you actually sell part or all of your home to the scheme provider, but have the guaranteed right to carry on living in it, and use the proceeds to buy an annuity or to invest in other income-producing investments. The scheme offers some variations: the income you get could be fixed or, in the case of at least one provider, part or all of the income can depend on changes in property prices.

There are a number of variations on the theme, some of which gave equity release schemes a bad name in the late 1980s. The very worst combined two high-risk products: the mortgage allowed you to

Balancing fun and security

Fact find: Jennifer is 61 and retired. She is single and has no dependants. She likes to travel and her main concern is to strike a sensible balance between enjoying her retirement to the full now and ensuring that she is financially secure in her later years. In view of this, she wonders whether the mix of her investments is appropriate.

Jennifer paid into her pension scheme for 28 years and gets a pension of £11,500 a year. This is increased annually in line with inflation up to a maximum of 10 per cent a year. She also receives a state pension of about £4,000 a year which is fully inflation-proofed, and a further £4,000 or so a year from a range of income-oriented investments.

With various other sources of income, including some freelance work, Jennifer has a total before-tax income of £22,000 a year. After tax, she is left with £19,000. This comfortably covers her spending, the largest item of which is £9,600 a year on holidays and weekends away.

Jennifer owns her own home outright. She has savings and investments worth roughly £160,000. Of this, £65,000 is in relatively low-risk deposit-type investments. These comprise eight accounts and bonds with various banks and building societies and four National Savings investments. She also has a TESSA.

A further £79,500 is invested in equities. She has ten share-based unit and investment trusts, some of which are held through PEPs, plus some Abbey National shares. Jennifer also has £10,000 invested in a guaranteed income bond and £6,000 in a corporate bond PEP.

Several of her investments are due to mature shortly and she needs to decide how to reinvest the proceeds.

Tip

If you are interested in taking out an equity release scheme, consider providers who are members of Safe Home Income Plans (SHIP).* Always take advice from your own solicitor before taking out the plan.

Financial plan: Some of Jennifer's deposits will have served her well in the past when interest rates were high. But the economy has moved into a different cycle. She should reduce the amount deposited in savings accounts to between £20,000 and £30,000. She should consolidate this in one or two accounts that pay above-average rates and allow ready access.

To ensure that the value of her income is maintained in future, she needs to invest for reasonable capital growth over the long term – equities give her the best chance of doing this. But to achieve a sensible spread of risk, Jennifer should choose medium-risk investments with the emphasis on providing income. She should put the money which had been on deposit into medium-risk unit and investment trusts which invest in UK corporate bonds, global bonds and/or the UK fixed-income sector. These trusts will provide income with some capital growth. They will spread risk, helping to protect Jennifer's assets if there is a downturn in the stock market. She should make full use of her yearly ISA allowances.

She should not reinvest the National Savings index-linked certificates which are about to mature – the return on the current issue is poor. Similarly, she should consider cashing in £6,000 presently invested in National Savings income bonds. Their return now looks uncompetitive and, for a taxpayer, they are inconvenient because interest is paid before tax is deducted. She should instead consider zero-dividend preference shares in investment trusts. They produce no income as such, but withdrawals of capital can be made by cashing in some of the shares at intervals. This 'income' will be tax-free provided Jennifer has unused capital gains tax allowance.

Investment Which? March 1999

defer some or all of the interest, with the interest being added to the outstanding loan; the investment gave you an income which depended on the performance of the stock market. When property prices collapsed and the stock market dipped, many planholders were left with unmanageable debts and the fear of their home being repossessed.

But there have always been perfectly sensible and sound versions of equity release schemes. In 1990 a group of companies formed

> **Warning**
>
> Beware of taking out an equity release scheme if you're getting income support, housing benefit or Council Tax benefit, as they are likely to be reduced.

Safe Home Income Plans (SHIP),* an organisation to promote the safer versions of equity release schemes.

You usually need to be aged at least 65 or 70 to be eligible for a scheme; at younger ages, the annuity rates would simply be too low to make the scheme worth while. You'll need to own your own home outright – usually a freehold house or a long leasehold house or flat (though freehold flats in Scotland might also be accepted). For reversion schemes, your home generally needs to be worth at least £40,000.

You should be aware that equity release schemes invariably give you a very poor deal compared with your other option for releasing capital – namely selling up and moving to a cheaper property. This is because the equity release company is advancing you money now that it will not get back until the scheme ends (usually on your death). The company charges you for that delay either through interest if it is a mortgage scheme or by scaling down the cash it gives you if it is a reversion scheme. For example, you might give up 80 per cent of the value of your home but in return receive a lump sum equal to only 40 per cent. But the older you are when you start a scheme the better the deal you should get.

Where you took out a mortgage-based plan before 9 March 1999, interest on the mortgage qualifies for tax relief, which, from 6 April 2000 onwards, is given at a set rate of 23 per cent on the first £30,000 of the loan. You will not lose the relief if you keep the plan going when you move home or if you switch to another mortgage lender without moving.

Schemes taken out on or after 9 March 1999 do not qualify for tax relief.

Chapter 19

Passing your money on

An integral part of financial planning as you get older is deciding what you want to happen to your wealth when you have died, and then ensuring that your wishes will actually be put into practice. But even when you are younger, you should give thought to this, especially if you have a family dependent on you. There are two aspects to your planning:

* setting out your wishes formally in a will
* ensuring that your assets do not disappear in unnecessary tax bills.

Below, we look at what happens if you don't make a will and how to go about drawing one up. On page 409, we look at the tax aspects of inheritance. Before coming to power, the Labour party was committed to reforming inheritance tax. However, by summer 2003, the Labour government had made no significant changes to the regime. This has left the position regarding inheritance tax uncertain and, while you should never rush into decisions about gifts and inheritance, there is a case for saying that well-thought-out plans should be executed sooner rather than later.

What happens if you don't make a will?

Everything you leave when you die, less anything you owe, is called your 'estate'. A will sets out what is to happen to your estate. It is a legal document which, although it can be changed after your death (see page 411), will normally be followed. A survey by NOP Research in 1998 found that only one in three adults in Great Britain has made a will. This proportion is largely unchanged since Mintel carried out an earlier survey which, in addition, found that about one-fifth of wills that have been made are out-of-date. Dying without a will (called dying 'intestate') can cause unnecessary hardship for your survivors:

- delays in trying to find out whether or not you did in fact leave a will and in tracing your possessions
- delays in the formalities required before your estate can be distributed
- your next of kin will usually be appointed to sort out your estate, and he or she might not be the best person to do the job
- the law dictates who will inherit your estate and in what proportions. The rules do not recognise unmarried partners (although a partner may be able to make a claim on your estate; see below)
- the law may require legally binding trusts to be set up. These may be unnecessarily restrictive and expensive, especially where only small sums are involved
- there may be inheritance tax on the estate which could have been avoided.

Another very important reason for making a will is so that you can say who you want to look after your children if you have a young family.

Who gets what if there is no will?

Dying intestate means that the intestacy rules state who will inherit your estate when you die. The charts on pages 404–6 show the effect of the intestacy rules on those living in England and Wales – although other people might also have a claim under the Inheritance (Provision for Family and Dependants) Act 1975: see below. For Northern Ireland and Scotland, see the box opposite.

Inheritance (Provision for Family and Dependants) Act 1975

Your dying intestate can pose particular problems for an unmarried partner, because he or she has no automatic rights under the intestacy rules. But if the partner can show that he or she lived with you as man or wife throughout the two years prior to your death, he or she can claim a share of your estate under this Act (which does not apply in Scotland, where a similar law is under consideration and might be introduced in 2003. If your partner had not been with you for the two years, he or she may still have a claim on your estate

Northern Ireland

The intestacy rules for Northern Ireland are broadly the same as those for England and Wales. But there are some important differences where you are married, have children and your estate is worth more than £125,000:

- If you have one child, your husband or wife gets half of any excess over £125,000. But, if you have two or more children, your husband or wife gets only one-third of the excess.
- Your husband or wife receives the excess over £125,000 outright rather than just a life interest.

Scotland

The rules are as follows:

- **married no children** Your husband or wife has 'prior rights' to the family home up to the value of £130,000 (or £130,000 cash if the home is worth more), furniture and household effects up to £22,000 and a cash sum up to £58,000. He or she has 'legal rights' to half the remaining 'moveable estate' (that is, excluding land and buildings). See below for the remaining estate.
- **married with children** Your husband or wife has prior rights to the family home up to the value of £130,000 (or £130,000 cash if the home is worth more), plus furniture and household effects up to £22,000 and a cash sum up to £35,000, plus legal rights to one-third of the moveable estate. The children also have legal rights to one-third of the moveable estate. See below for the remaining estate.
- **children but no husband or wife** The children have legal rights to half the moveable estate. See below for the remaining estate.
- **the remaining estate** Whatever remains after any prior and legal rights have been met passes to your survivors or relatives in the following order of priority: 1) any children or, if they have died, their children; 2) if there are no children but there are parents and/or brothers and sisters, half to the parents and half to the siblings; if a sibling has died, his or her place is taken by his or her children, if any; 3) if no parents, everything to the brothers and/or sisters; 4) if no brothers or sisters, parents take everything; 5) a surviving spouse; 6) uncles and aunts or, if they have died, their children; 7) grandparents; 8) brothers and/or sisters of grandparents or, if they have died, their children; 9) remoter ancestors. If you are survived by no family at all, the estate passes to the Crown.

Who gets what if you die intestate and you are married with no children (England & Wales)

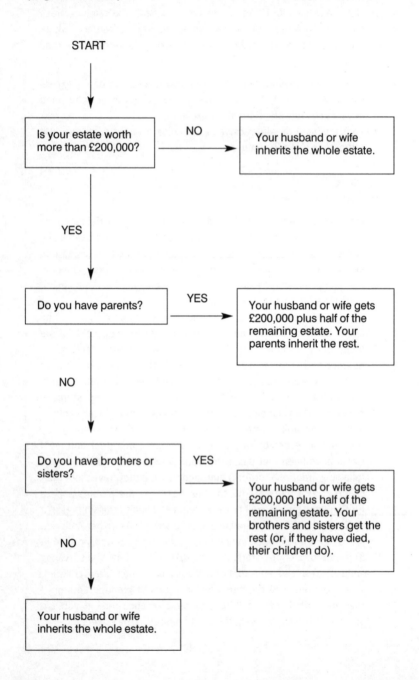

START

Is your estate worth more than £200,000?

NO → Your husband or wife inherits the whole estate.

YES

Do you have parents?

YES → Your husband or wife gets £200,000 plus half of the remaining estate. Your parents inherit the rest.

NO

Do you have brothers or sisters?

YES → Your husband or wife gets £200,000 plus half of the remaining estate. Your brothers and sisters get the rest (or, if they have died, their children do).

NO

Your husband or wife inherits the whole estate.

Who gets what if you die intestate and you have children (England & Wales)

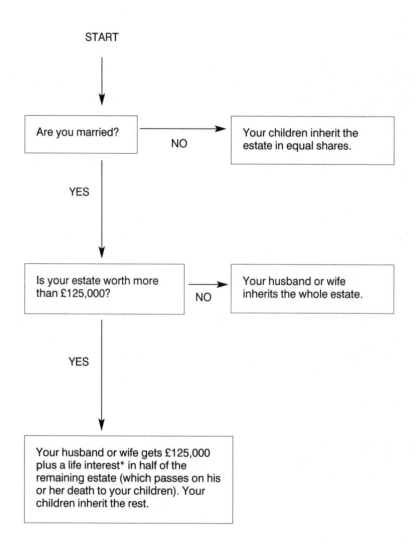

* A life interest gives you the right to the income produced by an asset or to use the asset during your lifetime, but you do not own the asset itself.

Who gets what if you die intestate and you have no close family (England & Wales)

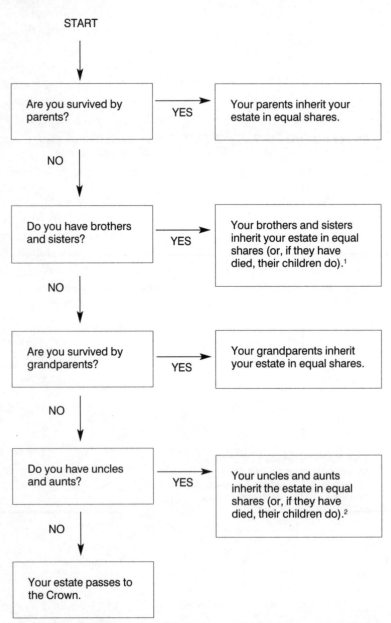

[1] If you have no full brother and sisters, any half-brothers and half-sisters inherit instead (or, if they have died, their children do).

[2] If you have no full uncles and aunts, any half-uncles and half-aunts inherit instead (or, if they have died, their children do).

by proving financial dependence on you. In either case, the claim must be made within six months of permission to distribute the estate being granted. It will then be considered by the courts. The whole procedure could take a long time, so it is much better that you make a will in the first place.

Similarly, if you write a will and use it to disinherit someone who is financially dependent on you, that person can (following your death) go to court and challenge the will. The court decides whether that person should have a share of your estate and how much this should be.

How to make a will

If your affairs are straightforward, you might consider making your own will using one of the d-i-y guides available: for example, *Make Your Will*, an action pack, published by Which? Books.* But be warned – solicitors claim they make more money out of unravelling d-i-y wills than they ever do drawing up professionally prepared ones! It is essential that the will makes your intentions absolutely clear. According to *The Guinness Book of Records*, the shortest-ever UK will simply said 'All for mother'. However, the gentleman concerned meant his wife, not his own mother. The will was contested in court (though eventually accepted), which goes to show that you need to take care over the wording of even the simplest will. Do not choose the d-i-y route if any of the following applies to you:

- your permanent home is outside England or Wales
- you have young children by a former marriage
- you run your own business or farm
- you are leaving 'heritage property' for the public benefit
- you have been married more than once and your ex-partner is still alive

---

Warning
If you do not make a will, your possessions will not necessarily be passed on in the way you would choose. This is a particular risk if you live with an unmarried partner. See above.

- you want to set up complicated trusts, for example for a disabled person
- you are involved with family trusts.

In any of these instances, go to a solicitor. For a straightforward will, a solicitor will charge around £60 or so. You will pay more for a more complicated will. Willwriting services are often cheaper, but a survey by *Which?* found that overall they offered the worst service when compared with solicitors, banks, building societies and insurance companies. Over a third of the wills drawn up by willwriting services were rated as poor, being overly reliant on standard formats and often failing to get the detail right. Some banks, building societies and insurance companies offer will preparation services, which came out consistently adequate in the *Which?* survey but were often lacking in depth and so failing to cover all eventualities. Wills from this source can also work out expensive later on if you have to use the organisation as executor.

Be wary of appointing a bank or solicitor to act as executor of your will. Another survey by *Which?* found that this can result in problems which your survivors may find hard to resolve. If you do appoint a bank or solicitor, you are their client and the beneficiaries of your will have no direct contract with the executor. This makes it hard, when you have passed away, for anyone to put pressure on a professional executor who is slow or unduly costly in administering your estate. Instead, consider appointing a couple of the beneficiaries, or other friends or relatives, as executors. In many cases, administering your estate will be a relatively straightforward procedure. If your executors do need professional help, they can always hire a solicitor. In that event, they – not you – will have a contract with the solicitor and can take action if they are not satisfied with the service they receive.

Make sure you keep your will up to date. Review it whenever your circumstances change and, in any case, every couple of years or so. An out-of-date will can cause terrible problems, with the 'wrong' people inheriting, and distressing and costly battles between your survivors, especially if you have divorced and remarried. In England and Wales, a will is usually automatically invalid if you subsequently marry. If you divorce (but not if you merely separate), any bequests to your former husband or wife automatically lapse but are instead subject to the intestacy laws with all the problems that they can entail although the rest of the will still stands. In Scotland, neither marriage nor divorce invalidates your will, although a new husband or wife can claim 'legal rights' from your estate (see page 403).

Warning
You can alter a will by adding a 'codicil' – a written amendment which must be signed and witnessed and should be kept with the will. But codicils can be lost, so unless the amendment is very slight it is better to draw up a fresh will when changes are needed.

Tax planning

Many people worry unnecessarily about tax taking a large slice of the inheritance they hope to leave to their families. In fact, under the regime in existence in 2003–4 only about five deaths out of every hundred trigger an inheritance tax bill. However, this proportion has been increasing steadily over the last few years and many families who would not consider themselves to be wealthy are being drawn into the inheritance tax net largely because of increases in the value of their home. Nevertheless, there might not be any inheritance tax to pay on your estate, because:

- tax is payable only if the value of your estate plus any taxable or potentially taxable gifts made in the preceding seven years come to more than a set 'tax-free slice', which is £255,000 in 2003–4
- some bequests are tax-free and are deducted from the value of your estate for tax purposes; these include bequests to charity and to your husband or wife.

If it does look likely that there will be inheritance tax on your estate, you can take certain steps during your lifetime to reduce or avoid the tax bill on death. But always bear in mind that ultimately inheritance tax is a problem for your heirs, not you. Do not jeopardise your present financial security simply to save your heirs some tax on their inheritance in the future. In particular, consider what resources you might need if you require specialist care in your old age – see Chapter 8.

Inheritance tax tips

Use your tax-free slice If you are married, you may be tempted to leave everything tax-free to your husband or wife. But because bequests to children and other relatives or friends are *not* tax-free, there could be a hefty tax bill when your husband or wife then dies and everything passes to other members of the family. If your husband or wife does not need all your money and assets, consider sharing them between your spouse and other family members, making sure that the bequests which are not tax-free fall within your available tax-free slice.

Make lifetime gifts Provided you can afford to make gifts during your lifetime, this is a good way to reduce the value of your estate, because many gifts are completely tax-free. Most other gifts between individuals count as potentially exempt transfers (PETs) and become taxable only if you die within seven years of making them (and, even then, only if the total of gifts made over the seven years up to the PET comes to more than the tax-free slice). Tax-free lifetime gifts include:

- gifts between husband and wife
- gifts to charities
- a regular pattern of gifts – for example, premiums for a life insurance policy – which count as normal spending out of your income
- any number of small gifts up to £250 per person
- wedding gifts up to certain limits
- up to £3,000 of any other gifts each year (or up to £6,000 if you did not use up the limit in the previous year).

Give away things whose value will rise The increase in value then benefits the person to whom you make the gift rather than swelling your estate.

Use life insurance You can pay the premiums (using one of the lifetime gift exemptions) on an insurance policy to benefit someone else. In this way, you can make an outright gift or you can ensure that the proceeds of the policy are available to pay an expected inheritance tax bill. Seven-year decreasing term insurance can be used to cover the potential tax bill on a PET.

More complex schemes If you have a large estate, you might be attracted to schemes which use loans, trusts and businesses to reduce the value of your estate. These can become complicated and, if not carefully set up, can fall foul of the tax rules, which disallow artificial methods of avoiding tax. Get professional advice.

Altering a will after death If all the beneficiaries of your will agree, they have two years following your death within which they can alter the bequests made under the will by drawing up a 'deed of variation'. This could be done to reduce or eliminate an onerous tax bill.

More information

To find out more about wills, see *Make Your Will* and *Wills and Probate*, both published by Which? Books.★ For a more detailed look at making gifts and bequests and the tax position, see *The Which? Guide to Giving and Inheriting*, also published by Which? Books.★ For anything beyond the simplest will or tax-saving scheme, get professional advice from a solicitor★ or accountant★. Consider choosing a member of the Society of Trust and Estate Practitioners★. The Capital Taxes Office – part of the Inland Revenue★ – produces a number of useful booklets about inheritance tax (see table below).

Useful leaflets about inheritance tax

Leaflet code	Leaflet name
IHT2	Inheritance tax on lifetime gifts
IHT3	Inheritance tax. An introduction
IHT15	Inheritance tax. How to calculate the liability
IHT16	Inheritance tax and settled property
IHT17	Inheritance tax. Businesses, farms and woodlands
IHT18	Inheritance tax. Foreign aspects

Inheritance issues

Henry Brown has three children, all under the age of 18. He will leave almost everything to his wife, Margaret, but if she dies at the same time or before him, he wants his children to inherit. Henry makes his wife an executor of his will, since she is the person who stands to gain most from the will. He also appoints as executor his friend Gordon Saunders, who will be guardian of his children if both he and his wife die. He appoints another friend as a 'reserve' executor. Apart from two small bequests, there are legacies for the executors as a reward for their efforts. Henry specifies that the residue should go to his wife, but that if she dies before him or within 30 days of him, it will be left for his children. If the children are under 18, the executors will act as trustees.

Make Your Own Will, An Action Pack from Which?

Sam dies and leaves his whole estate of £200,000 to his wife, Harriet. Since any gift to your spouse is tax-free, there is no inheritance tax on Sam's estate. When Harriet dies, her free estate is valued at £300,000 and is left completely to their only child, Phyllis. There is inheritance tax to pay on the estate, calculated as follows:

Value of free estate	£300,000
less tax-free slice	£255,000
	£45,000
Tax on £45,000 @ 40%	£18,000

However, suppose instead that Sam had left £100,000 to Phyllis (on which no IHT would be payable because it would be covered by the tax-free slice) and the remaining £100,000 to Harriet. On Harriet's death, her estate would have been valued at £200,000. Giving this to Phyllis would have been completely covered by Harriet's tax-free slice, so no IHT would be payable. Straightforward planning to make use of Sam's tax-free slice would save £18,000 in tax.

Based on *The Which? Guide to Giving and Inheriting*, updated to 2003–4

Appendix I

Targets and priorities

Work through this checklist. The left-hand column aims to help you identify your personal targets for Column 1. Columns 2 and 3 prompt you to note down your progress so far towards achieving each target. Where work remains to be done, Column 4 invites you to say what priority you give to each target; to do this, count how many targets you have identified, then try to put them in rank order: for example, if you have seven targets, give the most important target a score of one, the next most important a score of two, and so on. In Column 5, commit yourself to a date when you will review the target: this might, for example, coincide with the date on which you receive a statement for the product involved.

Nature of target Things to consider	1 Your specific targets	2 Are you already working towards this target?	3 Do you need to take additional steps to meet this target?	4 What priority do you give this target?	5 When do you next intend to review this target?
Protecting your family • Would your survivors need income? How much? • Would your survivors need capital? How much?					
Protecting your income • Do you have cover through your job? Is the cover adequate? • Do you have savings to fall back on? Are they enough? • Do you need to take out insurance? How much?					

Nature of target Things to consider	1 Your specific targets	2 Are you already working towards this target?	3 Do you need to take additional steps to meet this target?	4 What priority do you give this target?	5 When do you next intend to review this target?
Buying a home • Could you save money by switching your mortgage? Which type of mortgage do you want? Can you pay off part of your mortgage early?					
Care in old age • Are you happy to rely on the state?					
Treatment if you are ill • Are you happy to rely on the NHS? Could a delay waiting for treatment damage your finances?					

415

1 Nature of target Things to consider	1 Your specific targets	2 Are you already working towards this target?	3 Do you need to take additional steps to meet this target?	4 What priority do you give this target?	5 When do you next intend to review this target?
Investment targets List your targets – e.g. planning for school fees, saving for a holiday etc. – and consider the following questions for each one: • Do you want to invest for a lump sum? Over what period? How much can you invest? • Do you want to invest for an immediate income? How much can you invest? • Do you want to invest for an income later on? Over what period? How much can you invest?					

| Nature of target

Things to consider | 1
Your specific targets | 2
Are you already working towards this target? | 3
Do you need to take additional steps to meet this target? | 4
What priority do you give this target? | 5
When do you next intend to review this target? |
|---|---|---|---|---|---|
| **Passing your money on**
• Have you made a will?
Is your will up to date?

• Is there a risk that you might have to pay inheritance tax? Can you take steps now to reduce the possible tax?

• Do you want to take out life insurance to cover a potential tax bill? | | | | | |
| **OTHER** | | | | | |

Resources calculators

To establish what scope you have for meeting your targets, you need to assess what income you have at this point in time and how that income is already committed. This indicates whether you have a surplus you can use or a shortfall which needs to be tackled. Similarly, you need to consider what assets you have, what debts you have, how assets are already committed to your financial targets, how well they are committed and whether you would do better to reallocate them. Bear in mind that if you alter the way your assets are used, this may affect the income you receive. You can use these Calculators to help you do that.

Income Calculator

Monthly income and expenditure		Yourself	Your spouse/ partner
Income (gross)			
Earnings from job	a		
Profits from business	b		
Income from investments	c		
Pensions	d		
State benefits	e		
Other income	f		
Gross income (a + b + c + d + e + f)	A		
less National Insurance	g		

Monthly income and expenditure		Yourself	Your spouse/ partner
less income tax	h		
Net income (A – g – h)	B		
Expenditure			
Mortgage/rent	i		
Council tax	j		
Gas/water/electricity	k		
Telephone	l		
Food, drink and household items	m		
Cost of running car	n		
House insurance	o		
Life insurance	p		
Other insurance	q		
TV licence	r		
Clothes	s		
Credit card bill	t		
Other loan repayments	u		
Child-related costs: school fees, riding lessons, hobbies etc.	v		
Miscellaneous spending money	w		
Pension contributions	x		
Regular saving	y		
Other	z		
Total spending (i + j + k + l + m + n + o + p + q + r + s + t + u + v + w + x + y + z)	C		
Surplus or deficit (B – C)			

Asset Calculator

Assets and liabilities		Yourself		Your spouse/ partner	
		Value (£'00)	Target (from Appendix I), if applicable, to which the asset is committed	Value (£'00)	Target (from Appendix I), if applicable, to which the asset is committed
Your assets					
Your home	aa				
Contents of home and personal belongings	bb				
Your car(s)	cc				
Other property	dd				
Other valuables	ee				
Cash in bank/building society	ff				
National Savings investments	gg				
Gilts	hh				
Corporate bonds etc.	ii				
Other stocks	jj				
Shares (except investment trusts)	kk				
Unit trusts	ll				
Investment trusts	mm				
Investment-type life insurance	nn				
Other investments	oo				
Total assets (aa + bb + cc + dd + ee + ff + gg + hh + ii + jj + kk + ll +mm + nn + oo)	E				

Assets and liabilities	Yourself			Your spouse/ partner	
	Value (£'00)	Target (from Appendix I), if applicable, to which the asset is committed		Value (£'00)	Target (from Appendix I), if applicable, to which the asset is committed
Your liabilities					
Mortgage	pp				
Outstanding credit card debts	qq				
Other loans	rr				
Other liabilities (e.g. tax owed)	ss				
Total liabilities (pp + qq + rr + ss)	F				
Net assets (E – F)					

Appendix III

Useful Internet sites

Web safety

Before relying on information from a website or making any purchase over the Internet, take the following precautions:

- Before dealing, check with the FSA Register★ that the company concerned is authorised.
- Be very wary of dealing with companies based abroad – you will not usually get the same level of protection as you would dealing with a UK company. It may be very difficult or impossible to resolve any problems.
- Make sure you are satisfied that this is the *bona fide* website of the company concerned. Some fraudsters set up bogus websites that look like the real thing. If you have any doubts, don't deal through the website and contact the company another way.
- Don't do business through a website which does not give you real-world contact details (address and phone number). Check out the contact details with a separate source, such as *Yellow Pages*, to make sure they are genuine.
- Before buying over the Internet, make sure you have the full terms and conditions applying to the deal. Don't just read them on screen – print them out so you have a record of the particular terms you signed up to on that day. The terms and conditions on the website may have changed next time you visit the site.
- Be sceptical. If what's on offer sounds too good to be true, it is probably a scam. Check out the Financial Services Authority (FSA)★ website for consumer alerts warning you of current frauds and problems.

- Before buying, make sure the company has a system for confirming your purchase or order and allowing you to check that it has been processed.
- Make sure the site explains how it handles data you supply. Does it adequately protect your personal information? If you are not happy with the arrangement, don't give any personal information.
- Make sure the site explains the security measures it operates when you send personal details and debit- or credit-card numbers to its site. Before sending such details, you should move to a secure link. Secure links are indicated in a variety of ways – for example, a key or closed padlock on your browser toolbar or the letter 's' for 'secure' in the Internet address after the 'http' prefix.
- If you send credit- or debit-card details over a secure site, they should be reasonably protected from interception by fraudsters. In fact, because your card number is encrypted, it will generally be better protected than giving your number over the phone or by post. However, if you need to send your card number in an email, it could be vulnerable. Ideally you should not send confidential information by email at all. Some fraudsters use 'sniffer programs' which detect card-like strings of numbers. So protect your number by writing it in words or splitting it across more than one email.
- Make sure your computer is set on its highest security setting. Don't buy through a website if your computer finds a problem with the security measures.

Websites to check out

By its nature, the Internet is fast-changing. The following list is by no means comprehensive and, by the time you read this, some of the sites may have altered their content or changed their address. But this list will give you a starting point for finding the information you need. Most websites contain links to other relevant or similar sites which you can follow. But, if you have a particular company in mind and you do not know its web address, try typing in 'www.' followed by the company's name, finishing with '.co.uk' or '.com' – it often works. Otherwise, try the company name as a keyword in a search engine or see if there is a link from www.find.co.uk. For more detailed information about using the Internet to help you

manage your finances, see *The Which? Guide to Money on the Internet*
available from Which? Books.★

Organisation	Website address
Financial advice	
IFA Promotion	www.unbiased.co.uk
Institute of Financial Planning	www.financialplanning.org.uk
Matrix Data UK IFA Directory	www.ukifadirectory.co.uk
Society of Financial Advisers	www.sofa.org
Financial regulation	
Financial Services Authority	www.fsa.gov.uk
Check whether a firm is authorised (follow link to Firm & Person check)	www.fsa.gov.uk/consumer
Fund supermarkets	
Ample	www.iii.co.uk
Barclays Stockbrokers	www.barclays-stockbrokers.co.uk
BestInvest	www.bestinvest.co.uk
CharcolOnline	www.charcolonline.co.uk
Chase de Vere	www.chasedevere.co.uk
Egg	www.egg.com
Funds Direct	www.fundsdirect.co.uk
FundsNetwork	www.fidelity.co.uk
Hargreaves Lansdown	www.hargreaveslansdown.co.uk
Inter-alliance	www.inter-alliance.co.uk
Self Trade	www.selftrade.com/uk
TQ Direct Choice	www.tqonline.co.uk
Insurance	
Association of British Insurers	www.abi.org.uk
General Insurance Standards Council	www.gisc.co.uk
Mortgages, other loans and credit	
Charcol Online	www.charcolonline.co.uk
Council of Mortgage Lenders	www.cml.org.uk
Mortgage Code Compliance Board	www.mortgagecode.org.uk
Office of Fair Trading	www.oft.gov.uk
The Mortgage and Loan Group	www.mortgageandloangroup.co.uk
Online calculators and comparisons	
ABI/FSA Pension Calculator	www.pensioncalculator.org.uk
FSA Comparative Tables	www.fsa.gov.uk/tables
State Pension Age	www.thepensionservice.gov.uk/resource_centre/calc.asp
Switch with Which? (e.g. Mortgage calculator)	www.switchwithwhich.co.uk

Organisation	Website address

Pensions
Department of Work and Pensions	www.dwp.gov.uk/
Occupational Pensions Regulatory Authority	www.opra.gov.uk
OPRA Pension Schemes Registry	www.opra.gov.uk/registry/ regmenu.shtml
Pensions Advisory Service	www.opas.org.uk

Personal finance generally
Financial Services Authority	www.fsa.gov.uk/consumer
FT Your Money	http://news.ft.com/yourmoney
MoneyeXtra	www.moneyextra.com
Moneyfacts	www.moneyfacts.co.uk
Money Net	www.moneynet.co.uk
Money Supermarket	www.moneysupermarket.com
Which?	www.which.net

Savings
Banking Code Standards Board	www.bankingcode.org.uk
British Bankers' Association	www.bba.org.uk
Building Societies Association	www.bsa.org.uk
National Savings & Investments	www.nsandi.com

Search engines, etc.
Alta Vista	www.altavista.com
Financial Information Net Directory	www.find.co.uk
Google	www.google.co.uk
Yahoo	www.yahoo.co.uk

Shares and other investments (also see Fund supermarkets, above)
Association of Investment Trust Companies	www.itsonline.co.uk
Association of Private Client Investment Managers and Stockbrokers	www.apcims.co.uk
Debt Management Office (for information about gilts)	www.dmo.gov.uk
Ethical Investment Research Service	www.eiris.org
Euronext.Liffe (traded options etc)	www.liffe.com
Exchange Traded Funds	www.ishares.net
Financial Times	http://news.ft.com/home/uk
For real-time share price quotes	www.freequotes.co.uk
FTSE International (stock market indices)	www.ftse.com
Hemscott (for company information)	www.hemscott.net
Investment Management Association	www.investmentfunds.org.uk
London Stock Exchange	www.londonstockexchange.com
Motley Fool	www.fool.co.uk
NASDAQ (US stock market)	www.nasdaq.com

Organisation	Website address
Proshare	www.proshare.org.uk
Share Pages (for stock market information)	www.sharepages.com
Splits Online (for information about split-capital investment trusts)	www.splitsonline.co.uk
Standard & Poors (investment fund ratings and performance)	www.funds-sp.com
Trust Net (for information about all types of investment fund)	www.trustnet.co.uk

State pensions and benefits

Department for Work and Pensions	www.dwp.gov.uk
To obtain a retirement pension forecast	www.thepensionservice.gov.uk/ resource_centre/state–pen– forecast–br19.asp
Government website. Links to all departments	www.ukonline.gov.uk

Tax

HM Treasury (for Budget information etc)	www.hm-treasury.gov.uk
Inland Revenue	www.inlandrevenue.gov.uk

Addresses

Age Concern Information Line
Astral House
1268 London Road
London SW16 4ER
Tel: (0800) 009 966 (freephone)
Email: boonp@ace.org.uk
Website: www.ace.org.uk

Association of British Insurers (ABI)
51 Gresham Street
London EC2V 7HQ
Tel: 020–7600 3333
Email: info@abi.org.uk
Website: www.abi.org.uk

Association of Consulting Actuaries
1 Wardrobe Place
London EC4V 5AG
Tel: 020–7248 3163
Email: acahelp@aca.org.uk
Website: www.aca.org.uk

Association of Investment Trust Companies (AITC)
Durrant House
8–13 Chiswell Street
London EC1Y 4YY
Tel: 020–7282 5555
Email: enquiries@aitc.co.uk
Website: www.aitc.co.uk or
www.itsonline.co.uk

Association of Private Client Investment Managers and Stockbrokers (APCIMS)
112 Middlesex Street
London E1 7HY
Tel: 020–7247 7080
Email: info@apcims.co.uk
Website: www.apcims.co.uk

Bank of England Brokerage Service
Bank of England Registrar's Department
Southgate House
Southgate Street
Gloucester GL1 1UW
Tel: (01452) 398333
Fax: (01452) 398098
Email:
stockenquiries@bankofengland.co.uk
Website: www.bankofengland.co.uk
(follow link to Brokerage Service)

Banking Code Standards Board
33 St James's Square
London SW1Y 4JS
Tel: 020–7661 9694
Email: helpline@bcsb.org.uk
Website: www.bankingcode.org.uk

British Bankers' Association (BBA)
Pinners Hall
105–108 Old Broad Street
London EC2A 1EX
Tel: 020–7216 8816
Website: www.bba.org.uk

Ceefax
- BBC1 for share prices
- BBC2 for city news, share prices and stock exchanges

Citizens' Advice Bureaux
Look in *The Phone Book* under 'Citizens' Advice Bureau' for your local office
Website: www.adviceguide.org.uk

Consumer Credit Counselling Service
Wade House
Merrion Centre
Leeds LS2 8NG
Tel: (0800) 138 1111 (freephone)
Email: info@cccs.co.uk
Website: www.cccs.co.uk

County Court
Look in *The Phone Book* under 'Courts'

Debt Management Office (DMO)
Eastcheap Court
11 Philpot Lane
London EC3M 8UD
Tel: 020–7862 6500
Website: www.dmo.gov.uk

Department for Education and Skills
Information Line: (0800) 731 9133
Website: www.dfes.gov.uk

Department for Work and Pensions (DWP)
- *Benefit Enquiry Line*
  Victoria House
  9th Floor
  Ormskirk Road
  Preston
  Lancashire PR1 2QP
  Tel: 0800 88 22 00
  Email: Bel-Customer-Services@dwp.gsi.gov.uk
  Website: www.dwp.gov.uk
- *For a state retirement pension forecast*
  The Pension Forecasting Team
  The Pension Service
  Room TB001

Tyneview Park
Whitly Road
Newcastle upon Tyne
NE98 1BA
Website: http://www.thepensionservice.gov.uk/resource_centre/state-pen-forecast-br19.asp
- *For free pensions leaflets*
  Tel: (0845) 7 31 32 33
  Website: www.thepensionservice.gov.uk

Designated Professional Bodies (DPBs)
- Association of Chartered Certified Accountants (ACCA)
  29 Lincoln's Inn Fields
  London WC2A 3EE
  Tel: 020–7396 7000
  Website: www.acca.co.uk
- Institute of Chartered Accountants in England & Wales
  PO Box 433
  Chartered Accountants' Hall
  Moorgate Place
  London EC2P 2BJ
  Tel: 020–7920 8100
  Website: www.icaew.co.uk
- Institute of Chartered Accountants in Ireland (Dublin)
  CA House
  87–89 Pembroke Road
  Ballsbridge
  Dublin 4
  Republic of Ireland
  Tel: (00353) 1–637 7200
  Email: ca@icai.ie
  Website: www.icai.ie
- Institute of Chartered Accountants of Scotland
  CA House
  21 Haymarket Yards
  Edinburgh EH12 5BH
  Tel: 0131–347 0100
  Email: enquiries@icas.org.uk
  Website: www.icas.org.uk
- Law Society
  113 Chancery Lane
  London WC2A 1PL

Tel: 020–7242 1222
Email:
infoservices@lawsociety.org.uk
Website: www.lawsoc.org.uk
- Law Society of Scotland
26 Drumsheugh Gardens
Edinburgh EH3 7YR
Tel: 0131–226 7411
Fax: 0131–225 2934
Email: lawscot@lawscot.org.uk
Website: www.lawscot.org.uk
- Law Society of Northern Ireland
Law Society House
98 Victoria Street
Belfast BT1 3JZ
Tel: 028–90 231614
Fax: 028–90 232606
Email: info@lawsoc-ni.org
Website: www.lawsoc-ni.org
- Institute of Actuaries
Staple Inn Hall
High Holborn
London WC1V 7QL
Tel: 020–7632 2100
Email: institute@actuaries.org.uk
Website: www.actuaries.org.uk

Discount brokers (examples)
- Chase de Vere
Eastcheap Court
11 Philpot Lane
London EC3M 8AE
Tel: (0845) 6000–900
Email:
enquiry@chasedevere.co.uk
Website: www.chasedevere.co.uk
- Hargreaves Lansdown
Kendal House
Brighton Mews
Clifton
Bristol BS8 2NX
Tel: (0845) 345–0800
Website:
www.hargreaveslansdowne.co.uk

Fax Services
Giving information provided by
Moneyfacts (calls cost maximum 75p
per minute)

Savings accounts 090 607 607 11
National savings 090 607 607 12
Offshore savings 090 607 607 13
Mortgages 090 607 607 01
Pension annuities 090 607 607 31
Purchased life annuities
090 607 607 32
Guaranteed income bonds
090 607 607 14
With profits bonds 090 607 607 56
and 090 607 607 59
Term assurance (non-smokers)
090 607 607 52
Term assurance (smokers)
090 607 607 53

Finance and Leasing Association (FLA) Arbitration Scheme
Finance & Leasing Association
2nd Floor
Imperial House
15–19 Kingsway
London WC2B 6UN
Tel: 020–7836 6511
Email: info@fla.org.uk
Website: www.fla.org.uk

Financial Ombudsman Service (FOS)
South Quay Plaza
183 Marsh Wall
London E14 9SR
Tel: (0845) 080 1800 (local rate calls)
Email: enquiries@financial-ombudsman.org.uk
Website: www.financial-ombudsman.org.uk

Financial Services Authority (FSA)
25 The North Colonnade
Canary Wharf
London E14 5HS
Consumer Helpline: (0845) 606 1234
(local rate calls)
Email: consumerhelp@fsa.gov.uk
Website: www.fsa.gov.uk

Financial Services Compensation Scheme (FSCS)
7th Floor
Lloyds Chambers
Portsoken Street
London E1 8BN
Tel: 020–7892 7300
Email: enquiries@fscs.org.uk
Website: www.fscs.org.uk

Financial Times
• From newsagents
• Website: http: //news.ft.com
• Company report and accounts service
  Tel: 020–8391 6000
  Website: http: //ft.ar.wilink.com

FSA Register
• FSA Consumer Helpline:
  (0845) 606 1234 (local rate calls)
• Follow link to Firm & Person Check Service on www.fsa.gov.uk/consumer

Funeral Planning Authority
Harelands
22 Bentsbrook Park
North Holmwood
Dorking
Surrey RH5 4JN
Tel: (01306) 740878
E-mail: enquiries@funeralplanningauthority.com
Website – http://www.funeralplanningauthority.com

General Insurance Standards Council (GISC)
110 Cannon Street
London EC4N 6EU
Tel: 0845 601 2857
Tel (complaints): (0845) 601 2857
Email: enquiries@gisc.co.uk
Website: www.gisc.co.uk

Go Private
Tel: (0845) 604 0333 (local rate calls)
Website: www.goprivatehealth.co.uk

Growth Company Investor
95 Aldwych
London WC2B 4JF
Tel: 020–7430 9777 (subscriptions)
Website: www.growthcompany.co.uk

Health Care Navigator
Tel: (0870) 727 0140 (local rate calls)
Email: enquiries@healthcarenavigator.co.uk
Website: www.healthcarenavigator.co.uk

Help the Aged
207–221 Pentonville Road
London N1 9UZ
Tel: 020–7278 1114
Email: info@helptheaged.org.uk
Website: www.helptheaged.org.uk

IFA Promotion
17–19 Emery Road
Brislington
Bristol BS4 5PF
Tel: (0800) 085 3250 (freephone)
Website: www.unbiased.co.uk

IFAs specialising in annuities
• The Annuity Bureau
  The Tower
  11 York Road
  London SE1 7NX
  Tel: (0845) 602 6263
  Website: www.bureauxltd.com
• Annuity Direct
  32 Scrutton Street
  London EC2A 4RQ
  Tel: (0500) 5065 75
  Email: info@annuitydirect.co.uk
  Website: www.annuitydirect.co.uk

Independent financial adviser (IFA) – to find one

For list of advisers in your area, see separate entries for:
- IFA Promotion
- Institute of Financial Planning
- Matrix Date UK IFA Directory
- Society of Financial Analysts

Independent money advice centre (to find one)
- **Community Legal Service**

Can direct you to local solicitors and advice organisations in England and Wales that can give advice about legal and debt problems
CLS Directory Line: (0845) 608 1122
Website: www.justask.org.uk
- **See also separate entries for:**
- Citizens' Advice Bureaux
- Consumer Credit Counselling Service
- National Debtline

Independent Schools Council Information Service (ISCis)

Grosvenor Gardens House
35–37 Grosvenor Gardens
London SW1W 0BS
Tel: 020–7798 1500
Email: info@iscis.uk.net
Website: www.iscis.uk.net

Inland Revenue
- For local tax enquiry centre, look in *The Phone Book* under 'Inland Revenue'
- For your own tax office, as applicable, check your tax return or other correspondence, or ask your employer or the scheme paying your pension
- Website:
  www.inlandrevenue.gov.uk

Inland Revenue Capital Taxes Office
- England and Wales:
  Ferrers House
  PO Box 38
  Nottingham NG2 1BB

- Northern Ireland:
  Level 3
  Dorchester House
  52–58 Great Victoria Street
  Belfast BT2 7QL
- Scotland:
  Medrum House
  15 Drumsheugh Gardens
  Edinburgh EH3 7UG
  Tel: (0845) 30 20 900
- Website:
  www.inlandrevenue.gov.uk/cto

Institute of Financial Planning

Whitefriars Centre
Lewins Mead
Bristol BS1 2NT
Tel: 0117–945 2470
Website:
www.financialplanning.org.uk

Investment Management Association (IMA)

65 Kingsway
London WC2B 6TD
Tel: 020–8207 1361
Email: ima@investmentuk.org
Website:
www.investmentfunds.org.uk

Investors Chronicle
- From newsagents
- Subscriptions:
  P.O. Box 423
  Sittingbourne
  Kent
  ME9 8FA
  Tel: (0870) 240 6663
  Website:
  www.investorschronicle.co.uk
- Company report and accounts service:
  Tel: 020–8391 6000
  Website: http://ft.ar.wilink.com

Jobcentre Plus
Jobcentre Plus is replacing the services for people of working age that used to be available from social security offices. For local office, see Phone Book under 'Jobcentre Plus' or 'Social security'.

London Stock Exchange
Old Broad Street
London EC2N 1HP
Tel: 020–7797 1000
Email:
enquiries@londonstockexchange.com
Website:
www.londonstockexchange.com

Matrix Data IFA UK Directory
Website: www.ukifadirectory.co.uk

Money Management
- From newsagents
- Subscriptions/back issues:
  WDIS
  Units 12 & 13 Cranleigh Gardens
  Industrial Estate
  Southall
  Middlesex UB1 2DS
  Tel: 020–8606 7545

Money Management National Register of Independent Fee-Based Advisers
C/o Matrix Data Ltd
FREEPOST 22 (SW1565)
London W1E 1BR
Tel: (0870) 013 1925 (local rate calls)

Money Observer
- From newsagents
- For free copy:
  FREEPOST MB2019
  Garrard House
  2–6 Homesdale Road
  Bromley BR2 9BR
  Tel: (0870) 870 1324 (local rate calls)
- Email:
  money.observer@guardian.co.uk
- Website:
  www.moneyobserver.com

Moneyfacts and Moneyfacts Life & Pensions
- Try larger public reference libraries
- Subscriptions:
  Moneyfacts House
  66–70 Thorpe Road
  Norwich NR1 1BJ
  Tel: (0870) 2250 100
  Email:
  subscriptions@moneyfacts.co.uk
- Website: www.moneyfacts.co.uk

Moneywise
- From newsagents
- Subscriptions:
  Tel: (08701) 614411
  Website: www.moneywise.co.uk

Mortgage Code Arbitration Scheme (MCAS)
12 Bloomsbury Square
London WC1A 2LP
Tel: 020–7421 7444
Email: info@arbitrators.org
Website: www.arbitrators.org/DRS/
Schemes/Mortgage_code.htm

Mortgage Code Compliance Board
University Court
Stafford ST18 0GN
Tel: (01785) 218200
Email:
enquiries@mortgagecode.org.uk
Website: www.mortgagecode.org.uk

National Debtline
The Arch
48–52 Floodgate Street
Birmingham B5 5SL
Tel: (0808) 808 4000
Website: www.nationaldebtline.co.uk

National Savings & Investments
Sales Information
Freepost BJ2092
Blackpool FY3 9XR
Tel: (0845) 964 5000
Website: www.nsandi.com

Occupational Pensions Regulatory Authority (OPRA)
Invicta House
Trafalgar Place
Brighton BN1 4DW
Tel: (01273) 627600
Email: helpdesk@opra.gov.uk
Website: www.opra.gov.uk

Pension centre
The Pension Service (see below) is setting up a network of pension centres that will replace the current service from social security offices. For local office, see Phone Book under 'The Pension Service' or 'Social security'.

Pension Schemes Registry
PO Box 1NN
Newcastle upon Tyne NE99 1NN
Tel: 0191–225 6316
Website: www.opra.gov.uk/registry/regmenu.shtml

Pensions Advisory Service (OPAS)
11 Belgrave Road
London SW1V 1RB
Tel: (08456) 012 923
Email: enquiries@opas.org.uk
Website: www.opas.org.uk

Pensions Management
Subscriptions/back issues:
WDIS
Units 12 & 13 Cranleigh Gardens
Industrial Estate
Southall
Middlesex UB1 2DS
Tel: 020–8606 7545

Pensions Ombudsman
11 Belgrave Road
London SW1V 1RB
Tel: 020–7834 9144
Email: enquiries@pensions-ombudsman.org.uk
Website: www.pensions-ombudsman.org.uk

ProShare
Centurion House
24 Monument Street
London EC3R 8AQ
Tel: 020–7220 1730
Website: www.proshare.org.uk

Safe Home Income Plans (SHIP)
PO Box 516
Preston Central
Preston PR2 2XQ
Tel: (0870) 241 6060
Email: info@ship-ltd.org
• Website: www.ship-ltd.org

Shares Magazine
• From newsagents
• Subscriptions:
FREEPOST SEA 8221
Haywards Heath RH16 3BR
Tel: (01444) 475661
• Website:
www.moneyam.com/holding/sharesmag.php

Sheriff's Court
Look in *The Phone Book* under 'Courts'

Social security office
For local office, see Phone Book under 'Social security'.

Society of Financial Advisers (SOFA)
20 Aldermanbury
London EC2V 7HY
Tel: 020–8989 8464
Email: info@sofa.org
Website: www.sofa.org

Society of Pension Consultants
St Bartholomew House
92 Fleet Street
London EC4Y 1DG
Tel: 020–7353 1688
Website: www.spc.uk.com

***Society of Trust and Estate
Practitioners (STEP)***
26 Dover Street
London W1S 4LY
Tel: 020 7763 7152
E-mail: step@step.org
Website http://www.step.or

Stockbroker (to find one)
See separate entries for:
* Association of Personal Client
  Investment Managers and
  Stockbrokers
* London Stock Exchange

Teletext
* C4 for bonds, borrowing, city
  news, mortgages, savings and
  share prices
* Website: www.teletext.com

The Pinsent Company Guide
HS Financial Publishing Ltd
Arnold House
36–41 Holywell Lane
London EC2A 3SF
Tel: 020–7827 5678
Website: www.company-guide.co.uk

The Pension Service
* For your local pension centre, see
  phone book or website
Website:
www.thepensionservice.gov.uk

What Mortgage
* From newsagents
* Subscriptions:
  Tel: 020–7827 5454
* Website:
  www.whatmortgageonline.co.uk

Which? Books
Freepost
PO Box 44
Hertford X
SG14 1YB
Tel: (0800) 252 100
Website: www.which.net

Which? Magazine
Freepost
PO Box 44
Hertford X
SG14 1YB
Tel: (0800) 252 100
Website: www.which.net

Index